The Definitive Christian D. Larson Collection

6 Volumes
30 Titles

Compiled and Edited
by
David Allen

Copyright © 2014 by David Allen / Shanon Allen
All rights reserved. No part of this publication may be reproduced, distributed, or transmitted in any form or by any means, including photocopying, recording, or other electronic or mechanical methods, without the prior written permission of the publisher, except in the case of brief quotations embodied in critical reviews and certain other noncommercial uses permitted by copyright law.
Printed in the United States of America

Reprint

First Printing November 2014

ISBN: 978-0-9909643-3-9

Visit Us At **NevilleGoddardBooks.com** for a complete listing of all our books and **1000's of Free Books to Read online and download.**

Books include: The Power of I AM 1, 2, 3, The Neville Goddard Collection, Neville Goddard's Interpretation of Scripture, The Money Bible, The Creative Power of Thought, The Secrets, Mysteries & Powers of The Subconscious Mind, Your Inner Conversations are Creating Your World, The World is At Your Command - The Very Best of Neville Goddard, Imagining Creates Reality - 365 Mystical Daily Quotes, Imagination: The Redemptive Power in Man, Assumptions Harden Into Facts: The Book, David Allen - Your Faith Is Your Fortune, Your Unlimited Power

First Printing
Copyright © 2014

Foreword

The Definitive Christian D. Larson Collection is a 6 volume set of 30 titles from one of the most renowned and prolific new thought authors and lecturers of his day. No metaphysical, new thought, law of attraction collection would be complete without Christian D. Larson's books. Before Neville Goddard, before Ernest Holmes, before Joseph Murphy and Napoleon Hill and a host of many of the great authors and teachers of today, there was Christian D. Larson (1874 – 1954) who was credited by Horatio Dresser as being a founder in the New Thought movement.

Christian D. Larson books contain hidden secrets (hidden from the conscious minds of those not prepared to receive them) and treasures that you are unlikely to find anywhere else and if you do it is likely it originated from Christian D. Larson.

David Allen

All Christian D. Larson's books are in the public domain.

* Editors note: Some Christian D. Larson books were originally published without chapter titles. They were later added by other editors of Mr. Larson's works. To my knowledge none of them are copyrighted.

Christian D. Larson Titles
Volume - Original Year Published - Title

Vol. 1	1913	Brains and How to Get Them
Vol. 1	1912	Business Psychology
Vol. 1	1907	How Great Men Succeed
Vol. 1	1912	How the Mind Works
Vol. 2	1920	Concentration
Vol. 2	1912	How to Stay Well
Vol. 2	1908	How to Stay Young
Vol. 3	1908	The Great Within
Vol. 3	1912	The Mind Cure
Vol. 3	1912	What is Truth
Vol. 3	1912	Your Forces and How to Use Them
Vol. 4	**1916**	**The Good Side of Christian Science**
Vol. 4	**1912**	**The Ideal Made Real**
Vol. 4	**1910**	**Mastery of Fate**
Vol. 4	**1907**	**Mastery of Self**
Vol. 4	**1916**	**My Ideal of Marriage**
Vol. 4	**1916**	**Nothing Succeeds Like Success**
Vol. 4	**1916**	**Steps in Human Progress**
Vol. 5	1918	Healing Yourself
Vol. 5	1912	Just Be Glad
Vol. 5	1940	Leave it to God
Vol. 5	1908	On the Heights
Vol. 5	1910	Perfect Health
Vol. 5	1922	Practical Self-Help
Vol. 5	1912	Scientific Training of Children
Vol. 5	1912	Thinking for Results
Vol. 6	1912	The Hidden Secret
Vol. 6	1916	In Light of the Spirit
Vol. 6	1912	The Pathway of Roses
Vol. 6	1907	Poise and Power

Volume 4

The Good Side of Christian Science	6
The Ideal Made Real	40
Mastery of Fate	230
Mastery of Self	296
My Ideal of Marriage	363
Nothing Succeeds Like Success	423
Steps in Human Progress	448

The Good Side of Christian Science

The Good Side of Christian Science

IN taking up this subject, a subject that is attracting worldwide attention at the present time, I wish to say that I have the greatest regard and the highest admiration for the Christian Science movement as a movement, and for the principles upon which the movement is based; and the principal cause of my regard and admiration is this, that I admire everybody and everything that has a great purpose in view, and that works for it with all the power that life can give.

This is something that we all feel and, therefore, whenever we meet an individual with a lofty ideal, someone who knows what he wants, and works for it and lives for it under all sorts of circumstances, we cannot help admiring that individual. We may not always agree with him in every respect; and under certain circumstances it may be unwise to try to agree with him; still, we are bound to admire him to the very highest degree, even though he may not take as broad a view of some things as we would like.

It is the same with institutions and movements. If they have a great object, a great purpose, and a lofty goal, and not only live for their convictions, but actually make good in practical life, we are bound to admire them; especially where we realize that they are inspired with the highest form of sincerity.

In all departments of life it is the weaklings that we sometimes lose patience with, although we ought to be patient with everybody, knowing that it is difficult to find anyone who is not doing his best under the circumstances; still, where we find individuals or institutions that have no purpose in view and that are vacillating and uncertain in connection with everything that has real value in life, we cannot bestow upon them any great degree of admiration; in fact, we are liable to think of them as obstacles to the welfare of the world. This they may be in a sense; nevertheless, they need our sympathy instead of our criticism; but when we meet people who live for something — or institutions that work for something definite — something of extraordinary importance to human welfare, and actually make good in their purpose, we invariably give them our admiration; and in this age this spirit of admiration for the successful, for the true, for the sincere and the genuine is growing rapidly; and there is a psychological reason for this fact — something that we shall find it important to respect and admire if we have greater success or higher attainment in view.

In this connection we should remember that we never find successful people among those who are constantly criticizing or antagonizing, or who live in the spirit of destruction. The reason is, those people are not living or working in that vital current of life that is moving toward greater things. They are at war with themselves because at war with others; and no mind that is living in continual warfare can ever develop or produce anything of great worth in the world. We cannot afford, therefore, to live in the critical spirit under any circumstances; but when we enter the opposite spirit, that is, when we begin to admire and respect both individuals and institutions that are moving forward, that are successful, that are working for great things — it is then that we get into the great constructive current of life and begin to move with that current into the larger, the higher, the finer and the richer in all the domains of existence.

The best advice that we could give to any young man or woman would be this: "Look at those who have succeeded greatly and achieved largely; then find their secret and apply it in your own life, or improve upon it if you can; but pay no attention to the weakness of those who have failed or lost, because it is the ways of success and not the ways of failure that should be imitated or selected as ideals."

If all young men would take this advice they would place their minds in a strong, constructive current; and this current would gradually gain force and power so that in the course of time their mental capacity would be increased to a very large degree. In consequence, they would not only enter the pathway that invariably leads to success, but they would constantly increase all those elements of mind and talent that make for still greater success.

The spirit of the age is entering more and more into the understanding of this idea; that is, that the human mind, to be true to itself, must follow constructive lines invariably; and therefore we are learning to apply this idea more and more, not only to individuals, but to institutions and world movements, including religious movements, and all systems of thought in this same manner. We are beginning to overlook as far as possible their weak points and are beginning to give more and more credit to the good and the helpful elements that they all do surely contain. We know that all individuals and all institutions have weak points, but our purpose must be to search for their strong points, and then apply those strong points to ourselves, and improve upon them as far as we possibly can. This is the spirit of the present age; and it is in this spirit that we will consider, the Christian Science movement with a view of finding the reason why that movement has been so very successful along certain lines of action, and why it has accomplished so much regardless of obstacles and persecutions.

There is a strong tendency among a large number of people to criticize new religious institutions, because they say we have too many religions already. Their idea is that we should not formulate any new religious system, but rather aim to unite all religious systems into one; but here we should remember that the ideal of religious union, that is, combining all the churches into one institution, is a dream that will not be realized at present, nor would we want it to be realized for many a long day.

There are in the world something like two hundred different types of mentality in the present age, and each type needs a different form of worship and belief; that is, each type needs a method of its own for approaching the Absolute, or reaching up toward the higher and finer life; and therefore we need all these different systems so that these many types of mind may have modes of aspiration and worship that will suit their present state of development. In another century there may not be so many types of mind, because the farther the human race develops the closer we all come together in understanding and consciousness; but so long as all these many types do exist we need corresponding systems of belief, of worship, of study, of living.

We must not find fault, therefore, with the fact that there are so many religions in the world. They are all necessary just now. If we were to find fault at all it would be this, that most of those religions do not, to use an ordinary term, "make good" in their own field. In brief, they are not living up to their highest light, or trying to make the best use of the gifts and possibilities in their possession.

When we learn to take a broad and reasonable view of all things, we come to the conclusion that no system of thought or no organization should disappear so long as it has a mission, or so long as there is a field wherein it can find useful work; but we do demand that every church, every system of thought, every philosophy, every science, every form of worship make good in the field where it may find its mission at the present time. We cannot commend any institution that is only half alive, or that is wasting the larger part of its opportunity. Such institutions have no right to exist; but an institution that is true to its purpose, true to its mission, and that is turning on the full current, so to speak, of all its power, to the end that it may render the greatest service possible to those with whom it may be concerned — such an institution is absolutely necessary for the time being and cannot fail to win the highest respect of all men and women who have the greatest welfare of the human race at heart.

The fact is, however, that there are very few systems of thought, or religious institutions of the present day, that are really making good in their own field. Many of them are doing fairly well, but there are only a few that are really making full and effective application of the principles upon which they stand.

One of these exceptional few is the Christian Science Church. As an institution this church is certainly making full and effective application of its own principles; and therefore we cannot hesitate to express our greatest admiration and our highest regard once more. It is indeed more than can be said of most of the other religious institutions in the world today; and the fact that the Christian Science Church is making full and effective application of its principles is one reason why it is so successful; but there are many other reasons, and we wish to consider all these reasons carefully so that we may apply them in our own individual life, in our business, in our education, or in any field of religious study that we may undertake now or in the future.

However, before we proceed to examine the inner secret, so to speak, of the Christian Science movement, we should remember that this movement is not for everybody; but the same is true of trigonometry, of agriculture, of chemistry, of domestic science. They are not for everybody. They are for those who need them. The same is true of a great many things, and, in fact, of nearly all things. Every particular system or factor may fill a special place and supply the need of a certain type of mind; and so long as that particular movement, institution or factor does supply the need of a certain type of mind, we should be glad that it is here, and not under any circumstances find fault.

The Christian Science movement occupies a most important mission. It is doing a marvelous work for a certain type of mind; but it is suited only to that certain type, and therefore must not be looked upon as the last word in religion, in science or in truth. It has, like all other institutions, arisen for the purpose of supplying a certain need for the time being; but no institution in itself is permanent. All institutions are destined to give place to other institutions that will arise to supply the new needs of advancing humanity; but for the present age, and possibly for many centuries, the Christian Science movement will continue as a wonderful power for good in the lives of those thousands and thousands who may need that service that Christian Science alone can render.

The Good Side of Christian Science

WHEN we proceed to examine the Christian Science movement we should remember at the outset that whenever we consider a plant, or anything that has developed, we must not only consider the plant itself, but also the seed, and the soil, and the tiller of the soil. In considering this movement, therefore, we must consider, not simply the movement alone, but where and how it came into being; why it grew; and we should also consider the psychological side, because it is the psychological side that holds the secret everywhere.

When we turn our attention to the middle of the past century we find that the human mind was at that time in a peculiar condition, the cause of which may be found by going back to the early part of that century. In examining the mode of thought as it existed in the early part of the past century we find that a number of liberal movements were beginning to take shape and form, and that considerable unrest among a great many people was becoming evident where previously perfect satisfaction obtained with things as they were.

There was considerable preaching against the old order; and a great many minds, some of them spiritual and mental giants, arose in that day to champion mental liberty, arousing thereby a strong sentiment in favor of freedom from the creeds of the day and the awful dogmas that the race had inherited from the past. This commotion in the world of thought in this country continued until about the middle of the century, when some strange things happened — the appearance of various forms of mystical phenomena which literally shook the earth.

The appearance of these phenomena, largely physical in their nature, aroused more curiosity among those who had become dissatisfied with the old order; and people began to think and wonder more and more about the great question, "What is truth?" Thousands and tens of thousands became interested in the various psychical manifestations that appeared at the time, and that continued to mystify the human mind more and more up until the end of the century; and the question was everywhere if these phenomena did contain real truth, because if they did it was evident that the old order was composed of a huge bundle of mistakes. No definite conclusions, however, were formulated at the time; but all this study and research and investigation certainly did prepare the minds of thousands of people for something else, something that would satisfy where the old order had largely failed.

The various liberal movements that were active at the time satisfied a few people, but those movements were more intellectual than otherwise, and therefore were limited in their power to serve the needs of that vast host that was coming out from the old system of belief. The mystical movement that arose at the time with its strange phenomena created much curiosity and much thought, but somehow did not satisfy the yearnings of the soul. This movement did not bring a science, or a philosophy, or a religion that really touched the inner or higher side of existence; and in consequence the demand for something else continued.

If we should examine closely the state of mind of the civilized world at that period, we would meet with a most interesting study, and we would realize that that period did present the psychological moment for a religion, or a higher science, that could meet the requirements of that vast number who had freed themselves from the old, but who had not found anything to take its place. We shall not take time, however, to analyze the mind of that period, nor will this be necessary, because we are all familiar with conditions as they existed at that time. We all have read much about the various movements and conditions that swayed the thought of the rising humanity fifty or sixty years ago, and, therefore, we realize what excellent soil the mentality of that period had become for the reception of the right seed. In fact, it was the very best and the very richest soil that could be desired for something that contained a vital message — something that not only aimed to possess the truth, but that could prove its claims, with thorough satisfaction to all who were in need of that particular message, whatever it was to be.

It was in that soil that the seed of Christian Science was placed; and we understand fully that coming as it did at that time it found everything that could be desired for the development of a religious system of tremendous power and extraordinary proportions.

Where or how Mary Baker Eddy received her first insight into her system of thought does not matter. It is sufficient to know that she did discover a principle that has served as a solid foundation for the work of Christian Science, and will continue to serve in that manner so long as that particular movement is needed for the progress of the race. Whether she was inspired or whether she was simply endowed with an extraordinary perception of the situation so that she could understand both the requirements of the hour and the mode of supplying those requirements — this does not matter in the least, although we must admit that no one could have done what she did without being in very close contact with mental and spiritual light of a very extraordinary nature.

She took advantage of the situation in a manner that bespeaks the possession of remarkable genius along the line of her thought and undertakings; and the first stroke of genius that we find in her mode of action was in selecting the name that she did for her religion. There is indeed magic in that name. She combined the two most powerful words in the civilized world at the time, and we know these two words still are the most powerful known to the western half of the hemisphere. She did more than that. She gave a new and interior meaning, both to the word "Christian" and to the word "Science," thus doubling the spiritual power of the name she had chosen.

The word "Christianity" had been a power for nearly twenty centuries. It was a term with which all minds were familiar. It stood for something high, something wonderful, something that incorporated all the ideals, all the dreams and all the most sacred yearnings of the soul.

The term "Science" had for some time occupied a similar position, although in a different field. The scientific method had become very popular, especially in the practical world and in the educational world; and this method stood for truth positively demonstrated. All awakened minds, therefore, realized that whatever was scientific was true, and that science was in its own field a synonym for truth and demonstration. Accordingly, it was a word of remarkable power.

The founder of the Christian Science movement took those two terms, both of them the most powerful in their own realms, and combined them as the name of a new religion, a new church, a new path to emancipation; and we admit that no one but an extraordinary mind could have conceived of such an idea, or such a plan. Genius was certainly present in that mind to a remarkable degree, and we may also say that inspiration was present to a still greater degree.

In analyzing the meaning of the word "Christianity," the founder of this new religion manifested more evidence of genius and inspiration. The term "Christianity" had stood for something remarkable, but it had been associated with dark clouds, and had also been connected continually with sin, sickness, trouble, and the idea that this world is a vale of tears. The old Christian doctrine declared that it was necessary to bear these things while we remained upon earth, and that there was no way in which we might dispel the clouds. The Christian Science idea, however, took the opposite view, and literally blew the clouds away. This new religion declared that Christianity stood for freedom here and now; that salvation is not only for the future, but also for the present; and that salvation includes salvation from sickness, trouble, adversity, poverty and all the ills of life, here and now, upon this planet, in this sphere of existence.

This new interpretation brought relief to thousands and thousands, and it proved its doctrines by healing the sick, and emancipating people everywhere from all sorts of trouble, poverty, wrong, adversity, and in brief, all those conditions that had been looked upon as inevitable by the old order. This new religion went further and proved its belief by the Bible, illustrating the great fact, on every hand, that the Christ power can and should emancipate mankind here and now.

This was the message, and it was indeed a great and vital message, although others had given the same message to a certain extent for some years previously, but they had not presented that message in the same forceful manner, or under the same favorable conditions; and we know it makes all the difference in the world how truth is presented. A thousand men and women may proclaim certain new ideas to the world and still the world may not pay much attention; but when a genius appears on the scene, presenting those same ideas under the proper conditions and in the proper manner, the attention of the entire world is aroused, and we all understand the reason why. Two minds may present the same idea; with the one that idea may fall flat and produce no impression whatever, but with the other that idea may actually create a sensation. The result therefore from the coming of anything new, whether it be ordinary or extraordinary, will depend entirely upon how it is presented.

The founder of the Christian Science movement did not necessarily present something that no one had ever dreamed of before, but she did present it in a manner that was strikingly new, and under combinations and conditions that were destined to produce a sensation. In other words, she laid hold upon a marvelous idea and gave it to the world in such a way that the world could receive it and understand. It was a great stroke of genius; or we might say it was the work of exceptional inspiration. Which of the two it happened to be does not matter. It is results that we all seek, and we are not directly concerned with the definition, or the methods, or the plan.

In connection with the word "Science," the founder of this movement presented evidence of more genius. We know that that word represented facts, facts that could be demonstrated; but Mary Baker Eddy gave a new meaning to that word, and made it stand not simply for demonstration of physical facts, but also for the demonstration of truth in mind and spirit as well. She also made it stand for a certain mode of living, a mode that we have come to call constructive living, scientific living, or living and thinking according to science — science interpreted as a spiritual manifestation of truth as well as a manifestation of truth on all other planes. To be scientific, therefore, in this new science would be to establish all living and all thinking upon the principle of Divine Truth, and formulate all thought, all states of mind and all modes of living in perfect harmony with the principle of truth itself.

The idea is that Divine Truth contains within itself the principle of freedom, health, wholesomeness, power, emancipation; and therefore, in order to be scientific according to this new idea, every thought and every expression will have to give expression to that which was revealed by the understanding of the principle of truth — Absolute or Divine Truths Herein we find the necessity of considering the word; "error," which represents the sum-total of all such ideas as the mind of man may create when living in materiality, or in a state where the truth is misunderstood or not properly comprehended. To eliminate error, therefore, became one of the essentials in the emancipation of the mind from all adverse conditions that might exist either in the personality or in one's environments; and this we clearly understand because if we are to become scientific according to this new idea, we must think and express the principle of truth.

This new conception of science became a power, and for several reasons. In the first place, it was logical, that is, to those who were able to appreciate the fact that science was not necessarily confined to the physical realm, but that science stood for a principle and therefore would naturally belong in a larger measure to the spiritual realm.

In this connection we might pause and consider the criticism of those who have sometimes termed Christian Science "mere intellectual rubbish"; but no one will make that criticism unless he is confined exclusively to materiality. Anyone who is spiritually awakened, or whose mind has gained that broad conception of life where he is conscious in the spiritual as well as in the material — such a mind knows that the Christian Science interpretation of the term "science" is logical, and that it is absolutely true to the truth. We know, of course, there are a number of statements in "Science and Health" that are contradictory; but it certainly would not be possible to find any book written by human hand that would not contain some imperfections; on the whole, however, that book is a clear and lucid presentation of facts; and anyone who is trained in metaphysics, or who has the power to appreciate the metaphysical idea, can read that book from beginning to end and find it thoroughly logical, absolutely true to the truth.

This new interpretation of science also presented a new conception of life, and enlarged upon the power of science to such an extraordinary degree that anyone who might henceforth use the term science — using it in the consciousness of its new meaning — could not help but feel its wonderful power. It opened a way to the discernment of the inner side of things, the higher side, the finer side, and enabled the mind to enter into that finer spiritual conception of truth and reality that is absolutely indispensable to the understanding of real truth itself, as well as to the living of a life that may have truth and reality as its permanent foundation.

This new idea of science became powerful for another reason; and it is this, that when our thinking is scientific, that is, when we formulate thought and life in the image and likeness of our highest conception of Divine Truth, we are building up in the mind some very powerful forces — forces that are wholesome and constructive, and that invariably tend to make the whole of life a positive power for greater and greater good; and therefore anyone who lives according to science cannot fail to ascend steadily and surely into the consciousness of greater and greater good.

We know that when the mind is trained to think constructively, and think toward certain lofty ideals, and when that training is made so thorough that every element in the entire personality becomes inspired with a desire to work toward this lofty ideal — we find that the entire system begins to pass through a state of transformation; that is, both mind and body will find freedom from the lesser, from the adverse, or from the wrong, and will steadily change into the consciousness and realization of the wholesome, the true, the harmonious, and the ideal.

Herein we find the real secret of emancipation and also the real principle upon which science healing is based. It is not necessary, however, to analyze in detail the process of the scientific method, because we are all familiar with it; but we realize what an inspiration the word "science" becomes when this inner and larger meaning of science is fully understood; and it cannot fail to produce a deep and wonderful impression upon those who are prepared to understand its meaning in this higher and larger measure.

The first step, therefore, to be taken by the new movement was to combine those two wonderful words in one name, formulating thereby a religious system of thought and life that eliminated completely the dark clouds of false belief. The term "Christian" came to stand for emancipation, for health, for life, for freedom, for joy, for abundance, for the all good of all good things, here and now; and the word "science" came to stand for a new and marvelous method, a method that could be employed and demonstrated not only in the external world, but also in the worlds of mind and spirit. We understand, therefore, that such a combination of terms and ideas, appearing at the right time, at the psychological moment, at a time when thousands were in dire need of that great message the new movement came so fully prepared to present — we fully understand why the movement became such a power, and why it has succeeded to such a remarkable degree. But back of it all was a wonderful woman, a woman who has made her place in history, a place that will be absolutely secure for all time. She has won immortal fame, and she deserves it in the fullest measure of the term. To these facts we all agree, but what we wish to know in particular is the real reason why the Christian Science movement has become so powerful, and why it has succeeded to such a degree regardless of misunderstanding and opposition. We know that when we consider its origin, and the elements that went to make up the system in the beginning, we find many reasons why it necessarily would succeed; but those elements do not convey the real reason. To find the real reason we shall have to penetrate more deeply into the principles upon which the movement was based; and in this manner we shall discover something that will prove of exceptional importance to us all; that is, if we choose to apply practically and continually the secret we shall thus discover.

There are a great many things that could be mentioned if we were in search of the real reason why the Christian Science movement has been so successful, but the majority of these things would occupy a secondary position. There are two things, however, that occupy a most important position, and it is these two that are, more than all others, responsible for the success of the movement.

The first of these is the practice among Christian Scientists of living absolutely according to the metaphysical principle; and although we cannot say that their method of conforming to the metaphysical principle would constitute the highest light for everybody, still one thing is certain, and it is this, that any individual who realizes the power of Divine Truth, or that comprehends the metaphysical conception of life and who positively believes that the power of truth is sufficient to give him absolute freedom from any illness in life or bring to him anything that he may desire in life — anyone who believes this, and who depends absolutely upon that understanding, is going to accomplish far more than if he relied upon that understanding part of the time, and at other times employed other or lesser means.

The Good Side of Christian Science

We have heard a great deal in modern times about the possibility of combining the different systems of cure, and whether it might be all right to take medicine and at the same time apply metaphysical treatment. The fact is, however, that it will depend largely upon the individual. There are some individuals who are not very deeply impressed by anything, but whatever means they do employ may tend to help them through good suggestions. In other words, when they take medicine they believe that this will help, and of course it does help to the extent that they accept the suggestion of helpfulness received at the time. Then they may employ science treatment and may expect help in the same way, thereby giving themselves good suggestions once more.

With these people, however, it is all suggestion, and whatever help they secure, they secure through the power of suggestion; and there are a great many people connected with the Christian Science movement who get nothing but good suggestions out of the Christian Science movement. They have not entered into the metaphysics of life in any mode or manner. They do not understand the science of the system they have adopted because they have not entered inside, so to speak, of the beliefs or ideas they have adopted. The only good they secure from their association with the Christian Science movement is the effect of helpful, positive and optimistic suggestions; and we know that where minds are susceptible such an influence is always beneficial, but it is also superficial and has no permanent value anywhere.

It is largely the same with a great many people who study other lines of mental or spiritual or metaphysical systems. They are benefited whenever a good suggestion is given them; but in their case it is nothing more than suggestion. The help they receive is always temporary, and they have to be helped again and again by some individual who can give them good, strong suggestions in the same way as the physician gives a dose of medicine according to requirement.

All of this, however, is on the outside, and has nothing to do with the real understanding of Divine Truth; but let any individual get into the spirit of this understanding and enter into the consciousness of real metaphysics — then he will actually gain possession of the power of truth, the power of the spirit and the power of the Christ dwelling in man; and he will find that if he continues to depend absolutely upon that power regardless of circumstances he is going to have far greater results than he could possibly have by dividing his attention among a score of different methods or systems.

The law involved therein is very simple because we understand that when we depend absolutely upon higher power and have unbounded faith in that power, the mind will constantly reach out into higher and finer realization of that power, thereby gaining possession of a greater and greater measure of that power constantly; and we understand full well that whatever the condition may be, if we gain sufficient spiritual power we will be able to eliminate adverse conditions absolutely and realize perfect freedom. On the other hand, if we have faith in higher power only now and then, and then transfer our faith to something else at frequent intervals, the house will be divided against itself. Thus we do not have real faith in anything. We are simply trying them, so to speak, to see whether they will work; but the fact is that nothing will work for us unless we first proceed with unbounded faith in the method or the principle that we have elected to employ.

We find among Christian Scientists that a great many of them are actually expressing and depending absolutely upon the power of truth. They depend exclusively upon the principle upon which they stand; that is, a fair percentage of them do, although we know that the larger percentage live undoubtedly on the outside and secure results only through superficial suggestion. This larger number have not entered into the inner circle of truth, so to speak, and do not comprehend the spirit of truth nor the real significance of the Christian Science movement.

The real Christian Scientist, however, depends absolutely upon the power of truth, the power of the spirit, the power of the Christ — and lives, thinks and acts continually in the metaphysical state of mind, that state of mind in which the understanding of divine truth is absolutely genuine and pure.

In this connection we may ask a very important question; and the question is, if we, who do not belong to the Christian Science organization and have not adopted their system as a whole, — if we can employ the same method of depending absolutely upon the spirit and get the same results, without complying with the rules and regulations of that organization. It is a question that has been asked frequently, and there is but one answer, because we all know that the truth is not confined to any organization nor dependent upon the rules and regulations of any institution whatever. The truth is that any human soul who will depend absolutely upon the spirit of truth will receive the full power of the spirit of truth, and will secure the same results, whether he work alone or choose to unite with some institution. We must realize that we do not have to abide by any fixed system of belief or any mode of organization in order to come into the possession of the good, the true and the ideal.

It is not necessary to be loyal to this system or to that individual in order to receive spiritual power. All that is necessary is to enter into the metaphysical conception of life where we can understand truth in its purity, and thereby receive the full power of the spirit of truth; and when we do receive that power, depend absolutely upon the truth itself, never for one moment thinking that we shall have to employ something else.

The real Christian Scientists have taken this lofty position; and that is one of their great secrets. They do not compromise with the lesser under any circumstance. They take God at his word and expect him to answer every prayer here and now. We know, however, that there are not a great many people who do this. Most people pray and have faith in a measure; and then when they discover that results do not follow instantaneously, they call in a physician, or they proceed to give their attention to some other means. As a rule, they continue in this house-divided-against-itself attitude, never giving any method or process sufficient time to do its work. They are constantly scattering their forces, and therefore accomplish very little in the metaphysical or spiritual worlds.

In this connection we must not say that no one should ever call in a physician. The truth is, that if we are convinced that we are in need of a physician or that we need material help of any kind, we should seek such help at once. But the point is this: When we know that the power of the spirit can do anything for us, and when we have learned to live in a state of consciousness where we understand the truth so deeply and so perfectly that we know absolutely that the knowing of the truth can and does make for freedom invariably — if we depend absolutely upon the truth and the limitless power of the indwelling Christ, we shall find that the mere thought of seeking lesser means at any time is a waste of time. We shall gain far more and realize far greater results if we stand by the power of the truth under every circumstance, and depend so absolutely upon that power that our entire attention is directed upon the light of that understanding through which we gain possession of this power.

When we proceed to consider this phase of the subject another question may arise. We will suppose that we do depend upon the power of the spirit absolutely for a reasonable length of time; and when we do not secure results, should we then give up and try some other method? We admit this question involves a very fine point, and the answer would depend altogether upon the situation. We know that Jesus Christ did, at some times, or at any rate appeared to use material means, and used various methods at times that seemed different from the purely spiritual method. And we must admit that it is always well to consider the laws of nature in the truth as we did when we depended exclusively upon material methods. There can be no sympathy for people who purposely sit in a cold draft in order that they may be able later to demonstrate the power of science; or for people who eat anything they like in order to prove how easily they can overcome the ill effects.

The truth is, we have better use for our energy than that. Still if we realize that we are in the spirit, that we are influenced exclusively by the power of the spirit, literally filled with that power, we certainly cannot have any fear of drafts or anything else. Nevertheless, there is no need of subjecting the body to extra work under any circumstance. This entire field involves many fine points, and we shall have to judge for ourselves what we are going to do under these circumstances. At the present time we all have physical bodies, and we are surrounded with many conditions that are imperfect or adverse, so that we shall find it advisable to exercise all the wisdom we possess in order to adapt ourselves harmoniously to everything that may arise in this sphere of existence.

But regardless of this we know that the principal secret of the Christian Science movement is found in this: That they depend absolutely upon the power of the truth and the power of the indwelling Christ. They have taken God at his word, and expect him to answer every prayer without the least doubt. They believe that in the spirit and in the truth there is health and freedom for everybody; they expect to demonstrate health and freedom by living absolutely and continuously in the spirit of truth; and they have results, wonderful results. What they have accomplished is an illustration of what can be accomplished by devoted and consecrated concentration upon higher spiritual power. It is an illustration of what can be done when we follow the great statement, "Keep the eye single upon the Most High"; and those who understand the psychology of this process will realize at once why the Christian Science movement has accomplished so much and become such a marvelous power in the religious world today.

It is not necessary to analyze this phase of the subject further, because we know that people are coming more and more to the conclusion that after we have entered into the understanding of the greater, and after we have come to a place where we really know what higher power can do, it is certainly a waste of time to give any attention whatever to the lesser. And we are also coming more and more into the realization of the truth that the more devoted we are to the power of the spirit, and the more perfectly we live in the pure metaphysical understanding of Divine Truth, the greater will the power of the spirit manifest in us and through us. This is a principle we all understand; but it is something that we should not simply remember; it is something that deserves our deepest and most thorough attention.

The Good Side of Christian Science

Another principle of practice that has proven so highly important in the success of the Christian Science movement is that of giving absolute devotion to the great central idea of the system itself. The term "Christian Science" stands for a certain idea. That idea may be vague to some minds, but to those who really understand it, or who have looked into it carefully, it becomes an idea that represents something that is not only definite but something of marvelous meaning.

On every hand we hear people making the statement when in dangerous places, "Suppose we try science." That word has come to mean something special; and even the outside world is beginning to appreciate the fact that there is power back of the term " Science," although they may not understand where or how that power produces results.

The majority, however, among those who have gained some understanding of the principle of real science, believe firmly that the power existing or manifesting through science has the power to protect, to heal, to emancipate and to bring us every good thing in life. In other words, science, with its interior interpretation, represents a power that can make all things right here and now; and those who have entered into this interior interpretation actually feel that they are protected by something that is invincible, something that comes from a higher and unlimited source.

We find that Christian Scientists, as a rule, realize that the central idea of the system they have adopted contains a superior power, or is the channel through which superior power can be realized; and by concentrating attention upon that idea they enter more and more into the realization of the power itself, thereby securing all the protection, all the guidance and all the benefit that their understanding of the idea can produce for them as far as they have gone in their understanding at the present time.

The Good Side of Christian Science

There are quite a number, however, among the more devoted Christian Scientists that have concentrated their attention so exclusively upon this central idea that they have become fanatical, and therefore are becoming in a measure an obstacle to their own higher achievement. That, however, is another story, and is something that we need not enter into at the present time.

The principle is this, that whenever you have an ideal of enormous possibilities, and devote yourself absolutely to that ideal, that is, concentrate your whole life upon everything that is high, wonderful or marvelous in that ideal — then you not only place in action all the greater powers within yourself, but you also place yourself in a position where you are constantly reaching out and up into the higher and better understanding of all the powers and possibilities that do exist in that ideal. The result is that you will enter more and more into the inheritance of that ideal; and where that ideal involves the absolute understanding of Divine Truth you will enter more and more into the spirit of that truth, thereby fulfilling in your own life that wonderful statement, "Ye shall know the Truth, and the Truth shall make you free."

To state it differently, if you know of a certain power that can do certain things, and you devote yourself absolutely to that power all through your life, there is only one conclusion to come to, and it is this, that one of these days that power is going to return your favor. You will enter into the possession of that power, and all that is beautiful and marvelous in that power will become your own.

The Christian Scientists are proving this every day. They are devoting themselves absolutely to the great central principle of Divine Truth, and have consecrated themselves in every form and manner to the invincible power of Divine

The Good Side of Christian Science

Truth. The result is that that power is returning the favor; and therefore they are proving their religion in every form and manner.

In this connection, however, we must remember that the secret of the Christian Scientist will not be found in the belief that they know more than other people, although they certainly do know more than a great many people; but their secret is found in their tremendous devotion to a high spiritual idea and a high spiritual power. They do not comprehend the mysteries of life any more perfectly than other devoted students of the same subject, but they have entered into the metaphysical conception of truth; and this has given them the key to the real understanding of truth and the real power of the spirit. But this key is not the sole possession of the Christian Scientist, nor will it become, at any time, the sole possession of anyone organization.

The truth is that any individual who will enter into the metaphysical conception of truth and devote his life absolutely and exclusively to the spirit of the truth as discerned in the consciousness of pure metaphysics — let any individual take this same course, and he will also find the same key.

It is an illustration of tremendous concentration or consecration of the highest order. We know that concentration is the great key to achievement in all modes of demonstration; but we cannot apply the principle of concentration unless we have something upon which to concentrate that really does contain the power that we desire. And here we must also remember that concentration does not express its greatest power until it becomes consecration; that is, the attitude of mind must become metaphysical and spiritual, and must devote itself absolutely to the highest truth and the inner or spiritual significance of absolute truth.

We all will admit that one of the greatest lessons to be learned at the present time is this lesson of unprecedented spiritual concentration or consecration of Divine Truth as manifested in the Christian Science movement; and we all may say to ourselves, and wisely, "Go, and do likewise"; although we need not unite with that movement in order to demonstrate the same truth and the same power.

The Christian Science system is a system that is admirably adapted to a large number of people, but the way it is organized at the present time is not adapted to everybody; and when no organization or system of belief can possess the exclusive secret to the perfect understanding of truth, we realize that we may employ this same principle no matter where we may live or work, or through what system of belief we may prefer to express ourselves in this age.

When we study this wonderful subject, we find that certain interpretations of truth become, so to speak, channels or pathways toward that higher understanding or consciousness that we are in search of; and although there may be any number of such interpretations, complying with the various needs of various people, they all may lead to the same sublime source. Our first object therefore should be to learn the understanding of the great law, that law of life that we all must employ in our search for the realization of the whole truth concerning life; and whenever we do employ that law we will enter into the very truth that we desire, that we have searched for. And whenever we are in the truth, we know the truth, and accordingly gain the absolute freedom promised.

The Good Side of Christian Science

In this connection we should also remember the fact that it is not what we believe, or what institutions we belong to, or what systems we have adopted — it is not these things that bring results; it is what we do with the principle involved — that is what brings results.

In considering this subject further, we might ask another question; that is, how it happened that the Christian Science movement almost from the beginning entered into this wonderful secret — the application of the wonderful law of spiritual concentration or consecration; and we also might ask why they succeeded in finding the inner or metaphysical conception of truth and life — the consciousness of the purely metaphysical state, thought and being.

In answer, we know that there were various reasons. One reason was the way the movement began; and these two wonderful words, "Christian" and "Science," were so combined that their interior meaning made a powerful impression upon those people who were ready to appreciate that interior meaning, and who entered into that attitude of mind where their consciousness of the spiritual side became a reality.

And here let us consider a remarkable psychological law. Whenever you find the inner meaning of any principle, law or state of being, and are in a position to be deeply impressed by the inner meaning thus discerned, and furthermore consecrate attention with mind and soul and spirit upon this inner meaning, you will soon enter into the real consciousness of that interior state. You will find thereby that you have discovered a new world in the domains of mind and spirit, a world in which you may remain all your life if you continue to be true to the highest truth that you have discerned within that world.

The Good Side of Christian Science

The early Christian Scientists discerned the inner meaning of Christian Science; that is, the interior meaning of the central idea or principle that was represented by the Christian Science system. They were ready for it, inasmuch as they had outgrown literalism absolutely; and being ready for it — hungering and thirsting for the consciousness of the spirit, they absolutely consecrated mind and soul and spirit upon the great Light that had been revealed to them. Accordingly, they entered into the very life and spirit of that Light; and they found after they had passed through the "inner gates" that they were in an attitude of mind they had never known before. This attitude of mind we know to be the attitude of pure metaphysics; that is, an attitude that transcends all conditions and things — an attitude that involves an absolute consciousness of the reality of eternal being. They discovered that while in that attitude, usually termed "the spiritual understanding of Divine Truth," they were able to demonstrate the power of truth; and whenever we can demonstrate the power of truth we have an argument in favor of our position that is invincible.

The Christian Science method, therefore, of finding the interior significance and power of real truth was a method that demonstrated itself admirably. And here we may emphasize the fact that, as far as we know, the meaning of Christianity and the inner meaning of Science had never been combined before into one great spiritual idea; and therefore those who were ready, hungering and thirsting for the spiritual, would naturally enter into this new understanding with unbounded enthusiasm and limitless faith.

It would be possible, if we should so desire, to illustrate this process along psychological lines, and demonstrate all the laws involved, explaining every step made in a thoroughly scientific manner; but those of us who have more or less

The Good Side of Christian Science

discernment of the inner meaning of all great principles, can discern at once why the Christian Science movement gained at the very beginning a position that was indeed founded on the solid rock. The methods employed were methods based upon the great law of spiritual understanding; and they have produced remarkable results; but they are not the only methods, because the spiritual world is wonderfully rich. We may expect, therefore, that almost at any time in the future another method for approaching Divine Truth may be evolved, and another system of thought with another institution appearing to further that method throughout the world — an institution that may become far greater and far more powerful than the Christian Science movement is today.

The fact that there are ten times as many people outside the Christian Science Church as inside that church who are searching for the highest truth, not being satisfied with the Christian Science method, proves conclusively that there is an overwhelming demand for some other means or process through which the marvelous power of the spirit may be gained and demonstrated here and now; and we know that wherever the demand is sufficiently large, the supply must follow in due time.

The Christian Science movement has filled the spiritual wants, as well as the temporal wants of thousands and thousands of people; but that movement is not able to supply the spiritual or temporal wants of all the people who have awakened to the new light, the new time and the new order.

We realize therefore that if the law of demand and supply is to be true, and it always is true, the time is ripe for another spiritual movement, a movement that will far transcend the Christian Science movement, both in spirituality and in power.

When that movement shall arise no one can say at the present time; but there is one thing we should remember in our study of this great subject; and it is this, that whenever a group of people unite in harmony upon a certain idea, or a certain lofty goal, or a certain sublime principle, and proceed to work together with unbounded devotion for the realization of that principle, the power contained within that principle will, sooner or later, return the favor and bring those people the very thing they want.

We must remember the great law that whenever we find an ideal, or a wonderful spiritual light containing within itself remarkable powers and possibilities, and when we devote ourselves absolutely to that light, having unlimited faith in its power, the time will come, and come shortly, when the truth and the power of that light will begin to manifest in us; that is, the truth and the power of that light will begin to express itself in all our thought and action and enable us more and more to demonstrate the law according to our highest ideals and our most perfect faith.

There are a great many things that could be added to this study, but we are interested principally in the fundamental or inner secret of results everywhere. If any man or any institution is gaining ground we wish to know why; but we do not want to feel that we have to adopt the system of any particular individual or institution, or do what he is doing in exactly the same mode or manner, because we all are individuals, and will have to express our individuality more and more if we are to advance in the scale of life. But if any particular individual has an inner secret, we wish to learn and understand that secret. We wish to understand the reason why he is securing results. We wish to understand the psychological side everywhere, because we know that if the psychological side is studied carefully we shall learn exactly how these higher laws operate, why they succeed at certain times, or through certain people, and why they fail at other times. We know there are many things that will have to be considered in connection with any movement or principle that has achieved wonderfully; but the principal thing involved is this, that unlimited devotion to some sublime idea, some idea that stands for something remarkable, an idea that has a vital message, or an idea that contains the power to do things along new and wonderful lines — unlimited devotion to such an idea will invariably bring wonderful results; and the more perfectly we can enter into the metaphysical attitude as we proceed, thereby laying hold of the real understanding or principle itself, the greater will be the results we have in view.

Herewith we might inquire more thoroughly into the nature of the metaphysical attitude with a view of learning exactly why results invariably increase when we proceed through that attitude; but we appreciate the fact that this would involve a very large study, although it is a study that we must by no means ignore in the future. The majority of us, however, have had so much experience along this line that we can see at once the inner meaning of that phase of the subject. And here we may well repeat that any person, or any system, or any institution that has found this higher or inner meaning, and that is making full and effective application of the principle involved, must certainly receive our highest admiration.

In the first place, we cannot help giving our admiration to any individual or institution that is demonstrating the law in a wonderful manner; and, in the second place, we shall find it most profitable to admire and respect every individual or institution that is demonstrating in this manner; for the fact is that whenever we admire or appreciate the greater, we enter into the spirit of the greater, and therefore establish in our own lives an upward and onward tendency.

The Good Side of Christian Science

We affirm that each individual should do his best work under every circumstance, employing what method he may think best; and we do demand that every individual or institution do the very best that he can with the method that he has adopted. But the question is, if there are very many individuals or institutions that are really doing their best with what they have. And inasmuch as the Christian Science movement is certainly doing its very best with the principle and system it has adopted as its own, that movement deserves the highest admiration that can possibly be given by any and every human soul. True, there are other institutions that are just as devoted to their ideals and that are also trying to make full and effective application of the principles upon which they stand. To these we must also give our highest admiration, because they are all moving in the same direction, toward the same great goal, approaching the same great Light. And while we are moving upward and onward in this wonderful manner we want to realize the highest and greatest possibilities along our own lines of action, and not waste energy criticizing other individuals or institutions that may be using methods slightly different from our own.

This is certainly good sound doctrine, and it has deep psychological significance. We all should apply it therefore; and above all we should remember the one great principle once more, that whenever you discover any system of truth, or any great idea, or any wonderful power — then consecrate yourself absolutely to that idea or power, devoting yourself to the greatest and the highest that you can possibly discern in the life of that idea or power, and the result will be that that power will return the favor and do for you what you expected, or according to your faith; and inasmuch as spiritual power is limitless, there is nothing that that power cannot do. If we fail in its use, the fault is ours; we have not devoted ourselves absolutely to our highest understanding of spiritual power. We may have scattered our forces or worshiped too many lesser gods. Henceforth, however, let us worship the highest that we know, and worship absolutely by keeping the eye singly upon the great light and the one great power, inspiring our worship with a passion for the sublime — a passion so strong and so deep that it stirs every atom of the soul. The results will be exactly what we have expected; our prayers will be answered; our ideals will be made real; and everything that we have wanted or desired in life shall come to us according to our faith.

The Ideal Made Real

The Ideal Made Real

Table of Contents

Chapter 1 - The Ideal Made Real	42
Chapter 2 - How to Begin: The Prime Essentials	52
Chapter 3 - The First Steps in Ideal Living	66
Chapter 4 - The First Thought in Ideal Thinking	80
Chapter 5 - The Ideal and the Real Made One	92
Chapter 6 - The First Step Towards Complete Emancipation	104
Chapter 7 - Paths to Perpetual Increase	113
Chapter 8 - Consider the Lilies	121
Chapter 9 - Count It All Joy	134
Chapter 10 - The True Use of Kindness and Sympathy	142
Chapter 11 - Talk Health, Happiness and Prosperity	153
Chapter 12 - What Determines the Destiny of Man	160
Chapter 13 - To Him That Hath Shall Be Given	165
Chapter 14 - The Life That is Worth Living	172
Chapter 15 - When All Things Become Possible	179
Chapter 16 - The Art of Getting What is Wanted	189
Chapter 17 - Paths to Happiness	197
Chapter 18 - Creating Ideal Surroundings	208
Chapter 19 - Changing Your Own Fate	216
Chapter 20 - Building Your Own Ideal World	223

Chapter 1

The Ideal Made Real

To have ideals is not only simple but natural. It is just as natural for the mind to enter the ideal as it is to live. In fact, the ideal is an inseparable part of life; but to make the ideal real in every part of life is a problem, the solution of which appears to be anything but simple. To dream +of the fair, the high, the beautiful, the perfect, the sublime, that everyone can do; but everyone has not learned how to make his dreams come true, nor realize in the practical world what he has discerned in the transcendental world. The greatest philosophers and thinkers in history, with but few exceptions, have failed to apply their lofty ideas in practical living, not because they did not wish to but because they had not discovered the scientific relationship existing between the ideal world and the real world. The greatest thinker of the past century confessed that he did not know how to use in everyday life the remarkable laws and principles that he had discovered in the ideal. He knew, however, that those laws and principles could be applied; that the ideal could be made real, and he stated that he positively knew that others would discover the law of realization, and that methods would be found in the near future through which any ideal could be made real in practical life; and his prophecy has come true.

To understand the scientific relationship that exists between the real and the ideal, the mind must have both the power of interior insight and the power of scientific analysis, as well as the power of practical application; but we do not find, as a rule, the prophet and the scientist in the same mind. The man who has visions and the man who can do things do not usually dwell in the same personality; nevertheless, this is necessary. And every person can develop both the prophet and the scientist in himself. He can develop the power to see the ideal and also the power to make the ideal real. The large mind, the broad mind, the deep mind, the lofty mind, the properly developed mind can see both the outer and the inner side of things. Such a mind can see the ideal on high, and at the same time understand how to make real, tangible and practical what he has seen. The seeming gulf between the ideal and the real, between the soul's vision and the power of practical action is being bridged in thousands of minds today, and it is these minds who are gaining the power to make themselves and their own world as beautiful as the visions of the prophet; but the ideal life and the world beautiful are not for the few only. Everybody should learn how to find that path that leads from the imperfections of present conditions to the world of ideal conditions, the world of which we have all so frequently dreamed.

The problem is what beginners are to do with the beautiful thoughts and the tempting promises that are being scattered so widely at the present time. The average mind feels that the idealism of modern metaphysics has a substantial basis. He feels intuitively that it is true, and he discerns through the perceptions of his own soul that all these things that are claimed for applied metaphysics are possible. He inwardly knows that whatever the idealist declares can be done will be done, but the problem is how. The demand for simple methods is one of the greatest demands at the present time, methods that everyone can learn and that will enable any aspiring soul to begin at once to realize his ideals. Such methods, however, are easily formulated, and will be found in abundance on the following pages. These methods are based upon eternal laws; they are as simple as the multiplication table and will produce results with the same unerring precision. Any person with a reasonable amount of intelligence can apply them, and those who have an abundance of perseverance can, through these methods, make real practically all the ideals that they may have at the present time. Those who are more highly developed will find in these methods the secret through which their attainments and achievements will constantly verge on the borderland of the marvelous. In fact, when the simple law that unites the ideal and the real is understood and applied, it matters not how lofty our minds and our visions may be, we can make them all come true.

To proceed, the principal obstacle must first be removed; and this obstacle is the tendency to lose faith whenever we fail to make real the ideal the very moment we expect to do so. This tendency is present to some degree in nearly every mind that is working for greater things, and it postpones the day of realization whenever it is permitted to exercise its power of retrogression. Many a person has fallen into chronic despondency after having had a glimpse of the ideal, because it was so very beautiful, so very desirable, in fact, the only one thing that could satisfy, and yet seemingly so far away and so impossible to reach. But here is a place where we must exercise extraordinary faith. We must never recognize the gulf that seems to exist between our present state and the state we desire to reach. On the other hand, we must continue in the conviction that the gulf is only seeming and that we positively shall reach the ideal that appears in the splendors of what seems to be a distant future, although what actually is very near at hand.

Those who have more faith and more determination do not, as a rule, fall down when they meet this seeming gulf; they inwardly know that every ideal will sometime be realized. It could not be otherwise, because what we see in the distance is invariably something that lies in the pathway of our own eternal progress, and if we continue to move forward we must inevitably reach it. But even to these the ideal does at times appear to be very far away, and the time of waiting seems very long. They are frequently on the verge of giving up and fears arise at intervals that many unpleasant experiences may, after all, be met before the great day of realization is gained; however, we cannot afford to entertain such fears for a moment nor to think that anything unpleasant can transpire during the period of transition; that is, the passing from the imperfections of present conditions to the joys and delights of an ideal life. We must remember that fear and despondency invariably retard our progress, no matter what our object in view may be, and that discouragement is very liable to cause a break in the engine that is to take our train to the fair city we so long have desired to reach.

The time of waiting may seem long during such moments as come when the mind is down, but so long as the mind is on the heights the waiting time disappears, and the pleasure of pursuit comes to take its place. In this connection we should remember that the more frequently we permit the mind to fall down into fears and doubts the longer we shall have to wait for the realization of the ideal; and the more we live in the upper story of life the sooner we shall reach the goal in view. There are many who give up temporarily all efforts toward reaching their ideals, thinking it is impossible and that nothing is gained by trying, but such minds should realize that they are simply making their future progress more difficult by retarding their present progress. Such minds should realize the great fact that every ideal can be made real, because nothing is impossible.

To reach any desired goal the doing of certain things is necessary, but if those things are not done now they will have to be done later; besides, when we give up in the present we always make the obstacles in our way much greater than they were before. Those things that are necessary to promote our progress become more difficult to do the longer we remain in what may be termed the "giving up" attitude, and the reason why is found in the fact that the mind that gives up becomes smaller and smaller; it loses ability, capacity and power and becomes less and less competent to cope with the problems at hand. Whenever we give up we invariably fall down into a smaller mental state. When we cease to move forwards we begin to move backwards. We retard progression only when we cease to promote progression. On the other hand, so long as we continue to pursue the ideal we ascend into larger and larger mental states, and thus increase our power to make real the ideals that are before us. The belief that it is impossible to make real the ideal has no foundation whatever in truth. It is simply an illusion produced by fear and has no place in the exact science of life. When you discern an ideal you discover something that lies in your own onward path. Move forward and you simply cannot fail to reach it; but when you are to reach the coveted goal depends upon how rapidly you are moving now. Knowing this, and knowing that fear, doubt, discouragement and indifference invariably retard this forward movement, we shall find it most profitable to remove those mental states absolutely.

The true attitude is the attitude of positive conviction; that is, to live in the strong conviction that whatever we see before us in the ideal will positively be realized, sooner or later, if we only move forward, and we can make it sooner if we will move forward steadily, surely and rapidly during every moment of the great eternal now. To move forward steadily during the great eternal now is to realize now as much of the ideal as we care to appropriate now; no waiting therefore is necessary. To begin to move forward is to begin to make real the ideal, and we will realize in the now as much of the ideal as is necessary to make the now full and complete. To move forward steadily during the great eternal now is to eternally become more than you are; and to become

The Ideal Made Real

more than you are is to make yourself more and more like your ideal; and here is the great secret, because the principle is that you will realize your ideal when you become exactly like your ideal, and that you will realize as much of your ideal now as you develop in yourself now. The majority, however, feel that they can never become as perfect as their ideal; others, however, think that they can, and that they will sometime, but that it will require ages, and they dwell constantly upon the unpleasant belief that they may in the meantime have to pass through years and years of ordinary and undesirable experience; but they are mistaken, and besides, are retarding their own progress every moment by entertaining such thoughts.

If all the time and all the energy that is wasted in longing and longing, yearning and yearning were employed in scientific, practical self development, the average person would in a short time become as perfect as his ideal. He would thus realize his ideal, because we attract from the without what corresponds exactly to what is active in our own within. When we attain the ideal and the beautiful in our own natures, we shall meet the ideal and the beautiful wherever we may go in the world, and we will find the same things in the real that we dreamed of in the ideal. When we see an ideal we usually begin to long for it and hope that something remarkable may happen so as to bring it into our possession, and we thus continue to long and yearn and wait with periods of despondency intervening. We simply use up time and energy to no avail. When we see an ideal the proper course to pursue is to begin at once to develop that ideal in our own nature. We should never stop to wait and see whether it is coming true or not, and we should never stop to figure how much time it may require to reach our goal. The secret is, begin now to be like your ideals, and at the proper time that ideal will be made real.

The very moment you begin to rebuild yourself in the exact likeness of your ideal you will begin to realize your ideal, because we invariably gain possession of that of which we become conscious; and to begin to develop the ideal in ourselves is to begin to become conscious of the ideal. To give thought to time is to stop and measure time in consciousness, and every stop in consciousness means retarded progress. Real progress is eternal; it is a forward movement that is continuous now, and in the realization of such a progress no thought is ever given to time. To live in the life of eternal progress is to gain ground every moment. It means the perpetual increase of everything that has value, greatness and worth, and the mind that lives in such a life cannot possibly be discouraged or dissatisfied. Such a mind will not only live in the perpetual increase of everything that heart can wish for, but will also realize perpetually the greatest joy of all joys, the joy of going on. The discouraged mind is the mind that lives in the emptiness of life, but there can be no emptiness in that life that lives in the perpetual increase of all that is good and beautiful and ideal.

The only time that seems long is the time that is not well employed in continuous attainment, and the only waiting time, that seems the hardest time of all, is the time that is not fully consecrated to the highest purpose you have in view. When we understand that we all may have different ideals we will find that we have an undeveloped correspondent in ourselves to every ideal that we may discern, and if we proceed to develop these corresponding parts there will be some ideals realized every day. Today we may succeed in making real an ideal that we first discovered a year ago. Tomorrow we may reach a goal towards which we have been moving for years, and in a few days we may realize ideals that we have had in view during periods of time varying from a few weeks to several years; and if we are applying the principles that underlie the process of making real the ideal, we may at any time realize ideals of which we have dreamed for a life time. Consequently, when we approach this subject properly we shall daily come into the possession of something that is our own. All the beautiful things of which we have dreamed will be coming into our world and there will be new arrivals every day.

This is the life of the real idealist, and we cannot picture a life that is more complete and more satisfying; but it is not only complete in the present. It is constantly growing larger and more desirable, thus giving us daily a higher degree of satisfaction and joy. When we discern an ideal that ideal has come within the circle of our own capacity for development, and the power to develop that ideal in ourselves is therefore at hand. The mind never discerns those ideals that are beyond the possibility of present development. Thus we realize that when an ideal is discerned it is proof positive that we have the power to make it real now.

Those who have not found their ideals in any shape or form whatever have simply neglected to make their own ideal nature strong, positive and pronounced. To live in negative idealism is to continue to dream on without seeing a single dream come true; but when the ideals we discern in our own natures become strong, positive working forces our dreams will soon come true; our ideals will be realized one after the other until life becomes what it is intended to be, a perpetual ascension into all that is rich, beautiful and sublime.

Whether we speak of environments, attainments, achievements, possessions, circumstances, opportunities, friends, companions or the scores of things that belong in our world, the law is the same. We receive an ideal only when we become just like that ideal. If we seek better friends, we shall surely find them and retain them, if we develop higher and higher degrees of friendship. If we wish to associate with refined people, we must become more refined in action, thought and speech. If we wish to reach our ideals in the world of achievement, we must develop greater ability, capacity and power. If we desire better environments, we must not only learn to appreciate the beautiful, but must also develop the power to produce those things that have true quality, high worth and real superiority. The great secret is to become more useful in the world; that is, useful in the largest and highest sense of that term. He who gives his best to the world will receive the best in return.

The world needs able men and women; people who can do things that are thoroughly worthwhile; people who can think great thoughts and transform such thoughts into great deeds; and to secure such men and women the world will give anything that it may hold in its possession. To make real the ideal, proceed to develop greatness, superiority and high worth in yourself. Train the mind to dwell constantly upon the borderland of the highest ideals that you can possibly picture; but do not simply yearn for what you can see, and do not covet what has not yet become your own. Proceed to remake yourself into the likeness of that ideal and it will become your own.

To proceed with this great development, the whole of life must be changed to conform with the exact science of life; that is, that science that is based upon the physical and the metaphysical united as the one expression of all that is great and sublime in the soul. The new way of thinking about things, viewing things and doing things must be adopted in full, and this new way is based upon the principle that the ideal actually is real, and therefore should be approached not as a future possibility, but as a present actuality. Think of the ideal as if it were real and you will find it to be real. Meet all things as if they contained the ideal, and you will find that all things will present their ideals to you, not simply as

The Ideal Made Real

mere pictures, but as realities. View the whole of life from the heights of existence; then you will see things as they are and deal with things accordingly; you will see that side of the whole of existence that may be termed the better side, and in consequence, you will grow into the likeness of that better side. When you grow into the likeness of the better side of all things, you will attract the better side of all things, and the ideal in everything in the world will be made real in your world.

Chapter 2

How to Begin: The Prime Essentials

To formulate rules in detail that will apply to each individual case is neither possible nor necessary. All have not the same present needs nor the same previous training; but there are certain general principles that apply to all, and these, if followed according to the individual viewpoint, will produce the results desired. If the proper beginning is made, the subsequent results will not only be greater and be realized in less time, but much useless experience and delay will be avoided. These principles, or prime essentials, are as follows:

1. Learn to be still.

When you undertake to live an ideal life and seek to promote your advancement in every direction, you will find that much cannot be gained until your entire being is placed in a proper condition for growth; the reason being that the ideal is ever advancing toward higher ideals, and you must improve yourself before you can better your life. It has been found that all laws of growth require order, harmony and stillness for proper action; therefore, to live peacefully, think peacefully, act peacefully and speak peacefully are important essentials. This will not only put the entire being into proper condition for growth, but will also conserve energy, and when you begin to live the larger life you will want to use properly all your forces; neither misusing or wasting anything. To acquire stillness never "try hard," but simply exercise general self control in everything you do. Never be anxious about results, and they will come with less effort, and in less time. Whenever you have a moment to spare relax the whole person, mind and body; just let everything fall into the easiest position possible. Make no effort to relax, simply let go. So long as you try to relax you will not succeed. While in this relaxed condition be quiet; do not move a muscle; breathe deeply but gently, and think only of peace and stillness. Before you go to sleep at night relax your entire system, and fall asleep with peace in your mind; bathe your mind and body, so to speak, in the crystal sea of the beautiful calm. These methods alone will work wonders in a few weeks. While you are at work hold yourself from anxious hurry or disturbed action; work in the attitude of poise and you will accomplish much more in the same given time and you will be a far better workman. Train yourself to come into the realization of perfect peace by gently holding a deep strong desire for peace and by ordering all your actions to harmonize with the peaceful goal in view. The result will be "the peace that passeth understanding," and for this alone your gratitude will be both boundless and endless.

2. Rejoice and be glad.

Cheerfulness is not only a good medicine, but it is food for mind and body. The cheerful life will fill every atom with new life, and it is to the faculties of the mind what sunshine is to the flowers and trees. To be happy always is one of the greatest things that man can do, and there are few things that are more profitable in every sense of that term. No matter what comes, be glad; and live in the conviction that all things are working together for good to you. As your conviction is so is your faith; and as your faith is so it shall be unto you. When you live in the conviction that all things are working together for good you will cause all things to work together for good, and you will understand the reason why when you begin to apply the real science of ideal living. No matter how dark the cloud, look for the silver lining; it is there, and when you always look at the bright side of things you develop brightness in yourself. This brightness will strengthen all your faculties so that you can easily overcome what obstacles may be in your way, and thus gain the victory desired. Direct your attention constantly to the bright side of things; refuse absolutely to consider any other side. At first this may not be possible in the absolute sense, but perseverance never fails to win. However, do not try hard; gently direct your attention to the bright side and know that you can. Ere long it will be second nature for you to live on the sunny side. The value of this attainment is very great; first, because joyousness will increase life, power, energy and force; this we all know from personal experience, and we wish to have all the life and power that we can possibly secure; second, because the happiest soul never worries, which is great gain. Worry has crippled thousands of fine minds and brought millions to an early grave. We simply cannot afford to worry and must never do so under any condition whatever. If we have that habit we can remove it at once by the proper antidote, which is joyousness. After you have trained yourself to look only for the bright and the best, the bright and the best will come to you, because you will be using your powers to bring those very things to pass; therefore, rejoice and be glad every moment. Let your heart and your soul sing at all times. When you do not feel the joyous music within, produce it with your own imagination, and ere long it will come of itself with greater and greater abundance; your soul will want to sing because it feels music, and there are few joys that equal the joy that comes when music is felt in the soul. There are so many things that are sweet and beautiful in life that when we once find the key to harmony we shall always rejoice. In the meantime, be happy for the good you have found, and through that very attitude you will develop the power to attract better things than you ever had before. This personal existence is brimful of good things and happy souls will find them all.

3. **Love everybody and be kind.**

If you wish your path to be strewn with roses, just be kind. Give your best to the world, and the best will come to you without fail; if it does not come today, never mind; just go on being kind and refuse to consider disappointments. Never hold in mind those things that you do not wish to retain; you thus cause those things to pass away. This "shall also pass away" is true of everything that is not pleasant; but unpleasant things will not pass away so long as we hold them in thought. That which you let go from your mind will pass away from you entirely. Train yourself to be kindness in a permanent state of mind, because you cannot afford to criticize, condemn or be angry at any time. We know that anger not only disturbs the mind, but also destroys the cells of the body, and no one can be angry without losing a great deal of life and energy. To find fault never pays; it simply brings enmity, discord and criticisms; besides, the faults we constantly see in others will develop in ourselves. The critical mind is destructive and the critical attitude is weakening to the entire system; therefore, no one can be his best who permits himself to think or talk about the flaws of life. Be good and kind to everybody; it is one of the royal paths to happiness and peace. When anyone does wrong, do not condemn; help him out; help him find the better way. "Cast your bread upon the waters;" it will surely return; sometimes more quickly than you expect it. Therefore, give abundantly of all that is best in your life, and nothing is better than kindness and love. When you begin to live an ideal life you will desire more and more to live the largest life possible, and to accomplish this you must learn to be much to everybody. Your purpose must be to be useful in the largest and truest sense of that term; and nothing can promote this purpose so thoroughly and so extensively as universal kindness. This does not imply, however, that you are to permit yourself to be imposed upon or unjustly used by the unscrupulous. It is our duty, as well as our privilege to demand the right at all times, and to demand justice for everybody and from everybody, but this should be done in kindness, with the antagonistic attitude eliminated.

The love that loves everybody is not the love that seeks to gain personal possession of some object of affection. We refer to that larger kindness that excludes no one from our whole-souled good wishes. This form of love is the greatest power in the world, and the one who loves the most in this larger, truer sense will accomplish the most. The reason why is found in the fact that a great love invariably brings out all that is large, great and extraordinary in human nature. To state that the one who takes the greatest interest in the welfare of the world does the most to promote his own interests may seem to be a contradiction of terms; but it is true, and it proves conclusively that the one who gives his best to the world will invariably receive the best in return. Never permit yourself to say that you cannot love every creature that lives; say that you do love everything that lives, and mean it. What you say you are doing that you will find yourself doing. This greater love illumines the mind, gives new life to every fiber in your being, removes almost every burden and eases the whole path of existence. Love removes entirely all anger, hatred, revenge, ill will, and similar states, a matter of great importance, for no one can live an ideal life while such states of mind remain. To have a sweet temper and loving disposition and a kind heart is worth more than tons of gold. We are all finding this to be true, and we realize fully that the person who loves everybody with that larger loving kindness has taken a long step upward into that life that is real life. This is not mere sentiment, but the expression of an exact scientific fact. A strong, continuous love will bring all good to anyone who lives and acts as he inwardly feels.

4. Have faith in abundance.

Have faith in God; have faith in man; have faith in yourself; have faith in faith. Believe in everything, and you relate yourself to the best that is in everything. We all know the value of self confidence, but faith is infinitely deeper, larger and higher. Self confidence helps us to believe in ourselves, as we are at present, and thus helps us to make a better use of the talents we now possess; but faith elevates the mind into the consciousness of our larger and superior possibilities, and thus increases perpetually the power, the capacity and the efficiency of the talents we now possess. Faith brings out the best that is within us and puts that best to work now. He who follows faith may frequently go out upon the seeming void, but he always finds the solid rock, The reason is that faith has superior vision and goes instinctively to the very thing we desire to find. Faith does not expect things to come of themselves. Faith never stands and waits; it does things; but while at work believes that the goal will be reached and the undertaking accomplished. The person who works in the attitude of faith can never fail; because through faith he draws upon the inexhaustible. The person who works in the attitude of doubt can never be at his best. Through the feeling of doubt he lowers his own ability; he holds back his best power and employs but a portion of his capacity; but the one who works in faith will press on to the very limit of his present capacity and then go on further still, because the more faith he has the more fully he realizes that there is no limit to his capacity, that the seeming void that lies before is positively solid rock all the way and he may safely proceed. Whatever you do believe that you can succeed in; do not for a moment permit yourself to doubt; know that the Infinite is your source, that you live in the universal and have the boundless upon which to draw for supply. If people or things do not come up to your ideal never mind; give them time; continue to have faith in their better selves; they will also scale the heights. Expect them all to do their best, and most of them will do so now; the others will soon follow, if you live in the faith that they will. The unbounded faith of one soul can elevate the lives of thousands. This is a statement that is just as true as it is great, and we should constantly give it the highest place in mind. The man who has faith in the whole race is an inspiration to everybody. Many a person has risen rapidly in the scale because someone had faith in him. Faith is the greatest elevating power that we know in the world. Faith can convert any failure into success and can promote the advancement of everybody, no matter what the circumstances may be. Have faith in yourself and you will advance as you never advanced before. Have faith in others and they will inevitably follow. Have faith in the Infinite and the Supreme Power will always be with you. This power will see you through, whatever your goal may be. Therefore, if you would enter the new life, the better life, the ideal life, and inspire others to do the same, have faith in abundance.

5. Pray without ceasing.

The true prayer is the whole-souled desire for the larger, the higher and the better while the mind is stayed upon the Most High; and to pray without ceasing is to constantly live in that lofty desire. The forces of mind and body always follow our desires; therefore, if we would use our powers in building up a larger life we must have high desires and true desires. Turn your desires upward and keep them there; desire the greater things only; never desire anything less. Those powers within you will cause you to become as true, as great and as perfect as your heart has prayed that you might become. To cause our desires, thoughts and states of consciousness to rise to the very highest states of being, we should employ the silence daily; that is, we should enter into the absolute stillness of the secret life of the soul. Through

The Ideal Made Real

the silence we shall find the secret of secrets, the path to that inner world from which everything proceeds. To begin, be alone and comfortably seated. Or, you may enter the silence in association with someone that is in perfect harmony with yourself. Relax mind and body; close your eyes and be perfectly quiet; turn your attention upon the inner life of the soul and gently hold your mind upon the thoughts of stillness and peace. Affirm with deep, quiet feeling, "Peace is mine." "I AM resting in the stillness of the spirit." "I have entered the beautiful calm." "I AM one with the Infinite." "I AM in the kingdom of the great within." "I AM in the secret places of the Most High," and similar states. While you make these statements feel that you are peaceful and still and that you are now in that inner world where all is quiet and serene. When you feel this deep, sublime stillness you can use other affirmations according to your present needs. You may affirm that you are well and strong and happy and harmonious, and that you have full possession of all those qualities that you know have existence in real life. To feel the perfect peace of the soul, however, is the first essential. After that is attained your consciousness will deepen and you will enter the great within to a greater and greater degree.

While the mind is in this interior state of being every thought you think will be a power, and every desire you express will modify or change everything in your life according to the nature of that desire and in proportion to its depth and unity with the Supreme. For this reason you should train yourself to think only right thoughts and create only the truest desires while you are in the silent state. That which you think or do while in the silence will have a greater effect upon your life than that which you may attempt while on the surface of outer consciousness. Therefore, everything that is important should be taken into the silence and through the silence to the Infinite. This corresponds perfectly with the statement "Take it to the Lord in prayer." The real purpose of the silence is to enable the mind to enter the inner life and not only recreate all thought according to the higher truth, but to enter into a more perfect touch with the divine source of things. The silence should be entered every day for ten, twenty or thirty minutes. This is a daily practice of extreme value. Though you may not have any real results at first, simply continue; you will reach your goal. When you begin to become conscious of your interior life and begin to live more or less in touch with the world beautiful that is within you, you will find that you can live in this high, peaceful state the greater part of the time and thus be in the silence almost constantly. This is not only a most desirable attainment, but it is the one great attainment toward which every soul should work. When a person can live in these higher realms always and constantly, and desire the realization of the highest and the best that he knows, the prayer without ceasing, the true spiritual prayer is being fulfilled. Such a prayer will be answered eternally. Every day will bring us something that we truly wished for, and every moment will be supplied with all that is necessary to make the present full and complete.

6. Think the truth.

When we learn to think the truth we have actually come to the "parting of the ways." Here we find where the old leaves off and the new begins. In this state the wrong disappears and the right is discerned and realized in an ever increasing manner. The foundation of all truth is expressed in the basic statement "MAN IS A SPIRITUAL BEING CREATED IN THE IMAGE AND LIKENESS OF GOD". Being created in the image of God man is now divine and in possession of all the divine attributes. Each individual is now in possession of infinite wisdom, infinite power, infinite love, eternal life, perfect peace, everlasting joy, universal truth, universal freedom, universal good, divine wholeness, spotless virtue, boundless supply. True, these attributes exist principally in the potential state, that is, they are possibilities waiting in the within for unfoldment, development and expression; nevertheless, they do exist in every soul and to a degree that is limitless. Therefore, every soul does actually possess those attributes, and to speak the truth we must recognize their existence and even now claim their possession. To think the truth you must think that you are divine in your true being, and that you possess these attributes, because this is the truth. You are divine in your true being, because you are created in the image of God, and you do possess the divine attributes just mentioned because that which is divine must necessarily possess the attributes of the divine. To think contrary to this would be wrong thought, and from wrong thought comes all the wrong in the world. The average person does think contrary to this thought; therefore, he is almost constantly in bondage to sin, sickness or trouble of some kind. Divine wholeness, that is, perfect health of body and mind is yours now, always was and always will be; therefore it would be wrong for you to say, "I AM sick." Your real being is never sick, never will be, because it is divine and you are the real being; you are not the body; you possess a body, and that body may be indisposed, if you create wrong thought, but that body is not you.

You are a spiritual being created in the image of God, therefore you are always well. When sickness appears on the surface, that is, in the body, know that it is on the surface only; that sickness is not in you; you are real being, and in real being perfect health reigns absolutely and eternally. The sickness that sometimes appears in the body is the result of a recognition of untruth, either expressed in wrong thinking or wrong living. Right thought, that is, that thought that invariably follows the recognition of absolute truth, would not produce sickness; and no person could become sick that is always filled and protected with the power of right thought. When the light reigns supremely, darkness cannot enter. Wrong thought comes from a false conception of yourself, and false conceptions will continue to form in mind so long as you are ignorant of the truth. When you know the truth, that you are the image of God, perfect in your own true being, you will think this truth and all your thought will; consequently, only right conditions can exist in your life, and all will henceforth be well with you. When you see yourself as you are in your true being, that you are even now strong and well, in full possession of peace, love, power, wisdom, freedom and all the good that is in God, you will think of yourself accordingly and such thought is right thought. The result will be right conditions in mind and body.

From center to circumference your entire being will be well and perfect, as it always was and ever will be in the truth. To think the absolute truth at first seems a contradiction of known facts, because we are so used to judging from appearances, but when we find that appearances are simply the result of thought, that right thought produces good appearances, and wrong thought produces adverse appearances, and learn that true being is the image of God, we shall no longer see contradiction in thinking absolute truth. When we think the truth about ourselves we shall always think the truth about others; we shall, therefore, not think of them as they appear on the surface but as they are in the perfection of real spiritual being. We shall overlook, forgive and forget the wrong appearance, knowing that it is but a temporary effect of wrong thought, and we shall proceed to inspire everyone to change that appearance by thinking right thought, the thought of truth.

7. Live in the spirit.

To express this statement in its simplest terms, we would say that to live in the spirit is to live in the upper story of mind and thought, or to live on the good side, the bright side and the true side of everything. To the beginner this is sufficient, because this simple change in living must come before the higher spiritual consciousness can be realized; but the change though simple at first will completely revolutionize life. Ere long, however, the consciousness of the true side and the better side will become so clear that to live in the spirit will mean infinitely more than to simply dwell in the upper story of mind, and when this larger experience comes we shall know from our own illumined understanding what it means to live in the spirit. When we begin to think the truth all kinds of illusions and false beliefs will gradually vanish, and we shall not only understand that we are spiritual beings, but we shall feel that we are all that divine life can be. We shall positively know that we are eternal souls living in a spiritual world now, expressing ourselves in a physical world, and we shall realize that we are actually created in the image and likeness of the Infinite, united with the Infinite and living in the life of Infinite being.

Through the fuller realization of truth we will learn that the spiritual is not some vague, far away something that saints alone can know, but that spirit is the essence of all things, the very life of all things visible and invisible, and that spirit is in itself absolutely good and perfect. We will realize that there is but one substance from which all things proceed and that substance is the expression of spirit; we will see that there is but one life, the spiritual life, and that there is but one law, the eternal coming forth in a greater and greater measure of life. We will find that spirit is the basis of all things, the soul of all things, and that therefore all things are in reality very good and very beautiful. We will find through the spirit that evil is but a temporary condition produced by man's understanding of the goodness and the completeness of real being and that to so live that we realize the absolute goodness and the perfect harmony of the whole universe is to live in the spirit. When we realize this we are on the true side of all things and we feel that we are. When we are in harmony with all things we are in harmony with the Infinite and can feel His presence always; and we also find that to "dwell in the secret places of the Most High" is to realize that we are in that great sea of life, the great spiritual sea, the universal state of being, the world of divine existence. While we are in this upper state, that is, in the spirit, we are away from the false, and actually in the true. We are in the spirit, and from the light of the spirit we can see clearly the truth concerning everything.

From this place we may ascend to other and greater heights and enter into the ever increasing realms of life where existence becomes fairer and higher, too beautiful for tongue to ever describe. What is held in store for the soul that lives in the spirit, eternity alone can reveal, but that the life that is lived in the spirit is the only true life thousands have learned, both in this age and in ages gone by. To the beginner, however, the first essential is to get away from material life, that is, the common, the gross, the superficial, the ordinary, the perverted and the wrong; then to go up higher, to enter the world of light and live in the more beautiful realms of sublime existence. To live in the spirit, live in the highest and most perfect state now, and do not for a moment come down. At first this state will simply be a life that is finer, larger and more harmonious, where things move more smoothly and where the value of life seems to constantly increase; but ere long living in the spirit will mean far more than merely a pleasing state of existence, and the further we advance the more this wonderful life will be, until we begin to understand the great soul who declared: "Eye hath not seen nor ear heard, neither hath it entered into the heart of man what God has prepared for them that love Him." In this connection we must bear in mind that it is not necessary to reach the supreme heights in spiritual life before we can live in the spirit. We can live in the spirit no matter where we may be in the scale of life, because the spiritual life has just as many degrees as there are human souls. Live in the realization that this universe has soul, that this soul is divine, and that you live and move and have your being in that great soul. Realize this as fully as your present state of development will permit, and you have begun to live in the spirit.

The realization of the divinity of the soul side of all things will reveal to your mind the great truth that all things are perfect in their real state of being, and that the real of everything lives in a universe of spirit, a universe that is everywhere within us all and about us all. However, before we begin we must be convinced of the great truth that the spiritual life is not mere sentiment nor a mere feeling of mind and soul. The spiritual life is the real life, the foundation of all life, the essence of all life, the soul of all life, and every true statement concerning the spiritual life is an exact scientific fact readily demonstrated by anyone who will apply the principle. And happy is the soul that does apply this principle, for such a soul will find life in the spirit, not only to be real, but to be infinitely more perfect, more wonderful and more beautiful than anyone has ever dreamed.

Chapter 3

The First Steps in Ideal Living

Give your best to the world no matter how insignificant that best may be, and the world will invariably give its best to you. There was nothing great or remarkable about the widow's mite, but it did produce remarkable results, and the reason was she gave her very best. When we give our best we not only receive the best in return from the outer world, but we also receive the best from the inner world. When you give your best you bring forth your best, and it is the bringing forth of your best that causes you to become better and better. When you become better you will meet better people and enter into better environments, and everything in your life will change for the better, because like does attract like. To give much is to become much, provided we give our best and give with the heart. The giving that comes simply from the hand does not count, no matter how large it may be. It brings nothing back to us nor does it bring permanent good to anybody else. When you give your best you do not give from your oversupply or from that which you cannot use. If you have something that you cannot use, it does not belong to you, and you cannot give, in the true sense of the term, what is not your own. To give does not mean simply to give money, unless that is the best you have; but rather to give your own service, your own talents, your ability, your own true worth and your own real self. The man who lives a real life at all times and under all circumstances is giving his best and the very best possible that can be given. A real life truly lived in the world is a power, and the person who lives such a life is a power for good wherever he may be. The presence of such a person is an inspiration and a light, as we all know. The man who loves the whole world with heart and soul, and loves without ceasing is doing far more for the race than he who endows universities, and will receive a far greater reward. We must remember, however, that such a love is not mere sentiment. Real love is a power and will cause the person who has it to do his very best for everybody under every possible circumstance. That person whose heart is with the race will never be satisfied with inferior work. He will never shirk nor leave the problems of life to somebody else; he will go in and push wherever something good is being done, and he will constantly endeavor to render better and better service where ever his field of action may be Such a person will give his best to the world, whether he gives through the channels of art or mechanics, music or literature, physical labor or intellectual labor, ideas or real living. What he does will be the best, and what he receives in return will be the best that the world is able to give. Give the best that you are through every thought, word and deed; that is the principle; and your life will be constantly enriched both from without and from within. Through the daily application of this principle you will develop superiority in mind, soul, character and life, and the world will be better off because you are here.

Expect the best from everybody and everybody will do their best for you. There may be occasional exceptions to this rule, but through close examination we shall find that these exceptions are due solely to our own negligence in applying the law to every occasion. The man who expects the best from everybody and has faith in everybody will certainly receive more love, more kindness, better friendship, better service and more agreeable associates by far than the one who has little or no faith in anyone. But, our faith in people must be alive, and our expectations must have soul. To live constantly in the fear that people will do this or that, and that such and such mistakes may be made, is to live in a confused mental world, and where there is much confusion there will be many mistakes. Mental states are contagious; how that can be is not a matter for present discussion, but the fact that they are is extremely important, and we all know that they are; therefore, if we live in fear and confusion we will be a disturbing element among all those with whom we associate, and if our associates are not mentally strong and positive, they will be more or less confused by our presence, and they are very liable to produce the very mistakes we feared. On the other hand, when we have faith in people we help them to have faith in themselves, and the more faith a person has in himself the fewer his mistakes and the better his work. When we have faith in everybody and are constantly expecting the best from everybody we create wholesome conditions in our own minds, conditions that will tend to develop the best in ourselves; that person, however, who has no faith in others will soon lose faith in himself, and when he does there will be a turn for the worse in his life. True, he may continue to possess a mechanical self confidence or an exaggerated state of egotism, but such a state will soon produce a reaction, and failure will follow. The self confidence that brings out the best that is within us is always founded upon a living faith in the inherent greatness of man; therefore, no one can have real faith in himself unless he also has faith in the greater possibilities of the race, and no one can expect the best from himself and give soul to that expectation unless he also expects the best from others. This is a scientific fact that anyone can prove in his own daily experience. To expect the best from everybody will cause everybody to do their best for you. Look for the best everywhere and you will find the best wherever you go. Why this is so is a matter upon which fact that this law works that concerns us, and concerns us very much. Not everybody can fully understand why the best is always found by him who never looks for anything but the best, but everybody can look for the best everywhere and thereby find the best; and it is the finding of the best that attracts our attention. It is real results that we are looking for, and the simpler the method the better. The man who will constantly apply this law will not remain in undesirable environments very long, nor will he occupy an inferior position very long; better things will positively come his way and he will not have to wait an age for the change. The man who looks for the best is constantly thinking about the best and constantly impressing his mind with the best thought about everything; and since man is as he thinks we can readily understand why such a man will become better and better; therefore, by looking for the best everywhere he will not only find the best in the external world, but he will create the best in his mental world; this will give him a greater mind, which in turn will produce higher attainments and greater achievements. That man, however, who is always looking for the worst will constantly think about the worst and will fill his mind with inferior thoughts; that he, himself, will become inferior by such a process is a foregone conclusion. We shall positively find, sooner or later, what we constantly look for; it is, therefore, profitable to look for the best everywhere and at all times; we become like those things that we constantly and deeply think about; it is, therefore, profitable to think only of the best whatever may come or not. The average person may not find the best the very first day this principle is applied. Most of us have strayed so far away from this mode of thinking and living that it may take some time to get back to the path that leads to the best; but one thing is certain, whoever will look for the best everywhere, and continue to do so for a reasonable length of time, will find that path; besides, he will have more delightful experiences while he is training himself to apply this principle than he has had for any similar period before. This, however, will be only the beginning; the future has far greater things in store, if he will continue to look for the best and never look for anything else.

When things are not to your liking, like them as they are. In other words, while you are working for greater things make friends with the lesser things, and they will help you to reach your goal. The person who is dissatisfied with things as they are and discontented because things are not to his liking is standing in his own way. We cannot get away from present conditions so long as we antagonize those conditions, because we are held in bondage to that which we resist. If you want present conditions to become stepping stones to better things, you must get on the better side of present conditions, and you do that by liking things as they are while they remain with you. We must be in harmony with the present if we wish to advance, because in order to advance we must use the present, but we cannot use that with which we are not in harmony. This is a fact that deserves the most thorough attention and will, when understood, explain fully why the average person seems powerless to rise above his surroundings. We must be on friendly terms with everything that exists in our present world if we wish to gain possession of all the building material that our present world can give, and we cannot secure too much material if we desire to build a larger life and a greater future. That which we dislike becomes detrimental to us, no matter how good it may be; nevertheless, it will always be with us because it is impossible to eliminate permanently that which we antagonize; when we run away from it in one place we shall meet it elsewhere in some other form; but that which we love will constantly serve us and help us on to greater things; when it can serve us no longer it will disappear. To like those things, however, that are not to our liking may seem difficult, but the question is why they are not to our liking; when we know that everything in our present world is a stepping stone to something still better it will be natural for us to like everything. Those things may not come up to our ideals, but that is not their real purpose; it is not the mission of present things to serve as ideals, their mission is to help us to reach our ideals, and they positively can do this if we will take them into friendly cooperation. When you take a drive to an ideal country place you do not dislike the horse because he is not that country place; if you are humane, you will love that horse because he is willing and able to take you where you wish to go. If you should dislike and mistreat that horse or should fail to hitch him to the vehicle, you would not reach your destination. This, however, is the very thing that the average person does with the things of his present world; these things are the horses and the vehicles that can take us to the ideal places we desire to reach; but we must hitch them up; we must treat them right and use them. To cause all things that are about us now to work together with us, we must be in perfect harmony with them; we must like them as they are, and that becomes comparatively easy when we know that it is necessary for them to be what they are in order that they may serve as our stepping stones; if they were different there would be no stepping stones, and we would have to remain where we are. When we realize that everything that exists in our present world has the power to promote our advancement, if we properly use that power, and when we realize that it is necessary to be in harmony with all things to use the power that is within those things, we shall no longer dislike anything; we shall even make friends with adversity, because the power that is in adversity can be tamed by kindness and love; and when that power is tamed it becomes our own. These are great facts and easily demonstrated by anyone, and whoever will apply these principles will find that by liking everything that be finds he will secure the cooperation of everything, and anyone can move forward rapidly when all things are working with him; consequently, by liking what he finds he will find what he likes.

When you do not get what you want take what you can get and call it good. It is better to have something than nothing; besides, we must use what we can get before we can become so strong and so able that we can get whatever we may want. When a person fails to realize his ideals, there is a reason; usually the cause is this: he simply longs for the ideal but does not work himself up to the ideal. And to work himself up to the ideal he needs everything that he can get and use now; by taking what he can get he secures something to work with in promoting his present progress, and by looking upon this something as good he will turn it to good account. It is a well known fact that we get the best out of everything when we meet everything in the conviction that it is good for something, because this attitude invariably brings the mind into conscious touch with the real value of that which is met. What we constantly look for we are sure to find, therefore, by calling everything good that we get and by constantly looking for the real worth of that which we get, the good in everything that we get will be found; the result is that everything we receive or come in contact with will be good for something to us and will have something of value to give us. Gradually, the good will so accumulate that we shall have all that we want; life will be filled with that which has quality and worth, which means that the development towards greater worth will constantly take place, and development towards greater worth means the constant ascension into the realization of our ideals. By accepting and using the good that we can now secure we add so much to the worth of our own life that we become worthy of the greater good we may desire; in consequence, we shall positively receive it. This process may not satisfy those who expect to reach the top at once or expect to receive the better without making themselves better, but it will satisfy those who would rather move forward gradually and surely than stand empty handed waiting and waiting for ages hoping that some miraculous secret may be found through which everything can be accomplished at once. The idea, however, is not that we should meekly submit to things as they are and be satisfied with what little fate may seem willing to give us; that is the other extreme and is just as detrimental to human welfare. Take everything that legitimately comes your way; do not refuse it because it seems too small; take it and call it good, because it is good for something; then make the best possible use of it with a view of getting greater good through that use; expect everything to multiply in your hands; have that faith; accept little things, as well as large things in that conviction, and every good that you do accept will be instrumental in bringing greater good to you. To live in the attitude of turning everything to good account has a most wholesome effect upon mind and character, because that mental attitude will tend to turn everything within yourself to good account; the result will be the constant development of a finer character and a more capable mind. By combining all the results from this mode of living and by noting the greater results that will invariably come from these combined results we must conclude that the total gain will be great, and that he who turns to good account everything that comes into his life, will positively receive everything that he may require to live an ideal life.

Live in the cheerful world, even if you have to create such a world in your own imagination. Resolve to be happy regardless of what comes; you cannot afford to be otherwise. Count everything joy; meet everything in the spirit of joy, and expect everything to give you joy. By creating a cheerful world in your own imagination you develop the tendency to a sunny disposition, and by meeting everything in the attitude of joy you will soon meet only those things that naturally produce joy. Like does attract like. Much sunshine will gather more sunshine, and the happiest mind meets the most delightful experiences. When exceptions occur pass them by as of no consequence, because they are of no consequence to you; you are interested only in happy events; it is only such events that you desire to meet; therefore, there is no reason whatever why you should pay any attention to the other kind. It is a fact that the less attention we pay to unpleasant conditions the less unpleasantness we meet in life. That person who looks for the disagreeable everywhere and expects to find it everywhere will certainly find what he is looking for in most places, if not in all places. On the other hand, the person who expects only the pleasant will seldom find anything else. We attract what we think of the most. There is no better medicine than cheerfulness, especially for the circulation and the digestive functions. Keep your mind full of living joy and your circulation will be strong in every part of your being, and a strong full circulation is one of the secrets to perfect health. Another great secret to health is a good digestion, and it is well to remember that so long as you are thoroughly bright and happy you can digest almost anything. The greatest value of cheerfulness, however, is found in its effect upon the mind; that is, in its power to make faculties and talents grow, just as sunshine makes flowers grow. It is a well known fact that the most cheerful mind is the most brilliant mind, other things being equal, and that the brightest ideas always come when you are in the brightest frame of mind. This makes cheerfulness indispensable to those who wish to improve themselves and develop superior mental power. The depressed mind is always dull and never sees anything clearly; while the cheerful mind learns more readily, remembers more easily and understands more perfectly; but we must not conclude that cheerfulness is all that is necessary to the development of a fine intelligence; there must be mental power and mental quality as well; but the power and the quality of the mind, however great, cannot be fully expressed without an abundance of mental sunshine. Though the warmest sunshine may fail to make a gravel knoll productive, still the most fertile soil will remain barren so long as the sunshine is absent. There are thousands of fertile minds in the world that are almost wholly unproductive, because they lack mental sunshine. If these would cultivate real genuine mental brightness every part of the world would sparkle with brilliant ideas. What the acorn is to the oak bright ideas are to a great and successful life, and we all can produce bright ideas through the development of mental ability and the cultivation of mental sunshine. Cheerfulness keeps the body in the best condition and brings out the best that there is in the mind. To attain the cheerful state we must remember that it is a product of the inner life and does not come from circumstances or conditions; therefore, the first essential is to create a cheerful world in the imagination; picture in mind the brightest states of existence that you can think of and impress joy upon mind at all times; feel joy, think joy, and make every action of mind and body thrill with joy; ere long you will have created within yourself the subconscious cause of joy, and when this is done cheerfulness and brightness will become permanent elements in yourself.

Live in the present only, and seek to make the great eternal now as full and complete as possible. It is what we do for the present that counts; the past is gone, and the future is not ready to be acted upon. Give your time, your talent and your power to that which is now at hand and you will do things worthwhile, you will not waste thought upon what you expect to do, but you will turn all your energies upon that which you now can do; results will positively follow. The man who does things worthwhile in the present will not have to worry about the future; for such a man the future has rich rewards in abundance. The greater the present cause the greater the future effect. Nine tenths of the worries in the average life are simply about the future; all of these will be eliminated when we learn to live in the present only. Instead of giving anxious thought to the bridge we may have to cross we should give scientific thought to the increase of present ability and power; thus we make ourselves fully competent to master every occasion that we may meet. To judge the present. The present moment should be dealt cause if we are advancing, the present is not only larger than the past, but quite different in many if not all respects. To follow the past is to limit one's self to the lesser accomplishments of the past and thus prevent the very best from being attained in the present. The present moment should be dealt with according to the needs of the present moment regardless of what was done under similar conditions in the past. There is sufficient wisdom at hand now to solve all the problems of the present moment, if we will make full, practical application of that wisdom. He who lives for the present only will live a larger life, a happier life, a far more useful life; this is perfectly natural, because he will not scatter his forces over past ages and future ages, but will concentrate his whole life, all his power, all his ability upon that which he is trying to do now; he will be his best today, because he will give all of his best to the life of today, and he who is his best today will be still better tomorrow.

Never complain, criticize or condemn, but meet all things in a constructive attitude of mind. The critical mind is destructive to itself, and will in time become wholly incompetent to even produce logical criticism. To complain about everything is to constantly think about the inferior side of everything, thus impressing inferiority upon the mind; this will cause the entire process of thinking to become inferior; in consequence, the retrogression of the man himself will inevitably follow. Refuse to complain about anything; complaints never righted a wrong and never will. When you seek to gain justice through complaint you temporarily gain something in one place and permanently lose something in another; besides, you have harmed your own mind. The fact is that the more you complain the worse things will become; and the more you criticize what you meet today the more adverse and inferior will be the things you are to meet tomorrow. The reason why is simple; the complaining mind attracts the cheap and the common, and the critical spirit goes directly down into weakness and inferiority. However,

The Ideal Made Real

we must remember in this connection that there is a marked difference between the critical attitude and the discriminating attitude. When things are not right we should say so, but while saying so we should not enter into a "rip and tear" frame of mind; the facts should be stated firmly but gently and without the slightest trace of ill feeling or condemnation; simply discriminate between the white and the black and state the facts, but let no hurt whatever appear in your voice. What we say is important, but the way things are said is far more important; even truth itself, can be expressed in such a way that it hurts, harms and destroys; this, however, is not true expression. It is truth misdirected, and always produces undesirable effects. To state your wants in a friendly manner is not complaint, but when there are hurts and whines in your voice you are making complaints and you are harming yourself; besides, you are producing unfavorable impressions upon those with whom you come in contact. It is far better to have faith in people than to criticize and complain, even though everything seems to go wrong, because when we have faith in people we shall finally attract those who are after our own hearts, and who are competent to do things the way we wish to have them done. Instead of complaining, or stating that there is always something wrong, we should live constantly in the strong faith that everything is eternally coming right; we thus place ourselves in harmony with those laws that can and will make things right. This is no idle dream, nor shall we have to wait a long time to secure results. The very day we establish faith in the place of complaints, criticisms and distrust, the tide will turn; things will change for the better in our world, and continue to improve perpetually.

Make the best use of every occasion, and nothing but opportunities will come your way. He who makes the best of everything will attract the best of everything, and it is always an opportunity to meet the best. There are occasions that seem worthless, and the average person thinks he is wasting time while he is passing through such states, but no matter how worthless the occasion may seem to be the one who makes the best use of it while he is in it will get something of real value out of it; in addition, the experience will have exceptional worth, because whenever we try to turn an occasion to good account we turn everything in ourselves to good account. The person who makes the best use of every occasion is developing his mind and strengthening his own character every day; to such a person every occasion will become an opportunity and will consequently place him in touch with the greater world of opportunities. Much gathers more and many small opportunities will soon attract a number of larger ones; then comes promotion, advancement and perpetual increase. "To him that hath shall be given." Every event has the power to add to your life, and will add to your life, if you make the best use of what it has to give; this will constantly increase the power of your life, which will bring you into greater occasions and better opportunities than, you ever knew before. Make the best use of everything that comes your way; greater things will positively follow; that is the law, and he who daily applies this law has a brilliant future before him.

Never antagonize anything, neither in thought, word nor deed, but live in that attitude that is non resisting to evil while positively and continuously inclined towards the good. You give your energy to that which you resist; you thereby give life to the very thing you seek to destroy. To resist evil is to increase the power of evil, and at the same time take life and power away from that good which you wish to develop or promote. The antagonistic mind develops bitterness in itself and thereby becomes just as disagreeable as the thing disliked; frequently more so, and we cannot expect to be drawn into the more delightful elements of the ideal while we ourselves are becoming less and less ideal. To live in the antagonistic attitude is to perpetuate a destructive process throughout mind and body, and at the same time suffer a constant loss of energy. We therefore cannot afford to be antagonistic at any time, nor even righteously indignant, no matter how perfectly in the right we may be; though in this connection it is well to remember that indignation never can be righteous. There are a number of minds that have the habit of feeling an inner bitterness towards those beliefs or systems of thought which they cannot accept. Frequently there can be no logical grounds for such a feeling. In many instances it is simply hereditary, or the result of foundationless prejudice; nevertheless, it is there and is actually sapping life and power out of the mind that has it. This habit is therefore responsible for much mental weakness, inability and consequent failure; and as everything that tends to decrease the life and the power of the individual tends to shorten his life, as well as decrease the value and usefulness of his life, it is evident that we cannot afford to feel bitter toward any religion, any belief, any doctrine, any party or any person whatever; we harm ourselves by so doing and do not add to the welfare or happiness of anybody. Be on friendly terms with the entire universe and feel kindly towards every creature in existence; leave the ills of perverted life to die; let the "dead bury their dead." It is our privilege to press on and promote the greatest good that we know; and when we give our whole time and attention to the highest attainment of the greatest good, evil will die of itself. This is what it means to overcome evil with good, and it is the one perfect path to complete emancipation, both for the individual and for the race. If you wish to serve the race do not antagonize systems, doctrines, methods or beliefs; be an inspiration to the race by actually doing the very best you know now.

Chapter 4

The First Thought in Ideal Thinking

But seek ye first his kingdom, and his righteousness; and all these things shall be added unto you. Mat. 6: 33.

The kingdom of God is a spiritual kingdom within man and manifests through man as the spiritual life. His righteousness is the right use of all that is contained in the elements of the spiritual life. The spiritual life being the complete life, the full expression of life in body, mind and soul, it is evident that the right use of the spiritual life will produce and bring everything that man may need or desire. The source of everything has the power to produce everything, provided the power within that source is used according to exact spiritual law. The spiritual life being the source of all that is necessary to a full and perfect life, and the kingdom within being the source of the spiritual life, we can readily understand why the kingdom should be sought first; and also why everything that we may require will be added when the first thought is given to spiritual living, ideal thinking and righteous action. Righteous action, however, does not simply imply moral action, but the right use of the elements of life in all action.

The kingdom of God is the spiritual side of all things. This spiritual side is within the manifested or visible side; that is, everything is filled with an inner, finer something that is perfect and complete. Every part of the outer world is filled and permeated with an inner world, and everything that appears in the outer world is a partial manifestation or expression of what exists in a perfect and complete state in the inner world. This inner world is the kingdom referred to, and as it is inexhaustible in every sense of that term, there is nothing we cannot receive when we learn to draw upon the riches of this vast inner realm. In the life of man we have the outer and the inner worlds; the personal life in the without and the great spiritual life in the within. What appears in the outer world of man, that is, in his personal existence, is the result of what he has sought and brought forth from his inner world. According to one of the greatest of metaphysical laws we express whatever we become conscious of. We, therefore, understand clearly why the personal man, or his outer world, is the direct result of what he has become conscious of in his interior world. Man is what he is in the without, because he has sought the corresponding elements in the within, and he may change the without in any manner desired by seeking first in the within those qualities and attributes that he may desire.

To seek and find the within is to become conscious of the within, and what is thus sought and found will express itself in personal life; but its real value will depend upon whether it is properly used or not. To seek the richer kingdom within is the first essential, but to promote the righteous use of these greater riches is the second essential, and is just as important as the first. To give the first thought at all times to the great spiritual kingdom within, it is not necessary to withdraw attention from the outer world nor to deny one's self the good things that may exist in the outer world. To seek the kingdom first is to give one's strongest thought to the spiritual life, and to make spiritual thought the predominating thought in everything that one may do in life; in other words, live so closely to the spiritual kingdom within that you are fully conscious of that kingdom every moment, and depend absolutely upon supreme power to carry you through whatever you may undertake to do. To seek the kingdom first the heart must be in the spirit; that is, to live in the full realization of the inner spiritual life at all times must be the one predominating desire. However, the mental conception of the spiritual life must not be narrow, but must contain the perfection of everything that can possibly appear in life.

To think of the spiritual life as being distinct from mind and body, is to prevent the elements of the great interior life from being expressed in mind and body, and what is not expressed cannot be lived. The spiritual life in this larger sense must be thoroughly lived in mind and body. The power of the spiritual must be made the soul of all power, and the law of spiritual action must be made the rule and the guide in all action. When the spiritual is lived in all life the richness and the quality and the worth of the spiritual will be expressed in all life, and spiritual worth means the sum total of all worth. There are any number of minds in the world who now realize this greater worth and who have found the spiritual riches within to an extraordinary degree, but they have not in every instance sought righteousness; therefore, these spiritual riches have been of no use; frequently they have become obstacles in the living of a life of personal welfare and growth.

Real righteousness means right living and exact scientific thinking; that is, the correct expression of everything of which we are now conscious. To be righteous does not simply mean to be moral and truthful and just, but to live in harmony with all laws, physical, mental, moral and spiritual. To be in harmony with physical law, is to adapt one's self orderly to everything in the external world; to resist no exterior force, but to constructively use every exterior force in such a manner that perpetual physical development may take place. To be in harmony with mental laws is to promote scientific thinking; that is, to think the truth about everything and to see everything from the universal viewpoint. Scientific thinking is that mode of thinking that causes all the forces of mind and thought to constantly work for greater things. To be in harmony with moral laws is to live a life of complete purity; and purity in the true sense of the term is the doing of all things at the right time, in the right place and with the right motive; in other words, every action is a pure action that leads to higher and better things. All other actions are not pure, therefore not moral. To be in harmony with spiritual laws is to live in constant conscious touch with the inner or higher side of everything. To apply the spiritual law is to seek the spiritual first, no matter what the goal in view may be; to seek first the spiritual counterpart that is within everything, to make the spiritual thought the predominating thought and to dwell constantly in the spiritual attitude. We enter the spiritual attitude when we enter the upper story of the mind and mentally face that supreme side of life that is created in the likeness of the Supreme. Briefly stated, to be righteous is to be in harmony with the outer side of life, to think the truth, to live in real purity, to dwell on the spiritual heights and to give full and complete expression to the highest and the best of which we are now conscious. When this is done we shall rightly manifest whatever we may find in the kingdom within. Righteousness, however, is not a definite goal but a perpetual process of attainment that involves the entire being of man. The righteous man is right and perfect as far as he has ascended in the scale of life at present, though not simply in a moral sense, but in every sense, including body, mind and soul.

The righteous man is never weak, never sick, and is never in a state of discord or disorder. This is a great truth that we should not fail to remember. Sickness, weakness, discord and all other adverse conditions come from the violation of law somewhere in human life, but the righteous man violates no law. He is true to life as far as he has ascended in the scale of life. To be righteous in the absolute sense of the term is to use everything in our present world as God uses everything in His world, which means in harmony with its own nature, in harmony with its sphere of action, and in harmony with that law that leads upward and onward forever. Righteous action is that action that is always harmonious and that always works for better things, greater things, higher things. The great majority of those minds that are awakened to the reality of the spiritual side of things have already found an abundance of good things in the vast interior life that is ready for manifestation in personal life, but as most of these have neglected the law of real righteousness this abundance remains inactive in the potential state and all other things as promised are not added. That all other things will be added when His kingdom and His righteousness are sought first may not seem clear to everybody, because the kingdom of God has been looked upon as a faraway place that we are to enter when we leave the body, and righteousness has been looked upon as simply a moral, just and honest mode of living. But when we realize that the kingdom is the great spiritual world within us, and that from this world comes all wisdom, all power, all talent, all life; in brief, everything that we now possess in body, mind and soul, and that everything we are to receive in the future must come from the same source, we understand clearly why the kingdom must be sought first.

We cannot secure anything unless we go to the source, and the spiritual kingdom within us is the one only source of everything that is manifested in human life. When we desire more wisdom and a greater understanding it is evident that we can obtain these things only by entering real mental light, and that light is within us in the spirit. By entering into the consciousness of the illumined world within we naturally receive more light. We ourselves, become illumined to a degree, frequently to a great degree, and we thus gain the power to understand perfectly what we could neither desire nor comprehend before. When we seek more life and power we can find the greater life only in the eternal life, and the eternal life is the life of the spirit in the kingdom within. "They that wait upon the Lord shall renew their strength." To wait upon the Lord is to enter into the spiritual presence of the Infinite, and whenever we enter into the presence of the Infinite we enter into the life of the Infinite and we are thus filled through and through with the supreme power of that life.

When we enter into the spiritual kingdom within we enter into the Christ consciousness and in that consciousness we receive the life more abundant, because to be in the Christ consciousness is to be in the very spirit of the limitless life of the Christ. When we seek health we can find it in the kingdom, because in the spirit all is always well. There is a realm within man where perfect health reigns supremely and eternally. In that realm everything is always perfectly whole and to enter into that realm is to enter into absolute health and wholeness. No one who lives constantly in the spirit can possibly be sick, because sickness can no more enter the spiritual state than darkness can enter where there is absolute light. To enter the kingdom within is to enter health, happiness and harmony in the highest, largest degree; therefore, by seeking the kingdom, health will be added, happiness will be added, harmony will be added. It is impossible, however, to gain health, happiness and harmony, in the true sense, from any other source. But to seek these qualities in the kingdom is not sufficient. We must also seek righteousness or the right expressions of those things. If we misuse any organ, faculty, function or power anywhere in body, mind or soul, we cannot remain in health, no matter how spiritual we may try to be.

To enter the kingdom within is to enter the perpetual increase of power, because there is no limit to the power of the spirit, and the more power we enter into or become conscious of the more power we shall give to mind and body;

in consequence, the more spiritual we become the stronger we become, the more able we become, the more competent we become and the more we can accomplish whatever our work may be; and he who can do good work in the world invariably receives the good things of the world. To his life will be added all those things that can make personal existence rich and beautiful. To enter the kingdom within is to enter the life of freedom. There is no bondage in the spirit, and as we grow in the spirit we grow out of every form of bondage. One adverse condition after another disappears until absolute freedom is gained. Therefore, when we seek first His kingdom and His righteousness we shall find the life of complete emancipation. Perfect freedom in all things and at all times will positively be added.

There are thousands of aspiring souls in this age that are trying to develop their powers and talents so that they might be of greater use in the world, but if these would seek the kingdom first, they would find within themselves the real source of every talent; and as the only way to permanently increase anything is to increase the expressions of its source we understand perfectly why greatness can come only when we begin to live in the great within. We must always bear in mind that what we become conscious of we bring forth into personal expression, but we cannot become conscious of the larger source of any quality or talent unless we enter into the spirit of that quality and talent, and as the spirit of all things has its source of real existence in the kingdom within, we must enter this interior world if we wish to become conscious of a larger and a larger measure of those things that we wish to express.

That any person can improve his environment or overcome poverty by seeking the kingdom first may not seem possible, but the truth is that adverse conditions will positively disappear after one begins to actually live the full spiritual life. Poverty has two causes; lack of ability and the misplacing of ability. To improve ability to any degree the within must be awakened. We must learn to draw upon the inexhaustible sources of the inner life and become conscious of the greater capacity that lies latent within us. This is accomplished by seeking the kingdom first. By giving your first thought, your predominating thought to the great and mighty world within, your mind will gradually enter more deeply into the life of this inner world. You thus become conscious of the larger powers within, because consciousness always follows the predominating thought. What you think of the most develops in yourself. When you think the most of the spiritual, consciousness will follow your spiritual thought and thus enter more deeply into the spirit. The result is you become conscious of a larger spiritual domain every day, you become conscious of a greater capacity within yourself every day, and since you always express what you become conscious of you will cause greater ability and capacity to be developed and expressed in yourself every day; you thereby remove the first cause of poverty and place yourself in a position where you will be in greater demand, and the greater the demand for your service the greater will be your recompense.

There are a number of people who have misplaced their talents that may have considerable ability, but they are not in the work for which they are adapted, and therefore do not succeed. They may have been forced into their present positions by necessity, or they may have chosen their present places through inferior judgment, but both of these causes may be changed by seeking the kingdom first. When we enter the spiritual everything clears up. We not only see our mistakes, but also how to correct them; therefore, if you are in the wrong place, enter the spiritual light of the kingdom within, and you will see clearly where you belong. If you do not know whether you are in the proper sphere or not, enter the spirit. Constantly live in the spirit and you will soon know; you will also know when and how to change. By entering this state where the outlook is infinitely greater you will see opportunities, open doors, possibilities, and pastures green that you never saw before; and you will also see clearly which one you have the power and the capacity to take advantage of now. If you have been forced into the wrong place by necessity, the larger mental life that will come when you seek the kingdom will give you the power to command something better, and the superior wisdom that comes through the light of the spirit will guide you in your choice. Instead of adversity and constant need you will have peace, harmony and abundance. You will pass from the world of poverty and limitations to a world that can offer a future as brilliant as the sun.

The man who fights adversity and complains of his lot will continue in poverty and need. He will remain in mental darkness; he will be daily misled, and will always be doing the wrong thing at the wrong time. Such a life breeds ill luck and misfortune and perpetuates the poverty that already exists. However, let this person enter into harmony with his present fate, count everything joy, and realize that he can make his present misfortune a stepping stone to better things; then let him give his first thought to the kingdom, to the greater life and power and capacity within, to the superior creative powers of his own mind, those powers that are able even now to create for him a better fate, if he will but place before them a better pattern; the results will be peace of mind first, then hope of the better, then the vision of great changes near at hand, then the faith that the new life, the new time and the better days are now being created for his world. And when a person begins to inwardly feel that things are taking a turn, that better days are coming and that the good is beginning to accumulate in his life, the victory is nearly won. A little more faith and perseverance and the crowning day is at hand. From that moment all things will begin to work together for good things and for still greater things, providing the mind is held in constant conscious touch with the spiritual kingdom within, and all the laws of life are employed according to the highest ideal of righteousness.

Many a person, however, has failed while on the very verge of his victory, because he neglected the kingdom when he began to see the change coming. By giving his first thought to the material benefits that he expected to secure, his consciousness is taken away from the spirit and becomes confused in those things that had not as yet been placed in the true order of perpetual increase. The result is a scattering of forces and his loss upon the hold of the good things that were beginning to gravitate towards his world. While ascending this upward path we must at every step keep the eye single upon the kingdom, upon the spiritual, upon the larger and the higher life within. When the other things are being added we must not forget the kingdom and give our first thoughts to the other things. We shall enjoy these other things so much the more, if we continue to give the first thought to the spirit. This is evident, because while giving the first thought to the spirit everything that comes into our world will be spiritualized, refined and perfected, and will thus be given added power and worth. When we continue to give the first thought to the spiritual kingdom those other things that are added will enter our world at their best and we shall thus receive the best that those things may have to give.

We are always at our best when we are on the heights, and we gain the power to create, produce and attract those things from every part of life that correspond to the life on the heights. Therefore, by living on the heights in the spiritual kingdom we gain everything that we may require;

we gain the best of everything that we may require, and we are in that condition where we can make the best use of what comes, and enjoy what comes to the highest and most perfect degree. We can thus readily understand that when we seek the kingdom of God constantly, giving our first thought to the spiritual and seeking to live righteously according to this larger view of righteousness, all problems of life will be solved. All the crooked paths of life will be made straight; obstacles will disappear; our circumstances will change to correspond with our ideas, and we will daily enter into a better life and a greater state of existence than we ever knew before. The problems of the world can be solved in the same way. Therefore, the greatest thing that we can do for the human race is to make clear this law, that is, the law through which His kingdom and His righteousness may be sought first by any individual, no matter what the degree of that individual's understanding may be. To promote a real spiritual movement on the largest possible scale is to cause the ills of humanity to gradually, but surely, pass away. This planet will then become, not a vale of tears, but what it is intended to be, the kingdom of heaven realized upon earth.

The human race, however, is the product of human thought; therefore, the prime essential is to inspire the human mind with the power to give His kingdom and His righteousness the first thought. To make the ideal real upon earth, all thinking must be ideal; and to cause all things to become ideal the foundation of all things must be based upon pure spiritual thought; that is, every thought that is created in the mind must be animated with this great first thought, the thought of the kingdom within and the full righteous expression of that kingdom. When we seek first the kingdom and his righteousness all other things are added, not in some mysterious manner, nor do they come of themselves regardless of conscious effort to work in harmony with the law of life. We receive from the kingdom only what we are prepared to use in the living of a great life and in the doing of great and worthy things in the world. We receive only in proportion to what we give, and it is only as we work well that we produce great results; but by entering the spiritual life we receive everything that we may require in order to give as much as we may desire, to do as much as we may desire. We gain the power and the talent to do everything that is necessary to give worth and superiority to our entire state of existence. When we enter the spiritual life we gain every quality that is necessary in making life full and complete now, and we gain the power to produce and create in the external world whatever we may need or desire. In other words, we receive everything we want from within and we gain the power to produce everything we want in the without. We, therefore, need never take anxious thought about these other things. By seeking first His kingdom and His righteousness we shall positively receive these other things. The way will be open to all that is rich, beautiful and superior in life, and we shall be abundantly supplied with the best that life can give.

Chapter 5

The Ideal and the Real Made One

When the elements of the ideal are blended harmoniously with the elements of the real the two become one; the ideal becomes real and the real gives expression to the qualities of the ideal. To be in harmony with everything at all times and under all circumstances is therefore one of the great essentials in the living of that life that is constantly making real a larger and larger measure of the ideal; and so extremely important is continuous harmony that nothing should be permitted to produce confusion or discord for the slightest moment. Discord wastes energy, while harmony accumulates energy. If we wish to be strong in mind and body and do the best possible work, harmony is absolutely necessary and we must be in the best possible condition to make real the ideal. The person who lives in perpetual harmony with everything will accomplish from ten to one hundred per cent more than the average during any given period of time; a fact that gives the elements of harmony a most important place in life. When harmony is absent there is always a great deal of mental confusion, and a confused mind can never think clearly, therefore makes mistakes constantly. To establish complete and continuous mental harmony will reduce mistakes to a minimum in any mind; another fact that makes the attainment of harmony one of the great attainments.

The mind that is living in continuous harmony is realizing a great measure of heaven upon earth regardless of his personal attainments or external possessions. He has made real that ideal something that makes existence thoroughly worthwhile, and he is rich indeed. To live in harmony is to gain the joy everlasting, the contentment that is based upon the real value of life, and that satisfaction that grows larger and better for every day that passes by. On the other hand, to live in discord is to live in perpetual torment, even though our personal attainments may be great and our personal possessions as large as any mind could wish.

To live the good life, the ideal life, the beautiful life, we must be at peace with all things, including ourselves, and every thought, word and deed must be harmonious. Whatever we wish to do or be it is wisdom to make any sacrifice necessary for the sake of harmony, although that which we sacrifice for the sake of harmony is not a sacrifice. When we enter into harmony we will regain everything that we were willing to lose in order that we might possess harmony. When we establish ourselves in perfect harmony we shall be reunited with everything that we hold near and dear and the new unit will be far sweeter, far more beautiful than the one we had before. "My own shall come to me" is a favorite expression among all those who believe that every ideal can be made real, and many of these are waiting and watching for their own to come, wondering in the meantime what can be done to hasten that coming. There are many things to be done, however, but one of the most important is the attainment of harmony. No person who lives in perpetual harmony will be deprived very long of his own, whatever that own may be. Whatever you deserve, whatever you are entitled to, whatever belongs to you will soon appear in your world, if you are living in perfect harmony.

To enter harmony is to enter a new world where everything is better, where opportunities are greater and more numerous, and where persons, conditions and things are more agreeable. You will not only enter a better world, however, but the attitude of harmony will relate your life so perfectly to the good things in all worlds that may exist about you, that the best from every source will naturally gravitate towards your sphere of existence. But harmony will not only cause the good things of life to gravitate towards you; it will also cause you to radiate the good qualities in your own being and thus become a perpetual benediction to everybody. To be in the presence of a person who dwells serenely in the beautiful calm is, indeed, a privilege, especially to those who can appreciate the finer elements of a truly harmonious life. Whenever we are in touch with real harmony, whether it comes from the music of human life, the music of nature or the music of the spheres, we are one step nearer the Beautiful. We can therefore realize the great value of being able to actually live in perfect harmony at all times. The life of harmony is the foundation of happiness and health and is one of the greatest essentials to achievement and real success. When we look into the past we can always find that our failures originated in confusion; likewise our troubles and ills. On the other hand, all the good things that have happened to us in the past, or that are happening in the present, had their origin and their growth in the elements of continuous harmony; the ideal and the real were made one, and we consequently reached the goals we had in view.

The mind that works in perpetual harmony does more work and far better work than is possible in any other condition; besides, harmonious work is invariably conducive to higher development and growth. To work in harmony is to promote increase and development in all the qualities and powers of the personality; while to work in confusion is to weaken the entire system and thus originate causes that will terminate in failure. The majority state that they have no time for self development, but to live in harmony and work in harmony is to promote self development every moment, and this development will not be confined simply to those muscles or faculties that we use directly, but will express itself throughout the entire system; and the mind especially will, under such conditions, steadily gain both in power and in worth. In the presence of these facts we can realize readily that no person can afford to permit discord, disturbance or confusion at any time. The many declare, however, that they cannot help it, but we must help it and we can. There is no reason why our minds should be excited or our nerves upset at any time. We can prevent this just as easily as we can refuse to eat what we do not want.

To proceed, we must apply exact reason to this great subject. We should learn to understand that no wrong will be righted because we permit ourselves to "fly to pieces;" also that the act of becoming nervous over a trouble will never drive that trouble away. To live in a constant strain will not promote our purpose nor arrange matters the way we want them. This is a fact that we should impress deeply upon our minds, and then impress our minds to take another and a better course. The average person feels that it is a religious duty to be as excited as possible, and to string up all his nerves as high as possible, whenever he is passing through some exceptional event; in consequence, he spoils all or practically all of that which might have been gained; besides, he places his system in a condition where all sorts of ills may gain a foothold. There are many reasons why such a large number of undertakings fail, but one of the principal reasons is found in the fact that few people have learned to retain perfect harmony under all kinds of circumstances. Discord and confusion are usually present to a great degree, and in consequence, something almost invariably goes wrong. But when a person is in perfect harmony and does his very best, he will succeed at least in a measure every time, and he will thus prepare himself for the greater opportunities that are sure to follow: To believe that intelligent, well educated people almost daily break down over mere trifles is not mere simplicity, but the fact that it is the truth leads us to question why. Intelligence and education should give those who possess it the power to know better. Modern education, however, does not teach us how to use ourselves. We have learned how to mix material substances so as to satisfy every imaginable taste, and we have learned how to use the tangible forces of nature so as to construct almost anything we like in the physical world, but we have not learned how to combine the elements of mind so as to produce health, happiness, strength, brilliancy and harmony whenever we may so desire. A few, however, have made the attempt, but the elements of the mind will not combine for greater efficiency and higher states of expression unless the mind is in perfect harmony.

We have all learned to remember, but few have learned to think. To repeat verbatim what others have thought and said is counted knowledge and with such borrowed knowledge the majority imagine they are satisfied, the reason being they have not discovered the art of thinking thoughts of their own. This is an art that every person must learn; the sooner the better, if the ideal is to be made real. Original thinking is the secret of all greatness, all high attainments, all extraordinary achievements and all superior states of being; but no mind can create original thought until a high state of mental harmony is attained. To produce mental harmony we must first bear in mind the great fact that it is not what happens that disturbs us, but the way we think about that which happens; and our thought about anything depends upon our point of view. The way we look at things will determine whether the experience will produce discord or harmony, and it is in our power to look at things in any way that we may desire. When we are face to face with those things that usually upset the mind we should immediately turn our attention upon the life and the power that is back of the disturbing element, having the desire to find the better side of that life and power constantly in view. Everything has its better side, its ideal side, its calm and undisturbed side, and a mere desire to gain a glimpse of that better side will turn the mind away from confusion and cause attention to be centered upon that calm state that is being sought. This will decrease discord at once, and if applied the very moment we are aware of confusion we will entirely prevent any mental disturbance whatever. To meet all circumstances and events in this way is to develop in ourselves a harmonious attitude towards all things, and when we are established in this harmonious attitude nothing whatever disturbs us; no matter what may happen we will continue to remain in harmony, and will consequently be able to deal properly with whatever may happen.

The mind that is upset by confused circumstances will lose ground and fail, but the mind that continues calmly in harmony with everything, no matter what the circumstances may be, will master every occasion and steadily rise in the scale. He will continue to make real the ideal, because he is living in that harmonious state of being where the ideal and the real are harmoniously blended into one. To promote the highest and most perfect state of continuous harmony we must learn to meet those persons, things and events, with which we come in daily contact, in the right mental attitude. The result of such an attitude is determined directly by the nature of our own attitude of mind, and as we can express ourselves through any attitude we desire, it is in our power either to spoil the most promising prospects, or convert the most unpromising conditions into the greatest success. We should train ourselves to meet everything in that attitude of mind that expects all things to work out right. When we deeply and continually expect all things to work out right we relate ourselves more perfectly with that with which we come in contact; we take things, so to speak, the way they ought to be taken, and we thereby promote harmony and cooperation among all things concerned.

Though this be extremely important, it is insignificant, however, in comparison with another great fact in this connection; that is, the way things respond to the leading desires of the ruling mind; whether it is the exercise of the mysteries of mental force or the application of a mental law not generally understood, does not concern us just now; but it is a fact that things will do, as a rule what we persistently expect them to do. To understand why this is so may require some study of the great laws of mind and body, and everybody should seek to understand these laws perfectly; but in the meantime anyone can demonstrate the fact that things will work out right if we constantly expect them to do so. No matter what may happen we should continue in the faith that all things will come right, and as our faith is so it shall be. To place ourselves in perfect harmony with all things, the domineering attitude of mind must be eliminated completely. The mind that tries to domineer over things will not only lose control of things, but will lose control of its own faculties and forces. At first it may seem that the domineering mind gains ground, but the gain is only temporary. When the reaction comes, as it will, the loss will be far greater than the temporary gain. When you try to domineer over persons and things you gain possession and control of those things only that are too weak to control themselves. That is, you gain a temporary control over negatives, and negatives have no permanent value in your life; in fact, they soon prove themselves to be wholly detrimental. Occasionally a domineering mind may attract the attention of better things, but as soon as his domineering qualities are discovered those better things will part company with him at once. The law of attraction is at the foundation of all natural constructive processes; therefore, to promote construction, growth, advancement and real success we must work in harmony with that law. If we wish to attain the superior, we must become superior, because it is only like that attracts like. If we wish to gain the ideal, we must become ideal. If we wish to make real the ideal, we must live the ideal in the real. When you want good things, make yourself better, and better things will naturally be attracted to you; but good things do not submit to force. Therefore, to try to secure better things through forceful methods, or through the domineering attitude can only result in failure; such methods gain only the inferior, those things that can add neither to the welfare nor the happiness of anyone. This fact holds good, not only among individuals, but also among nations and institutions. The more domineering an institution is the more inferior are its members, and the more autocratic the nation the weaker its subjects. On the other hand, we find the best minds where the individual is left free to govern himself and where he is expected to act wisely, to be true to the best that is within him. In order that the individual may advance he must steadily grow in the mastery of himself, and must so relate himself to the best things in life that he will naturally attract the best things; but these two essentials are wholly interfered with by the domineering attitude. Such an attitude repels everything and everybody that has any worth. It spoils the forces of mind, thus weakening all the mental faculties, and it steadily undermines whatever self control a person might possess. Never try to control anything or domineer over anything, but aim to live in perpetual harmony with the highest, the truest and the best that is in everything.

Whatever happens we should approach that event in that attitude that believes it is all right. We should never permit the attitude that condemns, not even when the things concerned have proved themselves to be wrong. The attitude that condemns is detrimental to our own minds, because it invariably produces discord. When you meet all things in the expectation of finding them right, you always find something about them that is right. This something you may appropriate and thus gain good from everything that happens. That person, however, who expects to find most things wrong will fail to see the good that may exist among the things that come his way; therefore, he gains far less from life than his wiser neighbor. But what is equally important, the man who expects to find everything right wherever he may go, will gradually gravitate towards those people and circumstances that are right. The man who expects to find everything wrong usually finds what he expects. The effect of these two attitudes upon mind and character is even more important, because the man is as his mind and character, and as the man is so is his destiny. The man who expects to find most things wrong and meets the world in that attitude is constantly impressing the wrong upon his mind, and as we gradually grow into the likeness of that which we think of the most, he is building upon sinking sand. The mind that is constantly looking for the wrong cannot be wholesome. Such a mind is not in harmony with the law of growth, power, and ability; therefore, can never do its best. Unwholesome thoughts will steadily undermine the finest character and mind, and the world is full of illustrations. There is always something wrong in the life of that person who constantly expects to find things wrong, and the reason why is simple. His own expectations are reacting upon himself; by thinking about the wrong he is creating the wrong and thus bringing forth the wrong in every part of his life.

The man, however, who expects to find everything right and meets the world in that attitude is daily nourishing his mind with right thoughts, wholesome thoughts and constructive thoughts; he thinks the most of that which is right, and is therefore steadily growing more and more into the likeness of that which is right, perfect, worthy and good; he is daily changing for the better, and through this constant change he steadily rises in the scale and thereby meets the better and the better at every turn. By expecting to find everything right he finds more and more of that which is right, and as he is becoming stronger in mind, character and soul, he is affected less and less by those few things that may not be as they should be. When you meet a disappointment meet it in the conviction that it is all right, because through this attitude you enter into harmony with the power that is back of the event at hand, and you thus convert the disappointment into a channel through which greater good may be secured. Those who doubt this should try it.; they will find that it is based upon exact scientific facts Transcend disappointment, and all the powers of adversity will begin to rise with you and will begin to work with you and help you reach the goal you have in view. You will thus find that, it is all for the best, because through the right mental attitude you made everything work out in such a way that the best transpired as a final result.

To live in what may be termed the "all right" attitude, that is, in that attitude that expects to find everything all right and that constantly affirms that everything is all right, is to press on to the realization and the possession of those things that are as you wish them to be. Disappointments and failures, when met in this attitude, simply become open doors to new worlds where you find better opportunities and greater possibilities than you ever knew before. When the average person meets disappointment he usually declares, "Just my luck;" in other words, he enters that mental attitude that faces ill luck; he thus fails to see anything else but misfortune in that which has happened; and so long as that person, consciously or unconsciously expects misfortune, into more and more misfortune he will go. He who believes that he is fated to have bad luck will have bad luck in abundance. The reason is he lives in that mental attitude that places his mind in constant contact with those confused elements in the world that never create anything else but bad luck. That person, however, who thoroughly believes that everything that happens is simply a step to greater good, higher attainments and greater achievements, will steadily rise into those greater things that he expects to realize; the reason being that he is living in that mental attitude that places his mind in contact with the building power of life. Those powers will always build for greater things to those with whom they are in harmony, and we all can place ourselves in harmony with those powers; therefore, we can all move upward and onward forever, eternally making real more and more of that which is ideal.

What we expect comes if our expectation is filled with all the power of life and soul, and what we believe our fate to be, that is the kind of a fate we will create for ourselves. To meet ill luck in the belief that it is your luck, your particular kind of luck, and that it is natural for you to have that kind of luck is to stamp your own mind as an unlucky mind. This will produce chaotic thinking, which will cause you to do everything at the wrong time, and all your energies will be more or less misdirected; in consequence, bad luck and misfortune must necessarily follow. Bad luck comes from doing the wrong thing, or from being your worst; while good luck comes from being your best and from doing the right thing at the right time. It is therefore mere simplicity to create good luck at any time and in the measure that we may desire. The person that fears misfortune or expects misfortune and faces life in that attitude is concentrating attention upon misfortune; he thereby creates a world of misfortune in his own mind; and he who lives in mental misfortune will produce misfortune in his external life. Like causes produce like effects; and this explains why the things we fear always come upon us. We create mental causes for those things, and corresponding tangible effects always follow. Train the mind to expect the right and the best, regardless of present circumstances, conditions or events. Call everything good that is met. Declare that everything that happens, happens for the best. Meet everything in that frame of mind, and no matter how wrong or adverse conditions seem to be, you cause them all to work out right.

When the mind expects the best, has the faith that the right will prevail, and constantly faces the superior, the true mental attitude has been gained. Through that attitude all the forces of mind and all the powers of will become constructive, and will build for man the very thing that he expects or desires while his mind is fixed upon the ideal. He relates himself harmoniously to the best that is in all things and thus unites the ideal with the real in all things; and when the ideal becomes one with the real, the ideal desired becomes an actual fact in the real; and this is the goal every true idealist has in view. He takes those elements that have been revealed to him through the vision of the soul and blends them harmoniously with the actions of daily life. He thus brings the ideal down to earth and causes the real of everyday life to express the ideal in everything that he may undertake to do. His life, his thought, his action, his attainments, his achievements, all contain that happy state where the ideal and the real are made one. His dreams have become true. The visions of the soul are actually realized, and the tangible is animated with that ideal something that makes personal existence all that anyone could wish it to be.

Chapter 6

The First Step Towards Complete Emancipation

To forgive everybody for everything at all times, regardless of circumstances, is the first step towards complete emancipation. Heretofore, we have looked upon forgiveness as a virtue; now we know it to be a necessity. To those who possessed the spirit of forgiveness we have given our highest praise, and have thought of such people as being self sacrificing in the truest sense of that term. We did not know that the act of forgiving is the simplest way to lighten one's own burdens. According to our former conception of this subject, the man who forgives denies himself a privilege, the privilege of indignation and revenge; for this reason we have looked upon him as a hero or as a saint, thinking that it could not be otherwise than heroic and saintly to give up the supposed pleasure of meting out revenge to those who seemed to deserve it. According to the new view, however, the man who forgives is no more saintly than the one who insists upon keeping clean, because in reality the act of forgiving simply constitutes a complete mental bath. When you forgive everybody for everything you cleanse your mind completely of every wrong thought or adverse mental attitude that may exist in your consciousness. This explains why forgiveness is a necessity and why the man who forgives everything emancipates himself from all kinds of burdens. It is therefore profitable, most highly profitable, to forgive everybody, no matter what they have done, and this includes also ourselves. It is just as necessary to forgive ourselves as to forgive others, and the principal reason why forgiveness has seemed to be so difficult is because we have neglected to forgive ourselves.

We cannot let go of that which is not desired until we have acquired the mental art of letting go, and to acquire this art we must practice upon our own minds. That is, we must learn to let go from our own minds all those things that we do not wish to retain. When you forgive yourself completely you wash your mentality perfectly clean. You let go of everything in your mental system that is not good. You emancipate yourself completely. Whatever you held against yourself or others you now drop entirely out of your mind; in consequence, you are freed from your mental burdens, and when mental burdens disappear all other burdens will disappear also. The ills that we hold in mind are the only things that can actually burden our lives. Therefore, when we forgive everybody for every ill we ever knew we no longer hold a single ill in our own minds; we thus throw off every burden and are perfectly free. This also includes disease, because disease is nothing but a temporary effect of a wrong that we mentally hold in the system. Forgive everybody, including yourself, for everything, and all disease will vanish from your system. This may at first sight appear to be a startling statement, but it is the truth, and anyone can prove it to be the truth. "As a man thinketh in his heart so is he." Therefore, when every wrong is eliminated from the heart of man there can be no wrong in the man himself, and every wrong is eliminated from that heart that forgives everything in everyone. Many persons, however, will state that they hold no ill against anyone yet suffer just the same. So they may think, nevertheless they are mistaken and will see their mistakes when they learn the truth about mental laws. You may not hold direct ill against any person just now, but your mind has not always been absolutely pure and absolutely free from every wrong thought. You have had many wrong desires in your heart, and have had many mistaken ideas. To hold a mistaken idea is to hold a wrong in your heart. To have wrong desires is to hold ills against yourself, as well as others. To blame yourself, criticize yourself, feel provoked at yourself or condemn yourself for your shortcomings is to hold ills against yourself, and there are very few who are not doing this every day to some degree.

When we forgive all and still suffer we may not believe that forgiveness produces emancipation; but the fact is that suffering is impossible when forgiveness is absolute. When we forgive completely we shall also eliminate completely every trouble or ill that may exist in our world. When you have trouble forgive those who have caused the trouble; forgive yourself for permitting yourself to be troubled, and your troubles will pass away. When you have made a mistake do not condemn yourself or feel upset; simply forgive yourself, and resolve that you will never make the mistake again. As you make that resolution, desire more wisdom, and have the faith that you will secure the wisdom you require. "According to your faith so shall it be." There are many who will think that the practice of forgiving everybody for everything will produce mental indifference and thus weaken character, but it is the very opposite that will take place. To forgive is to eliminate the useless, everything that is not good; and to free the mind from obstacles and adverse conditions is to enable that mind to be its best, to express itself fully and completely. This will not only strengthen the character and enlarge the mind, but will cause the greatness of the soul to come forth. There is many a character that appears to be strong on account of its open hostility to wrongs, but such a character is not always strong. Too often it is composed of a few borrowed ideas about morality backed up by mere animal force.

The true character does not express hostility and does not resist or antagonize, but overcomes evil by giving all its power to the building of the good. A strong character meets evil with a silent indifference; that is, indifference in appearance only. The true character does not pass evil by because he does not care, but because he does care. He cares so much that he will not waste one single moment in prolonging the life of the wrong; therefore gives his whole time and attention to the making of good so strong that evil becomes absolutely powerless in the presence of that good. No intelligent person would antagonize darkness. By giving his time to the production of light he causes the darkness to disappear of itself.

When we apply the same principle to the elimination of evil a marvelous change for the better will come over the world. No person can forgive everybody for everything until he desires the best from every person and from every source. In other words, we cannot forgive the wrong until we desire the right. Therefore, the letting go of the inferior and the appropriation of the superior constitutes one and the same single mental process. We cannot eliminate darkness until we proceed to produce light, and it requires only the one act for removing the one and bringing forth the other. From these facts it is evident that when we let go of the wrong we gain more of that power that is right, and we thus increase the strength of character. To eliminate diseased conditions from the body will increase the strength of the body and will place the body in a position for further development, if we desire to promote such development. Likewise, to eliminate all ill feelings, all hatred, all wrong thoughts and all false beliefs from the mind will increase the power of the mind and place every mental faculty in proper condition for higher development. The same effect will be produced in the character, and all. awakened minds know that the greatness of the soul can begin to come forth only when we have completely forgiven everybody for everything.

The man who finds it easier to forgive than to condemn is on the verge of superior wisdom and higher spiritual power. He has entered the path to real greatness and may rapidly rise in the scale by applying the laws of true human development. Instead of producing weakness and indifference the act of absolute forgiveness will produce a more powerful character, a more brilliant mind and a greater soul. Try this method for a year. Forgive everybody for everything, no matter what happens, and do not forget to forgive yourself. You will then conclude that forgiveness, absolute forgiveness, is not only the path to complete emancipation, but is also the "gates ajar" to a better life, a larger life, a richer life, a more beautiful life than you ever knew before. You will find that you can instantaneously remove disease from the body, perversion and wrong from the mind by complete and unrestricted forgiveness; and you can in the same way steadily recreate yourself into a new and better being. Forgive the imperfect, and with heart and soul desire constantly the realization of the perfect; the imperfect will thus pass away and the more perfect will be realized in a greater and greater abundance.

Whatever our place in life may be, we must eliminate every burden of mind or body, if we wish to rise in the scale, and the first step in this direction is to forgive everybody for everything. When you begin to practice forgiveness on this extensive scale you will find obstacles disappearing one after the other. Those things that held you down will vanish and that which was constantly in your way will trouble you no more; your pathway will be cleared. You will have nothing more to contend with, and everything in your life will move smoothly and harmoniously towards greater and greater things. This is perfectly natural, because by forgiving everybody and everything you have let every form of evil go. You have invited all the good, and have therefore populated your own world with persons and things after your own heart. Through perpetual and complete forgiveness your mind will be kept perfectly clean. Not a single weed will ever appear in the beautiful garden of your mind, and so long as the mind is clean neither sickness nor adversity can exist in human life. This may be a strong statement, but those who will try the principle and continue to live it will find it to be the truth.

Since forgiveness is a necessity to all who wish to eliminate the lesser and retain the greater, or in other words make real the ideal, it will be highly important to present the simplest methods through which anyone may learn to practice this great art. It has been said that to know all is to forgive all; but it is not possible for anyone to know all. Therefore, if we wish to forgive absolutely, we must proceed along a different line. When we ask ourselves why people live, think and act as they do we meet the great law of cause and effect. In our study of this law we find that every cause is an effect of a previous cause, and that that previous cause is also an effect of a cause still more remote. We may continue to trace these causes and effects far back along the chain of events until we are lost in the dimness of the past; but what do we learn by such a process of analysis, nothing whatever. We fail to find anything definite about anybody, and consequently cannot fix the blame for anything; but it is not possible to justly blame anybody when we cannot fix the blame for anything. Therefore, we have only one alternative, and that is to forgive. We can never find the real cause of a single thing. We may first blame the individual, but when we discover the influence of environment, heredity and early training we cannot wholly blame the individual. If we blame the parents, we must find the reason why those parents were not different, also why previous generations were not different. If we accept the theory that the individual has lived before and that he came into his present environments because he was what he was in a previous state of existence, we must explain why he did not live a different life in that other existence; why did he act in such a manner in the past that he should merit adversity and weakness in the present. If he knew no better in the past., what is the reason that he did not know any better? If we accept the belief that we have all inherited our perverted tendencies from Adam and Eve, we must explain why those two souls were not strong enough to rise above temptation. If they were tempted, we must explain why; we must explain why the original man who was created in the image and likeness of God did not express his divine nature in the midst of temptation. But there is no way in which we can explain these things; therefore, to fix the blame for anything is absolutely impossible.

The more we try to find the original cause of anything the more convinced we become that to look for sin or the cause of sin is nothing but a waste of time. Every individual is himself a cause, and his life comes constantly in touch with a number of other causes; therefore, it is never possible to say which one of these causes or combination of these causes produced the original action. Back of every action we find other actions that lead us to the one that we may now consider, but we do not know how those other actions were produced. To trace them back to their original source simply leads us into what appears to be a beginningless beginning. For this reason it is the height of wisdom to let the "dead bury its dead," to let the past go, to forgive every sinner and forget every sin, and to use our time, talent and power for the building of more lofty mansions in the great eternal now. To look for the blame is to find that we are all more or less to blame, and also to find that there is no real fixed blame anywhere. We may then ask what we are to do with this great subject; are we to talk, theorize, speculate, condemn and punish? We know too well that all of that is but a waste of time. The sensible course to pursue is to forgive everybody for everything, to drop ills, mistakes, wrongs, disagreeable memories and proceed to use those laws of life that we understand now in making life better for everybody now.

The Ideal Made Real

The man who is habitually doing wrong is mentally or morally sick. Punishment is a waste of time; besides, it is absolutely wrong, and one wrong cannot remove another. Such a person should be taken where he can be healed and kept there until he is well. We should not hate him or condemn him any more than those who are physically sick. Sickness is sickness whether it appears in the body, the mind or the character, and he who is sick does not need a prison; he needs a physician. To absolutely remove this hatred for the wrongdoers in the world we must cultivate a higher order of love, that love that loves every living creature with the true love of the soul, and such a love is readily attained when we train ourselves to look for the ideal soul of life that exists in everything everywhere in the world. This idea may cause many to come to the conclusion that the act of forgiving the wrongdoer will have an undesirable effect upon society, because we may be liable to let people in general do as they please; but in this they are wholly mistaken. Reason declares that you cannot justly blame anyone, and love does not wish to blame anyone; forgiveness must therefore inevitably follow when reason and love are truly combined; but reason and love will never permit man in general to do as he pleases. When we love people we are not indifferent about their future: We do not wish them to go down grade. We want them to improve, to do the right and the best and we will do everything in our power to emancipate and elevate the entire race. Reason understands how the laws of life can be applied in producing those results we may have in view; therefore, the desires of love can be carried out through the understanding of reason, and thus every high purpose may be promoted by the right spirit and the proper methods. Others may declare that these methods are in advance of our time and cannot be carried out at present; therefore, it is useless to even talk about it. However, be that as it may, the fact remains that forgiveness is a necessity to the true life, the emancipated life, the superior life, the ideal life. For that reason every person who desires to make real the ideal in his world must begin to practice absolute forgiveness at once. If we can forgive everybody for everything now, we should do so, whether the world in general can do so or not. The man who wishes to move forward must not wait for the race. It is his privilege to go in advance of the race; thus he prepares the way for millions.

When he has demonstrated by example that there are better ways of living, the race will follow. What the few can do today the many will do tomorrow, but if the few should wait until tomorrow, the many would have to wait until the day following, or possibly longer still. Be what you can be now. Do what you can do now, no matter how far in advance of this age such actions may be. If you are capable of greater things today, you owe it to the race to demonstrate those greater things now. You sprung from the race. You are composed of the finer elements that exist in the race, and should consider it a privilege to cause those elements to shine as brilliantly as possible; and one of the greatest of all demonstrations in this age is that of absolute forgiveness, to demonstrate the power of forgiving everybody for everything at all times and under every possible circumstance. We therefore conclude that complete emancipation from everything that is not desired in life can be realized only when we forgive absolutely in this great universal sense; and when we have forgiven everybody for everything, then we can say with the great Master Mind, "My yoke is easy and my burden is light."

Chapter 7

Paths to Perpetual Increase

The universe is overflowing with all manner of good things and there is enough to supply every wish of every heart with abundance still remaining. How every heart is to proceed, however, that its every wish may be supplied, has been the problem, but the solution is simple. In consequence, everybody may rejoice. This world is not a "vale of tears," but is in truth a most delightful place, and is endowed with everything that is needful to make the life of man an endless song. We now know that we do not live to be miserable, but to rejoice. The bitterness that sometimes appears in life is not a real part of life. The greatness of existence alone is intended for man.

To know the bitter from the sweet and to appropriate the latter and always reject the former is a matter, however, that is not clearly understood. There may be thousands who know the bitter when they see it, but they do not always know how to reject it. To throw off the ills of life is an art that few have mastered. But those who can eliminate the wrong are not always able to distinguish the right from the wrong, the reason being that we have not looked at things from the viewpoint of that power that produces things. The philosophers, the theologians and the scientists, as a rule, make life very complex and difficult to live. Their profound expressions confuse the multitudes, while ills and troubles continue as before; but to live is simple. Even a child can be happy; it therefore should not be difficult for anyone else.

When we realize happiness in its highest, broadest sense, we find that it comes in its fullness only when we have everything that the heart desires; and since the desires of the heart increase in size and number with the enlargement of life, the joy of living will increase in proportion providing all the, desires of the heart are supplied. This fact, however, may at first sight seem to make happiness very difficult to secure. If we cannot enjoy the allness of joy until we have everything that heart can wish for, then happiness is far away; so it may seem, but things are not always what they seem. All things are possible, and the most difficult. things become comparatively easy when we know how; therefore, the way of wisdom is not to look for those difficulties that ignorance has connected with things, but look for that simplicity that is the soul of all knowledge. When we learn to do things as they should be done, all difficulties disappear, and even the largest life becomes simple.

The doing of things is the universal theme in this age. Those who simply tell us what to do are no longer acceptable. We want practical instructions that tell us how. The greatest man of this age and of the future will not be the one who can move as he wishes the emotions of multitudes by the magic art of eloquence and bring whole nations to his feet by the artistic juggling of eloquent phrases. The great man will henceforth be the man who can tell us how, and who can express himself so clearly that anyone can understand. This, however, we are now beginning to do, and ere long the many will come back to the truth itself and understand the real truth in all its original simplicity. The path of truth and life is perfectly straight and is illumined all the way. It is therefore simplicity itself to follow this path when we find it, but the many have strayed into the jungles of illusions and misconceptions. These must all come back to the simple path, and when they do the difficulty of living will wholly disappear.

To teach the race how to find the simple things, the true things and the real things is now the purpose of every original thinker, and whoever can add to the world's wisdom in this respect becomes a light to the race, indeed. One of the first principles in this new understanding of things is that which deals with man's power to place himself in perfect touch with the source of limitless supply; in other words to enter the path of perpetual increase. As previously stated, the world is overflowing with good things, because life is in touch with the limitless source of all good things, and there is so much of everything that the wish of every heart can be gratified. We do not have to take from another to have abundance, because there is more than sufficient for all. The fact that someone has abundance does not prove that he has taken some or all of his wealth from others, although this is what a great many believe to be the truth. Whenever we see someone in luxury we wonder where and how he got it, and we usually add that many are in poverty because this one is in wealth. Such doctrine, however, is not true.

It is thoroughly false from beginning to end. The world is not so poverty stricken that the few cannot have plenty without stealing from the many. The universe is not so bare and so limited that multitudes are reduced to want whenever a few persons undertake to surround themselves with those things that have beauty and worth. True, there is injustice in the world. There are people who have secured their wealth, not upon merit, but through the art of reducing others to want; but the remedy is not to be found in the doctrine that thousands must necessarily become poor when one becomes very rich.

This doctrine is an illusion, and illusions cannot serve as foundations for a better order. There is enough in life to give every living person all the wealth and all the luxury that he can possibly appropriate. God is rich; the universe is overflowing with abundance. If we have not everything that we want, there is a reason; there is some definite cause somewhere, either in ourselves or in our relations to the world, but this cause can be found and corrected; then we may proceed to take possession of our own. Among the many causes of poverty and the lack of a full supply there is one that has been entirely overlooked. To overcome this cause is to find one of the most important paths to perpetual increase, and the remedy lies within easy reach of everyone who has awakened to a degree the finer elements in his life.

There may be exceptions to the rule, but there are thousands who are living on the husks of existence because they were not grateful when the kernels were received. Multitudes continue in poverty from no other cause than a lack of gratitude, and other thousands who have almost everything that the heart may wish for do not reach the coveted goal of full supply because their gratitude is not complete.

We are now beginning to realize more and more that the greatest thing in the world is to live so closely to the Infinite that we constantly feel the power and the peace of His presence. In fact, this mode of living is the very secret of secrets revealing everything that the mind may wish to know or understand in order to make life what it is intended to be. We also realize that the more closely we live to the Infinite the more we shall receive of all good things, because all good things have their source in the Supreme; but how to enter into this life of supreme oneness with the Most High is a problem.

There are many things to be done in order to solve this problem, but there is no one thing that is more important in producing the required solution than deep, whole-souled gratitude. The soul that is always grateful lives nearer the true, the good, the beautiful and the perfect than anyone else in existence, and the more closely we live to the good and the beautiful the more we shall receive of all those things. The mind that dwells constantly in the presence of true worth is daily adding to his own worth. He is gradually and steadily appropriating that worth with which he is in constant contact; but we cannot enter into the real presence of true worth unless we fully appreciate the real worth of true worth; and all appreciation is based upon gratitude.

The more grateful we are for the good things that come to us now the more good things we shall receive in the future. This is a great metaphysical law, and we shall find it most profitable to comply exactly with this law, no matter what the circumstances may be. Be grateful for everything and you will constantly receive more of everything; thus the simple act of being grateful becomes a path to perpetual increase. The reason why is found in the fact that whenever you enter into the mental attitude of real gratitude your mind is drawn into much closer contact with that power that produces the good things received. In other words, to be grateful for what we have received is to draw more closely to the source of that which we receive. The good things that come to us come because we have properly employed certain laws, and when we are grateful for the results gained we enter into more perfect harmony with those laws and thus become able to employ those laws to still greater advantage in the immediate future. This anyone can understand, and those who do not know that gratitude produces this effect should try it and watch results.

The attitude of gratitude brings the whole mind into more perfect and more harmonious relations with all the laws and powers of life. The grateful mind gains a firmer hold, so to speak, upon those things in life that can produce increase. This is simply illustrated in personal experience where we find that we always feel nearer to that person to whom we express real gratitude. When you thank a person and truly mean it with heart and soul you feel nearer to that person than you ever did before. Likewise, when we express whole-souled thanksgiving to everything and everybody for everything that comes into life we draw closer and closer to all the elements and powers of life. In other words, we draw closer to the real source from which all good things in life proceed.

When we consider this principle from another point of view we find that the act of being grateful is an absolute necessity, if we wish to accomplish as much as we have the power to accomplish. To be grateful in this large, universal sense is to enter into harmony and contact with the greatest, the highest and the best in life. We thus gain possession of the superior elements of mind and soul and, in consequence, gain the power to become more and achieve more, no matter what our object or work may be. Everything that will place us in a more perfect relation with life, and thus enable us to appropriate the greater richness of life, should be employed with the greatest of earnestness, and deep whole-souled gratitude does possess a marvelous power in this respect. Its great value, however, is not confined to the laws just mentioned. Its power is exceptional in another and equally important field.

To be grateful is to think of the best, therefore the grateful mind keeps the eye constantly upon the best; and, according to another metaphysical law, we grow into the likeness of that which we think of the most. The mind that is always dissatisfied fixes attention upon the common, the ordinary and the inferior, and thus grows into the likeness of those things. The creative forces within us are constantly making us just like those things upon which we habitually concentrate attention. Therefore, to mentally dwell upon the inferior is to become inferior, while to keep the eye single upon the best is to daily become better. The grateful mind is constantly looking for the best, thus holding attention upon the best and daily growing into the likeness of the best. The grateful mind expects only good things, and will always secure good things out of everything that comes. What we constantly expect we receive, and when we constantly expect to get good out of everything we cause everything to produce good. Therefore, to the grateful mind all things will at all times work together for good, and this means perpetual increase in everything that can add to the happiness and the welfare of man.

This being true, and anyone can prove it to be true, the proper course to pursue is to cultivate the habit of being grateful for everything that comes. Give thanks eternally to the Most High for everything and feel deeply grateful every moment to every living creature. All things are so situated that they can be of some service to us, and all things have somewhere at sometime been instrumental in adding to our welfare. We must therefore, to be just and true, express perpetual gratitude to everything that has existence. Be thankful to yourself. Be thankful to every soul in the world, and most of all be thankful to the Creator of all that is. Live in perpetual thanksgiving to all the world, and express the deepest, sincerest, most whole-souled gratitude you can feel within whenever something of value comes into your life.

When other things come, pass them by; never mind them in the least. You know that the good in greater and greater abundance is eternally coming into your life, and for this give thanks with rejoicing; you know that every wish of the heart is being supplied; be thankful that this is true, and you will draw nearer and nearer to that place in life where that can be realized that you know is on the way to realization. Live according to this principle for a brief period of time, and the result will be that your life will change for the better to such a degree that you will feel infinitely more grateful than you ever felt before. You will then find that thanksgiving is a

The Ideal Made Real

necessary part of real living, and you will also find that the more grateful you are for every ideal that has been made real, the more power you gain to press on to those greater heights where you will find every ideal to be real. And when this realization begins you are on the path to perpetual increase, because the more you receive the more grateful you feel, and the more grateful you feel for that which has been received the more closely you will live to that Source that can give you more.

Chapter 8

Consider the Lilies

Consider the lilies of the field, how they grow; they toil not, neither do they spin; yet I say unto you, that even Solomon in all his glory was not arrayed like one of these. Matt. 6; 28, 29.

The greatest service that anyone can render to the race is to properly fill the place he occupies now, to be himself today; but it is not only others that will benefit by such individual actions. The individual himself will receive greater good from life through this method than through all other methods combined. The great secret of secrets is to live your own life in your own world as well as you possibly can now. In this age thousands are seeking the path of spiritual growth and high intellectual attainments, while millions are dreaming of the life beautiful; accordingly, systems almost without number are springing up everywhere, claiming to reveal the hidden path to these greater goals; but it is the truth that when everything has been said, the one statement that rises above them all is this: Be all that you are today and you shall be even more tomorrow. If you are in search of higher spiritual and intellectual attainments enter into every form of wisdom that surrounds you today and fill your life with as much spirit as you can possibly realize. If you wish to live an ideal life, then aim to make real the most beautiful life that you can think of today. If you are longing for greater accomplishments and a larger sphere of usefulness, then be your very best in the place that you occupy now.

The mighty oak grows great because it grows in the present; it does not think of the past or the future; it is what it is now; it does not wish to become mighty; it simply grows on silently and continually. The lily of the field is beautiful because it is perfectly satisfied to be a lily, but it is not satisfied to be less than all a lily can be. It does not strive or work hard to become beautiful; it simply goes on being what it is, and the result is it has been made immortal by the greatest mind that ever lived. When we follow the example of the lily we find the real secret of life, so simply and clearly stated that anyone can understand. Be what you are today. Do not be satisfied to be less than you can today and do not strive to be more. Progress, growth, advancement, attainment, these do not come through overreaching. The mind that overreaches will have a reaction; he will fall to the bottom and will have to begin all over again. Real attainment comes by being your best where you are just for today, by filling the present moment with all the life you are conscious of; no more. If you try to express more life than you can comfortably feel in consciousness, you are overreaching and you will have a fall. The great mistake of the age is to strive, to go about our work as if it were extremely difficult. The man who works the hardest usually accomplishes the least; while the truly great man is the man who has trained his life and his power to work through him.

The lilies of the field are not engaged in hard labor, and yet their usefulness cannot be measured; they are fulfilling their true purpose; they are making real the ideal in their own world and they are living inspirations to every soul in existence. They live to be beautiful and they become beautiful, not by being ambitious for beauty, but by permitting all the beauty they possess to come forth. What is within us is constantly pressing for expression. We do not have to call it forth nor labor so much to bring it into action. All we are required to do is to permit ourselves to be what we are, to permit what is within to express itself fully and completely. We do not have to work so hard to become great. We are all naturally great, and our potential greatness is ever ready to manifest, if we would only cease our striving and let life live. The lily is beautiful because it does not hinder its own inherent beauty from coming forth to be seen; but if the lily should take up the strenuous life it would in one generation become a despised weed. The human race today resembles in too many instances the useless weed. Millions in every generation come and go without accomplishing anything whatever. They do not even live a life that gives contentment. The reason is they strive too much, and in their striving destroy the very powers that can produce greatness. We have worked hard for results, not knowing that the only cause of results was within us, ready to produce the very results we desired, just for the asking. We have in many instances destroyed our brains trying to invent methods for producing health, happiness, power and success, not knowing that these things already existed within us in abundant supply, and that by wholesome thinking they would appear in full external expression.

The secret of secrets is to let the best within us have full right of way; this, however, most of us have failed to do. In consequence, the majority are undeveloped weaklings of little use to themselves or to the world. The lily permits that which is to have right of way. It does not interfere, but man does interfere. He usually refuses to accept the gifts which nature wishes to bestow upon him, and he hardly ever accepts assistance from a higher power. He sets out for himself and works himself into old age and death trying to gain what was actually given to him in the beginning. He leaves the real riches of life and enters the world of personal ambition expecting to find something better and create something superior through his own efforts, but he fails because man alone can do nothing. The average person does not realize that to create something from nothing is impossible, nor has he learned that the necessary something can come only from the life that is within. He may try to accomplish much and become much through personal ambition and hard work, but no one can build without material, and the material that is needed in building greatness can be secured only by giving right of way to the life and the power of the inner world. The man who expects to build greatness upon personal limitations will pass away in the effort, leaving his unfinished work to be taken up by someone else who will possibly build upon the same useless foundation. Thus one generation after another comes and goes, each expecting to succeed where predecessors failed; in the meantime very little is accomplished by man, and he fails to receive what infinite life is ever waiting to give.

This is the truth about man in general. The multitudes have come and gone during countless ages and have accomplished but little. There have been a few great exceptions in every age, but these were exceptions because they refused to follow the ways of the world. They learned the lesson that the lilies have taught, and they chose to let life live, to let the greatness from within come forth, to let power work, and to let that which is in the real of man have full right of way. When a person discovers what he is and permits that which he is to have full expression, his days of weariness, trouble and failure are gone. Henceforth he will live as the flower. His life will be full. He will fulfill his purpose and eternally become more and more of that which already is in the great within. When a flower, which has so little of soul within itself, can become so much by permitting itself to be itself, how much more might man become if he would permit himself to be himself. Man is created in the image of God, therefore marvels are hidden within his wonderful soul. When these marvels are given full expression then man begins to become that which the Infinite intended that he should be. In the soul of the lily is hidden the spirit of beauty; nothing more. But the lily does not hinder this spirit from appearing in visible form; therefore, it becomes an inspiration of joy to all the world. In the soul of man even the

Infinite is hidden; we can therefore imagine what man will become when he permits the spirit of divinity to express itself in his personal form. This is a great truth, indeed, and deserves constant attention from every mind that has learned to think.

We may believe that every step forward that we have taken has been produced through personal efforts and hard work, but in this we are mistaken.

In the first place, those achievements that have followed hard work are always insignificant and never of any permanent value, but those steps forward that have permanent value and that are truly great we find were taken during those moments when we permitted real life to live. We therefore find that striving accomplishes nothing, while we may through living, accomplish anything. There are times when many of us cease our strenuous labor for a few moments and unconsciously open our souls to that higher something that we feel so much the need of when wearied with misdirected labors, and the influx of real life that comes at such times is the cause of those real steps upward and onward that we have taken. At such times we chose to be like the lily; we permitted the good that was to come forth; we gave up, so to speak, to higher power and did not interfere with its highest, fullest expression. What we gain at such moments is always with us and never fails to give us strength, power and inspiration even when we decide for the time being to adopt the ways of the world once more. But since every step in advance comes when we refuse to go the way of the world, we should now understand that the way of the world is a mistake. We should therefore free ourselves from that mode of life, thought and action absolutely.

The world seeks to gain greater things through personal ambition and hard work. The true way to attain greater things is to permit the greatness that is within to have full expression; likewise when we seek health, happiness and harmony or a beautiful life, the true course is to permit those things to come forth and act through us; they are ready to appear. We do not have to work for them or strive so hard to secure them. They are now at hand and will express themselves through us the very moment we grant them permission. We have all discovered that whenever we become perfectly still and permit supreme life to live in us we can feel power accumulating in our system until we feel as if we could move mountains. We have also felt that while turning attention to the everlasting joy within and opening the mind fully to this joy that there came into being a state of happiness, comfort and contentment that seemed infinitely more perfect than the imagination has ever pictured the joys of heaven to be. Likewise when we failed to find health in the without or through external means we invariably found the precious gift coming from within, the moment we gave up, so to speak, to its wholesome life and power.

In this age personal ambition is one of the ruling factors, and nearly everybody is trying to outdo someone else. The result is we build up and tear down in the outer world, but as a race we improve but little. The great within is ignored, held back or prevented from free expression, while there are few things in the great without that are really worthwhile. There never was a time when we should consider the lilies of the field more than now. The human race is breaking itself down striving to gain hold upon phantoms, while the great prize that has already been given is lost sight of in the dust and confusion. But to inspire the present generation with a desire to return to nature and her beautiful ways cannot be done to any extent, however, except through living examples. It is the living of life that will change the life of the world. The world at large does not listen to reason, nor can those who are in the mad rush stop to think; besides, such minds are

The Ideal Made Real

not sufficiently clear to understand the principles upon which the living of life is based. Seeing is believing, as far as the world is concerned, and therefore they require living examples of those who have proven the superiority of the better way; accordingly, those who know how to live as the lilies live should consider it a privilege to place their light wherever it can be seen.

When you can prove through your own life and experience that personal ambition and hard work are not necessary to greater things, but are actual hindrances, and that greater things come of themselves to those who will permit themselves to be themselves, you have caused a great light to spring up, and few there are who will not see it. Those who take everything literally may wonder how anything can be accomplished without work, but they must bear in mind that there is work, and work. The work that is done by those who are down in the world's way is hard, wearing and tearing. It is destructive to human life and builds up one thing by tearing down another, and in the end it brings no lasting good, neither to the individual nor to the race; but the work that is done by those who have found the better way is neither hard nor wearisome. It is not done through strenuous living nor external striving, but is done by the power of the great within coming forth into expression in personal life. In this mode of work you first give your inner power right of way, then you direct it consciously and intelligently. You do not depend upon personal power and difficult personal efforts.

You place yourself in the hands of higher power, and as you receive higher power you cause it to do that which you wish to have done. You have all felt power working through you, and at such times work was pleasure. You gave the commands, of course, and you knew it was your own power, your own higher power, but no hard personal effort was required. You simply opened the way somehow, then decided firmly but gently what you wished to have done; and you could feel a mighty power coming forth, seemingly from an inexhaustible source, taking full possession of thought and muscle, and doing the very thing you desired to have done. After the work was finished you discovered it was superior work, and although you had engaged in the task for many hours you actually felt stronger than when you began.

The reason why is simple. You did not depend upon personal limitations and strenuous efforts; and you did not try to make those limitations do a great deal more than they had the capacity to do. You opened your life to all the power of your life and you thus received enough power to do what you wished to have done, and more; and so long as you have power to spare you can be neither weak nor tired. When the system is thoroughly full of energy, work is a pleasure; and so long as that fullness continues weariness is impossible; and there is enough power in real life to cause your system to be full of energy, and more, at all times no matter how much you may do or how great your task may be.

When we consider the lilies of the field, how they grow, we find that they naturally permit the life that is within them to unfold; they do not try to grow; they have, as everything has, the power of growth within them and they grow because they do not hinder that interior power and growth from having their way. Likewise, when we know that divinity reigns within us we do not have to work hard nor many years to reach that state. We will grow and develop, both mentally and spiritually, when we permit the divinity within to unfold. Everything seeks self expression. Nothing in nature, visible or invisible, will have to be forced into expression, because at the very heart of all things there is the deep, strong desire to come forth and be. Therefore, if we wish to ascend in the scale of life, we must cease those confused and destructive states of mind that hinder expression, and become as the lilies of the field. Give the life within permission to really live in us. The life within will live our life and give us a beautiful life. The power within will do our work and do that work extremely well. The divinity within will make us Godlike in all things, and never cease to give us the things of the spirit so long as we permit those things to come forth and abide in personal existence.

What we are required to do that such things may come to pass is to live, think and act in the likeness of the Infinite. God is, and He permits Himself to be what He is. Man must do likewise, and all shall be well with him. Those who do not understand may think that the individuality of man might diminish, if he were to give himself up to the life and the power within, but such a conclusion will disappear when we realize that the power from within is our own. We are simply causing ourselves to become more and more of what we already are in reality.

By giving free expression to our own higher, interior powers we naturally become more powerful, and by giving free expression to our own inherent divinity we naturally become more Godlike and more spiritual on every plane of being. The lilies of the field do not become inferior lilies by permitting the spirit of the beautiful to unfold from within their gentle lives. It is by this method that they become what they are, and they become so much that the glory of artificial man can never compare with theirs. It is the same with the human soul. The soul becomes great and beautiful by permitting its own greatness and loveliness to come forth unhindered and undisturbed.

Thousands of people are at present trying to develop higher powers. Many of these actually try to work hard in their efforts to gain the various gifts of mind and soul, and because they do not succeed to any great extent they frequently become discouraged and give up, wondering whether or not the real truth has been found. Others being ambitious to become great in the world try to employ spiritual laws in the furthering of their personal aims, but they find the reactions so disagreeable that the prize is not worth the labor. To fly to the top at once is the ruling passion among many and when they fail with whatever methods they may employ they conclude that what passes for truth is nothing but manmade doctrines.

The fact is, however, that the truth always appears to be the untruth when misdirected. To apply the principles of real truth in the furthering of any lofty aim we may have in mind, the first essential is to establish life in perfect touch with eternal life; the second essential is to positively determine what we expect to attain and become in actual personal living; and the third essential is to proceed in the attainment of health, happiness and harmony. Without health nothing of permanent value can be accomplished. Without happiness our talents will be as the flowers without sunshine, and without harmony most of the power we might receive would be thrown away.

To obtain health, happiness and harmony we need simply let life live. Real life already has these things, and when we let life live in us those things will be expressed through us. The next essential is to resolve that we will be fully contented simply to live. To shine in the world, to acquire fame or to do something wonderful that mankind may long remember us, that we will not think of. Many a person has worked hard for fame and died early, in obscurity. Fame in itself, however, is of no value. When you are neither happy nor well, fame cannot make your life worthwhile. If you are miserable, it will profit nothing if everybody may know your name. It is not the praise of man that we should seek, but the life of the Infinite. The praise of the world can give us nothing, but life from within can give us everything that the heart can wish for.

True fame comes to him who deserves it without his trying to get it, but those only can deserve the honor of the race who have always been their best, who have not neglected a single opportunity to be of service, and who have lived constantly for the one purpose of being an inspiration to every soul. We may look at this phase of the subject as we may, we can come to only one conclusion. He alone is great and deserving of honor who so lives that he always is all that God made him to be; and it is such a life that is lived by the lilies of the field. When man will be as true to his large world as the lilies are to their small world, mankind will become a race of gods indeed, and the Utopian dreams of the prophets will come true. This, however, the ordinary thinker may declare to be impossible, but nothing is impossible. If a flower can be true to itself in its world, man can be true to himself in his world.

Those who are accustomed to the worldly methods of thinking and working may feel that it is hardly possibly to apply these new ideas while associated with worldly minds, but we must remember that it is not where we work or at what we work, but how we work that determines what results are to be. To work so that you permit the boundless power within to work through you is the secret, and this will not only cause your work to be pleasant, but will also cause you to do better and better work every day. It is therefore the royal path to pleasantness today and greater things tomorrow. In the old way you are compelled to almost wear yourself out today in order that you might provide for tomorrow; but not so in the new. While you are providing for tomorrow you are not only enjoying life today, but you are, through the expression of greater and greater power from within, making yourself larger, stronger and greater today. In the development of talents you employ the same principle. You do not strive for greatness; you know that you are potentially great already, and by permitting this greatness to become alive in you, you will accomplish great things.

When you apply this principle in everything that you do, you will find your advancement to be steady and even rapid; you will move forward in all things, making the ideal real as you ascend in the scale. The very moment you find a new ideal you find that power within you that can make that ideal real; thus your advancement becomes continuous, your progress eternal. To live the life beautiful we simply let life live. We know that life itself is beautiful and when we permit that life that is beautiful to live in us, we will live consciously and personally the most beautiful life that we can picture in the ideal without making any personal effort to do so. When we begin to live, think and act according to these principles we feel that we are carried on and on by some mysterious presence that seems to be doing everything for us while giving us the pleasure and the glory. We soon learn, however, that this presence is ourself, our own larger, superior self created in the image of God.; therefore, able to do everything that we may wish to have done; and it is a joy, indeed, to feel everything moving so smoothly and gently, so harmoniously and pleasantly, and at the same time producing such great results.

To engage in some extraordinary work becomes one of our greatest pleasures, because nothing is hard or difficult anymore; obstacles disappear the very moment we enter their presence, and we realize inwardly that whatever we undertake to do will be accomplished. We no longer tremble when in the midst of events that require exceptional wisdom and power; we know that wisdom is ready to speak whatever may be necessary now, and that power is at hand to do whatever may be necessary to be done now. We are in touch with the greatness of the great within and may draw upon that great, inexhaustible source whatever we may need at any time. Fear takes flight, while faith becomes stronger, higher and more perfect; sorrow and despair are no more, because all things are working for the best. Even in the presence of death and loss we see more life and greater gain.

We know that what passes away merely ascends that it may live more and be itself in a larger, higher measure than it ever was before. We know that whatever comes will bring the new and the more beautiful. It could not be otherwise, because having chosen to be all that we are, the all can never cease to come, and the more the all continues to come the more the all will continue to bring. We have laid aside the illusions of the world and adopted the ways of truth. We have beheld the beauties of nature and have opened our minds to the visions of the soul. These have given us the secret, and like the lilies of the field, we have learned to be still and live.

Chapter 9

Count It All Joy

We meet something at almost every turn that we think ought to be different. If we have high ideals, we may not feel satisfied to permit those conditions to remain as they are; we may even complain or antagonize. On the other hand, if our ideals be low, we may feel wholly indifferent, but then we find that those things go from bad to worse. What we seek, however, is our present comfort on the one hand and the betterment of everything about us on the other hand, and we wish to know how this may be brought about in the midst of the confusion, the ignorance and the ills that we find in the world. When we are indifferent to the wrong it becomes worse; therefore, even for our own good we must do something with those adverse conditions that exist in the home, in society, or in the state. We must meet all those things and meet them properly, but the problem is, how?

To antagonize, criticize or condemn never helps matters in the least; besides, such states of mind are a detriment to one's own peace and health. The critical mind wears itself out while thinking about the wrong, but the wrong in the meantime goes on becoming worse. To feel disappointed because the universe does not move according to our fancy will not change the universe, but it will produce weakness in our own mind and body. That person who lives constantly in the world of despondency will soon lose all hold upon life; he consequently does nothing in the world but bring about the end of his own personal life. The usual way of dealing with the problems of life solves nothing. The ordinary way of meeting temptation gives the tempter greater power, while the person who tries to resist is usually entrapped in adversity and trouble. But St. Paul has told us what to do under all such circumstances. Count it all joy. That is the secret. Count it all joy no matter what may come, agreeing with all adversity at once, antagonizing nothing; condemning no one, leaving criticism alone. Never be disappointed or discouraged, and have nothing whatever to do with worry. Whatever comes, count it all joy. He who meets adversity in the attitude of peace, harmony and joy will turn enemies into friends and failures into greater good.

When things do not come your way, never mind. Continue to count everything joy, and everything will change in such a manner as to give you joy. If you are seeking the best, all things will work together in such a way as to give you the best, and your heart's desire shall be realized; possibly not today, but life is long; you can wait. That which is good is always good; it is always welcome whenever it comes. In the meantime you are living in harmony and joy, and that in itself is surely a great good. That person who lives constantly in gloom drives even the sunshine out of his own mind; the clouds of gloom are so heavy that he fails to see the brightness that is all about him. That person, however, who counts everything joy will change everything to brightness and thus receive joy from everything. When you fail to receive what you sought, never for a moment be disappointed. Count it all joy. In fact, be supremely happy; you have a reason so to be. When you fail to get what you seek it simply means that there is something still better in store for you; then why should you not count such an event great joy. This is always the case when your whole desire is to receive the best; and when you train yourself to count everything joy, your mind develops that desire that always desires the best.

When you seek only the best, the best only will come, and you must not feel disappointed when you are taken away from a hovel in order that you may enter a palace. When you meet enemies or adversaries do not resist them or enter into warfare; look for terms of agreement. Possibly they may seem to get the best of the bargain now, but you can afford to give them the terms they ask. The Infinite is your supply. When one door closes another opens, and if you depend upon the Supreme to open that other door, it will be a door opening into far greater and far better things than what you seemingly lost; besides, by being kind to your adversary you lifted yourself up. You are now a higher and a greater being. That means that you will now draw to yourself higher and better things; consequently, it was not the enemy that got the best terms; it was you.

Whatever you are called upon to do, do it and be happy. Count it all joy that you are given the opportunity to bring sunshine into dark places and develop your own latent power by doing what seemed difficult. You are equal to the occasion, if you think so; therefore you should consider it a privilege to prove it. The world is waiting for great souls, souls that are ready to do what others failed to accomplish. You can become one of these great souls by proving to yourself that you are equal to every occasion; and you will be equal to every occasion, if you count everything joy. When you are in the midst of temptations, rejoice with your whole heart. You have found a great opportunity to turn wrong into right, and to turn wrong into right is always a mark of greatness. Millions of people have died unhonored and unsung who might have arisen to greatness and become leaders and saviors in the world, if they would have demonstrated their superiority in the midst of temptation, tribulation and wrong. Look upon all temptations and troubles as opportunities to make wrong right, and be glad that such opportunities have been presented to you. Count it all joy; besides, the result will not only produce joy to yourself, but possibly to millions. He who changes wrong into right rises in the scale, and you can think of no greater good coming to you than this. He who remains below must be counted with the small and the ordinary. He who goes up higher shall gain everything that his heart may wish for. Therefore, whatever comes, or whatever you meet, or whatever you are called upon to do, proceed with peace and joy. Be glad that you have the opportunity to prove your own power, and thus elevate yourself thereby. Be supremely happy to know that you may change many things for the better through this attitude, and thus bless the lives of multitudes.

Train yourself to look at things according to this principle, and you will find that everything can produce joy. Everything can give cause for rejoicing; that is, providing everything is met in that attitude that counts everything joy. The same principle may be employed to great advantage in overcoming difficulties. When you are asked to do what seems to be very difficult, or when you are called upon to perform duties you do not like, never refuse. Count it all joy. To excuse yourself when such occasions appear is to lose most valuable opportunities.

Every person desires to make the most of himself, but to accomplish this all latent power must be awakened, and there is nothing that will bring forth our latent powers more thoroughly than the doing of what seems difficult. When you find yourself shrinking from certain tasks you have discovered a weak faculty within yourself. Refuse to let that faculty remain in such a condition. Go and do what you feared to do and let nothing hold you back. In this way the weak faculty will be made strong and your entire nature will pass through most valuable discipline and training. Nothing is really disagreeable unless we think so. That is, we may approach the disagreeable in such a way that it ceases to be disagreeable; and the secret is, count everything joy. You may enter darkness and gloom, but if you are living in a world of brightness and cheer, that darkness will not be darkness to you, nor will gloom enter your mind for a moment. You can remain in your own happy world, no matter what may happen, no matter what may take place in your immediate environment.

When you resolve to do certain things and proceed with a conviction that you will enjoy the work thoroughly, you will find real pleasure in that work; besides, you will do the work very well. Pleasure comes from within, and when the fountain of joy within is overflowing, it will give joy to everything that exists about us. To cause this fountain within to overflow at all times, count everything joy at all times. We should never look for weakness, but when we find it we should proceed at once to change it into strength. Whenever we meet difficulties, or whenever we are called upon to do what we dislike we have found a weakness. We may remove that weakness by doing with a will what the moment demands, and resolve to enjoy it. Never permit such occasions to pass by without being changed. The opportunity is too valuable. Whatever your present sphere of action may require of you, that you are able to do; and the present demand upon your life and your talents must be supplied by you if you would bring out the best that is in you, and make the great eternal now full and complete.

Tasks that seem difficult and demands that seem unreasonable are after all neither difficult nor unreasonable. They are simply golden opportunities for you to become what you never were before. They are but paths to greater achievements, sweeter joys and a larger life. Therefore, when you meet such occasions, count it all joy. When you fail to gain or realize in the present what you expected, do not feel disappointed. Make up your mind to be just as happy in those conditions that are, as you expect to be in those conditions that you are looking for. The feeling of disappointment is not produced by events. It is produced by your own attitude toward events. You can meet all events in such a frame of mind that you never feel disappointed in the least, and that frame of mind is the result of counting everything joy. When you know that eternity is long and that countless joys are in store for you, you will not feel sad now because one insignificant event has been postponed. And when you have full control of your mind you will have the power to produce just as much happiness in the absence of that event as in its presence, because events themselves cannot produce happiness.

The same is true of things. We do not gain joy from things, but from the way we think about things, and we can think as we choose at any time no matter what the circumstance may be. When the present demands happiness from something different than what you were looking for in the present, grasp the opportunity to prove that you are equal to this occasion. You thus develop latent ability. When you count everything joy you know that you can always produce joy. You know that whatever happens is best, because you have the power to cause it to become the best. The best always happens to those who seek only the best; therefore, whatever comes should be received as the best, and we must give it the opportunity to prove that it is better than anything that could have happened. You are not dependent upon events for happiness. Happiness does not come from what we do or where we go. Happiness comes from what we are now or what we create out of what is present now. Whether we be alone in a garret or in a gorgeous ball room the amount of happiness we are to receive in either place will depend entirely upon our own frame of mind. The frame of mind that you desire for the present moment you may have; if it does not come of itself, you can create it; you are the master.

When things do not come the way we like, we can like them the way they are coming. This is how we agree quickly with our adversaries; we thus receive the enemy instead of fighting the enemy; and that which we receive in the true attitude of mind becomes our own. Count everything joy and every adversity will give up its power to you. That which is evil becomes good when we meet it in such a way that we draw out of it the best that it may contain, and we always attract the best from everything when we meet everything in the conviction that all things work together for good. When nothing comes to give us happiness in the external we can open the fount of everlasting joy in the great within. The heaven of the soul is ever ready to open its pearly gates, but we must look towards the soul if we would pass through those gates. We shall fail to see the fountain of joy within, however, so long as our whole attention is fixed upon those worldly pleasures that failed to come into our world; but if we count everything joy we no longer feel disappointed about what did not happen; on the other hand we enter into that joyous state of mind that will place us in direct contact with the source of limitless joy within the mind. When people speak unkindly of you, you will become offended if you thought they spoke unkindly, but if your eyes are too pure to behold iniquity you will go on your way as if nothing had been said; you count everything joy and thus you will receive joy from your own lofty position in the matter.

When you are asked to do certain things do not proceed with a feeling that you are compelled to. Go and do it because you want to; say that you want to, and count it all joy. We should never say "I have a duty to perform," but rather, "Here is an opportunity which I have the privilege to embrace." Train yourself to want to do whatever your present sphere of life may demand. He who loves and thoroughly enjoys what he is doing today will be asked to do greater things tomorrow. The large soul never asks if things are unpleasant or difficult; such thoughts never enter his mind. Whatever he finds to do he proceeds to do, with his mind full. of will and his heart full of joy. If you dislike anybody, you have found a weakness in yourself. You have found a difficulty that must be overcome at once. Do not permit such obstacles to remain in your way. The soul that knows no weakness loves everything that God has created. The strong soul never considers those imperfections in life that man has created. Intelligence was not intended to be used in the study of nothingness, illusions or mistakes. When we hate anything we recognize the existence and the power of those things that have neither real existence nor real power; we therefore enter into a confused state of mind. What God has created we cannot help but love, but if we see something else and dislike that something else we are seeing something that God has not created. In other words, we are giving attention to illusions and mistakes, and the mind is not intended for that purpose. Remove the illusion by transforming that hate into love; this will change the point of view. You will thus see things from the upper side, the divine side, and when we look at things from the divine side we find that everything is altogether lovely.

Therefore, when you dislike anybody overcome that weakness by giving that person all the love of your heart. Love that person and mean it, no matter what he has said or done. There is nothing in the world that lifts the soul so high above darkness and illusion as strong, pure, spiritual love; and it is not difficult to love a person when you know that he is God's creation, while his mistakes are simply man's creation. Mistakes must be forgiven. Our desire is to do the will of God, and to do the will of God is to love every creature in existence, and to love everything as God loves everything.

Chapter 10

The True Use of Kindness and Sympathy

The ordinary use of sympathy is responsible for a very large portion of the ills and the troubles we find in the world; the reason being that nearly all suffering is mental before it is physical, and that mental suffering is almost invariably produced when we enter into sympathetic touch with the ills that we meet among relations, friends or associates. The average person would suffer but little if he suffered only from the troubles that arise in his own system. It is the pain that is felt through sympathy for others that gives him most of the burdens he finds it necessary to bear. It is considered a sign of kindness, goodness and high regard, however, to sympathize with others in this manner, or rather to suffer with others, but this is not the true use of kindness.

We do not help others by entering into the same weakness that is keeping them in a world of distress. We do not help the weak by becoming weak. We do not relieve sickness by becoming sick. We do not right the wrong by entering into the wrong, or doing wrong. We do not free man from failures by permitting ourselves to become failures. We do not emancipate those who are in bondage to sin by going and committing the same sin. This is very simple; but ordinary sympathy is based upon the idea that we sympathize with a person only when we suffer with that person. We expect to relieve pain by proceeding to produce the same pain in our own systems; but we cannot remove darkness by entering into the dark We can remove wrong only by removing the cause of that wrong, and to remove the cause of wrong we must produce the cause of right. Darkness disappears when we produce light; likewise, sickness and trouble will vanish when we produce health and harmony, but we cannot produce health and harmony by entering into disease and trouble. This, however, is what ordinary sympathy does; it has, therefore, failed to relieve the world. The ordinary use of sympathy multiplies suffering by making suffering contagious. It causes the suffering of the one to give pain to the many, and then in turn causes the pain of the many to give additional pain to each individual person whose sympathy is aroused in the same connection. We must remove everything that tends to make ills contagious, whether it is physical or mental, and it is very evident that ordinary sympathy does spread pains and ills to a very great degree. Therefore, one of the first essentials in producing emancipation or in making real the ideal is to find the true use of sympathy.

Sympathy itself must not be removed, because it is one of the highest virtues of the soul. The average person, however, misapplies this virtue continuously, and in consequence brings pains and ills both to himself and others, that could easily have been prevented. There is a better use for sympathy, and through this better use we cause all the good things in life to become contagious. Instead of entering into sympathetic touch with the weakness that may temporarily exist in the personality of man we enter into sympathetic touch with the strength that permanently exists in the soul of man. Instead of morbidly dwelling upon the ills and the wrongs which we find we proceed to gain the highest possible realization of the good, the right, the superior and the beautiful that we know has existence back of and above the superficial life of human nature. According to a metaphysical law, when we enter into mental contact with the good in man we awaken the power of that which is good in man, and the most perfect mental contact is produced by sympathy.

To sympathize with the soul is to increase the active power of the soul, because we always arouse into greater action that with which we sympathize, and when the active power of the soul is increased the weakness of the personality will become strength. To sympathize with the power of health and harmony in man will increase the power of health and harmony throughout his entire system and the elimination of sickness and trouble must inevitably follow. To sympathize with the pain a person may feel is to do nothing to relieve that person. You take the pain to yourself, but you do not take the pain away from the person with whom you sympathize. You thus double the suffering instead of removing it entirely, as you should. On the other hand, when we refuse to recognize the suffering itself and proceed to awaken in that person that something that can remove the suffering we protect ourselves from pain, while we actually do something to relieve that person from pain. We do not suffer with the person that suffers, but we do something to remove suffering absolutely from everybody concerned; instead of entering into the pain we take that person out of pain. That is sympathy that is sympathy. That is kindness that really results in a kind act. It does not weep, but does better. It removes both the cause and the effect of the weeping. It awakens that superior power in man that positively does produce emancipation. It does not cause suffering to be transmitted to a score of other persons who have done nothing to merit that suffering, but it stops the pain where it is and puts it out of existence absolutely.

Every form of suffering comes from the violation of some law in life. It is therefore wrong, but it cannot be righted by making a special effort to spread the results of that wrong among as many others as possible. This, however, ordinary sympathy does; it makes a special effort to make everybody feel bad because someone is not feeling as he should; but the pains of the many cannot give ease and comfort to the one, nor can many minds in bondage set one mind free. When anyone is feeling bad it will not help him to have a group of morbid minds suffer with him. When anyone is sorry it will not remove the cause of his grief to have others decide to be sorry also. Do something so that person will not feel bad any more. Take him out of his trouble. That is real sympathy; and while you are helping him out make him feel that your heart is as tender as tenderness itself. Do something so that the grief may be removed through the realization of that greater truth that knows that all is well. That is kindness worthy of the name.

Those, however, who are in the habit of sympathizing in the ordinary way may think the new way cold, and devoid of feeling or love, but the fact is that it is the ordinary form of sympathy that is devoid of love. When you love a person who is in pain you will not stand around and weep pretending that you are also feeling bad. You will put on the countenance of light and cheerfulness and actually do something tangible to remove his pain. That's love; and if you have real sympathy, you will minister to him with so much depth of feeling and tender kindness that you will touch the very innermost life of his soul. All love, all tenderness, all kindness and all real feeling come from the soul. Therefore, he whose sympathy is of the soul will receive his love and his kindness directly from the true source; in consequence, he will have more love and more kindness by far than the one whose sympathy is a form of morbid feeling.

The real purpose of true sympathy is twofold; first, to arouse in a greater measure that finer something in everybody with whom one may come in contact that will arouse this greater something, not only in others, but also in him who lives in this form of sympathy. In other words, to sympathize with the superior in man is to banish the wrong and the inferior by causing the expression of that divine something within that has the power to in life that is not only tender and sweet and beautiful, but is also immensely strong, strong with the strength of the Infinite; and second, to awaken everything in man that has quality, superiority and worth; that is, to make man feel the supreme power of his own inherent divinity. There is something in man that is greater than all weakness, all ills, all wrongs, and when this something is awakened, developed and expressed, all weakness, all ills and all wrongs must disappear. To sympathize with this greater something makes all things well. Such a sympathy will tend to build a stronger life, a better life, a superior life, a more beautiful life; and to give such a sympathy to everybody is kindness indeed.

There may seem to be kindness in weeping with those who weep, but it is a far greater kindness to give those people the power to banish their sorrows completely, and he who does this is not cold; he is the very essence of the highest and most beautiful love. There is no joy in having sorrow. There is no pleasure in having pain. Therefore, what greater good can man do for man than to help him gain complete emancipation from all those things, and this is the purpose of this higher use of sympathy. True sympathy is neither cold nor purely intellectual. It is real soul-feeling, while ordinary sympathy is simply a morbid mental feeling. True sympathy is the very fire of real spiritual love, because it springs from the very soul of love and is in constant touch with the unbounded power of that love. That such a sympathy should have extraordinary emancipating power is therefore most evident. The ordinary use of sympathy may appear to be kind. It may mean well, but it is usually misdirected kindness, and is nearly always weak. The higher use of sympathy, that is, the expression of divine sympathy, is not only kindness itself, but it has the spiritual understanding and the spiritual power to do what kindness wants to do. Ordinary kindness is usually crippled. It lacks both the power to do and the understanding to know what to do. The true sympathy, however, not only has the power to feel kindly, but has the power to act kindly. It not only gives love and makes everybody feel that they are in the presence of real love, but it also gives that something that can cause the purpose of love to come true. Real love invariably aims to produce comfort, peace and emancipation. That is its purpose, and real sympathy can fulfill that purpose. Therefore, this higher sympathy is the sympathy that is sympathy.

The same principle should be employed in the use of every form of emotion, because every emotion is a movement of the mind conveying mental elements and powers with certain definite objects in view. Therefore, the way the emotion acts will determine to a very great extent whether these mental powers will build for better things, or produce undesirable conditions. Those movements of the mind or emotions that express themselves in love, heartfelt joy and spiritual feeling have a beneficial effect; while that mental feeling that is usually termed emotionalism is never wholesome. True spiritual feeling is calm, but extremely beautiful and awakens orderly and harmoniously all the finer elements of human life. It is true spiritual feeling, or what may be termed emotions sublime, that gives action and expression to personal quality, mental worth and individual superiority. In other words, it is these actions of mind and soul that elevate thought, action, feeling, consciousness and desire above the planes of the ordinary. Such emotions should therefore be cultivated to the very highest and finest degree.

What is spoken of as heartfelt joy is that wholesome joy that comes directly from the heart and that has depth, reality and joyous feeling; but that joy that runs into uncontrolled ecstasy is never wholesome. Every feeling of joy that causes the mind to be carried away into excited or overwrought ecstasy is not joy, but mental intoxication. Such joy does not produce genuine happiness, and the reaction always disturbs the equilibrium of the wind. Depth of thought, clear thinking, intellectual brilliancy, good judgment, mental poise, all of these will diminish in the mind that indulges in uncontrolled ecstasy, emotionalism or pleasure that produces excitability and overwrought emotional feeling. The feeling of love, when it is love, is always wholesome and elevating, but passionate desire is weakening unless it is permeated through and through with genuine love. A deep, strong feeling of love will turn all desires, whether mental or physical, into constructive channels, but we must be certain that it is real love and not an artificial feeling temporarily produced by the misuse of the imagination. Here every mental movement that is intense, forced, overwrought or worked up to an abnormal pitch of excited enthusiasm leads to emotionalism, and emotionalism burns up energy. Nearly all kinds of nervous diseases can be traced directly or indirectly to emotionalism in one or more of its many forms; and as physical and mental weakness always follows the burning up of energy, a number of physical and mental ills can be traced to this source.

When emotionalism, fear, anger and worry are eliminated, all kinds of insanity and all kinds of nervous diseases will be things of the past; while the power, the capacity and the brilliancy of the average mind will increase to an extraordinary degree. Strong emotional feelings and intense enthusiasm will sometimes arouse a great deal of dormant, mental power. In consequence, people sometimes do exceptional things while under the emotional spell, but the entire process, as well as the final results, are very similar to that produced by alcoholic stimulants and other drugs. The system seems to be charged with a great deal of extra power for a while, but when the reaction comes the entire system becomes much weaker than it ever was before. The mind that permits itself to be aroused by intense, emotional feeling will gradually lose its power of clear thought. The understanding will become so weakened that the principles of real truth cannot be fully comprehended, while the judgment will follow more and more the illusions of an overwrought imagination. The fact that religious feeling among millions is so closely associated with this overwrought state of emotionalism proves the importance of a better understanding of the use of these finer mental elements. Emotionalism compels the mind to follow mere feeling, and mere feeling, when not properly blended with clear understanding, will be misdirected at every turn. Emotionalism also stupefies the finer perceptions by intoxicating the mind, and by burning up the finer mental energies; and since these finer perceptions are required to discern real truth we understand readily why highly emotional people cannot comprehend the principles of pure, spiritual metaphysics. Having been trained towards materialistic literalism instead of away from it, they are not to blame, however, for their present state and deserve no criticism. Nevertheless, those who wish to find real religion and real spirituality must learn to understand the psychology of emotion and must learn the true use of all the finer feelings of the mind.

There is something in man that is called religious feeling. It is present to a greater or lesser degree in everybody and cannot be removed, because it is a part of life itself. When in action, and it is never inactive very long, it expresses itself in some power of emotion. When this emotion or delicate mental movement is permitted to act without any definite purpose it becomes emotionalism; that is, mental energy running rampant, and becoming more and more intense until it destroys itself, as well as all the energy it originally contained. On the other hand, when this feeling is directed towards the highest and the most perfect conception of truth, life and being that the mind can possibly picture, all that is lofty, ideal and beautiful will be developed in the mind and soul of that individual. This is natural, because there is nothing that has greater developing power than deep, spiritual feeling; a fact that those who desire to develop remarkable ability, extraordinary talent and rare genius will do well to remember.

There is no mental faculty that is more readily affected by the emotions than the imagination, and since the imagination is such a very important faculty, no mental or physical action that in any way interferes with the constructive work of the imagination should be permitted. Emotionalism, however, invariably excites the imagination, and an excited imagination will imagine all sorts of things that are not true. The mind will thus be filled with illusions, and in consequence, false beliefs, wrong thoughts, perverted states and misdirected mental energy will follow. The result will be sickness, trouble, mistakes and failures in one or more of their many forms. It is now a well demonstrated truth that every thought has a definite power of its own, and, that power will produce its natural effect in some part of the human system. If the thought is not good the effect will naturally be undesirable, and conditions will be produced in mind or body that we do not want. But whatever we imagine, that we think; therefore, when we excite the imagination we imagine all manner of things that are untrue, unreal or abnormal; we produce false or perverted thought action in the mind; we think the wrong, and wrong thoughts invariably produce wrong conditions in mind or body, or both.

What we imagine we reproduce in ourselves to some degree, frequently to a marked degree; but an excited imagination simply cannot imagine what is good and wholesome. In every form of development, whether in the body, the mind or the soul, the imagining faculty is employed extensively. All growth is promoted by combining and recombining the elements of life in higher and higher forms, and since it is one of the functions of the imagination to produce these higher, more complex and more perfect combinations, development cannot take place unless the imagination works orderly, constructively and progressively. An excited imagination will produce false mental combinations or may waste energy by attempting to combine mental elements that will not combine. An orderly imagination may be likened to a skilled workman who builds a beautiful mansion out of his bricks, while an excited imagination might be likened to someone who can do nothing more than pile those bricks into a heap. The fact that emotionalism always excites the imagination proves therefore how impossible it is for minds with uncontrolled emotions to develop the greatness that is latent within them.

Another fact of great importance in this connection is that emotionalism will intensify every mental tendency that may be active in mind at the time. If there is a tendency towards abnormal desires, emotionalism will intensify those desires so that it will be very difficult to resist temptation should it appear. On the other hand, pure spiritual feeling would transmute those desires, and produce instead, an ascending tendency, thus leading all the forces of mind towards higher ground. To overcome emotionalism, intense mental feeling, anger, excitability and all overwrought or abnormal mental states, turn attention upon the spiritual heights of the soul whenever such mental feelings are felt. By training all mental feelings and emotions to move toward the deeper and the higher spiritual state of being these same feelings will become stronger, deeper, finer and more beautiful than they ever were before. We then establish the foundation upon which we can build an ideal character, and through such a character all the qualities of mind and soul can be used beneficially in the midst of every experience, whatever the nature of that experience may be.

To cause all the emotions to follow ascending tendencies will increase remarkably the power, the fineness, the life and the rapture of every phase of feeling, not only in the soul, but in the mind and the body as well. Every trace of coldness, indifference or lack of feeling will entirely disappear, and we shall develop instead that higher form of kindness, sympathy and spiritual emotion that is created in the likeness of divine emotion. Whoever employs this method will not permit his feelings to run wild at any time, but will cause the life and the power of every feeling to accumulate in his system. He will hold them all in poise and use their energies intelligently in the building up of his whole life and in adding to the joy, the rapture and the delight of the living of a full, strong, ever-ascending state of existence. That person who controls his feelings and turns all the energies of those feelings upon the spiritual heights of the soul will actually become a living flame of love, sympathy and sublime emotion. Such a person will enjoy everything intensely, but his joy will be in such a high state of harmony that he will waste nothing in his life; instead, all the elements and powers of his life will continue to accumulate, thus giving added strength, worth and superiority to everything that he may physically, mentally or spiritually possess.

Chapter 11

Talk Health, Happiness and Prosperity

Talk happiness. When things look dark, talk happiness. When things look bright, talk more happiness. When others are sad, insist on being glad. Talk happiness, and they will soon feel better. Talk happiness; it pays in every shape and form and manner. Give sunshine to others, and others will be more than pleased to give sunshine to you. Talk happiness, and your health will be better, your mind will be brighter and your personality far more attractive; but the qualities that happiness will give to you will also be given to those who have the pleasure to listen to you when you talk happiness.

Talk happiness, and you will always remain in a happy frame of mind. You will encourage thousands of others to do the same. You will become a fountain of joy in the midst of the garden of human life, and who can tell how many flowers of kindness and joy unfolded their rare and tender beauty because you were there. When others have lost courage, talk happiness. The future is bright for everybody. Talk happiness, and you turn on the light in their pathway, and they will see the better things that are before them. When the mind is depressed it is blinded; it sees only the darkness; but when the light of joy is admitted, everything is changed. Therefore, talk happiness to all persons and on all occasions.

We cannot have too much light in the world, and the more we talk happiness the more light we produce wherever we may be. What greater pleasure could anyone desire than to realize that he has eased the way of life for thousands and sent the sunbeams and joy into the mental world of tens of thousands? You can do this by talking happiness. Thus by constantly talking happiness you produce perpetual increase in your own happiness. What we give in abundance always returns in abundance; that is, when we give in the right spirit; and he who talks happiness is always in the right spirit. When in the midst of discord, trouble or confusion, talk happiness. Harmony will soon be restored. The majority can easily change their minds for the better when someone takes the lead. You can take the lead by talking happiness.

Talk prosperity. When times are not good, man himself must make them better, and he can make them better by doing his best and having faith in that power that produces prosperity. When men have faith in prosperity they will think prosperity, live prosperity and thus do that which produces prosperity; and you can give men faith in prosperity by constantly talking prosperity.

They may not listen at first, but perseverance always wins. Prosperity is extremely attractive, and the more you impress it upon the minds of others the more attractive it becomes until no one can resist it; and when we admit the idea of prosperity into our own minds we will from that moment begin to produce prosperity. Think prosperity, talk prosperity, and live prosperity; and you will rise in the scale no matter what the circumstances may be. Hold to the power that produces abundance by having unbounded faith in that power and you will overcome all adversity and reach the highest goal you have in view. The fear of failure produces more failure than all other causes combined. You can remove that fear by talking prosperity.

Talk health. It is the best medicine. When people stop talking sickness they will stop getting sick. Talk health and stay well. Talk health to the person who is sick and you will cause him to think health. He who thinks health will live health, and he who lives health will produce health. When your associates take delight in relating minutely everything they know about the ills of the community, purify the muddy waters of their conversation by talking health. Insist on talking health. Prove that there is more health than sickness, and that therefore health is the more important subject. The majority rules. Health is in the majority. Increase that majority by talking more health. Take the lead in this manner of conversation, and be positively determined to continue in the lead. Others will soon follow, and when they do, sickness will diminish more and more until it becomes practically unknown among those who have the privilege to live in your circle.

When the sins of the world are in evidence, talk virtue. When the power of virtue is in evidence, talk more virtue. Eternally emphasize the good; give it more and more power, and it will soon become sufficiently strong to produce that ideal of power that you wish to make real. Talk virtue, and people will think of virtue; they will dwell more and more upon the beauty of virtue. Ere long they will desire virtue, and that desire will become stronger and stronger until it thrills every atom in human life. To desire virtue is to become virtuous. To live for the attainment of purity is to place in action all the purifying elements in your being, and you will soon realize that perfectly clean condition that every awakened mind has learned to worship. You can purify the minds of thousands by constantly talking virtue, and these thousands will in turn convey the power of virtue to as many thousand times thousands more.

Talk virtue eternally and there is no end to the good that you may do. When the world seems bad, talk virtue. The power of good is not gone; it is just as great as it ever was, and it is here and there and everywhere. You can open the mind of man to the mighty influx of this power by eternally talking virtue. You can, through the proper use of your own words, change the tide of human thought. You can cause all mankind to desire virtue by forever talking virtue. On the surface many things may seem to be what they ought not to be, but the surface is not all there is. It is an insignificant part of the whole. There is a hidden richness in life that the many do not see, because their attention has never been turned in that direction. You can lead mankind into the gold mines of the mind and into the diamond fields of the soul, and the secret lies in the words you speak. You can guide the mind of man by the way you talk. Talking therefore should not be empty, but should ever have a sublime goal in view. Your words point the way and they who hear what you have to say will, to some degree, be influenced to go whatever way your words may point. Your power, therefore, in directing other minds towards greater and better things is hidden in every word you speak, and how important that this power be wisely employed.

We are responsible for every word we express. It will affect somebody either for good or otherwise. Talk sin, sickness and trouble, and you will cause many to go directly into more sin, sickness and trouble. Talk health, happiness and prosperity, and you will cause many to find health, happiness and prosperity in greater and greater abundance. When the world complains, do not forget to emphasize the great fact that universal good is even now at hand. The complaining mind wears colored glasses. He cannot see things as they are. You can help him to remove those glasses by calling his attention to the fact that things are not what they seem to him. Everything lies in the point of view. Look at things from the right point of view and you will be happy, cheerful and optimistic under all sorts of circumstances. But look at things from the wrong point of view, and you will see nothing clearly; everything will appear to be what it is not. You will thus live in confusion and your mistakes will be many. Remove this confusion by placing yourself in harmony with eternal good, and you can do this by talking about the good, thinking about the good and emphasizing most positively every expression of good with which you may come in contact. That which we think of and talk of constantly will multiply and grow in our own world.

Talk peace. You will thus not only prevent confusion, but you will remove those confused conditions that may already exist. You can still the storms of life everywhere by talking peace. When man thinks the most of peace he will be in peace, and he cannot fail to think of peace so long as he is faithfully talking peace. Talk success, and you will inspire everybody with the spirit of success. You will help to turn the energies of life upon the goal of success, and thus you will help all minds to move towards success. Never say that anything is impossible. Talk success, and you help to make everything possible. Everybody should succeed. It is not only the privilege of everybody to succeed, but every person, to be just to himself, must succeed. The fear of failure, however, is the greatest obstacle. You can remove that fear by talking success. Hold the idea of success before every mind with which you come in contact; you will thus become one of the greatest philanthropists in the world.

New and greater opportunities may be found everywhere. Talk of these things and forget the missteps of the past. We can leave the lesser that is behind only by pressing on towards the greater that is before. Talk success to everybody, and everybody will press on towards the greater goal of success. Be an inspiration among all minds; and you can be by holding up the light of success, prosperity and attainment at all times. Use your words in promoting advancement, in awakening new interest in the better side, the brighter side, the sunny side, and turn the mind of man upon those things that can be done. He can who thinks he can, and you help every person to think that he can by talking prosperity and success. Impress the greater upon every mind, and every mind will think the greater; and he who thinks the greater is constantly building for greater things. Emphasize the sunny side in all your speech and you provide a never failing antidote for complaints; and since the complaining mind soon becomes the retrogressing mind, this antidote has extreme value. It may change for the better the destiny of anyone when brought squarely before his attention, and this your words can do.

When one door closes another opens; sometimes several. This is the law of life. It is the expression of the law of eternal progress. The whole of nature desires to move forward eternally. The spirit of progress animates everything. Whenever a person loses an opportunity to move forward this great law proceeds to give him another. This proves that the universe is kind, that everything is for man and nothing against him. This being the truth, the man who talks health, happiness, prosperity, power and progress is working in harmony with the universe, and is helping to promote the great purpose of the universe; and who would not occupy a position of such value and importance? Whenever you talk trouble, failure, sickness or sin you arraign your own mind against the law of life and the purpose of the universe. You will thereby be against everything, and everything will, in consequence, be against you. You must, therefore, necessarily fail in everything you undertake to do. But how different everything will be when you turn and move in the other direction. Go with the universe, and all the power of the universe will go with you, and will help you to reach whatever object you may have is view.

Harmonize yourself with the laws of life and you will steadily rise in the scale of life. Nothing can hold you down. Everything you undertake to do you will accomplish, because everything will be with you. You will reach every ideal, and at the best time and under the best circumstances cause that ideal to become real. When you cease to talk failure and begin to talk success you invariably meet the turn in the lane. You find that a new world and a better future is in store. Things will take a turn when you take a turn, and you will take a turn when you begin to talk about those things that you desire to realize. Never talk about anything else. The way you talk you go. The way you talk others will go. Therefore, talk health, happiness and prosperity, and help everybody, yourself included, to move towards health, happiness and prosperity. The power of words is immense, both in the person that speaks and in the person that is spoken to. The simplest way to use this power is to train yourself to talk the things you want; talk the things that you expect or desire to realize; talk the things you wish to attain and accomplish. You thus cause the power of words to work for you and with you in gaining the goal you have in mind. Whatever comes, talk health, happiness and prosperity. Say that you are well; say that you are happy; say that you are prosperous. Emphasize everything that is good in life, and the power of the Supreme will cause your words to come true.

Chapter 12

What Determines the Destiny of Man

The destiny of every individual is being hourly created by himself, and what he is to create at any particular time is determined by those ideals that he entertains at that time. The future of a person is not preordained by some external power, nor is fate controlled by some strange, mysterious force that masterminds alone can comprehend and employ. It is ideals that control fate, and all minds have their ideals wherever in the scale of life they may be. To have ideals is not simply to have dreams or visions of that which lies beyond the attainments of the present; nor is idealism a system of ideas that the practical mind may not have the privilege to entertain. To have ideals is to have definite objects in view, be those objects very high or very low, or anywhere between those extremes.

The ideals of any mind are the real wants, the real desires or the real aims of that mind, and as every normal mind invariably lives, thinks and works for that which is wanted by his present state of existence, it is evident that every mind must necessarily, either consciously or unconsciously, follow his ideals. When those ideals are low, ordinary or inferior the individual will work for the ordinary and the inferior, and the products of his mind will correspond in quality with that for which he is working. Inferior causes will originate in his life and similar effects will follow; but when those ideals are high and superior, he will work for the superior; he will develop superiority in himself, and he will give superiority to everything that he may produce. Every action that he originates in his life will become a superior cause and will be followed by a similar effect.

The Ideal Made Real

The destiny of every individual is determined by what he is and by what he does; and what any individual is to be or do is determined by what he is living for, thinking for or working for. Man is not being made by some outside force. Man is making himself with the power of those forces and elements that he employs in his thought and his work; and in all his efforts, physical or mental, he invariably follows his ideals. He who lives, thinks and works for the superior becomes superior; he who works for less, becomes less. It is therefore evident that any individual may become more, achieve more, secure more and create for himself a greater and a greater destiny by simply beginning to live, think and work for a superior group of ideals. To have low ideals is to give the creative forces of the system something ordinary to work for. To have high ideals is to give those forces something extraordinary to work for, and the fate of man is the result of what his creative forces hourly produce. Every force in the human system is producing something, and that something will become a part of the individual. It is therefore evident that any individual can constantly improve the power, the quality and the worth of his being by directing the forces of his system to produce that which has quality and worth. These forces, however, are not directed or controlled by the will. It is the nature of the creative forces in man to produce what the mind desires, wants, needs or aspires to attain, and the desires and the aspirations of any mind are determined by the ideals that are entertained in that mind.

The forces of the system will begin to work for the superior when the mind begins to attain superior ideals, and since it is the product of these forces that determines both the nature and the destiny of man, a superior nature and a greater destiny may be secured by any individual who will adopt the highest and the most perfect system of idealism that he can possibly comprehend. To entertain superior ideals is to picture in mind and to hold constantly before mind the highest conception that can be formed of everything of which we may be conscious. To mentally dwell in those higher conceptions at all times is to cause the predominating ideas to become superior ideas, and it is the predominating ideas for which we live, think and work. When the ruling ideas of any mind are superior the creative force of that mind will produce the superior in every element, faculty, talent or power in that mind; greatness will thus be developed in that mind, and the great mind invariably creates a great destiny.

To entertain superior ideals is not to dream of the impossible, but to enter into mental contact with those greater possibilities that we are now able to discern; and to have the power to discern an ideal indicates that we have the power to realize that ideal. We do not become conscious of greater possibilities until we have developed sufficient capacity to work out those possibilities into practical, tangible results. Therefore, when we discern the greater we are ready to attain and achieve the greater; but before we can proceed to do what we are ready to do we must adopt superior ideals, and superior ideals only. When our ideals are superior we shall constantly think of the superior, because as our ideals are so is our thinking, and to constantly think of the superior is to steadily grow into the likeness of the superior.

When the ideals are very high all the forces of the system will move towards superior attainments; all things in the life of the individual will work together with greater and greater greatness in view, and continued advancement on a larger and larger scale must inevitably follow. To entertain superior ideals is not simply to desire some larger personal attainment or to mentally dwell in some belief that is different from the usual beliefs of the world. To entertain superior ideals is to think the very best thoughts and the very greatest thoughts about everything with which we come in contact. Superior idealism is not mere dreaming of the great and the beautiful, but is actual living in mental harmony with the very best we can find in all things, in all persons, in all circumstances and in all expressions of life. To live in mental harmony with the best we can find everywhere is to create the best in our own mentality and personality; and as we steadily grow into the likeness of that which we think of the most, we will, through ideal thinking, perpetually increase our power, capacity and worth. In consequence, we will naturally create a greater and a more worthy destiny.

The man who becomes much will achieve much, and great achievements invariably build a great destiny. To think of anything that is less than the best, or to mentally dwell with the inferior is to neutralize the effect of those superior ideals that we have begun to entertain. To secure the greatest results it is therefore absolutely necessary to entertain superior ideals only and to cease all recognition of inferiority or imperfection. The reason why the majority fail to secure any tangible results from higher ideals is because they entertain too many of the lower ideals at the same time. They may aim high; they may adore the beautiful; they may desire the perfect; they may live for the better and work for the greater, but they do not think their best thoughts about everything, and this is the reason why they do not reach the goal they have in view. Some of their forces are building for greater things, while other forces are building for lesser things, and a house divided against itself cannot stand.

Superior idealism contains no thought that is less than the very greatest and the very best that the most lofty states of mind can possibly produce, and it entertains no desire that has not the very greatest worth, the greatest power, and the highest attainment in view. Superior idealism does not recognize the power of evil in anything or in anybody; it knows that adverse conditions exist, but it gives the matter no conscious thought whatever. It is not possible to think the greatest thought about everything while mind is giving conscious attention to adversity or imperfection. The true idealist, therefore, gives conscious recognition to the power of good only, and he lives in the conviction that all things in his life are constantly working together for good. This conviction is not mere sentiment with the idealist. He knows that all things positively will work together for good when we recognize only the good, think only the good, desire only the good and expect only the good; likewise, he knows that all things positively will work together for greater things when all the powers of life, thought and action are concentrated upon the attainment and the achievement of greater things.

To apply the principles of superior idealism in all things means advancement in all things. To follow the superior ideal is to move towards the higher, the greater and the superior, and no one can continue very long in that movement without creating for himself a new world, a better environment and a greater destiny. To create a better future begin now to select a better group of ideals. Select the best and the greatest ideals that you can possibly find, and live those ideals absolutely. You will thus cause everything in your being to work for the higher, the better and the greater, and the things that you work for now will determine what the future is to be. Work for the greatest and the best that you know in the present, and you will create the very greatest and the very best for the future.

Chapter 13

To Him That Hath Shall Be Given

The statement that much gathers more is true on every plane of life and in every sphere of existence; and the converse that every loss leads to a greater loss is equally true; though we must remember that man can stop either process at any time or place. The further down you go the more rapidly you will move towards the depths, and the higher up you go the easier it becomes to go higher still. When you begin to gain you will gain more, because "To him that hath shall be given." When you begin to lose you will lose more, because from "Him that hath not, even that which he hath shall be taken away." This is a great metaphysical law, and being metaphysical, man has the power to use it in any way that he may desire. As man is in the within, so everything will be in his external world. Therefore, whether man is to lose or gain in the without depends upon whether he is losing or gaining in the within. The basis of all possession is found in the consciousness of man, and not in exterior circumstances, laws or conditions. If a man's consciousness is accumulative, he will positively accumulate, no matter where he may live; but whether his riches are to be physical, intellectual or spiritual will depend upon the construction of his mind. When the mind has the greatest development on the physical plane an accumulative consciousness will gather tangible possessions. When the mind has the greatest development on the intellectual or metaphysical plane, an accumulative consciousness will gather abundance of knowledge and wisdom. When the mind has the greatest development on the spiritual plane an accumulative consciousness will gather spiritual riches.

However competent you may be on the physical plane, if your consciousness is not accumulative, you will not gain possession of a great deal of this world's goods. Likewise, no matter how diligently you may search for wisdom in the higher spiritual possessions, if your consciousness is not accumulative you will gain but little. In fact, you will constantly lose the knowledge of truth on the one hand while trying to gain it on the other. Therefore, to gain abundance in the world of things or tangible possessions, the secret is to become competent in our chosen vocations, and then acquire an accumulative consciousness.

To gain the riches of the mind and the soul, the secret is to develop the same accumulative consciousness and to consecrate all the powers of mind and thought to spiritual things. There are thousands in this age who have consecrated their whole lives to the higher state of being, but there are very few who have gained the real riches of the spiritual kingdom, and the reason is they have neglected the development of the accumulative consciousness. In other words, they have overlooked the great law, "To him that bath shall be given." Those who have nothing will receive nothing, no matter how devotedly they may pray or how beautifully they may live. But to have is not simply to possess in the external sense. Those who are conscious of nothing have nothing. Those who are conscious of much have much, regardless of external possession. Before we can gain anything we must have something, and to have something is to be conscious of something.

We must be conscious of possession in the within before we can increase possession in any sphere of existence. All possession is based upon consciousness and is held by consciousness or lost by consciousness. All gain is the result of an accumulative consciousness. All loss is due to what may be termed the scattering consciousness; that is, that state of consciousness that lets go of everything that may come within its sphere. When you are conscious of something you are among those that hath and to you shall be given more. As soon as you gain conscious hold of things you will begin to gain possession of more and more things. As soon as you gain conscious hold upon wisdom and spiritual power, wisdom and spiritual power will be given to you in greater and greater abundance. On the other hand, when you begin to lose conscious hold of things, thoughts or powers, you will begin to lose more and more of those possessions, until all are gone.

When you inwardly feel that things are slipping away from you, you are losing your conscious hold of things, and all will finally be lost if you do not change your consciousness. When you inwardly feel that you are gaining more and more, or that things are beginning to gravitate towards your sphere of existence, more and more will be given to you until you have everything that you may desire. How we feel in the within is the secret, and it is this interior feeling that determines whether we are to be among those that have or among those that have not. When you feel in the within that you are gaining more you are among those that have, and to you shall be given more. When you feel in the within that you are losing what you have, you are among those that have not, and from you shall be taken away even that which you have. When we learn that mind is cause and that everything we gain may come from the action of mind as cause, we discover that all possession is dependent upon the attitude of mind, and since we have the power to hold the mind in any attitude desired, all the laws of gain and possession are in our own hands. When this discovery is made we begin to gain conscious possession of ourselves, and to him that hath himself all other things shall be given. To feel that you, yourself, are the power behind other powers, and that you may determine what is to come and what is to go, is to become conscious of the fact that you are something. You thus become conscious of something in yourself that is real, that is substantial and that is actually supreme in your world. To become conscious of something in yourself is to have something, and to have something is to gain more; consequently, by gaining consciousness of that something that is real in yourself you become one of those that hath. and to you shall be given.

To gain consciousness of the real in yourself is to gain consciousness of the real in life, and the more you feel the reality of life the more real life becomes. The result is that your consciousness of the reality of life becomes larger and larger; it comprehends more and takes in more. In other words, it is becoming accumulative. When this realization is attained you gain conscious hold upon life and are gradually gaining conscious hold upon everything that exists in life. This means a greater and greater mastery of life, and mastery is always followed by an increase in possession. Whatever you become conscious of in yourself, that you gain possession of in yourself. Whatever you gain possession of in yourself, that you can constructively employ in your sphere of existence, and whatever is constructively employed is productive; it produces something. Therefore, by becoming conscious of something you gain the power to produce something, and products on any plane constitute riches on that plane.

The more you become conscious of in yourself and in your life the greater your power to create and produce in your sphere of action, and the more wealth you produce the greater your possession, providing you have learned how to retain the products of your own talent. When we analyze these laws from another point of view we find the consciousness of the real in ourselves produces an ascending tendency in the mind, and whenever the mind begins to go up, the law of action and reaction will continue to press the mind up further and further indefinitely. Every upward action of mind, produces a reaction that pushes the mind upward still farther. As the mind is pushed upward a second upward action is expressed that is stronger than the first; this in turn produces a second reaction stronger than the first reaction, and the mind is pushed upward the second time much farther than it was the first time. The fact is, when the mind enters the ascending scale the law of action and reaction will perpetuate the ascension so long as the mind takes a conscious interest in the progress made; but the moment the mind loses interest in the movement the law will reverse itself and the mind enters the descending scale. Therefore, become conscious of the law in yourself and take a conscious interest in every step in advance that you make, and you will go up in the scale of life continually and indefinitely.

When the mind is in the ascending scale it is steadily becoming larger, more powerful and more competent, and will consequently be in demand where recompense is large and the opportunities more numerous. Such a mind will naturally gain step by step in rapid succession. To such a mind will be given more and more continually, because it has placed itself in the world of those who have. The great secret of gaining more, regardless of circumstances, is to continue perpetually to go up in mind. No matter how things are going about you, continue to go up in mind. Every upward step that is taken in mind adds power to mind, and this added power will produce added results in the tangible world. When these added results are observed mind gains more faith in itself, and more faith always brings more power. On the other hand, when we permit ourselves to go down in mind, because things seem to go down, we lose power. This loss of power will prevent us from doing our work properly or from using those things and conditions about us to the best advantage. In consequence, things will actually go down more and more; and if we permit this losing of ground to make us still more discouraged, we lose still more power, to be followed by still more adversity and loss. It is therefore evident that the way we go in mind everything in our world will go also, and that if we change our minds and stay changed, everything else will change and stay changed. If we continue to go up in mind, never permitting retrogression for a moment, everything in our world will continue to go up, and there will not even be signs of reverse, much less the loss of anything which we wish to retain.

When things seem to go wrong we should stay right and continue to stay right, and things will soon decide to come and be right also. This is a law that works and never fails to work. When we permit ourselves to go wrong because things seem to go wrong, we produce what may be termed the letting go attitude of mind, and when we cease to hold on to things, things will begin to slip away. We must hold on to things ourselves, if we wish to retain them for ourselves; and the secret of holding on to things is to continue positively in that attitude of mind that is perpetually going up into the larger and the greater. The laws of life will continue perpetually to give to those who have placed themselves in the receiving attitude, and those same laws will take away from those who have placed themselves in the losing attitude. When you create a turn in yourself you will feel that things are also taking a turn to a degree; and if you continue persistently in this feeling, everything in your life will positively take the turn that you have taken. As you go everything in your world will go, providing you continue to go; the law of action and reaction explains why. In the last analysis, however, everything depends upon whether consciousness determines how every force, element, power or faculty is to act, because they are all controlled by consciousness. When your consciousness does not have the proper hold on things, the power of your being will fail to gain the proper hold on things; but when your consciousness does possess this holding power, all the powers of your being will gain the same firm grip upon everything with which they may have to deal.

To establish the accumulative consciousness, that is, that consciousness that has complete hold on things, train yourself to inwardly feel that you have full possession of everything in your own being. Feel that you possess yourself. Affirm that you possess yourself. Think constantly of yourself as possessing yourself, everything that is in yourself, and you will soon be conscious of absolute self-possession. Some have this conscious feeling naturally, and they invariably gain vast possessions, either in tangible goods or in wisdom and higher spiritual powers. But everyone can develop this state of conscious possession of his whole self by remaining firm in the conviction that "All that I AM is mine." When you begin to feel that you possess yourself you actually have something in consciousness, and according to the laws of gain and possessions you will gain more and more without end. You are in the same consciousness with those who have, and to you will be given. You have established the inner cause of possession through the conscious possession of your entire inner life, and the effect of this cause, that is, the perpetual increase of external possession, must invariably follow. In brief, you have applied the great law "To Him That Hath Himself All Other Things Shall Be Given".

Chapter 14

The Life That is Worth Living

To the average person life means but little, because he has not discovered the greater possibilities of his real existence. He has been taught to think that to make a fortune or to make a name for himself are the only things worthwhile, and if he does not happen to have the necessary talent for these accomplishments there is nothing much else for him to do but to merely exist. However, if he has been touched with the force of ambition, or if he has had a glimpse of the ideal, mere existence does not satisfy, and the result is a life of unhappiness and dissatisfaction. But such a person must learn that there are other openings and opportunities in life besides mere existence, regardless of what the mental capacity of the individual may be. These other opportunities, when taken advantage of, will give just as much happiness, if not more, than what is secured by those who have won the admiration of the world; besides, when one learns to live for these other things real living becomes a fine art, and he begins to live a life that is really worthwhile. There is many a person whose present position in life depends almost wholly upon his financial returns, and if these are small, with no indications of immediate increase, his life seems to be almost, if not wholly, a barren waste; not because it is a barren waste, but because he has not found the real riches of existence. The trouble with this person is the point of view; he is depending upon things instead of depending upon himself. He must learn that there is something more to live for besides his salary and what his salary can buy. The value of the individual life is not measured by the quantity of possessions, but by the quality of existence. The value of life comes not from having much, but from being much; and happiness is invariably a state of mind coming, not from what a person has, but from what he is. We must remember, however, that he who is much will finally gain much, providing the powers in his possession are practically applied; and his gains will have high quality whether they be gains in the world of things or in the world of mind, consciousness and soul.

The problem for the average person to solve is what he actually can do with himself in his present position. He may not be earning much now, and his opportunities for earning more may not be clearly in evidence, but he is nevertheless living in a great sea of opportunities, many of which may be taken advantage of at once. The first of these is the opportunity to make of himself a great personality, and in taking advantage of this opportunity he should remember that to do great things in the world is not the only thing worthwhile. To be great in the world is of equal if not greater worth, and he who is now becoming great in his own life will, without fail, do great things in years to come. The majority of those who have practical capacity are making strenuous efforts to do something great, something startling, that will arrest the attention of the world; while those who do not possess this practical capacity are not satisfied because they are not similarly favored. In the meantime neither class gains happiness, and the best forces of life are employed in the making of things, most of which are valueless, while the making of great personalities is postponed to some future time.

The capacity to make great things is not the only capacity of value in the possession of man; but all minds do not possess this capacity; all minds, however, do possess the power to remake themselves in the exact likeness of all that is great and beautiful and ideal. Begin now to rebuild your own personality and proceed in the realization of the fact that you have the power to produce an edition DeLuxe out of your own present personal self. You could hardly find a purpose of greater interest and of greater possibility than this, and results will be secured from the very beginning. To find your own personality passing through a transformation process, bringing out into expression the finest and the best that you can picture in your ideals, is something that will add immensely to the joy and the worth of living. In fact, this alone would make life not only worth living, but so rich that every moment would become a source of unbounded satisfaction in itself.

The average person usually asks himself how much money he can make during the next ten years, but why should he not ask himself how much happiness he can enjoy during those same years, or how much brilliancy he can develop in his mind, or how much more beautiful he may become in body, character and soul? He would find that by living for these latter things he would not only perpetually enrich his life and live a life that is thoroughly worth living, but he would find that the earning of money would become much easier than if he simply lived for material gain alone. The ambition of the average person is to do something great in the world of things; but why is he not ambitious to do something great in the perfecting of his own being, the most wonderful world in the universe? Such ambitions are truly worth living for and working for, but our attention has not been called to their extraordinary possibilities; therefore, we have neglected the greater while wasting most of our energies on the lesser.

There are a number of ambitions outside of the usual ones that could engage our attention with the greatest of profit, because they not only have worth in themselves, but they lead to so many other things that have worth. The desire to secure as much out of life as life can possibly give will not only make living intensely interesting, but the more life a person can live the more power he will get. Live a great

The Ideal Made Real

life and you gain great power. The increase of your power will enable you to carry out a number of other ambitions, thus adding to the richness of your life from almost every imaginable source. When a person declares that his greatest ambition is to live he is taking the most interesting, the most satisfying, the most profitable and the most complete course in life that can possibly be selected. Living, itself, when made a fine art, is one continuous feast, and the fact that all increase of power comes from the increase of life makes the ambition to live not only the greatest ambition of all, but the means through which all other ambitions may be realized.

If your present life does not hold as much as you would wish, do not think of it as an empty state of existence. Do not depend upon those few things that you are receiving from the external world; but begin to draw upon the limitless life and power that exists in the vastness of your interior world. Then you will find something to live for. Then you will begin to live a life that is thoroughly worthwhile. Then you will find the real riches of existence, and you will also find that these riches will so increase your personal power and worth that you will become able to take advantage of those opportunities that lead to things of tangible worth.

When the world of things does not seem to hold any new opportunities for you resolve to grow more and more beautiful in body, character and soul with the passing of the years. Make this your ambition, and if you do your utmost to carry out this ambition, you will gain far more satisfaction from its realization than if you had amassed an immense fortune. Live to express in body, mind and soul all that is high and beautiful and ideal in your sublime nature, and you will not only give yourself unbounded joy, but you will become a great inspiration to the entire world. The life that is not expressed through the beautiful nor surrounded by the beautiful is not worth a great deal to the mind of man; but there is practically no end to the joy and richness that man may gain through that which is actually beautiful. The beautiful not only gives happiness, but it opens the mind of man to those higher realms from which proceed all that is worthy or great or ideal. To look upon the beautiful is to gain glimpses of that vast transcendent world where supreme life is working out the marvelous destiny of man. Therefore, there can be no greater ambition than to live for the purpose of giving higher and more ideal expression to the life of that sublime world.

To give expression in personal life to the great riches of the interior world is worth far more, both to yourself and to the race, than it is to gain possession of any number of things in the external world. The man who simply gains wealth never gains happiness; besides, he is soon forgotten. But the man who will live for the purpose of giving expression to mental and spiritual wealth will gain unlimited happiness, and his life will be so illustrious that his name will never be forgotten. And remember that no matter how insignificant your position in life may be today, or how small your income, or how limited your opportunities, you can begin this moment to give expression to the vast riches of your interior life; and before you take your departure from this sphere you may become such a great light in the world of higher illumined attainment that your accomplishments in this unique sphere of action will continue to inspire the world for ages yet to come.

To live for the purpose of developing the gold mines of the mind and the diamond fields of the soul, are ambitions that might engage the attention of millions who have found no satisfaction in the world of things; and to those who will make these their leading ambitions a rich future is certainly in store; and, in addition, the present will be filled to overflowing with almost everything that can give interest and happiness to life. To develop a charming personality, to live a long life, to live a happy life, and to retain your health, your youth and your vigor as long as you live, these are ambitions that anyone can work for with the greatest interest and profit; and to him who will accomplish these things the world will give more honor than it has given to its greatest musicians, its most brilliant orators or its most illustrious statesmen. To live for the purpose of unfolding the latent powers of your being is a work that will not only prove interesting to an exceptional degree, but will prove exceedingly rich in future possibilities. That there is practically no end to the possibilities that are latent in man is now the firm conviction of all real psychologists. Therefore, we need not weep because there are no more worlds to conquer. We are on the borderland of greater worlds than were ever dreamed of by the most illumined seers that the world has ever known.

We need not feel discouraged because our position in life seems uninteresting or insignificant. We have opportunities at our very door that are so great and so numerous that it will require an eternity to take advantage of them all. Though the external world may not as yet have given us much to live for, the internal world stands ready to lavish upon us so much that is rich and marvelous that not a single moment need be otherwise than a feast fit for the gods. The doors of this internal world are open, and he who will walk in will begin to live a life that is great, indeed.

When we look into life as life really is there is so much to live for and there is so much to accomplish and attain that even eternity seems too short. The problem to solve is to know the greatest thing we can do now; and the solution may be found by resolving to live for that which is nearest at hand, whatever that may be. Accept the greatest opportunity that you can take advantage of now, and then begin to live for the working out of everything that that opportunity may contain. Do not long for opportunities that are out of reach. The majority do this and thus waste their time. Do not wait for opportunities to do great things. The opportunity to make of yourself a great soul, a marvelous mind and a higher developed personality is at hand, and by taking advantage of this opportunity you will awaken within yourself those.

powers that can do great things. You will thus cause your present to become all that you may wish it to be; you will build for a future that which will be nothing less than extraordinary; and you will be living a life that is thoroughly worth living in the great eternal now. You will be making the ideal real at every step of the way, but every moment will lead you into worlds that are richer and realms that are fairer than you ever dreamed of before. It is therefore evident that when we learn to live the life that is really worth living, there is no reason whatever why a single moment should be empty, dull or uninteresting in the life of any person, because there is so much to live for that has real worth, so much to enjoy that holds real enjoyment, so much to do that is thoroughly worth doing; besides, the whole of life, when actually lived, is eternally alive with interest, ever revealing the splendor of its vast transcendent domains. And he who aims to live for the purpose of gaining the realization of, and the possession of, as many spheres of this life as possible will find full expression for every ambition and every aspiration that he can possibly arouse in his mind. Life to him will be a continuous feast and existence will become an endless advancement into the highest attainments and the greater achievements that even the most illustrious mind can picture as its goal.

Chapter 15

When All Things Become Possible

When the mind is placed in conscious contact with the limitless powers of universal life all things become possible, and faith is the secret. To have faith is to possess that interior insight through which we can discern the marvelous possibilities that are latent in the great within, and to possess the power to enter into the very life of the great within. To most minds there seems to be a veil in consciousness between the spheres of present understanding and the spheres of the higher wisdom, and though there are many who feel distinctly that there is something greater within them, yet it seems hidden, and they cannot discern it. Faith, however, has the power to perceive those greater things within that previously seemed hidden, and this is the reason why faith is the evidence of things not seen. Faith does not simply believe. It knows; it knows through higher insight, because faith is this higher insight. Faith is not blind, objective belief, but a higher development of consciousness through which the mind transcends the circumscribed and enters into the life of the boundless.

When faith is active consciousness is expanded so much that it breaks all bounds and penetrates even those realms that objective man has never heard of before. In this way new truth and discoveries are brought to light, and this is how man gains the understanding of what previously seemed to be beyond his comprehension. When we define faith as that power in mind through which consciousness can penetrate into the larger sphere of life we perceive readily why almost anything can be accomplished through faith, and we also understand why no one can afford to work without faith. When consciousness enters a larger sphere of action its capacity is naturally increased, and the greater power that can be drawn upon in performing any kind of work increases in proportion; likewise, the knowing how to work will be promoted in the same manner. To do anything successfully one must know how to do it and have the power to do what one knows should be done, and both these essentials are increased in proportion to the enlargement of consciousness. One of the principal metaphysical laws declares that whatever you become conscious of you express through your personality; therefore, according to this law more life, more power and more wisdom will come into actual possession in the personal life as we become conscious of more and more of these things in the mental life; in other words, the ideal is made real.

The art of extending consciousness into the realms of unlimited life and power and wisdom is the secret through which all great attainments and great achievements become possible; but without faith this enlargement of consciousness cannot take place, because faith is that power that perceives and enters into the greater things that are still before us. Faith looks into the beyond of every faculty, talent or power and perceives that there is much more of these same talents and powers further on. In fact, there is no visible limit to anything when viewed through the eyes of faith. Consciousness does not extend itself in any direction until it feels that there will be tangible grounds upon which to proceed. You can become conscious only of those things that seem real; therefore, to extend your consciousness in any direction you must secure evidence of the fact that there is more reality in that direction; and here we find the great mission of faith. Faith supplies this evidence. Faith looks further on into the beyond and sees real reality at every step, and proves to consciousness that things not seen are thoroughly substantial. Faith discerns that there is no danger in going on and on because there is solid ground all the way, no matter how far into the limitless we may wish to

The Ideal Made Real

go; there is no danger of being lost in an empty void by following faith. Instead, faith gives us a positive assurance of finding more life, more power, more wisdom and a fairer state of existence than we ever knew before.

The practical value of faith is therefore to be found in its power to enlarge all the faculties and spheres of action in the mind of man, and as this enlargement can go on indefinitely, as there is no end to the visible, we conclude that anything can be accomplished by following faith. No matter how much wisdom or power we may require to reach the goal we have in view we can finally secure the required amount through the perpetual enlargement of consciousness. This is evident, and since faith is that something in mind that leads consciousness on and on into larger fields of action it becomes indispensable to all growth, to all great achievements, to all high attainments and to the realization of all true ideals. The man who has no faith in himself can neither improve himself nor his work. When nothing is added to his ability, capacity or skill there can be nothing added to the quality or the quantity of what he is doing. The effect will not improve until we have improved the cause; and man himself is the cause of everything that appears in his life.

Modern psychology, however, has discovered and conclusively demonstrated that no faculty can be improved until the conscious sphere of action of that faculty is enlarged and thoroughly developed. Therefore, to promote the efficiency of any faculty the conscious action of that faculty must become larger and imbued with more life. This is the fundamental principle in all advancement, but consciousness will not enlarge its sphere of action until it perceives that there is reality beyond its present sphere, and it is only through the interior insight of faith that the greater reality existing beyond present limitations is discovered to be real. The lack of this interior insight among the great majority is the principal obstacle that prevents them from becoming more than they are. Their minds have not the power to see the potential side of their larger nature. They are aware of the objective only and can do only as much as the limited power of the objective will permit. But they are not aware of the fact that there is limitless power within, nor do they realize that they can draw upon this great interior power and thus accomplish not only more and more, but everything that they may now have in view. Not having the power to look beyond present attainment, the little world in which they live is all that is real to them. Occasionally there is a dream or a vision of greatness, but it soon fades away, and in those rare instances when the high vision continues for some time the knowledge of how to make real the ideal is usually not at hand.

The human race is divided into three classes; first, those who live in the limited world and never see anything beyond the limited; second, those who live in the limited world but have occasional glimpses of greater things, though having neither the knowledge nor the power to make their dreams come true; and third, those who are constantly passing from the lesser to the greater, making real every ideal as soon as it comes within the world of their conscious comprehension. The last group is small, but there are millions today who are on the verge of a larger sphere of existence, and for this reason we should usher into the world at once a greater movement for the promotion of faith than has ever been known before. It is more faith that these millions need in order to enter into the beautiful life they can see before them. It is more faith they must have before they can become as much as they desire to be. It is faith, and faith alone, that can give them the power to do what this great sphere of existence may require.

The Ideal Made Real

To make real the ideal in any life faith must be combined with work, and no work should be undertaken unless it can be animated thoroughly with the power of faith. The reason why is found in the fact that all practical action is weak or strong, depending upon the capacity of that part of the mind which directly controls that action; and the capacity of the mind increases in proportion to the attainment of faith. To accomplish what we have in view, it is not only necessary to know how to go about our work, but it is necessary to have sufficient power, and faith is the open door to more and more power.

The very moment you obtain more faith you feel stronger; you are then certain of results and the very best results; and the reason why is found in the fact that faith always connects the mind with the larger, the greater and the inexhaustible. On the other hand, you may have an abundance of energy, but do not see clearly how to apply that energy in such a way that results will be as desired; again the remedy is more faith. Faith elevates the mind and lifts consciousness up above doubt, uncertainty and confusion. When you go up into faith you enter the light and can see clearly how to proceed; but in this connection we must avoid a very common mistake. When we discover the remarkable power of faith there is a tendency to depend upon faith exclusively and ignore other faculties. We sometimes come to the conclusion that it matters little how we work or think or act so long as we have an abundance of faith, because faith will cause everything to come right. The fact, however, that we sometimes come to this conclusion proves that we have not found real faith, because when we have an abundance of real faith we can see clearly the great truth that all thought and action must be right to secure results, and that all faculties and powers must be employed in their highest states of efficiency if we wish to make real the ideal. Though it is absolutely necessary to have the

The Ideal Made Real

vision, still the vision is not sufficient in itself. After the vision has been discovered in the ideal it must be made real; the principle must be applied; the new discovery must be worked out in practical action; but these things require both fine intelligence and practical skill.

Faith without works is dead, because it does nothing, uses nothing, creates nothing; it is as if it were not; and works without faith are so insignificant and ordinary that they are usually very little better than nothing. But when work and faith are combined then everything becomes possible. The power of faith is placed in action; work becomes greater and greater, and whatever our purpose may be we shall positively scale the heights. The great principle is to combine unlimited faith with skillful work. Work with all the skill that you can possibly cultivate, but inspire all your efforts with the mighty soul of a limitless faith. Become as learned, as intellectual and as highly developed in mind as possible, but animate your prodigious intellect with the supreme spirit of faith. Faith does not come to take the place of art, skill or intellect.

Faith comes to give real soul to art, skill and intellect. Faith comes to fill all physical and mental action with renewed life and power. It comes to open that door through which all our efforts may pass to higher and greater things. Faith is not simply for the moral and spiritual life; is not simply for what is sometimes called higher endeavor. It is for all endeavor, and it has the power to push all endeavor with such energy and force that we simply must succeed, no matter what our work may be. The man who has faith in his work, faith in himself, faith in the human race and faith in the Supreme, that man simply cannot fail, if he gives the full power of his faith to everything that he undertakes to do.

The Ideal Made Real

We must eliminate the idea that faith is something apart from everyday life, and that it is something for the future salvation of the soul only. We have held to that belief so long that real faith has actually been separated from human existence, and we find very few people today who really know what faith actually is. The fact is that if you are not giving your faith to everything you do, be it physical, mental or spiritual, you have not as yet obtained any faith. When faith comes it never comes to give greater power to a part of your life. It comes to give supreme power to all your life, and it comes to push all your work towards higher efficiency and greater results. When you have real faith you never undertake anything without first placing your entire being in the very highest attitude of faith. Even the most trivial things you do are done invariably in the spirit of faith. This is very important, because by training yourself to be at your best in little things it soon becomes second nature for you to be your best in all things, and when you are called upon to do something of exceptional importance, something that may seem very difficult, you do not fall down; you are fully equal to the occasion. The more we exercise faith the more it develops; it is therefore profitable to use faith at all times and in everything that we do.

When we know that faith is that something that takes mind into the superior side of life and thus places in action superior powers it is not difficult to understand how to proceed when we place ourselves in faith. As we think more and more of this higher side of our nature, this better side, this wonderful side, we gradually become conscious of its remarkable possibilities and soon we can feel the power of superiority becoming stronger and stronger in everything that we do in mind or body. To develop the power of faith the first thing to do is to train the mind to hold attention constantly upon the limitless side of life; that is, to live in the upper story of being and to think as much as possible about the true idea of faith, as well as the interior essence of faith itself. When you begin to see clearly that faith is this higher development of mind, this insight that leads to higher wisdom, greater power and more abundant life, you actually find yourself entering into the realization of those greater things whenever you think of faith. By concentrating your attention upon the inner meaning of faith your mind becomes clearer, your faculties become stronger and your entire being feels the presence of more life; and that you can do much better work while in this condition is too evident to require any more elucidation. While in the attitude of faith you cannot only do your present work better, but you will steadily develop the ability and the capacity to do more difficult work, work that will prove more useful to the community and more remunerative to yourself. The world wants everything well done and is more than willing to pay for good work. We are all seeking the best and the majority aim consciously or unconsciously to give their best, but without faith it is not possible for anyone to be his best, give his best, or do his best.

Do your best and the best will come to you in return. The universe is founded upon justice, and justice will positively be done to you if you have faith in justice. Everything in life is moving towards greater worth, and since justice is universal, the greater the worth of a man the greater the value of those things that he will receive in life. The worthy soul is always rich in those things that have real worth; and when we learn to harmonize ourselves more fully with all the laws of existence we shall place ourselves in that condition where we not only can give more that has worth but will also receive everything of worth that actually is our own. Whether you are working in the commercial world, the professional world, the artistic world, the intellectual world; in brief, whatever your work may be, to have the best results you must have faith, and it is practical results in practical everyday life that determines how rapidly and how perfectly the ideal shall be made real in your own world. Whoever will do his present work as well as he possibly can, and continue to work in the highest attitude of faith will positively advance and perpetually continue to advance. He may not have accomplished much thus far; but if he takes this course, combining efficient work with supreme faith, he certainly has a splendid future before him.

If your present work is not to your liking do not plan to change at once. First proceed with your present work in this higher attitude of faith. You may thus find your present work to be the very work you want; or your present work, if it is not what is intended for you, will become the open door through which you will reach that field of action that will be to your liking, providing you animate your present work with all the faith that you can possibly realize. Make yourself the best of your kind whatever your sphere of action may be, because by so doing you are not only increasing the number of great minds in the world, but you are adding immeasurably to the world's welfare and joy; and he who combines his work with limitless faith will become the greatest and the best in his sphere. In the application of faith, however, the whole of attention must not be directed upon the improvement of your work, but more especially upon the improvement of yourself. The more you improve the better work you can do, but while you are improving yourself your improvement will be incomplete and insufficient unless you each day practically employ in your work what you have developed in yourself. Give the power of every moment to greater attainment in yourself and to greater achievement in your present occupation, and you will fulfill that dual purpose in life that invariably leads to the heights. Develop more power, more ability and more faith and combine these in everything that you do. Through the power of faith you will not only discern higher and higher ideals, but you will also give greater capacity to your practical ability. In other words, you will not only gain the power to see the ideal, but you will gain the power to practically apply what you have seen; you will make tangible in real life what the visions of the soul have revealed in the ideal life; and as you grow in faith, so great will this power become that there is no ideal you cannot make real. You will have placed yourself in touch with limitless power, the power of the Supreme, and therefore to you, all things will become possible.

Chapter 16

The Art of Getting What is Wanted

We frequently hear the statement "I never received what I wanted until the time came when I did not care for it and did not need it." This statement may in most instances be based upon an unguided imagination, though this is not always the case, because there are thousands of people who actually have this very experience. They never get what they want until the desire for it, as well as the need of it, have disappeared. There may be occasional exceptions, but the rule is that what we persistently desire we shall sooner or later receive. Too often it is later, the reason being that most desires are purely personal and are not inspired by those real needs that may exist in the great eternal now. Mere personal desires are usually out of harmony with the present process of soul-growth, and therefore there is no supply in our immediate mental vicinity for what those desires naturally need. This is the reason why more time is required for the fulfilling of these desires, and frequently the time required is so long that when the desire is fulfilled we do not need it any more. When we desire only those things that are best for us now, that is, those things that are necessary to a full and complete life in the present, we shall receive what we desire at the very time when those things are needed. What is best for us now is ready in the mental world to be expressed through us. Every demand has its own supply in the immediate vicinity, and every demand will find or attract its own supply without any delay whatever, but the demand must be natural, not artificial.

The average person is full of artificial desires, desires that have been suggested by what other people possess or require. But the question is not what we need now to compete with other people so as to make more extravagant external appearances than other people. The question is, what do we need now to make our present life as full, as complete and as perfect as it possibly can be made now. Ask yourself this question and your artificial desires will disappear. In the first place, you will try to ascertain what you are living for, and what may be required to promote that purpose of life that may seem true to your deeper thought on the subject. In the second place, you will realize that since it is the present and the present only for which you are living you will concentrate your attention upon the living of life now. This will bring the whole power of desire down upon the present moment and engage all the forces of life to work for the perfection of the present moment. The result will be the elimination of nearly everything that is foreign to your present state of existence.

To know what to desire and what to ignore in the present may seem to be a problem, but it is easily solved by depending upon the demands of the soul instead of the demands of the person. The desires of the average person are almost constantly colored or modified by suggestions from the artificial life of the world; they are therefore not normal and are not true to real life. The desires of the soul, however, are always true and are always in harmony with the greatest good and the highest welfare of the entire being of man in his present sphere. It is the soul that lives; therefore the soul can feel truly what is necessary to fullness and completeness in present life. Real life never lives for the past or for the future. Real life lives now, and therefore knows the needs of life now. It is the soul that grows and develops; therefore the soul can feel what is required to promote present development. For these reasons it is perfectly safe to follow the desires of the soul and those desires only; it will mean the best of everything for body, mind and spirit, and the right things will appear in the right places at the right time.

The Ideal Made Real

We live not to acquire things nor to provide for an extravagant personal appearance. We live to become more than we are. We live to live a larger and a greater life perpetually; therefore every desire must desire only those things that are conducive to growth, advancement, attainment and superior states of existence. The expression of desire, however, must not confound cause with effect, but must so place every desire that the power of cause invariably precedes the appearance of effect. To promote advancement in life we must advance in our own conscious beings before true advancement in the external world can follow. Forced advancement is artificial, and is detrimental to the permanent welfare of the soul. Do not push the person forward. Live to give greater expression to the soul and you will develop all the power that is necessary to push the person forward towards any lofty goal you may have in view. Become more than you are from the within, and external environments, demands and opportunities will ask you to come forward. Thus you promote true advancement.

There are a number of people who believe that to follow the desires of the soul is to be led into poverty, and hardships in general, but those who have this belief know practically nothing about the real nature of the soul. He who follows the desires of the soul will be led away from sickness, trouble and poverty and will enter into the possession of the best of everything, physical, mental and spiritual. This is natural, because the ruling desire of the soul is to promote the attainment of greater power, greater ability, a larger life, superior qualities and greater capacity so that things may be done that are really worthwhile. The soul lives to unfold the limitless possibilities that are latent in the within. Therefore, to live the life of the soul and follow the desires of the soul is to become greater, more able, more competent and more worthy every day. By developing greater power in yourself you overcome sickness and trouble; and by constantly increasing your ability, your talent and your genius you pass from poverty to abundance, no matter where you may live or what your work may be.

The man who lives to perfect his entire being will naturally desire only those things that are conducive to the growth and the development that he is trying to promote, and such desires will be supplied without delay, because they are natural, and they are in harmony with real life. What life may require now that life can receive now. This is the law. But every artificial desire that we may hold in mind interferes with the workings of this law, and since the average person is full of artificial desires he usually fails to receive what is needed to promote the welfare of real life. Every desire that is held in mind uses up energy; therefore, if the desire is artificial, all that energy is thrown away, or it may be employed in creating something that we have no use for when it does come. It has been very wisely stated that a strong mind should weigh matters with the greatest of care before uttering a single prayer, because most of the prayers of such a mind are answered; and should he pray for something that he cares nothing for when it does come be will have a burden instead of a blessing.

The majority are entirely too reckless about their desires; they desire things because they want them at the time, but do not stop to think whether the things desired will prove satisfactory or not when they are received; and since we usually get, sooner or later, what we persistently desire, the art of knowing what to desire is an art, the development of which becomes extremely important. It is not an act of wisdom to pray for future blessings or to entertain desires that will not be fulfilled until some future time. When the future comes you may have advanced so far, or changed so much, that the needs of your life will be entirely different from what they are in the present. Let every desire be just for today, and let that desire be prompted by the ruling desire of your life; that is, the desire to become a more powerful personality, a stronger character, a more brilliant mind and a greater soul. Live perpetually in the desire that you will receive the best that life can give today, that all things will work together for good to you now, and that everything necessary to the promotion of your highest welfare will come in abundance during the great eternal now. Make this desire so strong that your heart and soul are in it with all the power of life, and let every present moment be deeply inspired by the very spirit of this desire. The result will be that the best of everything will constantly be coming into your world, and everything that may be necessary to make your life full and complete now will be added in an ever increasing abundance.

In this connection we must remember that is not best for anyone to pass through sickness, trouble and misfortune. When people have misfortune they sometimes console themselves with the belief that it is all for the best, but this is not the truth; though we can and should turn every adverse circumstance to good account. When you come into trouble you have not been living for the best. You have made mistakes or entertained artificial desires, and that is why trouble came. Had you lived in the faith that all things are working together for good, nothing but good would have come; and had you lived in the strong desire for the best and the best only, you would have received the very best that you could appreciate and enjoy now. The belief that we have to pass through trouble to reach peace and comfort is an illusion that we have inherited from the dark ages, and the belief that we are purified through the fires of adversity is another illusion coming from the same source. We are purified by passing through a perpetual refining process, and this process is the result of consciousness gaining a deeper, a higher, a truer and a more beautiful conception of that divinity in man that is created in the image and likeness of the Supreme; and it is well to remember that this refining process can live and act only where there is peace of mind, harmony of life and the joy of the spirit.

Higher states of life do not come by passing through adversity but by living the soul-life so completely that you are never affected by adversity. The peace that passeth understanding does not come from the act of overcoming trouble, but is the product of that state of mind that is so high and so strong that it is never moved by trouble. The greatest victory does not come through successful warfare, but through a life that is so high and in such perfect harmony with all things that it wars against nothing, resists nothing, antagonizes nothing, pursues nothing, overcomes nothing. The life that is above things does not have to overcome things, and it is such a life that brings real peace, true joy and sublime harmony. The belief that we have to fight for our rights is another illusion; likewise, the belief that wrongs have to be overcome. The higher law declares, be right in all things and you will have your rights in all things. Be above all things and you will not have to overcome anything. Live in the spirit of the limitless supply and you will not have to demand anything from any source, because you will be in the life of abundance.

There is value in the silent demand, but it is not the highest thought. The highest thought is to desire with heart and soul whatever we may need now, and live in the absolute conviction that all natural demands are supplied now; then we shall not have to make any demands whatever, silent or audible. A mental demand usually becomes a forced mental process, and such a process, though it may succeed temporarily, as all forced actions do, will finally fail; and when it does fail the mind will not be as high in the scale as it was before. The highest state is pure realization, a state where we realize that everything is at hand for us now and will be expressed the very moment we desire its tangible possession. Here we must remember never to turn our desires into mental demands, but to make every desire an inward soul feeling united perfectly with faith. The highest desire is always transformed into a whole-souled gratitude, even before the desire has been outwardly fulfilled, because when the desire is high in the spirit of faith it knows at once the prayer will be answered, and consequently gives thanks from the very depths of the heart.

The prayer that is uttered through the spirit of faith and through the soul of thanksgiving, the two united in one, is always answered, whether it be uttered silently or audibly. The desires that are felt in such a prayer are inspired by the divinity that dwells within and are therefore true to real life. They are soul desires. They belong to the present and will be fulfilled in the present at the very time when we want them and need them. When we fail to get what is wanted, our wants are either artificial or so full of false and perverted wants that the law of supply is prevented from doing its proper work for us. Under such conditions it is necessary to ask the great question, "What am I living for!" Then eliminate those desires that are suggested by the world, and retain only those that desire the highest state of perfection for the whole man. It is the truth that when man seeks first the kingdom of the true life, the perfect life, all other things needful to such a life will be added. He who desires more life will receive more life, and with the greater life comes the greater power, that power with which man may create his own destiny and make everything in his life as he wishes it to be. In order to get what is wanted or what is needed the usual process of desire must be reversed. Instead of desiring things, desire that greater life and that greater power that can produce things. First, desire life, power, ability, greatness, superiority, high personal worth, and exceptional spiritual attainments. Never desire definite environments, special things or certain fixed conditions. Leave those things to Higher Power, because when Higher Power begins to act you will receive the very best environments, the richest things and the most perfect conditions that you can possibly enjoy. Desire real life first, and all that is beautiful and perfect in the living of such a life in body, mind and soul, will invariably be added. Follow the desires of the soul and you will receive everything that is necessary, not only for the life of the soul but for the life of mind and body as well. Seek the Source of all good things and you will receive all good things.

Chapter 17

Paths to Happiness

To be happy is the privilege of everybody, and everybody may be happy at all times and under all circumstances through the knowing and living of a few simple principles. The reason why happiness is not as universal and as abundant as it might be is because the majority seek happiness for itself alone. Happiness is an effect. It comes from a definite cause. Therefore, if we would obtain happiness we must not seek happiness for itself, but seek that something that produces happiness. He who seeks happiness directly, who desires happiness for the sake of gaining happiness or who works directly for the attainment of happiness will find but little real joy in his life. To seek happiness is to fail to find it, but to seek the cause of happiness is to find it in an ever increasing measure. Happiness, however, is not the result of anyone single cause. It is the result of many ideal states of being grouped together into one harmonious whole. In brief, happiness is the result of true being perfectly lived upon all planes of consciousness. Happiness does not come from having much, but from being much; therefore, anything that will tend to bring forth into tangible expression more and more of the real being of man will add to his joy. To promote the larger and larger expression of the real being of man; in other words, to promote the living in the real of more and more of the ideal, a number of methods may be presented; but as happiness is based upon simplicity, methods for producing the cause of happiness must also be based upon simplicity, therefore only those principles that are purely fundamental need be employed. These principles however must not be applied singly. It is necessary to combine them all in practical everyday living, and when this is done, more and more happiness will invariably follow. The principles necessary to the perpetual increase of happiness are as follows:

1. Live the simple life.

The complex life is not only a burden to existence, but is invariably an obstacle to the highest attainments and welfare of man; and the majority, even among those whose tangible possessions are very insignificant, are living a complex life; but when the average person is told to remove complexity from his world and adopt simplicity he almost invariably destroys the beauty of life. The art of living a life that is both simple and beautiful is an art that few have mastered, though it is by no means difficult. Most of the life that is called simple is positively devoid of beauty and has nothing whatever that is attractive about it. In fact, it is positively a detriment both to happiness and advancement. To live the simple life is not to return to primitive conditions nor to decide to be satisfied with nothing, or next to nothing. It is possible to live the simple life in the midst of all the luxuries that wealth can buy, because simplicity does not spring from the quantity of possession but from the arrangement of possession. The central idea in the living of a simple life is to eliminate nonessentials. The question should be, "Which of the things that are about me do I need to promote the greatest welfare of my life?" To answer this question will not be difficult, because almost anyone can determine at first thought what is needed and what is not needed to a complete life. When the decision is made, nonessentials should be removed as quickly as possible. True, we must avoid extremes, and whatever we do we must do nothing to decrease the beauty or the harmony of life.

There are a great many things in the world of the average person that he simply thinks he needs, though he knows that those things never did anything but retard his progress.

It therefore necessary to remove nonessentials from the mind before we attempt to simplify our immediate surroundings. The simple life is a beautiful life, with all burdens removed, and it is only the unnecessary that is burdensome. To live the simple life, surround yourself only with those things that are directly conducive to your welfare, but do not consider it necessary to limit the quantity of those things. Surround yourself with everything that is necessary to promote your welfare, no matter how much it may be, although do not place in your world a single thing that is not a direct power for good in your world. You thus establish the harmony of simplicity without placing any limitations whatever upon your possessions, your welfare or your highest need. You thus eliminate everything that may act as a burden; and we can readily understand that when all burdens are removed from life the happiness of life will be increased to a very great degree.

2. Live the serene life.

Be calm, peaceful, quiet and undisturbed in all things and at all times. Confusion and hurry waste energy, and it is a well known fact that depression and gloom are produced, in most instances, simply by the energy of the system running low. The serene life, if lived in poise, will keep the system brimful of energy at all tunes, and so long as you are filled through and through with life and energy you will be full of spirit and joy. Our saddest moments are usually the direct results of reactions from turbulent thinking and living; therefore, such moments will be eliminated completely when thinking and living are made peaceful and serene. It is not necessary to live the strenuous life in order to accomplish a great deal, although on the other hand it is not quantity but quality that we seek. Our object should not be to do many things, but to do good things. If we can do many things that are good, very well, but we must have duality first in the mind; the quantity will increase as we grow in capacity, and there is nothing that promotes the increase of mental and physical capacity more than calm, serene living. The sweetest joys that the mind can feel usually come from those deep peaceful realizations of the soul when all is quiet and serene. Therefore, to cultivate the habit of living always in this beautiful calm will invariably add happiness to happiness every day of continued existence.

3. Be in love with the world.

He who loves much will be loved much in return, and there is nothing in the world that can give more joy and higher joy than an abundance of real love. The selfish love, that is only personal, and that must be gratified to be enjoyed, gives but a passing pleasure, the reaction of which is always pain. When we love with such a love we are always unhappy when not directly loved in return, and the purely selfish love never brings real love in return. When we love everybody with the pure love of the soul, that love that does not ask to be loved in return but loves because it is loved, we shall positively be loved in return; and not simply by a few here and there, but by great numbers. To feel that you are loved unselfishly, that you are loved not because anything is expected in return, but because the love is there and must come to feel this love is a source of joy which cannot be measured, and this joy everybody can receive in abundance now. The simple secret is to love the whole world at all times and under every circumstance; love everybody with heart and soul and mean it, and everything that happens to you will add both to the pleasure of the mind and to the more lofty joys of the soul.

4. Be useful.

"Give to the world the best that you have and the best will come to you." Hold nothing back. If you have something that you can share with the world, let everybody have it today. Do all that you can for everybody, not because you expect reward, but because it is a part of your nature. Be all that you can be and do all that you can do. Never say, "I will do only as much as I AM paid for." Such an attitude has kept many a person in poverty for life. Reward is an effect, not a cause. Do not place the reward first, and the service second. Increase your service and the reward will increase in proportion; you will thus not only place yourself in a position where you can secure more and more of the good things of life, but you will live in that position where you are bringing into expression more and more of the good things that exist in your own life. And we must remember that the greatest joy does not come from gaining good things from the without, but from the expression of good things from the within; and when both of these are combined harmoniously we shall secure all the joys of life, the joys that come from the outer world and the joys that come from the beauty and the splendor of the inner world. To combine these in your life, be useful; express your best; be your best; do your best. You thus bring forth riches from within and attract riches from without. Give richly of the best you have and good things in an ever increasing number will constantly flow into your life. That deep soul-satisfaction that comes to mind when we have rendered valuable service to man is entirely too good to be ignored; it is one of the deepest and highest joys that man can know. Those people who are the most valuable wherever they go are always the happiest, and we all can be of service in a thousand ways; therefore, we may add to our happiness in just as many ways, if we will always remember to be and do the best we can wherever we may go in the world.

5. Think and speak the beautiful only.

Every word or thought that you express will return to you. Never say anything to make others discouraged or unhappy; it will come back to yourself. He who gives unhappiness to others is giving unhappiness to himself. He who adds to the joys of others is perpetually adding to his own joy. You can say something good about everybody. Then say it. It will give joy to everybody concerned, yourself included. Think only of the beautiful side of everybody. Everybody has a beautiful side. Find it and think of that only. You will thus live in the world of the beautiful, and he who lives in the world of the beautiful is always happy. Speak kindly and pleasantly to everybody; think kindly and pleasantly of everybody, and your days of gloom will be gone. When every word is animated with the spirit of kindness and joy, you will not only increase the power of joy in your own life, but you will be sowing the seeds of joy in the garden of the universal life; and one of these days you will reap abundantly from what you have sown. Let this sowing time be continuous and the harvest will be continuous; thus you will be reaping a harvest of boundless joy every day of your endless existence.

6. Forgive and forget everything that seems wrong.

We have spent many a weary day simply because we persisted in remembering something that was unpleasant. Forget the wrong and it will disturb you no more. Forgive others for what they have done and you will have no unpleasant memories to cloud the sky of your mental world. When people speak unkindly of you, never mind. Let them say what they, like, if they must. Nothing can harm you but your own wrong thinking and living. If people do not treat you right remember they would act differently if they knew better, and you know better than to become offended. So therefore forgive it all and resolve to be happy. Forgive everybody for what is not right and forget everything that is not conducive to the right. You have no time to brood over ills and troubles that exist only in your memory. Your memory is created for a better purpose. Remember the good, the true and the beautiful; this is one of the greatest secrets of perpetual happiness. When you forgive those who have wronged you, you usually come to a place where you think more of those very persons than you ever did before, and when you come to that place you will realize a joy that is far too sweet and beautiful for pen to ever describe. It seems to be a blessing coming direct from heaven and it does not go away. This fact proves that he who learns to forgive rises in the scale of life. He who can forget and forgive the wrongs of the lowlands of undeveloped life, invariably ascends to the heights, and it is upon the heights that we find real happiness. Such is the reward of forgiveness. It will therefore not be difficult to forgive when we know that the results are so rich and so beautiful; indeed, to forgive and forget everything that seems wrong will thus become a coveted pleasure.

7. Be perfectly contented with the present.

We have heard a great deal about the value of divine discontent, but discontent is never divine any more than indignation is ever righteous. Perfect contentment is one of the highest states of the soul and is one of those attainments that invariably follows ideal living. Discontent, however, in any of its shapes or forms, always indicates that we are not on the true path. So long as there is discontent there is something wrong in our living, but the moment this wrong is righted perpetual contentment will be realized. If your present lot is not what you wish it to be, discontent will not make it better. Be perfectly content with the present and create more lofty mansions for the future; thus you will not only improve your condition every year, but you will be supremely happy every day. The more perfect your present contentment the more power you will have to create for yourself a greater future, and the more mental light you will have to build wisely for days to come. The more contentment you realize in your mind the more brightness and strength there will be in your mind.

Find the good that you already possess, then enjoy it. Better things are even now on the way and through the harmony of contentment you will be prepared to receive them. You will also be in that higher state of mental discernment where you can know good things when you see them. Many people are so much disturbed by the discord of discontent that they are unable to recognize the good things already in their world; thus they add doubly to the cause of discontent. Contentment, however, does not mean to be so satisfied with present conditions that we do not care to change them. True contentment not only appreciates the full value of the present, but also appreciates those greater powers in life that can perpetually add to the value of the present; therefore, the contented mind gains everything that life can give in the great eternal now, while at the same time perpetually increasing the richness, the worth and the beauty of the great eternal now. To be contented, find fault with nothing. Those things that are not quite right can be made better. Proceed to make them better, and one of the greatest joys of life comes directly from that action of life that is causing things to become better. The process of growth and advancement is invariably conducive to joy; therefore, if we cease finding fault, and use all our time in promoting improvement, we will find sources of happiness in every imperfection that we may meet in life. In other words, when we aim to improve everything that we meet, we bring out all the good that is latent in our world, and to increase the expression of the good in our world is to increase our own measure of joy.

8. Seek the ideal.

Look for the ideal everywhere; live in ideal environments when possible; but if not possible in an external sense create for yourself an ideal environment in the internal sense. Live in ideal mental worlds no matter what external worlds may be. Associate as much as possible with ideal people, and if you are living an ideal life in your own mental and spiritual life, you will attract ideal people wherever you go. And one of the greatest joys of life is to associate with those who are living in lofty realms. We have no time to give to the common and the ordinary. We want the best. We deserve the best, and we can secure the best by seeking the best and the best only. Live your own ideal life. Seek the ideal both in the within and in the without, and aim to make the ideal real in every thought, word and deed; you will thus cause every moment to add to your joy.

9. Develop the whole man.

To promote an orderly growth throughout your entire being is highly important, and to establish perfect harmony of action among all the various members of mind and body is indispensable to happiness. Develop everything in your nature and place all the elements in your being in perfect harmony. You will thus ascend perpetually to higher states of being and greater realms of joy. Much of the discord and unhappiness that comes into life is the direct result of one-sidedness and undevelopment, and these can be permanently removed only through the orderly development of the whole man. Body, mind and soul must be perfectly balanced in every sense of that term. The more perfectly you are balanced the greater will be your joy, because a balanced nature is conducive to harmony, and harmony is conducive to happiness.

10. Open the mind to beautiful thoughts only.

The world is full of thoughts, all kinds of thoughts, but only those that are invited will come to you. There is nothing that affects life more than the thoughts we think; and the thoughts we are to think will depend almost entirely upon our mental attitude towards that which we meet in life. When we resolve to receive only beautiful thoughts from everything with which we come in contact the change for the better in life will be simply remarkable. All things will become new. We will actually enter a new heaven and a new earth, and the joys of existence will multiply many times.

11. Be in touch with the harmony of life.

The universe is full of music, and happy is the soul that can hear the symphonies of heaven; he can find no greater joy. Every soul that has been in tune with higher things is familiar with that deep pleasure that comes to mind when the sensations of sublime harmony sweetly thrill every fiber of being; and we can all so live that we can be in tune with the music of the spheres. When you learn how to place yourself in harmony with the music of life you may for hours at a time remain within the gates of everlasting joy, and you may enter into the very life of that sublime something which eye has not seen nor ear heard. It is then that you understand why the kingdom of heaven is within and why all souls that have found that inner life is radiant with joy. Here is happiness without measure, happiness that you may enjoy anywhere and at any time. No matter what your environments may be, enter into these lofty realms and you will be the happiest soul in the world.

12. Consecrate every moment to the higher life.

The mind that is ever ascending can never be sad. Perpetual ascension means perpetual joy. The happiest moments that come to you are those moments that come when you see yourself rising in the scale of sublime existence. You are then ascending to the heights. You are entering into the cosmic realms, those realms where joy is supreme; and one single moment in that lofty realm gives more happiness than we can imagine were a million heavens united in one. It is in these realms that we enter the secret places of the Most High, and to enter into that sublime state is to gain all the happiness that life can give and have that happiness while eternity shall continue to be.

Chapter 18

Creating Ideal Surroundings

We all believed, not so very long ago, that the circumstances in which each individual was placed were produced by inevitable fate, and that the individual himself could not change them, but would have to remain where he was until something in his favor happened from external sources. What was to cause that something to happen we did not know, nor did we give the matter much thought. We believed more or less in chance and luck, and had no definite conception of the underlying laws of things. But now many of us have changed our minds, as we have received a great deal of new light on this most important subject. The many, however, are still in the old belief; they are ignorant of the fact that man can create his own destiny, and that fate, circumstances and environments are but the products of man himself, acting alone, or in association with others. But this is the fact, and it can be scientifically demonstrated by anyone under any circumstance.

This new idea that man can change his surroundings or transport himself to more agreeable environments through the use of psychological and metaphysical laws may seem unthinkable and farfetched to a great degree; but when we study the subject with care we find that the principles, laws and methods involved are not only natural but thoroughly substantial and can be applied in tangible everyday affairs. If the surroundings in which you live are not what you wish them to be, know that you can change them. You can make those surroundings ideal. You can make those surroundings better and better at every step in your advancement, thus making real higher and higher ideals in your life. This is a positive truth and should be impressed so deeply upon every mind that no former belief on the subject can cause us to doubt our possession of this power for a moment. The importance of thus impressing this fact upon the mind becomes very evident when we understand that no matter how much we may know, we will have no results so long as we are in doubt as to whether what we have undertaken is really possible or not. There are thousands of people who believe, in a measure, that they can better their own conditions and they understand fully all the principles involved, but they have no satisfactory results because one moment they believe that the change is possible while at the next moment they entertain doubts. To have real results in any undertaking, especially in the changing of one's surroundings, one must believe with his whole heart that he can, and he must constantly employ all the necessary principles in that conviction. No undertaking ever succeeded that was not animated through and through with the positive faith that it could be done, and such a faith is simply indispensable if you wish to create ideal surroundings for yourself, because the process depends directly upon the way you think. You must think that you can so as to fully annihilate the belief that you cannot. Know that you can, and in that attitude continue to apply the necessary methods. Let nothing disturb your faith in the possibility of what you have undertaken to do in this respect, and you will positively succeed.

To create ideal surroundings, the first essential is to gain a clear understanding of what actually constitutes your surroundings. The world in which you live is a state of many elements, factors, forces and activities. The physical environment with all its various phases and conditions has been considered the most important, but this is not necessarily true, because the mental environment is just as much a part of the world in which you live as the physical. The term "world" is not confined simply to visible things; it also includes states of mind, mental tendencies, thoughts, desires, motives and all the different phases of consciousness. The place in which you live physically, the place in which you live mentally, the place in which you live morally and spiritually, these places combined constitute the world in which you live. All of these states and conditions are necessary parts of your surroundings, and it is your purpose to make these necessary parts as beautiful, as perfect and as ideal as possible.

The place where you work with your hands and with your brain is a part of your world, but the same is true of the place where you work in your dreams, in your aspirations and in your ideals. The circumstances and events of your life, physically and mentally; the opportunities that are constantly passing your way; the people you meet in your work; the people you think of in your thoughts; the people you associate with and friends that are near; the various elements of nature, both visible and invisible; the many groups of things in all their various phases that you come in contact with in your daily living; all of these belong in your world. To enter into details it would be possible to mention many hundreds of different elements or factors that compose the world in which the average person lives; but to be brief we can say that your world is composed of everything that enters your life, your home, your experience, your thought and your dreams of the ideal. All of these play their part in bringing to you the good that you may desire or the ills that you may receive. Consequently, since the world in which you live is so very complex and since so much of it belongs to the mental side of life, the process of change must necessarily involve mental laws, as well as physical laws; but here the majority have made their mistake.

Many great reformers and human benefactors have tried to emancipate the race through the change of exterior laws and external conditions alone, forgetting that most of the troubles of man and nearly all of his failures have their origin in the misuse of the mind. We all know that mind is the most prominent factor in the life of man, and yet this factor has been almost entirely overlooked in our former efforts to change the conditions of the race. Everything that man does begins in his mind; therefore, every change that is to take place in the life of man must begin in his mind. This being true, we understand readily why modern metaphysics and the new psychology can provide the long looked for essentials to human emancipation and advancement. When we examine all the various things that go to make up the world in which we live we may find it difficult to discover the real source of them all. How they were produced; who produced them; why they happened to come to us, or why we went to them; these are problems that we are called upon to solve before we can begin to create ideal surroundings.

To solve these problems the first great fact to realize is that we are the creators of our own environments; but at first sight this fact may not be readily accepted, because there are so many things that seem to be the creation of others. There are two kinds of creation, however, the direct and the indirect. In direct creation you create with the forces of your own life, your own thought and your own actions, and your own creations are patterned after the ideas in your own mind; but in what is termed indirect creation someone else creates what you desire. It is your creation, however, in a certain sense, because it was your desire that called it forth. To state the fact in another manner, the world in which you live may be your own direct creation or it may be the creation of another, but you went into that other one's world to live. In the majority of cases, the world in which the individual lives is produced partly by his own efforts and partly by the efforts of others, though there is nothing in his world that he has not desired or called forth in some manner and at some time during his existence. There are a number of people who are living in worlds created almost entirely by others; in fact, the world of the average person is three-fourths the creation of the race mind; but the question is, why does a person enter into a world that is created by others; why does he not live exclusively in a world created by himself?

There are many fine minds who are living in the world of the submerged tenth, but they did not create that world. That inferior state existed long before the birth of its present inhabitants; but why have those gone to live there who were not born there, and why have those who were born there not gone away to some better world of their own superior creation? Why do the people who live in that inferior world continue to perpetuate all its conditions? No world can continue to exist unless the people who live in that world continue to create those conditions that make up that world. Then why do not those people who live in the world of the submerged tenth cease the creating of that inferior world and begin the creation of the superior world when we know they have the power to do so? These are great questions, but they all have very simple answers. To answer these questions the first great fact to be realized is that the mind of man is the most important factor in everything that he does, and since no person can change his environments until he changes his actions we realize that the first step to be taken is the change of mind. Learn to change your mind for the better, and you will soon learn how to change your surroundings for the better. Before you proceed, however, there is another important condition to be considered; it is the fact that a portion of what is found in our world is created by ourselves, while the rest is the product of those minds with which we work or live. In the home each individual contributes to the qualities of the world which all the members of that home have in common, but each individual lives in a mental world distinctly his own, unless he is so negative that he has not a single individual purpose or thought. When the mental world of each individual is developed to a high degree it will become so strong that the fate of that individual will not be affected by the adverse conditions that may exist in the home.

The same is true of the environments that we meet in our places of work. No man need be affected very long by adverse surroundings or obstacles that he may meet in his work. He will finally become so strong that he can overcome every adversity that may exist in his physical world and thus gain entrance to better surroundings. However, we can readily see how a great deal of discord can be produced in a home or in our place of work where the different members are not in harmony with each other, and we can also understand how the events, circumstances and conditions of all those members, as well as each individual member, will be affected more or less by that in harmony; providing however, that each individual is not developing that power of his mental world that can finally overcome all adversity. We can also understand how harmony and cooperation in a home or in a place of work would become a powerful force for good in the life of each individual concerned. Where a few are gathered in the right attitude there immense power will be developed; in fact, sufficient power to do almost anything that those few may wish to have done. This has been fully demonstrated a number of times; therefore, where many minds are associated in the creation of a world in which all will live, more or less, these higher mental laws should be fully understood and most thoroughly applied.

To enter a world that does not correspond with yourself and to go in and live where you do not naturally belong is to go astray, and such an action will not only cause all the forces and elements of your life to be misdirected, but you will place yourself in that position where nothing that is your own can come to you. There are vast multitudes, however, who have gone astray in this manner, and that is the reason why we find so many people who are misplaced, who do not realize their ideals, and who have not the privilege to enjoy their own. But we may ask, why do people go astray in this manner; why do we associate with people that do not belong in our world; why do we enter environments that do not correspond to our nature; why do we enter vocations for which we are not adapted, and why do we pursue plans, ideas and ambitions that lead us directly away from the very thing that our state of development requires? These are questions that we must answer, because no one can get the greatest good out of life or make the most of himself unless he lives in a world where he truly belongs. It is only when you live in a world created by yourself or in a world that others have created in harmony with you that you can be your real self, and since one must be truly himself to be wholly free and to promote his own advancement naturally and completely the subject is of great importance.

There are two reasons why we stray from our own true world and enter worlds where we do not belong; first, because we frequently permit the inferior side of our nature to predominate; and second, because we permit the senses to guide us in almost everything that we do. No person who has qualifications for the living of life in a superior world will ever enter an inferior world if he does not permit inferior desires to lead him into destructive paths; and no person, no matter what his work may be, will go down the scale so long as he follows the highest mental and spiritual light that he can possibly see during his most lofty moments. Follow the highest and the best that is in you, and you will constantly ascend into higher and better worlds; all your creative forces will thus build for you better and better surroundings, because so long as you are rising in the scale everything in your life in the external as well as in the internal must necessarily improve continuously. There is no need whatever of any person ever entering an inferior world. No one need pass into environments and surroundings that are less desirable than the ones in which he is living now. In fact, a person may take the opposite course. Endeavor constantly to attain superiority and you will steadily work yourself up into superiority, and as you become superior you will find an entrance into those worlds, those environments and those surroundings that are superior. There is a higher light, a better understanding within yourself that will guide you correctly in all your associations with people and environments. Do not follow physical desires or physical senses; let these be servants in the hands of higher wisdom. Follow this higher wisdom and you will make few mistakes, if any. You will constantly pass into better and better surroundings, because you will constantly pass into a higher, a better and a superior life. To follow the highest and the best that is within you under all circumstances does not constitute supernaturalism. It is simply good sense enlarged, and those who take this course will continue to make real the ideal in everything that may exist in the world in which they live. In consequence, both the mental world and the physical world in which we live will perpetually change for the better; and all our surroundings will improve accordingly, becoming more and more ideal until everything that exists about us is as beautiful as the visions of the soul.

Chapter 19

Changing Your Own Fate

When you discover that you are living in a world that you did not create and that does not correspond with your ideals, there is a tendency to break loose from external conditions at the earliest possible moment; but this tendency must be checked. Nothing is gained through an attempt to change from one world of effect to another world of effect without first changing the cause. The majority believe that, when things are wrong in the outer world the only remedy is to change external conditions; but the fact is that external conditions are simply effects from internal causes, and so long as those internal causes remain the same, no attempt to change external conditions will prove of permanent value. So long as there are adverse causes in your inner life there will be adverse effects in your outer life, no matter how many times you may change from one condition to another or from one place to another.

When you begin to seek emancipation from the false world in which you are living now; in other words, when you begin to take positive measures to change your own fate, the first thing to do is to resolve not to make any forceful effort to change external conditions without first changing the inner cause of those conditions. Let outer things be as they are for the time being and continue to remain where you are until you can open a door to better things; but while you are waiting for this door to open do not be idle in any manner whatever. Although you are letting things be as they are in the external sense, and although you are not forcing yourself into different places or circumstances, still your purpose must be to entirely remake yourself. You came into this false state of life because you were misled by your own judgment, and if you should break loose, this same judgment will mislead you again; you will thus pass from one world that is not your own into some other world that is not your own, and there will be no improvement in the change.

If you have not improved yourself in any manner whatever, your judgment will be just as inferior and unreliable as it was before, and no attempt to follow this judgment into different conditions will help matters in the least. Your object is not to set yourself free from the false world in which you are living now and then enter some other world that is not your own. You are not ready to move, neither physically nor mentally, until you have created a world of your own just as you would have it in your present state of development. Therefore, all thought of change will but divert your attention from the real purpose in view. So long as you are constantly thinking about external changes your mind cannot concentrate upon internal changes. So long as you are trying to change external conditions you cannot change yourself, and as you, yourself, are the cause of the new world which you are trying to create, you must recreate yourself before you can create the external world as desired.

To change your fate begin with yourself. If the environments in which you live are beneath your ideal, nothing can be gained by leaving those environments until the way is opened naturally to better things. If you simply get up and leave, you will gravitate into something elsewhere that will be just as uncongenial as those conditions you left behind. First, find the reason why you are living in your present adverse environments, then proceed to remove that cause. There may be many reasons, but in most cases the principal reason is a lack of ability or the lack of power to apply the ability you possess. In such a case you must remove inability by becoming more proficient, and as soon as you are competent to render better service you will readily find a better place. This means larger remuneration, and you will thus be able to secure more desirable surroundings. The many, however, will think that to promote sufficient improvement so as to command greater recompense, and do so in a short time, is practically impossible under the average conditions; but all difficulties that may be met in this connection may be readily removed through the principles of modern metaphysics.

Continuous improvement in everything pertaining to the life, the power, the capacity or the mentality of the individual can be readily promoted by anyone and decided results secured in a very short time. Therefore, no person need remain in adverse or limited conditions. He can, through the awakening and the expression of the best that is in himself, become competent to take advantage of greater opportunities and thus change his fate, his future and his destiny.

If you wish to improve your physical environments, remain content where you are while you develop the power to earn and create better environments. Contentment with things as they are and harmony with everything about you are indispensable essentials if you wish to increase your ability, your capacity and your worth. To continue to kick against the pricks is to remain where pricks are abundant; but when we cease this mode of action and begin to polish off all the rough corners of our nature and improve ourselves in every manner possible, things will take a turn. We will leave the world of pricks and enter a smoother path. The polished man is admitted to the polished world where there are no rough places and where adverse conditions are few, if existing at all.

When circumstances are against you, do not contend with circumstances. So long as we contend with things, things will contend with us. Do not resist present conditions;

you prolong their existence by so doing. Whatever comes, meet all things in the attitude of perfect harmony and you will find that all things, even the most adverse, can be readily handled and turned to good account. We all know the marvelous power of the man who can harmonize contending factions, be they in his own life or in his circumstances. He not only gains good from everything that he meets, but he becomes a most highly respected personage, and is sought wherever opportunities are great and where great things are to be accomplished.

Learn to harmonize the contending factions in your own life and experience, and you will find yourself entering new worlds where circumstances are more congenial and opportunities far greater. You will thus meet more desirable events, more desirable people, and superior advantages of every description will appear in your pathway. If your present friends are not to your liking admire them nevertheless for every good quality that they may possess. Emphasize their good qualities and ignore everything in their nature that seems inferior. This will help you to develop superior qualities in yourself; and this is extremely important, because as you develop superiority you prepare yourself for places higher up in the scale.

Make yourself over, so to speak, in your own friendship; increase your personal worth; polish your own character; refine your mind, and make real more and more of the ideal; double and treble your love and your kindness and constantly increase your admiration for everything that has real quality and high worth. Continue thus until you have results, whether those results begin to come at once or not; they will positively come ere long, and the things that you develop in yourself you will meet in your external world. Change yourself for the better in every shape and manner, and you change your fate for the better, but the change that you produce in yourself must not simply be negative in its action. It is the positive character, the positive mind, the positive personality that meets in the external world what has been developed in the internal world. The fact that a change in yourself can produce a similar change in your fate, your environments, your circumstances, in brief, everything in your outer world, may not seem clear at first.; but it is easily demonstrated to be the truth when we analyze the relationship that exists between man and the world in which he lives.

Everything that exists in your outer world has a correspondent in your inner world. This inner correspondent is the cause that has either created or attracted its external counterpart, and the process is easily understood. To state it briefly, environment corresponds with ability. Circumstances are the aggregation of events brought about by your own actions and associations and friends, which follow the law of like attracting like. That environment is the direct effect of ability may not seem true when we observe that there are many people living in luxury that have practically no ability, but we must first demonstrate that these people have no ability.

We shall find that those who have actually accumulated their own wealth have ability, in fact, exceptional ability, though they may not always have employed it according to the exact principles of justice. On the other hand, when we understand the process of creation we shall find that ability employed according to principle will produce far greater results than when it is employed unjustly. Therefore, the law underlying the power of ability to create its own environment acts wholly in the favor of him who lives according to the highest ideals of life.

This fact becomes more evident when we discern that success is not measured simply by the accumulation of things, but also by the accumulation of those elements in life that pertain to quality and worth in man's interior nature. It is wealth in the mental and the spiritual worlds that has the greatest value or the greatest power in promoting the welfare and the happiness of man, and this higher wealth can be accumulated only by those who are living according to their ideals. However, the accumulation of mental and spiritual wealth will have a direct tendency to increase the power and the capacity of practical ability, and practical ability when scientifically applied will tend to increase tangible wealth; that is, to improve the value and the worth of external environments.

When we consider this subject from the universal viewpoint we shall find a perfect correspondent existing between the size of a man's possessions, physical, mental and spiritual, and the size of his brains, taking the term "brains" to signify ability, capacity and worth in the largest sense; but the size of brains can be increased perpetually. We therefore conclude that possessions in the larger sense can be increased perpetually, and he who is perpetually increasing his possessions on all the planes of his life is constantly changing his fate for the better. We shall also find that when a person increases the power of his own life he will bring about, through his own actions, new events, and these new events will produce new circumstances.

To change circumstances is to change fate; and whatever the change may be in fate, circumstances or events it will be a change for the better, if the increase of power is applied according to the principles of ideals. Again, when a person develops quality and superiority in himself he will, through the law of attraction, meet friends and associations that are after his own heart. In other words, he will enter a world where his ideals, both as to persons and as to things, are constantly being made real in every sphere of his present state of existence. He is thus creating for himself a better fate in every sense of the term and opening doors and pathways to a larger and a more beautiful future than he has ever realized before; but the beginning is in himself; in fact, every change for the better must begin within the life of man himself, and whoever will begin to change for the better in the within will positively realize greater and greater changes for the better in the without.

Chapter 20

Building Your Own Ideal World

To build your own ideal world, the first essential is to begin to build in the real everything that you can discern in the ideal; and the second essential is to continue to rebuild your ideal world according to higher and higher ideals. However congenial or desirable or perfect our world may be, we should continue to improve upon it constantly. When we cease to promote progression we return to the ways of retrogression. One of the principal causes of undesirable environments or unexpected reverses among the more capable is found in the tendency to "stop, rest and enjoy" what we have gained whenever conditions are fairly satisfactory. It is the mind that is ever creating the new and ever recreating everything according to higher ideals that is always free and that is always enjoying the best. No one can be in bondage to the lesser who is constantly rising out of the lesser, and he who is ever growing into the best is constantly enjoying the best. In the last analysis, retrogression is the only cause of bondage, while constant progression is the only cause of perfect freedom; and constant progression is promoted by the continuous recreation of everything in your world according to higher and higher ideals.

To begin, your entire mentality must be changed and constantly changed so as to correspond perfectly with your newest thoughts on every subject and your highest ideals of everything that you can discern in your life. The mind is the cause and is the source of every force that can act as a cause of whatever may be developed, expressed or worked out through yourself into your external world. Therefore, begin with the mind and with all the elements of the mind. All desires, motives and ambitions must be concentrated upon the larger and the perfect in their various spheres of action.

All the mental states must be in harmony with each other, and with the outer as well as the inner conditions of life. All mental qualities must be expanded and enlarged constantly, and consciousness must be trained to act perpetually upon the verge of the limitless. The entire world of thought must be perpetually renewed, enlarged and perfected, and every step taken in the mental world must be practically expressed and applied in the outer world. In order to bring all the creative forces of mind into harmony with the goal in view the ideal wished to be realized must be thoroughly established in consciousness, and the goal in view must be constantly held before the mental vision. In the rebuilding of your own world one of the principal causes of failure will be found in a tendency to change your plans, motives or desires; therefore, do not permit yourself to entertain one group of desires today and a different group tomorrow, and do not permit your faith to fall into periodical states of doubt. Decide upon what you wish to do, accomplish, promote and attain, and proceed to live, think and work for those things, regardless of what may happen. The powers within you follow the predominating states of mind, and when these states are constantly changing, the creative forces will be employed simply in taking initial steps, but never in completing anything. On the other hand, when your mental states, desires, motives, plans, etc., continue to concentrate upon the one supreme goal in view your creative forces will perpetually build towards that goal, and you will be daily rebuilding your entire world according to the higher, the better and the greater that you have in view. There are thousands of fine minds that are down in the scale today and cannot get up, because they are constantly changing their plans, motives and desires. To create a new world you must fix in your mind what you wish to create, and then continue to build until the complete structure is finished. Recreate your present world, then constantly make it better, larger and more beautiful. All the elements of your mind, both conscious and subconscious, must be constantly inspired with your highest thought of the larger, the better and the more beautiful. Not a single thought should enter your mind that is inferior or in the least beneath your ideal of life, and not a single moment of discouragement or doubt should ever be permitted. Fix your mind on the soul's vision and hold it there through all sorts of circumstances or conditions. Do not waver for a moment. Keep the eye single upon the heights and all the powers of your being will build that great world that you can see in your mental vision as you concentrate attention upon the heights.

The mind must be clean, strong and high. It is the mind that does things. It is the mind that originates things. Therefore, if you wish to build for yourself an ideal world, the mind must be ideal in every sense of the term, and every element of the mind must always be its best and act at its best. To promote the right use of mind the imagination must be guided with the greatest of care. The imagination is one of the most important powers in the mind. The imagination when misdirected can produce more ills than any other faculty, and when properly directed can produce greater good than any other faculty. In fact, the imagination when scientifically applied becomes a marvelous power in the great creative process of the vast mental domain. Train the imagination to picture, not only the goal you have in view but all the highest ideals that you can possibly imagine as might exist within the realms of that goal. Train the imaging faculty to impress upon the mind only those superior qualities that you wish to incorporate in your new world, and whatever you impress upon the mind will be created in your mental world. To create superior qualities in the mental world means that you will create, as well as attract, the superior in your outer world, and you thus promote the building of an ideal world.

The Ideal Made Real

To build your own ideal world, the more opportunities that you can take advantage of the better, but opportunities come only to those who have demonstrated their worth. Prove to the world that you have worth, and you can have your choice of almost any opportunity that the world can offer. There is nothing that is in greater demand than great men and women, minds of ability and power, people who can do things. The great mind is constantly in the presence of opportunities to change his environment and his field of action; therefore, he may enter into a new world almost any time. Those opportunities, however, do not come of themselves; they come because he has made himself equal to those opportunities. Make yourself equal to the best and you will meet the best. This is a law that is universal and is never known to fail. Make yourself a great power in your present sphere of action. Learn to do things better than they have ever been done before. Produce something for the world that the world wants and the gates to new and greater opportunities will open for you. Henceforth, you may secure almost anything that you may wish, and all the elements that may be necessary for you to employ in order to build the ideal world you have in mind may be readily obtained because you have placed yourself in touch with the limitless supply of the best that life can give.

Those who are in search for new and greater opportunities should eliminate the belief that the best things have been said, that all great things have been done and that all remarkable discoveries have been made. The fact is we are just in the A B C of literature, invention, art, music, industrial achievements and extraordinary human attainments. The human race is now on the verge of hundreds of undeveloped fields that have just been discovered, and they have more possibilities in store than we have ever dreamed. Many of these possibilities when developed will supply the world with the very things that the present development of the race is demanding in every expression of thought and desire. It is therefore easier to attain greatness, and do something of exceptional value at the present time than it ever was before. The opportunities of this age are very numerous, and some of them hold possibilities that are actually marvelous. Those who will prepare themselves to meet the requirements of this age will therefore find a number of rich fields already at hand, and all minds can prepare themselves as required. Every person of moderate intelligence can, in a short time, place himself in the path of some of these new opportunities, and all minds can find better opportunities in their present spheres if they will proceed to become more than they are.

Train all the elements of your being to work towards a higher goal and you will bring forth into expression those greater powers that will make for you a mentality that the world will demand for its highest places of action and achievement. When you proceed to build in yourself an ideal mental world, a mental world of power, ability, capacity and high worth you will find it necessary to adapt this mental world to the external world in such a way as to promote harmony of action. The added power of your new mental world must work in harmony with your external world if practical results are to be secured. Circumstances come from personal actions; therefore, to change circumstances, personal actions must be changed, and to change personal actions your ideal mental life must be expressed in your personal life, and to this end the development of a high degree of harmony becomes necessary. Harmony, however, will not only promote the united action of the inner world with the outer world, but will also tend to eliminate mistakes from personal actions, and when we eliminate, mistakes from personal actions we will cease to produce adverse circumstances. When you are in perfect harmony with yourself and everything you eliminate mental confusion. You thus place your mind in that position where you can think clearly, reason logically and judge wisely. The result is, you will do the right thing at the right time. The elements of your life will be properly blended, and this is necessary in order to create an ideal world.

Another essential in the practical application of your ideals to real life is the development of what may be termed interior insight. This faculty will guide you perfectly in your expression of the finer things of life through the tangible things of life; in other words, you will see clearly how to combine the ideal with those actions that are promoted for the purpose of rebuilding the real. To combine the ideal with the real and make the two one, we must come into the closest possible relationship with the finer things in life and learn to use that phase of mind that is always in a cleared-up condition. The lower story of the mind is often darkened with false conclusions about things, and is frequently more or less filled with ideas that have been impressed through the senses; but in the upper story we can see things, as they are; we can think clearly, and invariably come to the right conclusions. The power to think in the upper story of the mind, the cleared-up side of consciousness where the sun is always shining and where there are no clouds, is called interior insight. This interior insight not only discerns the ideal, but can discern the practical possibilities that every ideal may contain, and we make the ideal real when we proceed to develop and apply in actual life those practical possibilities that our ideals may contain. Interior insight will also elevate all our mental faculties and cause those faculties to function with far greater efficiency. In fact, the entire mind will be lifted up into a state of greater power, greater brilliancy and greater ability for high and efficient mental expression.

The Ideal Made Real

To develop interior insight, aim to use consciousness in the discernment of what may be termed the spirit of all things. Do not simply think of things as they appear on the surface, but try to think of things as they are in the spirit of their interior existence. The mere effort to do this will develop the power to look through things or to look into things; and the growth of this power promotes interior insight. You may thus discern clearly the real worth and the real possibilities that exist in the lofty goal that you have in view, and by keeping the eye single upon that lofty goal, never wavering for a moment, all the powers of your being will work together and build for those greater things that you can see upon the heights of that goal. Thus your entire world in the within as well as in the without will constantly be recreated and rebuilt according to the likeness of your supreme ideals; in consequence, you will not only build for yourself an ideal world, but you will be building for yourself a world that is ever becoming more and more ideal, and to live in such a world is ideal living indeed. The world that is ever becoming more and more ideal is the world in which to live, and the power to create such a world is now at hand in every human mind.

Mastery of Fate

Mastery of Fate

Table of Contents

Chapter 1 - Mastery of Fate   232
Chapter 2 - The State of Self-Supremacy   238
Chapter 3 - Superior Thoughts   247
Chapter 4 - Creating the Spirit of Success   253
Chapter 5 - We Can Create Any Fate   260
Chapter 6 - He Can Who Thinks He Can   265
Chapter 7 - Express Your Individuality   269
Chapter 8 - The Four Parts of Fate   275
Chapter 9 - Making the Ideal Real   279
Chapter 10 - Directing Creative Forces   284
Chapter 11 - How to Develop Internal Insight   288
Chapter 12 - Character, Ability and Faith   292

Chapter 1

Mastery of Fate

WHAT man is, and what man does, determines in what conditions, circumstances and environments he shall be placed. And since man can change both himself and his actions, he can determine what his fate is to be.

To change himself, man must change his thought, because man is as he thinks; and to change his actions, he must change the purpose of his life, because every action is consciously or unconsciously inspired by the purpose held in view.

To change his thought, man must be able to determine what impressions are to form in his mind, because every thought is created in the likeness of a mental impression. To choose his own mental impressions, man must learn to govern the objective senses, and must acquire the art of original thought.

Everything that enters the mind through the physical senses will produce impressions upon the mind, unless prevented by original thought. These impressions will be direct reflections of the environment from whence they came; and since thoughts will be created in the exact likeness of these impressions, so long as man permits environment to impress the mind, his thoughts will be exactly like his environment: and since man becomes like the thoughts he thinks, he will also become like his environment.

But man, in this way, not only grows into the likeness of his environment, but is, in addition, controlled by his environment, because his thoughts, desires, motives and

Mastery of Fate

actions are suggested to him by the impressions that he willingly accepts from environment.

Therefore, one of the first essentials in the mastery of fate is to learn to govern the physical senses so thoroughly, that no impression can enter mind from without, unless it is consciously desired.

This is accomplished by holding the mind in a strong, firm, positive attitude at all times, but especially while surrounded by conditions that are inferior.

This attitude will bring the senses under the supremacy of the subconscious will, and will finally produce a state of mind that never responds to impressions from without unless directed to do so. To overcome the tendency of the physical senses to accept, indiscriminately, all sorts of impressions from without, mind should, at frequent intervals, employ the physical senses in trying to detect the superior possibilities that may be latent in the various surrounding conditions. And gradually, the senses themselves will become selective, and will instantaneously inform the mind whenever an undesirable impression demands admission.

While the senses are being employed in the search of superior possibilities, the impressions thus received should be analyzed, and recombined in the constructive states of consciousness, and according to the mind's own original conception. This will promote original thinking, which will, in turn, counteract the tendency of the objective side of mind to receive suggestions from without. Every original thought that mind may create, will to a degree, change man and remake him according to what he inwardly desires to be; because every original thought is patterned after man's conception of himself when he is at his best.

Mastery of Fate

Thoughts inspired by environment are inferior or superior, according to what the environment may be; but an original thought is always superior, because it is inspired by man himself while the superior elements of his being are predominant.

When every thought that mind creates is an original thought, man will constantly grow in greatness, superiority and worth; and when all these original thoughts are created with the same purpose in view, man will become exactly what is indicated by that purpose.

Therefore, since man can base thinking upon any purpose that he may desire, he can, through original thinking, become whatever he may choose to become.

Fate is the result of man's being and doing; a direct effect of the life and the works of the individual; a natural creation of man; and the creation is always the image and likeness of the creator.

Therefore, when man, through original thinking, acquires the power to become what he chooses to become, his fate will of itself change as man changes; and through this law he can create for himself any fate desired.

That man will consciously and naturally create his own fate when he gains the power to recreate himself as he desires to be, is evident for various reasons. And the power to recreate himself is simply the power of original thought. Because man becomes like the thoughts he thinks, and original thoughts are created in the likeness of man's ideal impressions of his superior self.

Mastery of Fate

That the fate of each individual person is the direct, or indirect result of what that person is and does, can be demonstrated by the following self-evident facts:

1. The mental world in which a person lives is the exact reflection of what that person is, feels and thinks; therefore, when a superior life and worthier thoughts are attained, the mental world will also change accordingly.

2. The circumstances and conditions of man's physical world are the direct or indirect effects of the active elements in his mental world; a fact we shall thoroughly demonstrate in the following pages.

3. Like attracts like; therefore, the associations of man are after his own kind; and as he changes for the better he will attract, and be attracted into better associations.

4. The events that transpire in the life of man are the consequences of his own efforts to express himself in his individual world of action. Therefore, what happens to any person is the reaction of what that person has previously said or done.

This being true, man has the power to cause any event to transpire that he may decide upon; though to accomplish this it is necessary to understand the law of action and reaction as applied both to the physical and metaphysical worlds.

When man begins to recreate himself, he will rise superior to his present position; and since new and better opportunities always appear when man proves himself superior to his present position, he can, by changing himself as he desires, call forth any opportunity that he may desire.

To have the privilege to take advantage of better opportunities, is the direct path to better conditions, better circumstances and better environments; and since man can create this privilege at will, he can create his own fate, his own future, his own destiny.

However, the secret of creating this privilege at will, lies in man's power to form only such impressions upon his mind as will originate constructive thought. Because when all the thought he thinks is constructive, every mental process will be a building process, and will constantly increase the ability, the capacity and the personal worth of man himself. This in turn makes man competent to accept the larger places that are waiting everywhere for minds with sufficient capability to fill them.

Every thought has creative power; and this power will express itself according to the desire that was in mind when the thought was created. Therefore, if every thought is to express its creative power in the building up of man, mind must constantly be filled with the spirit of that purpose. When the desire for growth and superior attainment does not predominate in mind, the greater part of the creative energy of thought will misdirect, and artificial mental conditions will form, only to act as obstacles to man's welfare and advancement.

The creative power of thought is the only power employed in the construction and reconstruction of man; and for this reason man is as he thinks.

Consequently, when man thinks what he desires to think, he will become what he desires to become. But to think what he desires to think, he must consciously govern the process through which impressions are formed upon mind.

Mastery of Fate

To govern this process is to have the power to exclude any impression from without that is not desired, and to completely impress upon mind every original thought that may be formed; thus giving mind the power to think only what it consciously chooses to think.

Before man can govern this process, he must understand the difference between the two leading attitudes of mind the attitude of self-submission, and the attitude of self-supremacy; and must learn how to completely eliminate the former, and how to establish all life, all thought, and all action absolutely upon the latter.

When this is done, no impression can form upon mind without man's conscious permission; and complete control of the creative power of thought is permanently secured.

To master the creative power of thought is to master the personal self; and to master the personal self is to master fate.

Chapter 2

The State of Self-Supremacy

MAN is inherently master over everything in his own life, because the principle of his being contains the possibility of complete mastership; and the realization of this principle produces the attitude of self-supremacy.

While mind is in this attitude, only those impressions are formed that are consciously selected; consequently, only those thoughts are created that conform to the purpose that may predominate in mind at the time.

To remain constantly in the attitude of self-supremacy, is therefore the secret of original thinking; and since the mastery of fate comes directly from original thinking, everything that interferes with the attitude of self-supremacy must be eliminated completely.

The most serious obstacle to this attitude is the belief that man is, for the greater part, the product of his environment; and that man cannot change to any extent until a change is first produced in his environment.

The result of this belief is the attitude of self-submission; and the more deeply this belief is felt, the more completely does man submit himself to the influence of his surroundings.

While mind is in this attitude, it has only a partial control over the process of thinking; it accepts willingly every impression that may enter through the senses, and permits the creation of thought in the likeness of those impressions without the slightest discrimination.

Mastery of Fate

To remove the attitude of self-submission, man must cease to believe that he is controlled by environment, and must establish all his thinking upon the conviction that he is inherently master over his entire domain.

This, however, may appear to be not only impossible, but absurd, when considered in the presence of the fact that man is controlled by environment. To tell a man to cease to believe as true that which he knows to be true, may not, at first sight seem to contain any reason; but at second sight it proves itself to mean the same as to tell a man to leave the darkness and enter the light.

When man ceases to believe that he is controlled by environment, he departs from a belief that is detrimental; and when he begins to realize that he has the power to completely control himself, he enters a conviction that is favorable to the highest degree.

While he is in the attitude of self-submission, he is controlled by environment, and the belief that he is thus controlled, is true to him. But when he enters the attitude of self-supremacy, he is not controlled by environment; therefore, the belief that he is controlled by environment is no longer true to him. While we are in the dark, we can truthfully say that we are in darkness; but when we enter the light, we cannot say, truthfully, that we are in darkness.

There is such a thing as being influenced by conditions that exist in our surroundings; but when we transcend that influence we are in it no more; therefore, to say that we are in it when we are out of it, is to contradict ourselves. And we equally contradict ourselves when we state that we are controlled by environment after we are convinced that we are inherently masters of everything in the personal life. What is not true to us now, we should not admit now, even though it had been true to us for all previous time.

To state that you are controlled by environment, and to permit that belief to possess your mind, is to submit yourself almost completely to the control of environment.

To recognize the principle of your being, and to realize that within that principle the power of complete supremacy does exist; to establish yourself absolutely upon that principle, and to state that you are not controlled by environment, is to depart from the control of environment.

While you are conscious of the principle of self-supremacy, you are unconscious of the influence of environment; therefore, to speak the truth, you must declare that you are complete master in your own domain.

When you know that the possibility of self-supremacy is within you, you cannot state truthfully that it is not there; and to state, in the presence of your knowledge of self-supremacy, that you are controlled by environment, is the same as to state that there is no self-supremacy. The very moment that you admit the possibility of self-supremacy, the control of environment is no longer a real fact to you; because in the state of self-supremacy, it is not possible for the control of environment to exist.

When man discovers the state of self-supremacy, he can no longer believe in the control of environment as a principle; and is therefore compelled to declare that the control of environment is no longer true to him. And, as he is permitted to speak only for himself, and judge only his own life, he must refuse absolutely to believe in the control of environment under any condition whatever.

Mastery of Fate

To believe that others are controlled by environment, is to judge where he has no authority, and also to place himself once again in the belief that environment controls man. To place himself in that belief is to enter the attitude of self-submission, and submit himself to the influence of everything that enters his sphere of existence.

It is therefore evident that the principal reason why those who know of self-supremacy do not master fate, is because they are not true to their own convictions. They believe that the principle of self-supremacy exists, but they also believe that the control of environment exists. They try to believe both to be true at the same time, which is impossible.

If the one exists as a living power in the life of a person, the other does not exist in the life of that person. It would be just as reasonable to believe that light and darkness could exist in the same place at the same time.

To try to believe in the idea of self-supremacy and the control of environment at the same time, is to live in confusion; and he who lives in confusion controls practically nothing. He is therefore more or less controlled by everything. When man is convinced that he is, in himself, master over his life, he can no longer believe that his life is controlled by environment. He must absolutely reject the latter belief; both cannot be true to anyone mind; therefore, every mind must decide which one of these beliefs to accept as absolutely true, and which one to reject as absolutely untrue.

The mind that does not wholly reject one of the two, is trying to serve two masters, which is impossible. He who tries to serve two masters will serve the one only, and that one will be the false one; because whoever tries to serve two masters is false to himself, and will consequently serve that which is false. In this connection it may be questioned how we know that the principle of self-supremacy does exist; and how we know that complete mastership is inherent in man.

But we do know; because man does exercise complete mastership over certain parts of his being at certain times; and the fact that he does this proves the existence of the principle.

If the principle of self-supremacy did not exist, man could not exercise complete control over anything at any time; but every mind demonstrates supremacy many times every hour.

The mastership exercised over mind and body in various ways may be confined to limited spheres of action; but within those spheres of action the mastership is complete. And those spheres will expand constantly as the principle of self-supremacy is applied on a larger and a larger scale.

Since the principle of complete control exists in man, there is a way to apply that principle in everything, and at all times. But to accomplish this, the attitude of self-supremacy must prevail at all times, and under all conditions.

While man is in the attitude of self-supremacy, he exercises complete control over certain things in his life; but when he enters the belief that he is controlled or influenced by other things, he leaves the attitude of self-supremacy, and ceases to exercise his complete control.

In the present state of human development, the average mind is so constituted that it oscillates from one state to another, remaining the greater part of the time in the attitude of self-submission; due principally to the fact that we are seldom absolutely true to the higher conviction, and also because we try to think that both beliefs are true at the same time.

Consequently, the great essential for man in his present state is to accept the high conviction as an absolute truth, and be true to that truth every moment of existence.

To be true to that truth he must refuse absolutely to believe that he can be controlled or influenced by anything or anybody. He must depart completely from the belief in the control of other powers, and must recognize in himself the only power to control the power to control completely, everything in his own domain.

Nor is this a contradiction, because when man enters the consciousness of self-supremacy, he cannot submit his self to any outside influence; therefore, there are no outside influences in action in his life. And when this is the case he cannot believe in the existence of outside influences, as far as he is concerned. When nothing is trying to control him, he cannot truthfully say that he is being controlled, nor even that he is liable to be controlled.

When man is in a state of self-supremacy, he is in a state where no, influence from without exists; he is in a world where the power of self-mastery is the only controlling power; therefore, he cannot truthfully recognize any other.

While in the attitude of self-submission, your mind is open to all kinds of impressions from without; and consequently, your thinking will be suggested to you by your environment. The result is that you will become like your environment, and will think, act and live as your environment may suggest.

Mastery of Fate

If your environment be inferior, you will think inferior thoughts, live an inferior life, and commit deeds that are low or perverse, so long as you are in the attitude of self-submission. But if you should submit yourself to a better environment, your life, thoughts, and deeds would naturally become better. In each case you would be the representation of the impressions that enter through the senses.

However, the very moment you pass from a superior environment to one that is inferior, you will begin to change for the worse, unless you have in the meantime attained a degree of self-supremacy. To enter a superior environment will not of itself develop self-supremacy, nor the art of original thinking; because so long as you permit yourself to be influenced by environment, you prevent your mind from gaining consciousness of the principle of self-supremacy.

A change of environment, therefore, will not give man the power to master his fate. This power comes only through a change of thought.

While in the attitude of self-supremacy your mind is not open to impressions from any source; but you can place your mind, at will, in the responsive attitude, so that it may receive impressions from any source that you may select.

By proper selection, consciousness can, in this way, be trained to express itself only through those mental channels that reach the superior side of things, and thereby come in contact with the unlimited possibilities of things.

From impressions received through this contact with unlimited possibilities, mind will be able to form original thoughts that embody superior powers and attainments; and as man becomes like his thoughts, he will, through this process, become superior.

Mastery of Fate

Instead of being controlled by the impressions received from environment, he will control those impressions, and use them as material in the construction of his own larger life, and the greater destiny that must follow.

While mind is in the attitude of self-supremacy, man's contact with the world will not affect him contrary to the way he desires to be affected; because he controls the impressions that come from without, and can completely change their natures before they are accepted in consciousness. Or, he may refuse to accept them entirely.

In the midst of adversity he does not permit the adverseness of the circumstances to impress his mind, but opens his mind to be impressed by the great power that is back of the adversity. His mind is not impressed by the misdirection of power, but by the power itself.

Therefore, instead of being disturbed, he is made stronger.

There is something of value to be gained from every disagreeable condition, because within every condition there is power, and there are always greater possibilities latent than the surface indicates.

Through original thinking these greater possibilities are discerned; and when mind is in the attitude of self-supremacy, it may choose to be impressed by the greater possibilities only, thus providing more material for the reconstruction of man, and his destiny, on a larger and superior scale.

It is therefore evident that self-supremacy is indispensable; and it is attained by placing all life, all thought and all action upon the principle that man is

Mastery of Fate

inherently master over everything in his life; and by refusing absolutely to believe that we can be controlled by environment under any condition whatever.

Mastery of Fate

Chapter 3

Superior Thoughts

THE statement that the conditions and circumstances of man's physical world are the direct, or indirect effects of the active elements in his mental world, is fully demonstrated by comparing the external and internal phases of life in any person. The correspondence between the two is exact. Every misfortune in the life of any individual, barring accidents produced by nature, can be traced to incompetence in some way, or to the misapplication of ability. And even those adverse conditions that come from nature's seeming irregularities can be wholly avoided through the development of superior insight.

The largest number of misfortunes comes from doing the wrong thing at the wrong time; and this is caused by confusion in the mental world, or by an obtuse judgment.

The mind that is constantly in a state of poise and harmony, judges well, and will never misdirect any thought, force or action. Therefore, by cultivating those states, anyone can gain the power to do the right thing at the right time.

A great many conditions that surround the average individual are not produced by himself and for this reason he does not hold himself responsible; but when a person enters circumstances that have been created by others, he simply enters something that corresponds with his own mental world.

No person with normal mind will voluntarily enter conditions that are inferior, or that do not correspond in any way to himself. The fact that he accepts, or borrows the environments produced by others, proves that he either belongs there, or that he does not know where he belongs.

When we enter blindly into disagreeable circumstances, our own blindness is at fault; therefore, the external circumstance is the indirect effect of a certain action in our own minds.

A person with great ability, who can practically apply his ability, will never be found at work where recompense is inadequate. Though a person with great ability who does not possess the practical element, may remain in a position that is inferior. In this case ability is misdirected, and the person's own mentality is the indirect cause of the undesirable circumstance.

The mind that is gentle, orderly and beautiful in character will inspire admiration in many places where associations are exactly to his liking. He is wanted among the best of his kind, and has the privilege to select the characters of his social world. Others may call him fortunate, but he has attracted ideal associations because he himself can give ideal companionship. Having developed a worthy mind, he belongs where minds of worth congregate; and through such associations gains inspiration for the development of still greater worth. This not only promotes his advancement in his field of action, but enables him to attract, meet and enjoy still better associations in the future.

When a beautiful character is found among inferior associations, the cause is usually a lack of positive quality. A number of beautiful characters are purely negative, and are therefore hiding the greater part of their true worth. They are far better than they appear to be, and they possess more than they use; but as it is only what we use that counts, such characters will be found in associations that measure exactly, not with what they are, but with what they use and express.

A genius may have no opportunity to employ his great ability; and if so, there is a reason. If he is really competent, there are a hundred excellent places open to him; but if he has only genius and little or no talent, he is not competent. If he has only the capacity, but not the art of turning his power to practical use, he can do nothing of value; and it is results that merit the good places in life.

His misfortune is therefore not due to any exterior adversity, but is caused directly by a state of his own mind.

His misfortune, however, will vanish, and great and good things come instead, when he transforms his genius into talent, and learns to do something that the world wants done.

There is many a skilled workman who keeps himself down because he is constantly out of harmony with his associations. By resisting everything and antagonizing everybody, he keeps his own inferior side always in view. His skill is submerged beneath his personal inferiority, and he is judged, not by what he hides, but by the imperfections that he willingly presents to the world.

A man who persists in revealing nothing but his inferior side, cannot expect promotion; to promote such a man would be a loss to the institution; and those in authority usually feel this fact instinctively. Every enterprise is continued for results; therefore, everything that interferes with results should be eliminated. To give a conspicuous place to someone who breeds discord, hatred and confusion, will positively interfere with results; therefore, such a person

Mastery of Fate

does not justly deserve promotion, no matter how perfect his individual product may be.

The man who is against the world will array the world against himself, and must take the consequences. His fate will not be pleasant, but he alone is to blame.

To do good work is necessary; but it is also necessary to make good as a man, if the best places are to be secured. Therefore, hide your inferior side until you have destroyed it entirely. Surround your skillful labor with a personal atmosphere that breeds harmony, wholesomeness and character, and the best position in your field of action will be opened to you.

There are thousands of people who claim they have not secured a fair chance; but if that be true, the mental worlds of those very persons are the causes. There is something in their mental makeup that places their ability and skill in a false light before the world.

The same is true of the man who is constantly misunderstood. He is not revealing himself as he really is; his real nature is misdirected during the process of expression, and everybody is deceived. That something that produces the deception exists in the person's own mind, and so long as that something remains, he will misplace himself, and will not meet the friends nor the opportunities that really are his own.

The misplacing of oneself is due to a lack of judgment, or to a malarrangement of one's personal powers and characteristics.

But judgment can be remarkably improved in anyone through the development of original thinking and interior insight; and the various powers of the person can be placed in perfect order and harmony with each other through the practice of bringing out the greater possibilities in every phase of being.

The habit of permitting everything we come in contact with to impress our minds, and suggest this course or that method is responsible for a great deal of misdirected effort; therefore, the attitude of self-supremacy becomes indispensable.

A large number of people have been induced to enter circumstances where they do not belong, through the exercise of an abnormal sympathy. Such a sympathy, called forth by a few selfish friends, has also kept many a great mind working in a narrow field, while scores of large, and even extraordinary opportunities were constantly waiting.

To correct this condition, train yourself to sympathize only with the superior side of people and the greater possibilities of things.

When you sympathize naturally and constantly with the superior side of people, all the desires of mind will gradually fix their attention upon the superior; and when all the desires of mind desire the superior you will be irresistibly drawn into superior association. And nothing, not even old abnormal sympathies can keep you away from your own.

When you sympathize with the greater possibilities in things, your attention will be constantly turned upon the greater; your mind will be more and more impressed with the greater, until every thought becomes a power for greatness; and with this power you will move into greatness, regardless of any obstacle that may appear in the way.

Mastery of Fate

The power of sympathy is one of the greatest powers of attraction in existence; therefore, when we sympathize only with the superior, we will be drawn into superiority, and this will steadily change our environments for the better. Thus, by producing a change in the mental world, we can revolutionize the external world.

When life is viewed comprehensively, it becomes very evident that the actions of the person determine what the external conditions and circumstances of that person are to be; but every personal action is caused by a mental action; therefore, the change of environment must be preceded by a change of mind.

To master thought is to master fate; but thought cannot be mastered until mind acts exclusively upon the principle that man is inherently complete master over his entire domain.

The strongest evidence that can be produced in favor of the statement that man's circumstances are caused by the active elements of his mental world, is that of creative ability, because it is being demonstrated every day that the man with a strong creative mind has destiny at his feet.

Creative ability can absolutely change all circumstances; but it is not an external power; it is simply an active element in mind.

Chapter 4

Creating the Spirit of Success

THE mastery of fate implies the constant improvement of everything in one's world physical or mental; and since the improvement of one's exterior environment requires financial increase, the problem of recompense and reward must be solved.

There are vast numbers who claim they are not being remunerated according to their worth, and this claim is keeping the industrial world in constant turmoil.

The result is detrimental to everybody, whether they are directly connected with industrial activity or not. Therefore, to find a solution for the problem would be one of the greatest discoveries that could possibly be made.

That a great deal of injustice exists in the world, is true; and that many who are strong are taking advantage of multitudes that are weak, is also true; but there is a peaceful way for every individual to secure his own. And it remains wholly with the individual.

There is no remedy in sight that the whole world can adopt, through which industrial justice can be established by law; but each individual can so relate himself to the world that his recompense will correspond exactly with his worth. To do this he must neither undervalue nor overvalue his work; and he must not compare his legitimate efforts with the efforts of those who employ questionable means. There are a great many who think they are worth more than they really are, because they compare themselves with the unscrupulous.

Mastery of Fate

When a certain person gains great wealth through illegitimate means, many imagine that they ought to gain as much; they are just as good and just as able as he, and work equally as hard.

But in the mastery of fate all kinds of unjust methods must be eliminated completely, because in the creation of one's future there must be no flaws, or the entire structure may have to be discarded.

There is no wisdom in making any comparison between oneself and the man who is gaining wealth by undermining his own future welfare. We do not care for the destiny of such a personage, and there is only loss in store for those who imitate his ways.

Whether we are gaining as much as this one or that one is not the question at all; the question is, are we receiving what we are actually worth? If we are not, we must find the cause, and the way to remove that cause.

If you are receiving all that you deserve, make yourself more deserving, and you will receive more; but if you are not receiving your share, learn the reason why. If you are to blame, change yourself; if your present work is to blame, use your present work as a steppingstone to something better.

The average person, who thinks he is underpaid, will find himself to be the real cause; therefore, the change of himself is the remedy. And he is usually to blame in this respect, that he overvalues his work and undervalues himself.

No one can advance in life unless he values himself correctly. The man who lives a "common" life, and continues in "ordinary" attitudes of mind will stay "down," no matter how hard he works or how well he performs his particular labor. For this there are several reasons.

It is not simply the visible product of brains or skill that the world pays for; the world also pays for what man contributes to life.

If your personal life is inferior, you give your vocation the stamp of inferiority; and a "common" atmosphere, so detrimental to the progress of any enterprise, goes with you, wherever you may be employed.

If you carry an atmosphere of worth, advancement is in store without fail, because the world does recognize worth, and pays well to secure it.

It is not only the work, but the life that surrounds that work that counts. It is not only the idea, but the words through which it is expressed that carry conviction. And it is not only the ability of the man, but the way he presents that ability that commands attention from the world.

When you present your ability in a crude, common attitude, and present yourself in an atmosphere of inferiority, you are hiding the larger part of your worth, your ability and your skill. And you will be paid only for that which the world can see.

The rays of a skilled mind or a brilliant intellect cannot be seen at first sight, through the dense atmosphere of personal recklessness and crudeness; and the world does not possess the second sight.

But no man can surround himself with a clear atmosphere an atmosphere that reveals the best there is in him unless he values himself, and aims to express his real worth in every thought and action. If a man has superior ability, let him demonstrate by his own presence that he is neither common, inferior nor ordinary. The world demands demonstration; and anyone can detect a real man, no matter what clothes he may wear.

The world is constantly in search of competent men, and when you prove yourself to be competent, you will have more rare opportunities than you can fill.

When the average man begins to live, and takes just as much pride in living a real life as he does in producing a good machine, the industrial world will be revolutionized for the better, and every man will receive all that he knows he is worth.

To value yourself correctly, understand the unbounded possibilities that are latent within you, and live in the realization of the greater things that you know you have the power to do. This will produce in mind the consciousness of superiority, and through this consciousness, superior impressions will be formed in mind. From these impressions will come superior thoughts; which in turn will develop superiority in you; because a man is as he thinks.

The principal reason why a man who is down, remains there, and continues to appear as ordinary as his environment, is because he permits his mind to be impressed with everything that his environment may suggest. His thoughts are therefore the reflections of his surroundings, and he is like his thoughts.

Therefore, the man who would become different from his environment must learn the art of original thinking, and must enter the attitude of self-supremacy.

Mastery of Fate

The principal reason why a man is underpaid is because he does not value himself, and therefore hides behind personal inferiority the greater part of his ability.

Another reason is because he works only for the wages that are coming to himself. He refuses to do more than is absolutely necessary, lest someone might be benefited. This attitude produces the cramped condition, which in turn reacts upon the purse.

The man who is afraid to do too much, usually fails to do enough; at any rate, he produces that impression, and his recompense is lowered accordingly.

On the other hand, the man who does his best at all times, regardless of the scale of wages, not only produces an excellent impression everywhere, but makes those in authority feel that he wants the enterprise to succeed. He is therefore better paid, because such men are valuable. They are wanted everywhere, not because they do more than they are paid for, but because they are a living power for success wherever they are called upon to act.

The spirit of success breeds success; and the man who takes a living interest in the enterprise for which he works, even doing more than he is expected to do when the occasion demands, is creating the spirit of success, and will soon share in the greater success that follows.

Among the underpaid, by far the largest number is composed of those who submit absolutely to their present conditions, and therefore remain not only in bondage to unscrupulous taskmasters, but also to their own environments and mental limitations.

Mastery of Fate

They are the many weak, of whom some of the strong take advantage; and it is in behalf of these that reformers demand a change in the order of things. But it is not a change in the order of things that the world requires; it is a change of mind. And when the change of mind is produced, all other necessary changes will inevitably follow.

If you are underpaid because you have submitted to the power of the unscrupulous, cease to live in the attitude of mental submission. Do not antagonize the powers to which you have submitted, and do not resist your present condition. In your external life continue as usual for a period; but change absolutely your internal life.

What we resist we fear; and we always continue in bondage to that which we fear.

What we antagonize, we meet on the inferior side, and thus enter into contact with the very things we desire to avoid. We shall never get rid of the inferior so long as we resist the inferior; and whatever stays with us will impress our minds. Therefore, by resisting the inferior, we produce inferiority in ourselves.

Begin your emancipation by removing your attitude of self-submission; cease to believe that you must remain down where you are. Change your mind; know that inherently you are master over everything in your own domain, and resolve to exercise your supremacy. Refuse to be impressed by your environment; and learn to impress your own mind with superior impressions only. Recreate your own mind according to a higher standard of power, ability and character; thus you will recreate both yourself and your surroundings; because by making yourself stronger and more competent, you will be wanted where surroundings are better, and recompense greater.

Mastery of Fate

The reason why those who are mentally weak remain in submission to inferior environments, is because they either do not attempt to become strong, or because they use up their mental powers resisting adversity.

Every person, no matter how submerged he may be, who will arouse his own interior strength, exercise his own supremacy over his thoughts, thus thinking his own superior thought, will gradually rise out of his condition; and before long he will find both emancipation and the reward of a better place in life. This is the only orderly method to freedom; and will produce permanent freedom. And it is the only natural method to greater gain and better conditions.

However, attention must not be centered too much upon mere financial gain. The principle is abundance of everything that is necessary to produce a complete life on all conscious planes; and the perpetual increase of all these things as life eternally advances.

But these things man himself must create; and creative power increases through the development of character, ability and self-supremacy.

Chapter 5

We Can Create Any Fate

TO master fate it is necessary to approach all the elements of fate in the proper mental attitudes; because since everything in the external world responds to the active forces in one's mental world, these forces should so act as to call forth only the response desired.

The idea of mastery will arouse in the average mind a tendency to control objective things with the will; but we must remember that fate is not controlled; fate is created.

When we can create any fate that we may desire, we have mastered fate; but not until then.

The mastery of fate does not call for the controlling actions of the will, but for the constructive actions of the creative energies; and since the domineering use of the will scatters creative energy, such an attitude of mind must never be permitted.

All desire to control or influence persons or things must be eliminated completely, because such a course will only defeat our purpose.

We do not master fate by compelling things to come our way; or by persuading persons to promote our objects in view. Things will come of themselves when we demonstrate our ability to use things; and persons will cooperate with us in every way possible when we prove the superiority of both ourselves and our work.

The weakest mind of all is the domineering mind, and since such a mind has but little creative energy, the man who domineers cannot fulfill, legitimately, a single desire. And what he does control through force, will later on react to his own downfall.

It is the meek that inherit the earth, because such minds have the greatest creative power. What we create, we inherit; no more, no less. Therefore, when we gain the power to create much, we shall inherit much.

To meet everything in the attitude of harmony is of the highest importance, because whatever we enter into harmony with, while in a state of aspiration, that we meet on the superior side.

The qualities that we enter into mental contact with, we absorb; therefore, it is a great advantage to mentally meet the superior only.

When we constantly aspire, and live in harmony with everything, we enter into true relationship with the better qualities that are latent in every person or condition with which we come in contact; and consequently permit the superior things in life to impress our minds at every turn. And the value of having only superior impressions in mind is so great that it cannot be calculated.

Superior impressions originate superior thoughts; and as man is as he thinks, superior thoughts will develop superiority in him. And the superior man creates a superior fate, a better future and a more wonderful destiny.

By entering into harmony with all things, and by constantly dwelling in the aspiring attitude, you absorb the good qualities from your enemies and your adversaries. And since evil is only the good perverted, when you take the good out of anything, there is nothing left to be perverted;

Mastery of Fate

consequently there can exist no more enmity nor adversity in that place.

Absorb the good power that is back of adversity, and adversity ceases to be. In this way, we can truthfully say, "We have met the enemy, and they are ours," because the very life of that which was against us has been appropriated by ourselves and engaged to work for our interest and promotion.

This principle, if carried out in every detail of life, would completely revolutionize physical and mental existence; and would reduce trouble, discord, adversity and enmity to practically nothing. The most disagreeable circumstances will change and become models of perfection simply through our attitude in calling forth the superior side; and when we enter into harmony with any circumstance while we are in the aspiring state of mind, we call forth the superior qualities of that circumstance, and the greater possibilities that are always latent everywhere.

When we meet circumstances of any description, we should never resist the undesirable elements, if there be any; nor find fault with the deficiency; but should search immediately for the possibilities. The questions are, what that circumstance can give; and how we may secure everything of worth that it can give.

Every circumstance you meet contains something for you; because it is made to enrich your life, to serve you, and to promote your welfare in every way possible.

By meeting a circumstance in the harmony of aspiration you call forth its real possibilities, and especially if you look directly for those possibilities. When you take an active interest and a friendly interest in the constructive powers of

Mastery of Fate

a circumstance, those powers will place themselves in your hands, and every disagreeable element will disappear.

By taking the best out of every circumstance, and by transmuting all the forces you meet so that they become your forces, you add so much to your present life that you rise readily to a higher position, where superior circumstances and still greater possibilities will be met.

Any circumstance can be changed, if constantly approached in this way; or you will change so much that far better circumstances will be ready to receive you.

Directly connected with the attitude of harmony is the attitude of love; and the way we love, as well as what we love, is of the highest importance in the mastery of fate.

The law is that we steadily grow into the likeness of that which we love; and the reason is that what we love is so deeply impressed upon mind that it never fails to reproduce itself in thought.

Anything that enters mind while mind is in the state of deep feeling, is deeply impressed; and it is the deepest impressions that serve as patterns for the creative energies.

Love only that which has high worth, and never permit the common, the ordinary or the inferior to enter the world of feeling.

Love the true side of life; love the soul side of persons; and love the greater possibilities that are latent in circumstances, conditions and things. And love these things with a passion that thrills every atom in your being. The result will be simply remarkable.

Mastery of Fate

Where the heart is, there we concentrate; and where we concentrate we give our life, our thought, our ability and our power. Therefore, if we wish to build up the superior, we must deeply love the high, the true and the worthy, wherever these may be found.

When difficulties are met, they should be met in the attitude of joy; and we should look upon the experience as a privilege through which greater power may be brought into evidence.

To count everything joy is not a mere sentiment, but the application of a great scientific principle. The mind that meets everything in joy, conquers every time, because the attitude of joy is an ascending attitude; it transcends, and goes above that with which it comes in contact.

Therefore, whatever we meet in the attitude of joy, we rise above; and whatever we rise above, that we overcome in every instance.

The feeling of joy is also expansive, enlarging and constructive, and is a developing power of extreme value.

To count everything joy may at first seem difficult; but when we realize that the attitude of real joy rises above everything, and overcomes everything by taking life to a higher level, we shall soon find it easier and more natural to meet everything in joy than otherwise.

Chapter 6

He Can Who Thinks He Can

A GREAT many new ideas of extreme value have recently appeared in current thought, but one of the most valuable is the idea that "he can who thinks he can;" and in the mastery of fate it will not only be necessary to keep this idea constantly in mind, but also to make the fullest possible use of the law upon which this idea is based.

To accomplish anything, ability is required; and it has been demonstrated that when man thinks he can do a certain thing, he increases the power and the capacity of that faculty which is required in doing what he thinks he can do.

To illustrate: When you think that you can succeed in business, you cause your business ability to develop, because by thinking that you can succeed in business you draw all the creative energies of the system into the business faculties, and consequently those faculties will be developed; and as those faculties are being developed, you gain that ability which positively can produce success in business.

You develop the power to do certain things by constantly thinking that you can do those things, because the law is that wherever in mind we concentrate attention, there development will take place; and we naturally concentrate upon that faculty that is required in the doing of that which we think we can do.

If you think that you can compose music, and continue to think that you can, you will develop that musical faculty that can compose music. Even though you may not have the slightest talent in that direction now, by thinking constantly that you can compose music you will develop that talent.

Mastery of Fate

Results may begin to appear in a few months, or it may require a few years; nevertheless, if you continue to think that you can compose music, you will, in a few years be able to do so. Later on, you can develop into a rare musical genius.

Persistence, however, is required and all thought must be concentrated daily upon that one accomplishment. But this will not be difficult, because before long the entire mind will form a tendency to accumulate all its power and creative energy in the region of that one faculty; and constant development will take place both consciously and unconsciously.

Whatever a man desires to do, if he thinks that he can, he will develop the necessary power, and when the necessary power and ability are gained, the tangible results inevitably follow.

The secret is persistence. After you have decided what you want to do, begin to think that you can, and continue without ceasing to think that you can. Pay no attention to temporary failures; know that you can, and continue to think that you can.

To continue in the consciousness of the law that underlies this idea will bring greater results and more rapid results, because in that case you will consciously direct the developing process, and you will know that to think you can is to develop the power that can.

To keep constantly before mind the idea that "he can who thinks he can," will steadily increase the qualities of faith, self-confidence, perseverance and persistence; and whoever develops these qualities to a greater and greater degree will move forward without fail.

Mastery of Fate

Therefore, to live in the conviction that "he can who thinks he can," will not only increase ability along the desired lines, but will also produce the power to push that ability into a living, tangible action.

In addition to thinking that you can do, try to do; put into practice at once what power and ability you possess, and by continuing to think that you can do more, you will develop the power to do more. To keep before mind the idea that "he can who thinks he can" will also hold attention upon the high ideals we have in view, and this is extremely important.

The fact is if we do not give ideal models to the creative energies of mind, those energies will employ whatever passes before them, as the senses admit all sorts of impressions from without.

The creative energies of mind are constantly producing thought, and these thoughts will be produced in the likeness of the deepest, the clearest and the most predominant mental impressions. Therefore, it is absolutely necessary that the predominant impressions be those into the likeness of which we desire to grow, because, as the impressions are, so are the thoughts; and as the thoughts are, so is man.

When man thinks that he will succeed, the predominant impression is the idea of success. All his thoughts will therefore contain the elements of success, and the forces that can produce success; and he himself, will become thoroughly saturated with the very life of success.

Nothing succeeds like success; therefore, the, man that is filled with the spirit of success can never fail; and what is more, the forces that contain the elements of success will give that man the very qualifications that are essential to success, because like produces like.

And again, the faculty required to produce the success desired, will be the one upon which all these success energies will be concentrated.

When a man has the ability to do certain things, those things will be done; that is a foregone conclusion; and the ability to do what we want to do, comes when we constantly and persistently think that we can do what we want to do.

In the mastery of fate, the law upon which this idea is based will be found indispensable; because, since fate is created, and not controlled, all the elements of fate will have to be constantly recreated.

But no one can do this unless he thinks he can. To change many of the circumstances and conditions that now may surround us, requires more ability and power than we now possess; and to secure this greater power we must proceed to change and improve everything in our world by working in the conviction that we can.

By constantly thinking that we can change all our conditions, we gain a power to produce that change, and will consequently reach our goal.

The man who faces his environment with the belief that he is helpless before so many insurmountable obstacles, will remain where he is; but the man who thinks he can, will proceed to surmount everything, overcome everything, change everything and improve everything; and by constantly thinking he can, he will gain the power to do what he thinks he can do.

Chapter 7

Express Your Individuality

THE purpose of life is continuous advancement, and this necessitates the constant appropriation of the new, and the constant elimination of the old. To promote the first essential, a practical system of ideals is required; and to promote the second, we must master the art of letting go.

If we desire the new to be created, the creative process of mind must be supplied with new and better impressions. Should we fail to do this, the creative energies will employ the old ideas, or impressions that are suggested from without.

In the mastery of fate, one of the greatest essentials is to prevent environment from impressing the mind; and to prevent this, your mind should be filled with your own ideal impressions. But this is not possible to any satisfactory degree unless a definite system of idealism is adopted, because no impression will become strong and predominant unless it is given constant attention.

In this connection, the true use of the imagination becomes extremely important. Everything that we imagine we impress upon mind; therefore, through the imagination we can work ourselves into almost any condition or state of being. In meeting circumstances and events imagination can be made to serve a most valuable service, and thus become directly instrumental in changing environment and fate.

When adversity comes we usually try to find the silver lining; but when we fail to find this, discouragement follows, which in turn but intensifies the darkness and the trouble.

However, we can create a silver lining with the imagination that will serve the same purpose; because when we picture the better side of things, and keep mind steadily upon that picture, the better will impress itself upon the mind. The result is that our thoughts change for the better, and we improve with our thoughts; and the improvement of man means the improvement of his environment. Anyone who is in trouble can work himself out by creating in his imagination the silver lining of emancipation, and keeping the eye single upon that ideal picture.

Anyone who wishes to change his fate can do so by imaging upon mind a different fate, and by keeping that image so constantly before mind that every thought becomes the likeness of the new fate.

The law is that the external world of man changes when his mental world changes; and through the constructive use of the imagination the mental world can be changed in any way that we may desire. When failure seems near, we should image success, refusing absolutely to think of the dark side. By imaging success, we impress upon mind the idea of success; thoughts will be created containing the elements of success, and from these thoughts we shall receive the power that can produce success. Any threatening failure can be overcome and entirely averted by this simple process, providing we live and work as we think.

By training the imagination to serve the system of ideals that we may have adopted, we shah soon gain full control of the process that forms impressions upon mind; and when this is accomplished every high ideal, every great purpose and every superior quality that we have in mind will be so well impressed upon the mental creative process that perpetual growth into every desirable condition must positively take place.

Mastery of Fate

But to promote this advancement, we must learn to let go completely of everything that has served its purpose, or that in any way interferes with the steady progress of the whole man.

To acquire the art of letting go is an accomplishment with few equals, and is easily attained by learning to act upon the subjective side of everything in our own systems. It is the subjective side that holds; therefore, the subjective side alone can let go. The subjective contains the root of every thought, every desire, every tendency, every physical condition and every mental state that exists in the human system; it is the foundation of everything in the personal man, and originates the cause of everything that takes place in the life of man.

Whatever we place in the hands of the subjective, the subjective will continue to hold until it is called upon to let go. Every cause that gains a foothold in the subjective will continue to produce its effects, until the subjective is directed to have it removed; and every impression that is formed upon the subjective will continue to act as a pattern for the creation of thought until a different impression is formed in its place. To know how to deal with the subjective is therefore one of the greatest essentials; and the reason why so few have the power to master their fate is because the conscious direction of the subjective is almost unknown.

Mind has two sides, the outer and the inner; or the objective and the subjective. The objective is the conscious mind; the subjective is the subconscious mind. The objective acts; the subjective reacts. The objective mind gives orders; the subjective carries them out. The objective selects the seed and places that seed in the subjective; and the subjective causes that seed to grow and bear fruit after its kind. Whatever the objective desires to have done, the subjective has the power to do, and will do, if properly directed; though it must be properly and consciously directed.

In the average mind the subjective is directed ignorantly and irregularly; sometimes for good, more frequently otherwise. Therefore, the results are as they are; uncertain, unsatisfactory and limited. However, when we learn to direct the subjective consciously and with method, we shall be able to produce any result desired, at any time desired.

To direct the subjective, the will must be employed, as it must be in all forms of direction; and in the use of the will is where the real secret is found. The will must not act upon the external phase of any idea, desire or condition, but must intentionally act upon the internal side only.

When you move a muscle, the will acts upon the subjective side of that muscle. If the will should act upon the objective side, the muscle would become stiff, unable to move at all. Likewise, when the will acts upon the objective side of any idea, desire, tendency, habit, mental state or physical condition, no change whatever will take place. But the very moment that the will acts upon the subjective side of those things, they will begin to change according to the desire predominant in mind at the time.

Therefore whatever we wish to remove from the subjective, we should direct the will intentionally upon the subjective side of that which we desire to remove, and desire deeply to have that something removed.

It may require some training to master this process, but when the process is mastered, we can drop anything from mind instantaneously. Any idea, any habit, any desire, any state of discord or confusion, any diseased condition all can be eliminated completely from the system, when we acquire the art of letting go.

To train the objective mind to act directly upon the subjective, consciousness should be more thoroughly developed in the realms of the finer feelings and the finer elements of life. Efforts should be made to come in touch with the higher vibrations in the system, because whenever we act in the higher vibrations, we act upon the subjective.

Whatever we desire the subjective to do while we act in the finer feeling of the higher vibrations that the subjective will proceed to do.

To act consciously and directly upon the subjective will also deepen the realization of life, which is extremely important; because the deepest life gives the strongest power, and in the creation of a greater destiny we need all the power we can secure.

When this deepening of life is continued in the serene attitude, mind is kept constantly in touch with the source of unbounded power, and thus receives as much power each day as may be required. This brings us to one of the greatest essentials in the mastery of fate living; because there is nothing that contributes so much to the supremacy of man as a real, full life.

To bring out the best that is within him, man must not merely exist; he must live. When man actually lives he is what he is, and is all that he is. He does not try to be something else, or someone else. He does not imitate, but continues to be himself. And this is one of the secrets in the creation of a greater destiny.

Mastery of Fate

The average person does not try to be himself, but tries constantly to imitate. He does not try to bring out his own individuality, but tries to fashion his personality and personal life according to some exterior model that is supposed to be the standard in the world's eye. The result is, he misplaces himself; because a person is always misplaced and misdirected when he tries to imitate the life of another; and no misplaced person can master his own fate.

Such a mind goes willingly and unconsciously into all sorts of foreign conditions, and then wonders what he has done to bring about such a mixed and undesirable fate.

When the individual tries to be himself, he will begin to act wholly in his own world, the only world where he can be his very best. And by trying to be himself, he begins to draw upon the unbounded possibilities that exist within himself, thus making himself a larger and a greater being constantly.

The individual that tries to imitate persons or environments does not express himself; therefore, his own hidden powers continue to lie dormant.

To express one's own individuality, and to be oneself, the greatest essential is to live real life; the life that is felt in the depth of inner consciousness.

To be yourself, be all that you are where you are, and greater spheres of action will constantly open before you. Be satisfied to be what you are, but do not be satisfied to be less than all that you are.

When one begins to live in the depth of real life, and begins to draw upon his own inexhaustible self, he will find that he is so much that there is no end to the possibilities that exist in his own life and his own world.

Chapter 8

The Four Parts of Fate

EVERY person finds himself in a certain environment, in a certain physical condition, in certain mental states, with certain abilities and opportunities, and with certain obstacles and limitations. In a world with others, he finds himself in a world of his own; and he calls this world his fate. But what is the cause of it all?

He knows that he is responsible for some of it, but he is quite sure he is not responsible for all of it. But who is? He wishes to know, in order that he may eliminate the undesirable, and constantly improve upon that which he wishes to retain.

When we analyze fate we find that it has four distinct parts, each of which comes from its own individual cause.

The first is the creations of nature that man has voluntarily entered into; the second is the creations of the race that man as an individual has accepted as his own; the third is the creations of certain individuals to which man has closely related himself; and the fourth is the creations of the individual himself.

That man voluntarily entered into the first three, is a fact easily demonstrated; though he might not have been wide awake when he did so. Those parts of your fate that you have not created, you have selected; though too often you made your selection in the dark.

In the mastery of fate it is therefore not only necessary to produce the very highest creations through your own creative efforts, but it is also necessary to obtain that wisdom, or interior insight through which the proper selections may be made from those other sources that do invariably contribute to your fate.

Those creations of nature that we may find in our own environment, are filled with unlimited possibilities, whether they appear favorable or not. What they are to do to us depends upon what we decide to do with them.

We may take the elements of nature and convert them into high and constructive uses, or we may permit ourselves to remain in bondage to those elements. The bondage, however, is not produced by nature, but the way we relate ourselves to nature.

To master that part of fate that we receive from nature, the secret is to be in harmony with nature at all times, and under all conditions, and to try constantly to employ constructively every element in nature with which we may come in contact.

That part of fate that has been received from the race is called heredity, and is usually looked upon as a permanent factor in life; but there is no heredity that cannot be changed.

Acquire the art of letting those things go that you do not want, and proceed to improve upon those that you do want.

Use undeveloped hereditary conditions as channels through which to reach the greater things you have in view. Back of every condition there is a power; that power can be developed, and when it is, the old, inferior condition disappears.

What is called the "world," with all its perversions and obstacles, is simply raw material, out of which the strong mind can build almost anything that he may desire. But the "world" must not be met in the belief that things as they are, are permanent and insurmountable; but as the builder meets his material.

Work in the idea that "he can who thinks he can;" develop interior insight so that you may know how to select the material you desire; and develop your mind into a strong mind by entering the attitude of self-supremacy.

We have the same mental power over circumstances and conditions as we have physical power over iron, lumber and coal. Every event that transpires in daily life contains an opportunity; but we must have the insight to see it, and the power to employ it.

The creation of those individuals with whom we come in personal contact, constitute frequently a predominating factor in our destiny, because since we are more or less wedded to our associations, our minds accept impressions from such sources to a very great degree; but this interferes with original thinking, and consequently, with our own mastery of fate.

Therefore, that part of fate that we receive from friends, relatives and personal associations, must be carefully selected through insight and through the principle that "when we become better, we meet better people." Instead of being indiscriminately influenced by our friends, we should accept their mental gifts as we accept their hospitable repast to be masticated, digested and assimilated by ourselves.

What to do with close relations that refuse to cooperate with us, is a great problem that becomes extremely simple when we decide to live our own life in such a way that no person's liberty or idea of liberty is disturbed.

Be a model character that does things; and everybody will soon go with you to the superior life you have in view.

Give your best to everybody and the best will certainly come to you if you give the law the time required, and do not force changes by impatience and lack of faith. Change yourself, and all other desirable changes must positively follow.

Chapter 9

Making the Ideal Real

EVERY factor in the fate of man responds to the life of man; and every element in the life of man is governed, directed, changed or modified by the thought of man. Therefore, as thought goes, so will the creative causes of fate go also. For this reason, if fate is to be improved, thought must move upward and onward; and since thought follows ideals, to him who would master his fate, ideals become indispensable.

But it is not only necessary to have ideals; it is also necessary to make real our ideals. This, however, seems difficult for the average person to do, because between the real and the ideal there appears to be a gulf that he does not know how to bridge.

Even many of the greatest philosophers in the world have failed to realize in a practical way what their finer perceptions had discovered; though this is not strange, because it is the prophetic faculty that sees the ideal, and the scientific faculty that makes the ideal real; and these two faculties are not always found in the same man.

The complete man, however, has both; and he who would master his fate must be complete. By the prophetic faculty we do not me the power to discern the future, because with the future we are not concerned; we are living in the eternal now and in the eternal now we shall always continue to live.

The prophetic faculty is the power to look back of things, within things and above things; thus discerning basic laws, fundamental principles and the unbounded possibilities that exist everywhere. It is seeing the ideal; and the ideal is not a mere mental picture, but the discovery of something higher, something better and something greater than what is actually realized now. The prophetic faculty discovers what can be done now if we choose to do it.

This faculty is developed through the constructive use of the imagination, the constant use of interior insight, and the practice of looking for the greater possibilities in everything with which we come in contact.

The mere discovery of the great is not sufficient; the ideal must be made real. It is not the dreaming of things, but the doing of things that produces a better fate and a larger destiny. But we must perceive the greater things before we can do the greater things; and to perceive the greater things is to have ideals. To make real the ideal, the scientific faculty is required; and this faculty develops through scientific thinking and through the practical application of every principle and law discovered.

To make real the ideal, the first essential is to remove from consciousness the gulf that seems to exist between present attainment and the greater possibilities. Refuse to think of this gulf, because to think of it is to impress the mind with the idea that the greater is beyond us. This impression will prevent mind from reaching the greater, and will also produce frequent states of despair. Such states not only weaken mind, but cause man to give himself up to the influence of environment.

A discouraged mind, submitting itself to environment, is impressed with failure, weakness, inferiority, and the tendency to go down grade; while the mind that is to master fate must go the other way. To remove the seeming gulf from mind, turn attention not only upon the ideal you desire to reach, but try to see the ideal of yourself as well. By so doing you impress the ideal of yourself upon your mind; thoughts like the ideal self will be created, and your personal self becomes like the thoughts you think. Consequently, by a simple process, the personal self is made to improve constantly, daily becoming more and more like the ideal.

To realize constant personal advancement is to prevent all thoughts of discouragement, and also to enter the power of that law through which gain promotes gain, and much gathers more.

The law is that you begin to realize the ideal in your personal life when the personal self begins to grow into the likeness of the ideal. Therefore, to yearn for ideals while nothing is being done to make yourself more ideal, is to continue to keep yourself away from your ideal.

It is like that attracts like, and only those who are alike will be drawn into the same world; consequently, to live in the same world with your ideal, you must become like your ideal. The ideal cannot come down to you; ideals never move that way; but you can go up to your ideal, and that is the true way for you to move.

To make any part of the personal self ideal, place before the creative powers of mind the corresponding ideal of your true self; and it must be remembered that your true self is not something distinct from your ideal self, because the two are one.

The ideal of yourself is you; you are the ideal side of yourself; the actual or external side of yourself is only a partial expression of the ideal or true self. The ideal side of man is the complete side; and the complete side is you. You are not the incomplete side, because if you were there would be no source for anything in your being; not even the incomplete or external side would have a source, and consequently could not exist.

Incompleteness cannot come from incompleteness, because an incompleteness is a partial effect of a complete cause. Incompleteness can come only from completeness; therefore, the fact that the personal self is incomplete proves that it comes from a self that is complete; and since you, yourself, cannot be complete and incomplete at the same time, you, yourself, must be the complete self, while the personal self is but a partial expression of the completeness that exists in you.

When you see this clearly, you will know that you are already ideal; that is, complete, and in possession of unlimited possibilities; and when you know that you are ideal, you will think of yourself as ideal. You will impress the ideal, and the greater possibilities upon mind, and your thoughts will not only be ideal, but will contain the power of the greater possibilities. This power will be expressed in the personal self, because the power of every thought is expressed in the personal self; consequently, the personal self will become larger, greater and more perfect, constantly making real the ideal.

To realize your ideal it is not necessary to change your present environment, or to adopt some radical mode of living; nor is it necessary to be transported to some other sphere.

The ideals that you see are in your own path, directly before you, and will positively be reached through a forward movement. We cannot see the ideals of another mind; therefore, the ideals that you see are in your own path, and can be reached by you. The secret is to move forward in your own life. Be yourself, and bring out all that exists in yourself, and you will gain both the power and the ability to reach what you have in view.

There will be no waiting time; and it is not necessary to become absolutely perfect to make real the ideal. The very moment you begin to develop the personal self into the likeness of the ideal self, the ideal life will begin to become real in the personal life; and the mind that impresses itself only with its own selected and superior impressions, will develop the personal self with the greatest rapidity.

To make real the ideal, the principle is to make everything in your life more and more like the ideal. Ideal friendship brings ideal friends; refinement in action, thought and speech brings refined people; greater ability brings greater results in the world of achievement; and better environments come when we develop the power to create the better. A beautiful mental life produces a beautiful physical existence; and by giving the best to the world, the best will surely return.

Chapter 10

Directing Creative Forces

FATE is created by the powers in man; therefore, in order to master fate, man must acquire control over the creative forces in his being. And this is accomplished, not by trying to control these forces, but by changing their courses.

Every force in the system moves through the field of consciousness, and by training the will to act upon consciousness so as to open or close the channels of consciousness in any place, the different forces in the system can be directed wherever desired.

No force can be driven. We cannot drive the force of electricity; but by providing suitable conductors, electricity will go wherever it is wanted, because we have the power to move the conductors about as we like.

The channels of consciousness, more correctly designated the tendencies of mind, are the conductors of the creative forces of the system; therefore, by regulating the tendencies of mind we may cause all, or any desired part of our creative power to accumulate at any time in any place of mind or body.

To regulate the tendencies of mind, the will must act upon the finer or inner side of consciousness; and whatever the will wills to have done while acting upon the finer side, the same will be done. To reach this finer side, mind must enter a perpetual refining process, and must establish this process in every part of the system. Create a strong desire to transform, refine and improve everything with which you come in contact, and the finer consciousness will develop steadily. This is the first essential.

The second essential is to properly meet the forces that come into your life, because every force that comes, comes to act; and how it is met will determine whether its action upon you will be favorable or not.

When you meet a force, you must do something with it, or it will do something with you; you must direct it, or it will pass through your system aimlessly and be lost. Or, if it is an undeveloped force, as most forces are, you will permit the formation of adverse conditions by permitting such a force to pass through your world unguided.

It is the nature of all forces to do things; they cannot be idle; therefore, if you do not give them something definite to build, they will build aimlessly, or destroy ruthlessly.

We are constantly in the midst of powerful forces, and they are all at our command when we know how to command them; but they do not pass under our dominion until they enter our systems.

It is the forces that pass through our own systems that we can direct; and when these are properly, directed, anything we desire to have done can be done; because an enormous amount of energy is generated in the average person, and hourly passes through the person.

When we learn to direct and constructively employ all those forces, it matters not whether we have highly developed parents or not; whether we have a good ancestry or not; whether we were born under favorable conditions or not; whether we have any talents and opportunities or not; we can make ourselves over absolutely; we can change and improve everything in ourselves and in our environments,

Mastery of Fate

and proceed in the creation and realization of a great and superior destiny.

When we place ourselves in a favorable attitude towards all the forces that enter the system, and learn how to direct those forces into favorable channels of construction, every force that passes through the system will become favorable to us, no matter where it comes from, nor how unfavorable it may be before it enters our favorable world.

The secret is to make your own system a transforming, refining and transmuting power. Establish in your system two predominating tendencies and desires to refine everything and to construct superiority out of everything. And every force that enters your system will become a superior constructive power for you; and will build up your talents, promote your purpose, and change your fate as you wish it to be.

The whole world of power is ready to build for the man that is thoroughly permeated with the desire to become more and accomplish more; therefore, the man who lives constantly in the spirit of transformation will reach the highest goal he has in view.

Make no effort to control or influence any force within yourself, or outside of yourself. Simply control yourself to remain constantly in constructive touch with the finer vibrations of the world of force.

It is necessary to meet every force in the serene attitude, and to feel an interior oneness with the real life of all power. When you feel this deeper unity, every force will unite with you, work for you, and promote your purpose.

Mastery of Fate

When the presence of a force is felt in the system, we should enter into mental touch with the inner, finer side of that force, and hold strongly in mind what we desire to accomplish. This will produce the tendency required, and the force will follow the new channel, to do what we desire to have done. To develop this finer and interior feeling, enter into constant sympathy with the inner life of everything, and be always in poise. Employ the finer senses of perception, discernment and deep feeling as frequently as possible, and try every day to feel through your entire system.

Concentrate several times daily upon the higher vibrations that are back of, within and above every atom in your being; and whenever you use the will, turn attention upon the soul or real substance of things.

Chapter 11

How to Develop Internal Insight

THE creative forces that are generated in man, and the cosmic forces that work through man are fundamental causes of fate; therefore, if man would master his fate, he must consciously direct these so that the creations may be what he desires. When he fails to do this, the creative forces will be directed or influenced by suggestions from external conditions and environments; and this is what takes place in the life of the average person; therefore, his fate is so uncertain, so mixed and so unlike his secret ideal.

The methods presented in the previous chapter will enable anyone to get into that state of consciousness where the forces of the system can be turned in any direction; but after a power is under our control, we want to use it wisely, and to the very best advantage.

Good judgment, reason, understanding, and a brilliant intellect will serve this purpose to a degree; but to make the very best use of every power, under every circumstance, another faculty is required. The necessary faculty is interior insight; or the power to discern the causes, principles and laws that lie beneath the surface. It is that sense that all possess to a degree, that feels and knows how things are going, and how they ought to go; and may therefore be called the inside secret of all success, of all great attainments and achievements.

It is through this faculty that man does the right thing at the right time, with or without the aid of external evidence.

The great minds who have taken advantage of exceptional opportunities at the psychological moment, have been prompted to do so by this very faculty; and what is usually termed extraordinary good fortune is but the result of actions that interior insight was instrumental in producing.

No one has ever reached the pinnacle of attainment and achievement without this faculty, and no one ever will. In the absence of interior insight, the greater part of the best ability would be misdirected, and most of the powers of the system would be lost.

Interior insight is not a faculty that has to be acquired; everybody has it to a considerable degree; it is only necessary that it be further developed and consciously employed. And as it deals directly with the finer forces of life, discerning the nature, the present movements and the latent possibilities of those forces, it is in connection with the world of those forces that the faculty must be exercised for greater efficiency.

To bring this faculty into full expression so it may be employed with accuracy in any field desired, the first essential is to exercise interior insight at every possible opportunity. Not that its verdict should be invariably accepted; but its verdict should always be sought. It will be profitable to do this even in minute and unimportant daily affairs, because it is by discerning the law of action in small things, that we gain the power to discern the same law in greater things.

When this faculty is developed, we shall no longer judge according to appearances, and be misled; but we shall judge according to the real facts that are at the foundation of things; and since it is the underlying causes that must be dealt with in the mastery of fate, interior insight becomes indispensable.

Mastery of Fate

Whenever you are in the midst of changes, or have anything to decide, expect to discern the proper course, and decide correctly through the action of interior insight. And have perfect faith in the power of this faculty at all times. This will not only strengthen the faculty, but will in most instances produce the decision desired.

When conflicting ideas come at such times, enter into a deep, serene state of mind, forgetting the various ideas received, and desiring with the whole of life to discern what you wish to know. Remain in this attitude for days if necessary, or until you receive only one leading decision on the subject. You will get it, and the strong, prolonged effort will have developed your interior insight to a remarkable degree.

To determine the reliability of an idea received through insight, test it with reason, from every point of view; and if it continues to remain a predominant conviction, it is the truth of which you are in search. While expecting information through this faculty, mind should be kept as quiet and as elevated in thought as possible. All sentimental or emotional feelings should be avoided, and the imagination must be perfectly still.

The upward look of mind, devoid of restless yearning, but fully serene and responsive, is the true attitude.

Expect to receive the desired information from the superior wisdom of your higher mentality, and know that there positively is such a wisdom.

While expecting this superior wisdom to unfold what you desire to know, be positive to your environment and to everything in the without. Do not permit the senses to suggest anything on the subject. But be responsive to your interior life; that is, feel in the within that your mind is open to the real wisdom from the within.

Never doubt the existence of the superior wisdom within. This will close the mind to that wisdom. You know that there is such a wisdom; you have evidence to prove it every day; and the more faith you have in its reality, the more perfectly will your mind respond to its unfoldment. Another essential to the full expression of interior insight is to refine the physical brain so that the finer mental actions may produce perceptible impressions. This is accomplished by awakening the finer forces of the system, and directing those forces through a deep, serene concentration, upon every part of the brain. This exercise should be taken for a few minutes, several times a day; and the more highly refined you feel throughout the system at the time, the greater the results.

In the use of interior insight, reason and objective understanding should not be ignored, because the best results are secured when the exterior and interior aspects of judgment are developed simultaneously and used together at all times. In this way the mind acquires the power to discern the internal causes on the one hand, and on the other, understands how to adapt the present movements of those causes to present exterior conditions. This brings the ideal and the practical into united action at every turn, which is absolutely necessary.

While exercising the faculty of interior insight, the predominant effort should be to see through things; because the predominant desire, if continued, is always realized.

Chapter 12

Character, Ability and Faith

THE place that each individual is to occupy in the world is determined principally by character and ability; there are other factors, all of which have been mentioned, but these two predominate. When character is absent, the powers of mind or body will be turned into wrong channels, because nothing in the being of man can go right unless it passes through the life of character.

When ability is absent, man becomes a negative personality, incapable of creating a single course of individual action, and is consequently influenced and controlled by everything with which he comes in contact.

The reason why so many beautiful characters are found in undesirable environments is because they lack positive creative ability.

It is ability that supplies the power to do things; and it is character that directs the power so that the things done will be worthy and true.

By character, however, we do not mean simply a state of being good in the ordinary sense of that term; nor is it a mere attitude of mind that holds preference for the right.

Character is an established quality of being, based upon the principle of absolute right. It is a living power with divine consciousness as its source; it is a life that is right, and that thrills every atom in being with the force of justice, righteousness and truth.

Mastery of Fate

Character is a permanent attainment; it cannot be shaken; it cannot, under any consideration, be influenced from without; but it can at all times be unfolded from within.

That character should be necessary in the mastery of fate, is evident when we realize that all the creative powers of man must express themselves through the principle of the absolutely right, if they are to create a better and a greater destiny; because it is through character alone that the right expression of any force or any talent can take place.

Develop ability, and develop character, and you have the foundation for any fate you may desire to create. You have that something that wins every time, regardless of seeming exceptions.

With character and ability combined, no one can fail; and with a high development of these two, anyone can attain, not only great things, but the very greatest of all things.

To promote the highest development and the most thorough use of character and ability, faith becomes indispensable.

Faith awakens everything within us that is superior, and brings out the best that is within. Faith unites man with the Infinite; and no one can accomplish the great things in life unless he works constantly in oneness with the Infinite. No mind can do much without the Supreme; and no one can do his best in any sphere of action unless he lives so near to the Supreme that the divine presence is consciously felt at all times.

We are helped by a higher power, and we can receive far greater assistance and far superior assistance from this same source when our faith is high and strong.

Mastery of Fate

A highly developed mind may accomplish much without faith, but with faith that same mind can accomplish a great deal more; and the same is true of every mind in every stage of development. Faith increases the power, the capacity and the efficiency of everything and everybody.

One of the greatest essentials in the mastery of fate is to have a high goal, a definite goal, and to keep the eye single upon this goal. And there is nothing that causes the mind to aim as high as faith. Faith goes out upon the boundlessness of all things; it passes by the borderland and proves there is no borderland. It demonstrates conclusively that all things are possible, and that there is no end to the path of attainment; and what is more, it demonstrates that this path to greater and greater attainment is substantial and sound all the way.

There is no seeming void; all is solid rock; therefore, it is perfectly safe to go out anywhere into the universal. In the eyes of faith, there is no gulf between the small and the great; from the smaller to the greater there is a path of smooth and solid rock, and anyone may safely reach the greater by simply pressing on.

To master fate, the mind must be determined to reach the highest goal in view, and should realize that the goal can be reached that it is being reached. And there is nothing that makes the mind more determined to reach the heights than a strong, living faith.

Faith sees the heights; faith knows they are there, and can be reached. Therefore, to a mind that would create a grander fate, nothing is more valuable than faith.

To attain faith we must understand that it is not blind belief; it is not belief at all. Faith is a live conviction,

Mastery of Fate

illumined knowledge received at first hand through the awakening of that power within that sees, knows and understands the spirit of things.

Consequently, faith not only awakens higher and mightier powers, and illumines the mind with light, wisdom and truth of incalculable value, but it also brings mind into perfect touch with those laws and principles that lie at the very foundation of all life, all attainment, all achievement, and all change; and it is these laws that mind must employ if fate is to be mastered, and a greater destiny created.

To attain faith, have faith; have faith in the Supreme; have faith in man; have faith in yourself; have faith in everything in the universe; and above all, have faith in faith.

Last, but not least, the man who would master his fate must do things in love. A tangible fate is the result of tangible deeds; but no tangible deed can contribute to a better fate unless is it the product of love.

Desire to do things with a desire that sets every fiber in being aflame; love everything, is being done, with a love that is the living power of the soul itself; and give yourself, your largest self, your whole self to your life and your work. And what you give that will be your fate.

Mastery of Self

Mastery of Self

MAN is made, for attainment and achievement; to ever become greater and greater than he is now — that is the purpose of his life; and to promote that purpose he must ever advance in the mastery of self. To move forward in the path of attainment, everything in the being of man must be employed constructively; every process in mind or body must become a building process, and all the elements and forces in the human system must work together towards the great goal in view; but to direct the whole of self to work for a greater self demands the mastery of self.

No power in man can do what it is created to do, and what it has the capacity to do, until it is directed by man himself; powers, elements, forces, and things are at the disposal of man; they can do only what he directs them to do; they respond only to his control, but before man can gain the power to master forces and things, he must gain the power to master himself.

When man has gained the power to control himself he can control everything in his world without trying to control anything. It is therefore evident that he who is trying to control everything has not learned how to control anything. The true master never tries to master anything, not even himself. He does not have to try to be a master — he is a master. Nor is it necessary to try to be a master in order to reach that state where one is a master; in fact, no person can learn to control himself so long as he tries to control himself. To eliminate every desire to master oneself is the first step towards the attainment of the mastery of self. He who does not wish to control anything is alone prepared to gain the power to control everything.

He who tries to control himself, or who tries to control anything that exists outside of himself gives everything in his being the tendency to work towards the surface; the power

Mastery of Self

that produces the mastery of self, however, can only be gained by training the mind to move in the opposite direction. To master self is to have the power to produce any effect desired in any part of mind or body, and to produce any effect desired it is necessary to produce the corresponding cause; but to produce any cause the mind must act in the world of cause — a world which exists, not on the surface of thought or being, but in the great within.

The harder one tries to control himself the nearer to the surface will the mind act, and the further will mental action be separated from that interior mental state from which one may gain the power to control himself.

He who tries to attain the mastery of self will act entirely upon the outer mental world of effect, and will therefore be unable to create the cause that can produce the mastery of self. The mind must act back of, beneath and above the effect in order to change or produce the cause.

The state of self-mastery is an effect; it is the result of certain attainments; therefore, to produce the state of self-mastery, one must not act upon the state of self-mastery, but must proceed to promote those attainments that naturally result in self-mastery.

It is not possible, however, to promote these attainments while the mind is trying to exercise control over things; to try to control things is to think about things and act directly upon things, and no mind that is acting upon things can act upon the power that controls things.

Each power in the being of man will, when expressed, do the very thing that it is naturally adapted for; that is, it will produce its own natural effect; therefore, to secure any desired effect, the secret is to awaken that power that will, of itself, produce that effect.

However, to awaken any power in the being of man, the mind must act directly upon that state where the power originates; and every power in man originates in the great within. There is an inner source of everything that appears in the human personality, and to master self is to have the power to cause this inner source to bring forth into the personal self whatever we desire to have expressed through the self.

What the self is to be, and to do, is determined by what is expressed through the self; therefore, when we can cause the inner source to bring forth into the self whatever we may desire, the self will be and do whatever we may desire. And when we can cause the self to be what we wish it to be, and do what we wish it to do, at any time and under any circumstance, then it is that we have gained the mastery of self.

Mastery of Self

THE mastery of self is an attainment that has no end. Though everything in mind and body may be mastered today, tomorrow will bring forth from the great within new forces, new talents, new powers, and new fields of consciousness, all of which demand control and direction if they are to serve their purpose and be of the greatest possible use to man.

Everything that exists in the being of man is created for some purpose, and the whole of life is not lived as it is intended to be lived unless every such purpose is fulfilled; but nothing in man can fulfill its purpose unless it is mastered by the ruling power in man.

The attainment of self-mastery is therefore indispensable to the living of life, and the promotion of the greatest welfare of the whole of life.

Those elements, forces, faculties, talents, and functions that are only partially under control do not serve the life of man as extensively as they might; in fact, many of these, even those that we have been conscious of for ages, serve us but little; and the cause is deficiency in the art of self-mastery.

There are only a few minds that accomplish as much with their talents as it is possible to accomplish at present; the majority, even among the most gifted, seldom use their ability in its full capacity because they have only a limited control over that ability.

That person who has perfect control of himself can accomplish from two to five times as much with a given talent as those who have no more self-control than is found among the average.

Mastery of Self

To those who seek to attain much and achieve much, self-mastery is therefore invaluable, though it is equally important in the minor affairs of every-day life; a fact that will readily be admitted when we realize how much distress comes hourly to millions because they cannot control their feelings, emotions, thoughts, and actions.

A large share of the mistakes that are made every moment, can be traced directly to a lack of self-control; and the same can be said of sickness, trouble and failure. To have health, happiness and harmony, peace, power and plenty, self-mastery, to a high degree, is necessary; in brief, the only life that is worthwhile is the life that is lived in the mastery of self.

To attain the mastery of self, it is first necessary to establish firmly in mind the fundamental purpose of mastery. This is extremely important, because to proceed with the wrong purpose in view is to make every effort useless. This, however, is what has been done by nearly everyone who has undertaken the attainment of self-mastery; and nearly all the books that have been written on the subject have been based upon the wrong purpose; they have therefore retarded the very thing which they aimed to promote.

This being true, it is simple to understand why it is practically impossible to find a single person who has attained complete mastery over self.

Nearly every system purporting to teach the art of self-mastery has been based upon the purpose of controlling something, or exercising arbitrary rulership over mind, body, circumstances, and things. But so long as the mind is trying to control something, the power that can control that something will not be gained.

Mastery of Self

We must remember, at the very beginning, that before the power of self-mastery can be developed and the state of complete mastery attained, all desire to exercise control over anything or anybody must be eliminated absolutely.

The purpose of self-mastery is to give the mind the power to make the fullest and the most perfect use of all the gifts that one may possess now; to be one's best in every sense of the term, at all times, and under all circumstances; to fulfill the purpose of life thoroughly during every passing moment; to live a larger life, a better life, and a more beautiful life every day; to be all that one can be now, and to do all that one can do now; to bring forth continually the very best that may exist in the great within, and to use that best in such a way that the very best will always come to pass.

The true purpose of self-mastery is to make yourself more perfect, more competent, and more useful. In other words, to become much and accomplish much, in order that you may not only be your complete self, but also be an inspiration to all those who believe in the new race, the superior race, the race of mental mastery and soul-supremacy.

Mastery of Self

THE problem of causing everything in life to become right will easily be solved when man becomes great enough to produce only that which is right; and this greatness will inevitably come when the mastery of self is attained.

That man may become infinitely more than he is now, and that he can do far greater things than has ever been done before, we know with a certainty; we also know that it is the purpose of human life to go on to greatness and greater greatness, but every step must be preceded by another degree in the mastery of self.

When we understand life we invariably gain a strong desire to develop superiority; first, because it is right to attain superiority, and second, because we may thereby inspire thousands to press on to those same magnificent heights.

We desire to demonstrate superiority, however, not for the sake of applause, but to prove by example what man can do. We seek greatness, not that we may rule over anything or anybody, but that we may fulfill the law of life which declares that man is created to become greater and greater so long as eternity shall continue to be.

Our object is not to control those things that exist about us, but to develop those things that exist within us. We seek the fullness of life, and the power to be of the greatest possible use in life; and we seek self-mastery because through mastery alone can these things be promoted to the very highest degree.

When the true purpose of self-mastery is firmly established in mind, we may proceed to develop the power that does produce self-mastery; but the true purpose must never be ignored, because growth in mastery will awaken new forces, new states of consciousness, and new possibilities, and these must all be properly directed.

The higher the power the stronger its force; therefore, the higher we go in the scale of attainment the more important it becomes to properly direct everything.

The misdirection of the higher forces will not only produce all manner of ills, troubles, and failures, but will produce mental phenomena that is misleading. The understanding of truth or any phase of truth will thereby become extremely difficult; in fact, it will be practically impossible to know the real truth about anything so long as such misdirections prevail;

To avoid absolutely the misdirection of any power, fix attention upon development; seek the mastery of self and everything that exists in yourself because you desire to promote greatness in yourself, and you will continue to remain on the right path.

When every thought is animated with a strong desire for a more perfect body, a larger mind, and a more beautiful soul, every effort towards the attainment of self-mastery will become constructive, and only good results can possibly follow.

The less you think about the outer self, and the more you think about the inner self, the better, because it is through the perfect expression of the inner self that you will gain the power to master the outer self.

To clearly, firmly, and permanently establish in mind what one desires to master is extremely important; also, what self- control will mean when it is attained, and what

Mastery of Self

will happen to mind and body when the power of mastery is exercised.

There is a current belief among many that to master oneself is to have the power to interfere with natural functions at will; to suspend the action of this or that organ without producing serious results, and to violate natural laws without having to under- go any of the natural consequences. Others believe that mastery consists in the forceful control of anything and everything that may exist in one's system or in one's circumstances; but such conclusions are the very opposites to the truth.

The majority, however, entertain those very ideas concerning self-mastery; and this is one of the principal reasons why their efforts to attain self-mastery cannot possibly succeed.

He who has attained the mastery of self never tries to suspend the action of any organ; he never thinks of interfering with natural functions in any way whatever, nor does he ignore or violate a single natural law. He never tries to control anything or anybody, not even himself. In fact, the desire to control has been eliminated completely from his mind. His object is not to control himself, but to make the best possible use of himself; and to try to exercise control over something is to interfere with the best use of that something.

The greatest use of self comes directly from the greatest mastery of self, but it is not possible to attain the greatest mastery of self unless the greatest use of self is made the one sole purpose in view.

He who has no desire to control anything, but is inspired with a strong, irresistible desire to make the greatest use of everything, has entered the path to the mastery of self. Without trying to control anything, everything will naturally and willingly come under his control, and will do whatsoever he may wish to have done.

Mastery of Self

TO master oneself means to direct all the elements, forces, functions, and faculties in the system for the purpose of promoting their natural activities to the highest degree of perfection. To master one's desires does not mean to suspend those desires, but to give those desires more life and power than ever before, and then direct them into channels of action where the greatest and best results can be obtained under present circumstances.

When you have a desire to do a certain thing and the force of that desire is at hand in the system ready to act, but present circumstances will not permit the expression of that desire, instead of suspending that desire, thereby wasting the energy that was ready for action, you simply turn the force of that desire into some other channel. In this way, valuable results may be secured from the force of every desire that appears in the system, whether the original impulse of that desire can be carried out or not.

Whenever a desire is crushed or suspended all the energy that was alive in that desire will be wasted; and the same waste takes place when a desire is carried in the system for hours, days or weeks, to wear itself out, so to speak, without having its active power turned into any channel of constructive action.

To feel a desire is simply to feel the presence of energy; a desire conveys to the mind the fact that there is energy in the system ready to do something; and if this energy is not given the opportunity to do something it will be wasted.

Through the attainment of self-mastery all the energy that comes into action in the system can be turned into any channel of constructive expression that may be convenient at the time; in fact, to master a desire does not mean to suspend that desire so that it is not felt any more, but to change the course of the force that is active in that desire, so that something of value may be accomplished now while that force is in working condition.

The master-mind never destroys a single desire; he not even thinks of putting down a single feeling that may arise in the system; when he cannot carry out the original desire, or when he finds that the original desire is not normal, which is frequently the case, he redirects the forces that are felt in the system causing them to do something else, something that is normal, and that is possible now.

To master the natural functions is not to interfere with the purpose of those functions, but to promote that purpose to the very highest degree of perfection.

You can master a natural function when you can cause that function to perform its work perfectly under all sorts of conditions, and thereafter, to continue to further perfect the perfection of its perfect work.

To master the organs and functions of digestion does not mean that you can cause those organs to digest anything that you might take into the system; self-mastery does not violate law, neither does it willfully admit an enemy in order that it may demonstrate its power to overcome that enemy. Self-mastery does not resist what is not wanted, but gives man the power to create and secure that which is wanted.

To master the organs of digestion would mean to keep those organs continually in such a perfect state of action that whatever the system needs could be digested perfectly, and without the slightest unpleasant sensation at any time or under any circumstance.

Mastery of Self

To master the heart does not mean that you can increase or decrease the heart-beats at will, but that you can keep the heart constantly in its true, normal action, no matter how much confusion or excitement there may be in your immediate environment.

The attainment of mastery, therefore, does not mean to interfere with natural action, but to promote natural action to the highest possible degree of perfection.

The idea of mastery is perfect action of all things at all times, regardless of circum- stances or events. When you attain self- mastery, all things in your system will be doing their work perfectly, at all times, no matter what your work or your environment may be. And, in addition, this perfect action will constantly develop higher degrees of perfect action.

To master the elements and the forces of the system is not only to promote normal action in the chemical world, but to increase the quality and the power of that action by producing new and superior compounds.

Every mind forms different compounds, unconsciously, as the various grades of vibration are entered by the predominating mental states; but what is formed unconsciously is not always desirable, and when it is desirable it is always inferior to what might have been produced through a similar, intelligently directed conscious action.

Mental states of anger usually produce poisonous elements in the system, while states of fear and depression convert healthy tissues into useless, foreign matter. Such matter always clogs the system, thus interfering with natural functions, and producing, directly or indirectly, a number of ills.

Mental states that are lofty, true, and constructive produce chemical compounds in the system that are nourishing and vitalizing, and that have a strong, refining tendency.

Through the power of self-mastery, undesirable compounds may be prevented entirely because the mind that masters self will not create other than wholesome mental states. Through the same power we may so direct and blend the elements of the system that the formation of the most beneficial and the most highly refined compounds may be constantly taking place.

The possibilities of this law are marvelous to say the least; it is through this law that false chemical conditions in the system may be transformed instantaneously into normal and wholesome actions, and it is through this law that all the elements of the physical body may be constantly refined, until absolute regeneration and spiritualization has taken place.

Through this law the physical body can be developed to the very highest degree of purity, wholeness, refinement, and perfection, and made as beautiful as the Ideal Form itself. The application of this law, however, is possible only to those who have attained the mastery of self.

Mastery of Self

TO master the forces of the system, the principal object in view is to gain power to accumulate those forces in any part of mind or body where important work is to be done now; because, by giving all the power at hand now to the work we are doing now, that work will invariably result in a superior product.

To employ this method at all times would not only cause all things to be done well, but all things would constantly be done better, and failure would be a thing of the past.

If we would give the greater part of our active energy to the organs of digestion during meals, and for a short time after meals, we should never have anything but the most perfect digestion. If we would give all the forces of intelligence and genius to the faculty that is in action now, that faculty would invariably do the work of genius, and would never fail to improve upon its own previous record.

The possibilities of self-mastery as applied to the forces of the system are therefore extraordinary; but we cannot master the forces of the system by trying to control those forces, to master any force, the will must act, not upon the force itself, but upon the interior cause of that force.

In the mastery of faculties, the purpose must be expansion and enlargement of conscious action; the average mind needs expansion of consciousness because most of its faculties are too small to give expression to all the energy of the system when concentration and accumulation take place. When this expansion has begun, however, quality, efficiency, and volume may always be secured through the action of any faculty or talent.

Consequently, in the mental world one of the principal objects of self-mastery will be to lead consciousness into the realization of new and greater realms of perception and illumination, and to awaken a greater and greater measure of the great within.

The first real step in the mastery of self is to eliminate all desire to control what is exterior to yourself. Train your mind to desire only the mastery of your own being, and refuse absolutely to even think of con- trolling anything else. We cannot possibly master ourselves so long as there is the slightest desire to control others.

This may seem to be a contradiction of terms, because when one is master, he ought to be master of everything, whether it be in the without or in the within. But though mastery implies the mastery of everything, the fact must not be forgotten that the mastery of the without is simply an effect of the mastery of the within.

The mastery of environments, circumstances, and external things, naturally follows when one has mastered himself; but so long as we try to control external things we can. not control ourselves, because we cannot produce causes while trying to interfere with effects.

The mastery of self can only be attained through the control of the inner side of mind, consciousness, thought, and action; and to control the inner side constantly, the whole of attention must constantly be given to the inner side.

You control the exterior by causing the interior to become exactly what you wish the exterior to be. The principle is, produce the cause you want and you will have the effect you want. The cause can be produced only by acting upon the subjective, because it is only the subjective side that has the power to originate cause; and to act upon

Mastery of Self

the subjective, the forces of the mind must be trained to move towards the within.

However, whenever we try to control that which is exterior to ourselves, the forces of the mind will begin to move towards the without; and it is not possible for the forces of mind to go in while they are going out, neither can the tendency to act upon the within be established in mind so long as the outward movement of mind is permitted in the least.

The mind of the average person has already a strong tendency to move towards the surface; therefore, to remove that tendency completely, the opposite tendency must be given the whole of attention; all the forces of mind must move towards the within at all times, and attention must be concentrated upon the subjective side absolutely without any cessation whatever.

It is not possible to form a tendency towards the inner life while the mind is acting more or less upon external things; a tendency is a continuous movement in a certain direction; therefore, while the mind is acting more or less upon the surface, the continuous movement towards the within will be interrupted and there will be no tendency towards the within.

We cannot train mental tendencies to move in opposite directions; no two forces, directly opposed to each other, can exist in the mind at the same time.

If the entire mind is to be harmonious and constructive, all the forces of the mind must move towards the within; that is, they must move into the mind and not out of the mind. The person, however, who is trying to control external things while he is trying to develop the mastery of self, will cause his mind to be divided against itself. He will consequently control nothing.

When we realize the difference between the control of self and the control of others, and how they are direct opposites in purpose and action, we shall understand why the two cannot exist in the mind together. And since the methods employed in the control of persons and things are antagonistic to those employed in the control of self, it will not be possible to develop self-mastery so long as there is the least attempt to influence others.

It may seem impossible, however, to deal with other minds, especially with younger minds, without exercising some form of influence; but we must remember that there is a great difference between trying to control a mind and trying to instruct a mind.

To control a mind is to compel that mind to neglect its own power; to instruct a mind is to inspire in that mind the desire to use its own power.

To train another mind in the line of right thought and action, do not try to compel that mind to think right or act right; place before that mind ideas that will naturally produce right thought and right action. And this can be done without having the slightest desire to influence or control.

It is upon this principle that the new education is based — the education that will not simply train small minds to remember what great minds have thought, but will train all small minds to become great minds.

Mastery of Self

GREAT is the mind that can leave everybody alone, that can be friendly to those who think what he cannot accept, and that can desire with his whole heart to have everybody be free to be themselves; but it is necessary to have such a mind if we would attain mastery of self.

If we are not to influence anyone it may be a problem to know how far we may go in persuading others to examine the desirability of the good things we have found in life. There is a natural tendency among us all to wish that everybody had all the good that we have, but we frequently go too far in trying to make people accept what they cannot appreciate. From this we observe that the human race is not depraved at all, but is somewhat lacking in judgment.

The best way and the simplest way to persuade others to take advantage of the good that you may have found, is to prove in your own life that what you have found is better.

Never try to compel others to change; leave them free to change naturally and orderly because they want to; and they will want to change when they find that your change was worthwhile.

To inspire in others a desire to change for the better is truly noble; but this you can do only by leaving them alone, and becoming more noble yourself.

Make the most of yourself in your way, and leave everybody free to make the most of themselves in their way; they will when they find that it is better to enter the greater than to remain in the lesser; and that that is better you can prove by the way you live.

All minds want the best, and they will soon know the best when it is constantly before them as a living reality.

People may not accept your theories, but if your life is better than theirs, they will soon do their utmost to live as you do.

After all, what would one have? Is it not life, the best life, the most beautiful life that we all seek?

To completely eliminate all desire to control persons and things, impress upon mind the great fact that it is not what others do, but what you, yourself do, that determines whether good or ill shall come to you.

When this fact is realized, your one desire will be to perfect your own life, thought, and action; you will find that the mastery of yourself will require all of your time and the whole of your attention, and you will interfere with others no more.

The true understanding of freedom will also help a great deal in removing the desire to interfere with others. When one finds that he cannot receive what he is not willing to give, and that so long as we deny freedom to others, others cannot give freedom to us, the relations between man and man become so clear that anyone can understand how to relate himself to the human race.

The best way, however, is to have so much faith in others that you know they will do the best they can without your telling them to do so. Such a faith may not always bring forth the best from everybody, but it will produce a strong tendency in that direction; and besides, it will make of you a superior being. You will advance constantly through such a faith, and thousands will follow your example.

To eliminate all desire to control others, however, is not the only essential; you must also eliminate all desire to control your own person. Nor is this a contradiction; to control the person you must act upon that inner power that can control the person; but it is not possible to act upon the power that is back of the person while attention is centered upon the person itself.

You cannot control the within while trying to control the without; the within is the world of cause, while the person is but the effect of what is being expressed from the inner cause.

As the subjective is, so is the objective; the subjective is the inner life, and originates everything that appears in the objective or outer life.

We must not try to control the person, whether that person belongs to us or to some other soul.

True, we are to master the person, but we cannot master the person by concentrating attention upon the person; we master the person by expressing through the person those conditions and actions that we desire to see in the person, and those can be brought forth only from the within.

You can produce any change desired in the person by creating the cause of that change in the subconscious; and you can make the person express any desired action by creating the subconscious cause of that action. Nothing can be done, however, in the person, or through the person, unless the necessary cause is first produced in the subconscious, or what is frequently termed the subjective side of mind.

It is therefore evident that all effort to control the person or act upon the person, is wasted effort; results can be secured in the person only through that action that deals with the power back of the person, because what this power does, that the person will do also.

Mastery of Self

THE mastery of self implies the power to make the greatest and the best use of self, and to exercise this power is the real purpose of mastery; therefore, those mental states through which this power can act with the greatest efficiency must be cultivated.

The first essential mental state is harmony; complete and universal harmony, harmony with oneself, with everybody, and with everything.

To be in harmony is to be properly related to that with which we may come in contact; and to be properly related to anything is to meet that something in its own world without disregarding the purpose of our world.

To be in harmony with everything is to adapt yourself to everything, and though this is an art requiring much thought and effort, it is absolutely necessary, because when one is not in harmony he is in discord, and discord misdirects energy.

To cultivate harmony, concentrate attention frequently upon the interior principle of harmony, the soul of harmony as it exists in the ideal within.

There is a state in the within that not only is in harmony, but that is harmony; and to mentally grow in the consciousness of that state is to unfold the life of harmony throughout one's entire personality.

The second essential mental state is poise, and its chief value in self-mastery is the part it plays in holding together the energies of the system.

The mastery of self implies the possession of self, the conscious possession of one's entire self; that is, the holding together of the various activities, forces, and elements in the system so that they may all work in unison in promoting the purpose the mind may now have in view. And this is poise.

Through the law of harmony you may change your mental attitudes at will, because when the consciousness of harmony is attained, you have not only the power to change your attitude so as to harmonize yourself with everything, but you also discern instantaneously when to change, and in what way.

Through the law of poise, however, you gain the power to prevent mental change, which at times, and in a certain sense is absolutely necessary.

To be ever the same and yet never the same is to be on the perfect path to the greater life. All the energies of the system must be held together in poise even when you are changing your mental attitudes to harmonize with something that is different.

Every change demands a law through which to produce its change; but this law does not change. The law is ever the same, and yet he who applies this law will be never the same.

The attitude of poise is the changeless attitude through which all energies must pass if constructive results and change for the better are to be secured. It is therefore indispensable to the attainment of self-mastery, because to master the forces of the system is to have conscious possession of those forces, and that is poise.

To cultivate the attitude of poise, combine in consciousness the feeling of power and the feeling of peace. To feel immensely strong, and perfectly serene at the same time, is to be in poise. The feeling of poise produces the feeling of self-possession, and to concentrate attention frequently upon our most perfect mental conception of the state of self- possession will develop the attitude of poise.

The third essential mental state is non- resistance; and the value of this state in the mastery of self is beyond measure.

To practice resistance is to direct attention upon the objective; it is trying to force things, and this causes the mind to act directly upon things; consciousness is brought to the surface, and the mental forces will begin to move towards the without instead of towards the within.

What we try to resist we try to control; and so long as we try to control anything we cannot attain the mastery of self.

The mental actions of resistance employ the external will altogether, something that must be eliminated completely before mastery can take place.

The external will, that is, ordinary will-power, is one of the principal obstacles to the attainment of self-mastery, and so long as we practice resistance this will-power will live and grow.

The stronger the power of the ordinary will, the larger will be the time required to attain the mastery of self, unless that form of will-power is eliminated completely at the beginning. Resistance, however, is the chief promoter of this form of will-power; therefore, non- resistance must be made the one great rule in everything, whether in life, thought, or action.

To practice resistance is to try to overcome by going against; to practice non-resistance is to overcome by going above. Resistance wastes its energy by fighting what it does not want; non-resistance leaves behind what it does not want, and proceeds serenely to employ its energy in creating what it does want.

It is therefore evident that resistance never can succeed while non-resistance always does succeed. To enter the attitude of non-resistance is not to bring your life to a standstill, nor to fold your arms, permitting persons, circumstances, and things to do to you what they like. Non-resistance is a forward movement, while resistance is never anything but retrogression.

The non-resisting mind does not antagonize the wrongs that are behind, and all wrongs are behind, but proceeds in peace to realize the greater good that is before.

The attitude of non-resistance makes man a stronger individuality, and he who becomes stronger will not remain in the hands of the weaker.

To resist what is against us is to continue to be small, and he who is small cannot overcome those obstacles that may seem to be great.

Resistance scatters and wastes energy; non-resistance accumulates and constructively employs energy. Therefore, to practice the former is to remain weak, while to practice the latter is to develop strength and power in greater and greater measure.

To use your power in resisting wrongs is to continue in bondage to those wrongs, because we give our power to that which we resist. To use your power for self-development and self-mastery is to rise superior to every circumstance and condition, which means inevitable victory and complete emancipation.

Mastery of Self

THE fourth essential mental state is receptivity, or the attitude of responsiveness — that attitude that places the mind in perfect touch with everything that it may desire to receive.

The objective or personal life is controlled by causing the objective to respond to the subjective, and there is positively no other law through which the person may be controlled.

It is not necessary to act upon the person to control the person, nor would such action produce any results whatever; the person will respond only to that which is taking place in the within; therefore, to create the desired subjective action, and train the person to respond to that action, is to secure the desired objective action.

The mastery of the personal self depends entirely upon the degree of responsiveness that exists in the person; but how can responsiveness be cultivated in the person if we are not to act upon the person? And if this quality is developed from within, how can the person, in the beginning, respond even to responsiveness?

The fact is that receptivity has its existence primarily in consciousness, and as consciousness fills the personal self, everything that is developed in consciousness will be active in the person.

When you become conscious of the state of receptivity, the person will respond to everything with which you may come in contact, whether the contact be with the without or with the within.

The receptive mind is easily influenced and affected by everything, both good and otherwise; for this reason, no mind should place itself in sympathetic contact with environments that are contrary to its own ideals.

What enters mind from adverse environments or inferior associations will manifest in the person according to the degree of receptivity that may be present at the time; but since it is possible to control the attitude of receptivity so that we come in mental contact only with that which is desirable, every person may determine what he is to receive, and what he is not to receive, from the physical or mental worlds in which he may be living now.

The power that environment may exercise in the life of any person depends entirely upon himself, how receptive he may happen to be; but since anyone can train himself to respond only to those things that are superior to himself, he may eliminate completely every form of influence that may come from those circumstances, persons, or things that are inferior.

It is absolutely necessary that the person should respond to the mind if it is to be mastered by the mind, but since the person, when highly receptive, will respond to everything that enters the mind, nothing that is inferior or undesirable must be permitted to enter the mind.

To prevent this, however, another, and a corresponding state of mind, viz., positiveness, must be cultivated.

The person that is not receptive is barely alive, and can accomplish nothing of real value? receptivity is, therefore, indispensable, and the fact that the receptive person responds to that which is not good, as well as to that which is good, should not cause any hesitancy in the cultivation of receptivity.

Mastery of Self

The person does not respond directly to anything that exists in the without, but only to that which has first entered the mind, and the mind has the power to select from every source what it wants to accept, and reject what it does not wish to use.

To cultivate the state of receptivity, en-courage the actions of the finer forces and the finer vibrations in the system. Whenever these forces are felt, the mind should become quiet and should enter more deeply into the feeling of those forces.

It is the finer forces to which the person responds; therefore, to promote the development of receptivity the action of these forces should be increased perpetually through the entire personality.

Another essential to the cultivation of receptivity is to enter into the closest possible mental touch with the finer elements that permeate all things; mentally live with the soul of things; and this is the true receptivity.

When we realize the great value of receptivity, and find that the person can respond to the low as well as to the high, it becomes necessary to find a method through which this delicate faculty may be so guarded and directed that it will respond only to the superior.

In other words, how shall the mind protect itself from being impressed with the many inferior things with which we come in daily contact?

What we see, hear, or feel, or meet in any way, produces some impression upon the mind; in fact, everything that enters through the senses will impress the mind, and every impression, if sufficiently strong, will affect the mind, and then the person.

We cannot close our eyes to what we see; we must, therefore, find a method through which we may prevent what we do see from impressing the mind when we so elect.

We want all our senses to be thoroughly alive, and we want consciousness to be wide-awake to everything that is taking place in our present state of existence, but we also want the power to close the mental door to every impression from without that is not worthy of being entertained.

This power is found in the state of positiveness, the fifth essential mental state.

So long as the mind is in a positive state, nothing can impress the mind unless that impression is deeply desired, and the reason why is simple.

It is the creative energies of mind that produce the mental impressions, but these energies will do only what they are directed to do by the vibrations that enter the mind. These vibrations may come from without, through the senses, or they may come from within, through the mind's own thinking, and the creative energies will obey those vibrations that have the greatest power.

When the vibrations from without are the strongest, as is the case in the average mind, the creative energies will proceed to form impressions, states, conditions, and thoughts that are exactly similar to the ideas that are being conveyed by the vibrations from without; and the mental world will be created in the likeness of the exterior environment.

However, when the mind is in a positive state, the vibrations from within are the strongest, and no vibration from without can produce an impression upon the mind unless the mental door is consciously opened to that particular idea.

When you are in a positive state, nothing that you may see, hear, or feel will impress your mind unless you so desire. It is there- fore evident that so long as you remain in a positive state, you will never be controlled by environments, circumstances, persons, or things.

Positiveness is that state wherein the mind generates its own vibrations and its own mental life; forms its own mental attitudes, thinks consciously its own thoughts, and is so strong in its own individualized being that no power can act in the mental domain unless it is wanted.

To be positive, however, does not mean to domineer over anything, but to feel the fullness of invincible life and power, and to fill the mind with the fullness of that life and power.

You do not have to exercise control over the forces of the mind; you do not have to compel the creative energies to ignore the vibrations, the influences, and the ideas that come from without; it is simply necessary to fill your own mind with your own mental vibrations, and to make those vibrations stronger than those that may try to enter from without.

So long as you fill your mind with your own mental vibrations, and you always do when in a positive state, the creative energies will produce only those thoughts and impressions that you desire to have produced; the desires of your own true self will be obeyed by the powers within you, and those desires alone.

Mastery of Self

The value of positiveness lies, first, in its power to protect the mind from being impressed by inferior, external conditions; and secondly, in its power to keep the creative energies under the complete control of the mind.

The positive mind has the power to think whatever it may want to think, and this is the real secret of the mastery of self.

He alone can master himself who can master his mind; and he alone can master his mind who can think what he wants to think, at any time and under any circumstance.

To develop positiveness, simply be positive at all times; that is the whole secret, and it is something that anyone can do with perfect ease.

Feel the fullness of invincible life and power, and fill your mind with this life and power. Resist nothing, domineer over nothing, and try to control nothing. Feel positively that you are a master, because that is what you are.

The sixth essential mental state to the attainment of the mastery of self, is the consciousness of superiority.

It is not possible to attain self-mastery so long as one thinks that he is an inferior creature, because through that thought mind goes down and functions below its true level. We can control only that which we have risen above; therefore, no mastery is possible until we live in the mental world of superiority.

The idea, however, is not that we are to think of ourselves as being superior to others; we know that the same superiority that exists in us exists in every person, and it is this superiority into which we desire to enter.

The idea is to dwell constantly upon the mountain top of your being; to live consciously and perpetually at the very apex of all your aspirations, and to constantly function in the most perfect spheres of those present possibilities that you can now realize.

The purpose of self-mastery is to make all of life just as high as our highest vision of the ideal; and we have attained mastery when we can make everything in life become exactly what we wish it to be.

The act of mastering oneself implies the power to bring oneself up to the state of superiority; to make everything superior to what it was, and then press on to still greater heights.

The purpose of mastery is not to control faculties, talents, forces, or elements, but to direct them all towards greater attainments and greater achievements — towards superiority.

It is not possible, however, to cause everything in one's being to move towards superiority unless the mind is established in the consciousness of superiority; to produce mental tendencies towards the superior, consciousness must feel the life, the spirit, and the soul of the superior, and this feeling may be cultivated by frequently concentrating attention upon the most perfect conception of superiority that the mind can possibly form.

Whatever we frequently think of, with depth and feeling, that we shall gain the consciousness of; this is a law through which any hidden secret may be brought into the light of a clear, positive understanding.

Mastery of Self

The seventh essential mental state is the realization of supremacy; the knowing of the truth that you, yourself, are the supreme ruler over everything in your being and in your world.

We must remove the idea of exercising control over the person through the use of objective will-power, and in the place of that idea establish the realization of supremacy.

When one knows that he is the supreme master of his being, he rules supremely without trying to do so; and herein we learn why he who has attained the mastery of self never tries to master or control anything, not even himself.

It is not necessary to try to be that which you are; and as you are created with the power to master yourself, you do not have to try, at any time, to master yourself. You are the supreme master of your being, and to think the truth, you must think of yourself as such.

He is what he is who knows that he is • and he who knows what he is, does what he can do by the virtue of being what he is.

He who knows that he is supreme in his own being exercises supremacy by the virtue of being supreme. He who is supreme cannot do otherwise but exercise supremacy; and since man is supreme in his own being he must necessarily exercise supremacy in his own being; that is, when he knows that he is what he is.

Man in the real is a master; therefore, when in the consciousness of the real, he does master; and does not have to try. He who tries to be a master does not know that he really is a master; when he knows that he is, he will do that which he has the power to do, not by trying, but by doing what he is in being.

The sun does not try to shine; it is light; therefore, it does shine. The sun does not have to control the sunbeams: the sun creates the sunbeams by being the cause of sunbeams; the sunbeams are created to give light because they proceed from that which is light; and that which is created to give light will give light because it is light; it will not have to be controlled to do so.

A piece of ice is cold, therefore, it makes everything cold with which it comes in contact; it does not have to try to produce cold. It is not necessary for any force or element in nature to try to produce in itself that which already exists in itself; neither is it necessary for man to try to do this.

So long as we try to master ourselves we shall not succeed in mastering anything; but when we discover that we in truth are masters, we shall succeed in mastering everything without trying in the least to do so.

The realization of supremacy is therefore of the highest value, because this realization will reveal man to himself. He will know that he is supreme in his own being; he will know that he is created with that power, and when man knows what he is he will act accordingly.

To cultivate the mental state of supremacy, impress the mind as frequently as possible with the truth that you are supreme in your own being. If you were not, you could not exist; your being would be chaos; the fact that you exist as an individualized entity proves that you are supreme in the being of that entity, and to be just to yourself you must exercise the whole of that power.

Therefore, to impress the mind with the idea that you are supreme in your being, is simply to train your mind to understand a great truth; and when that truth is realized, the realization of supremacy will have been attained; you will know what you are and you will act with supremacy in everything that is done within yourself.

When the mind acts with supremacy in the within, all the creations of mind will be patterned after the highest ideals that may now exist in consciousness; and the progress of the individual will be remarkable.

The reason why so many fail to reach their ideals is because they do not act with supremacy in the inner world of creation; they, therefore, do not recreate themselves in the likeness of their ideals, and no person can realize his ideals until he grows into the exact likeness of those ideals.

When the mind has not attained the consciousness of supremacy it cannot act with supremacy; the creative energies will, consequently, follow lower ideals, and will not do what is wanted done.

To enter fully into the consciousness of supremacy, all knowledge that reveals the unlimited possibilities of man will prove of great value, because the more deeply we can penetrate the greatness already existing within us, the more firmly we can establish the consciousness of supremacy.

To constantly feel that one is supreme in his own domain is absolutely necessary, and as this feeling would simply be the conscious expression of what is the truth, no one should hesitate for a moment to enter that attitude, and to dwell therein forever.

Mastery of Self

The person may feel weak, but that does not prove that you are weak; the weakness of the person is felt because you have failed to bring forth your own real strength.

Know that you are strong, and all weakness will disappear; know that you are supreme in your own domain, and you will rule supremely in your own domain. You will rule with supreme power because you are the individualization of supreme power.

Mastery of Self

HAVING established the mind in the seven states that are necessary to the attainment of self-mastery, the next essential is to train the will to perform its true function.

To begin, we must discard the current belief that the will was made to rule? the very opposite is its function; the true will never attempts to rule anything, but holds itself constantly in that attitude through which it can be ruled by the mind's highest conception of law, principle, and truth.

Man attains self-mastery not by trying to rule, but by permitting himself to be ruled by that which is greater than his present conception of himself.

That personality is always the most powerful that lets go of its own personal power and gives itself up completely to superior power.

He who is willing to lose the smaller life for the sake of the larger, will gain the larger; and he who is willing to lose his limited personal power for the sake of unlimited impersonal power, will gain the unlimited.

In like manner, he who disposes of the will that tries to rule, for the sake of the will that is the ruler, will receive the latter, which is the real will. And this is necessary, because the mastery of self cannot be attained so long as willpower is exercised in the usual way. The true will never tries to rule; it already is the ruling power; and it never tries to gain supremacy; it already is supreme.

Since the true will already is supreme, it would be a misuse of will to try to become supreme. Through such actions an inferior imitation of the real will would be employed, and that imitation would not contain any will-power whatever, but would simply be some aimless use of superficial mental force.

What is usually termed the personal will, that is, that something that we employ when we try to rule or domineer, is not will-power in any form; the personal will is nothing but the misuse of mental forces.

In the average person the real will is never employed; what passes for will in those minds is a more or less uncertain expression of those states of consciousness that have gained some imperfect conception of the real will.

Through every mental conception of the will a temporary state of consciousness is established having a tendency to direct, and to take initial steps. This is natural, be- cause since the will itself is the ruling power every mental conception of the will would have a tendency to rule.

Each mental conception of the will bears a slight resemblance to the will, and receives a tendency to act accordingly. Consequently, a mental conception of the will, by virtue of this slight resemblance, imitates the will with imperfect attempts to rule.

When we take initial steps, we are said to use the will, but we do not; we simply express our latest mental conception of the will; and since all such conceptions have tendencies to rule, direct, or take initial steps, initial steps, however imperfect, will accordingly be taken.

It is the truth, well-known to everybody, that the average initial step is a mistake; and it could not very well be otherwise, because it is not taken by the real will, but by an inferior imitation. It is also well known that most of our

Mastery of Self

attempts at exercising the power to rule are complete failures, and lead both object and subject into confusion.

It is also the truth, easily demonstrated, that practically all the mistakes of the world come originally from the tendency of the mind to follow imitations of the will instead of the real will itself.

The ills of life are wholly due to the mistakes we make when trying to control and direct our actions by the personal will; while the great and the good things that are done are done only when the mind gives way to a superior power, and acts under the direction and inspiration of the supreme will.

The pronounced individualist may object to the idea that we are to give up to a superior power, but such objections will disappear when we realize that this superior power is our own power, and that we are simply discarding the false and the limited in order that we may take possession of the limitless and the true.

In like manner, all objections to the idea that the will must place itself in that attitude where it can be ruled by the superior, will disappear when we realize that through that attitude of the will, the will is permitted to be itself.

In order that the will may be itself, it should make no effort to rule, but should remain what it is — the power that does rule.

The will is properly performing its true function when it is eternally giving way to the superior; that is, the superior that is in itself, that is in man, and that is in the expression of the infinite in man.

The true function of the will is to hold the mind in such a state that the higher may find a full and free expression at all times. In other words, to keep the mind open to the perpetual influx of life and power from on high — that is what the true will is created to do; and that is sufficient; the mind that is constantly being filled with the superior, will receive everything that it may desire to receive because the superior contains everything.

Such a mind will also become what it may wish to become, because to be filled with the superior is to become superior. It will also achieve anything that may be undertaken, because there is no limit to the power from which the superior eternally proceeds.

The difference, therefore, between the real will and its man-made imitations is immense, and anyone can understand that man has nothing to lose and everything to gain by eliminating the latter and giving up completely to the power of the former.

Mastery of Self

THE purpose of the personal will is to try to compel things to do thus or so; but this is not necessary, neither can anything but undesirable results proceed from such efforts.

Things will do that which they are created to do when left to themselves; and since everything has the inherent right to be itself and itself only, we cannot try to make them do or be different without violating the law of freedom.

When we desire different things we should cause different things to be created, and not try to make things already created different from what they are. This, however, is constantly being done; the result is, we not only misplace things, but we interfere, more or less, with the natural inclinations and best motives of nearly every person with whom we come in contact.

This practice leads to the violation of the law of freedom on every hand, and since we cannot expect to receive from others what we do not wish to give to others, there can be no freedom for ourselves until we interfere with persons and things no more.

The leading purpose of the personal will is to change things in the without; to try to make over what has already been created. In brief, the ordinary will-power is simply a meddler, and is engaged principally in the work of interference, trying to prevent per- sons and things from being themselves.

This purpose, however is contrary to all the laws of life, because the very first principle in life is to give everything the freedom to be what it is.

When we wish to change things we must not misplace them, but proceed to transmute them; and transmutation is brought about, not by interfering with the present external condition of things, but through the expression of superior power into the interior life of things.

When things are not as they should be, we can change them, not by trying to remake the present external condition of things, but by creating a new internal condition for things.

We remove evil, not by resistance nor by interference, but by permitting evil to be itself, which is nothing. Evil, being mere nothingness or emptiness, would never disturb us if we did not make " something " out of it.

The more we interfere with evil the more we make of evil and the more we disturb the development of the good, thus retarding the growth of the very thing that can remove evil.

We cannot remove evil; this the good alone can do; but we can create the good in sufficient abundance to cause all evil to disappear.

We have no time to create the good while constantly interfering with evil; and since it is the creation of the good and the good alone that can remove evil, we understand perfectly why we should not disturb the tares.

We have given ages of time to the pulling up of tares, but there are just as many tares in the world now as there ever were. Nothing has been gained; we have not removed the ills of life by constantly interfering with those ills; the method is a complete failure, and should be abandoned absolutely.

It can be demonstrated conclusively that evil invariably disappears when left to itself, to be itself, which is nothing; but to leave evil alone, the mind must give the whole of its attention to the creation of the good.

Mastery of Self

The personal will, however, cannot leave evil alone; its nature is to interfere; therefore, it must be eliminated, and the entire mind placed absolutely in the hands of Supreme Will.

When we compare, briefly, the two methods for dealing with adverse conditions, we find that the old method, the method of the personal will, through a constant interference with evil, never succeeds in eliminating evil, while the new method, through a constant creation of the good, soon eliminates all the evil there is.

Employ the new method, and evil will continue but a short time, and it is no more; but so long as the old method is employed, evil will live and grow, with no promise of cessation whatever.

When we examine evil we find that it is a condition of emptiness or incompleteness, and can live only until the fullness and the completeness of the opposite good appears.

The harvest of tares, which we have been told not to prevent, is therefore not some future fixed time, but any time when the true life-forces of growth are made sufficiently strong to bring evil conditions to an end.

This end can be brought about by any person, in his own life, at any time, by the giving of all his power and the whole of his attention to the creation of those good things that are necessary to fill the conditions of nothingness that may exist in the world.

The harvest of tares, that is, the end of evil conditions in any personal life, can be produced at once, and complete emancipation secured now; but the personal will must first give way to the ruling power of the real will.

Mastery of Self

To use the will for the purpose of interfering with things, as they are, not only perpetuates evil, but also prevents everything in life from being its best.

Nothing can be its best unless it is given freedom to be itself, its true and complete self; and in order that we may enter that attitude wherein we naturally give all things the freedom to be themselves, we must permit both the perfect and the imperfect to be what they are.

Our tendency to interfere with the imperfect will disappear of itself when we realize that the imperfect will not pass away until we create something better to take its place.

However, to create that something better it is necessary to attain a higher understanding of the superior, and also to bring into action the finer creative forces. The present states of mind must give place to states that have all the essentials required for the creation of the better; but this becomes possible only when the will is employed in its true function.

+

Mastery of Self

THE purpose of self-mastery is the attainment of superiority; to employ all the elements of being in such a way that perpetual growth becomes the principal factor in existence.

You have attained mastery of all the forces and elements of your being when you have caused all of these to work together constantly for the higher development of your entire self.

To simply make certain forces in your system obey your desires does not indicate any degree of self-mastery; in fact, every attempt to control your forces according to personal desires will pervert the will, and thus prevent the attainment of mastery. But when any force has been made constructive and constructive only, then you are the master of that force.

It is the true purpose of all forces to be constructive; they are, therefore, not in their true sphere of action until they have become permanently constructive; and he who has accomplished this has mastered the powers of his being.

To master yourself is to cause all things in yourself to enter their true sphere of action, and the very moment that the will proceeds to direct all things in being into their true spheres of action, the first step in mastership has been attained.

The will cannot direct things, however, until it has given up completely to that superior power that is the ruling power, and its direction of things into their true spheres of action consists in the placing of things in the hands of this same power.

When analyzing the true will and its true function, we find that its one and only purpose is to act upon consciousness; not to control consciousness, but to act upon consciousness.

The will was not made to act upon the body, nor upon any of the forces and elements in the body; neither was it made to act upon the mind, nor upon any of the states, the tendencies, or the desires of the mind.

The will should act upon consciousness only, and the reason why is found in the fact that everything that appears in body or mind is but the effect of conscious states.

Whatever you become conscious of, that you will express in the personality, and mind and body will become what those expressions are. The conditions of those expressions will be externalized in the personality, and the person will feel, act, and behave exactly as those expressions feel, act, and behave.

Every change that actually takes place in consciousness will produce a corresponding change in the personality, and every step in advance that is realized in consciousness will cause the personality to advance and develop in a similar manner.

Every cause that is formed in consciousness will produce its own effect in the personality, and as any cause desired may be produced in consciousness, any effect desired may be secured in mind or body.

There is nothing, however, except the true will that can produce causes in consciousness, therefore the will must be trained for this work.

In training the will for practical purposes, the mind should be centered as much as possible upon the true

Mastery of Self

function of the will; the personal will should be ignored completely, and no thought whatever should be given to the exercise of control over anything, nor should the slightest desire to rule be permitted.

To feel a desire to rule, control, antagonize, or resist, means that the true will is not recognized, and that the mind is permitting itself to be misled by inferior imitations.

The true will always moves towards the superior; it acts upon consciousness for the purpose of causing consciousness to gain a higher and a larger conception of the superior, and as these superior conceptions are realized in mind, they become patterns for the creative energies. Superior thoughts, desires, tendencies, actions, and conditions will thereby be created throughout the entire system.

The will is created to take the initial step in everything that transpires in human existence; and since all the elements of life follow the will, it is of the highest importance that every step be a step in advance, because if it is not, the elements of life will produce the inferior; retrogression will then take place, and the very things that are not wanted will appear in life.

However, when the will is true every step that is taken will be a step in advance, a step towards the consciousness of greater superiority; the true will is superior, therefore can will to act only in the life of superiority.

The will is superior now; it is above all other functions and attributes; nothing takes place until the will acts; it is the master over all, and therefore occupies the highest place in mind. Consequently, when we recognize the will in its true state, we recognize something that is superior, and all our thoughts will ascend towards the superior.

When all the actions of mind are moving towards the superior, greatness is being developed and the purpose of mastery is being fulfilled.

We master any particular part of the system when that part is made to perform its true function under all sorts of conditions; and we further master the same part when we have trained it to perform its function much better than it ever did before.

To cause this perfect action, and the more perfect action, to take place in any particular part of the system, this action must first be Caused in consciousness, because each part of the system simply carries out what consciousness holds for it to do. The various forces, elements, organs, and states are mere channels of expression for conscious action.

Change a certain phase of consciousness, and the corresponding mental or physical expression changes likewise? but no change can possibly take place in any part of the personality until the necessary change is produced in consciousness; and nothing can produce this change in consciousness but the true action of the true will.

The prevailing state of consciousness is the only one cause in the personal being of man; all other things are effects of this one cause; it is therefore useless for the will to act upon anything else but consciousness, because it is only through consciousness that the purpose of the will can be promoted.

Mastery of Self

To train the will to will in harmony with the real will, form in mind a clear conception of the real will; then will only the larger, the higher, and the better.

As the consciousness of the real will is developed, the will-power becomes immensely strong; and there are two reasons why; first, because the true will does not destroy its strength through the desire to rule; and second, because it gives itself up to the influx of real power — the power that proceeds from the source of limitless power.

As this power fills the system more and more, a deep stillness is gained, a state of being that is not only perfectly serene, but immensely strong; peace and power united; and when this state of being is felt, one may know that the path to self-mastery has been found.

To enter this state is to begin the mastery of self, and to continue in this state is to continue to develop the mastery of self to the very highest possible degree.

To step outside of this state is to cease, for the time being, to master oneself, and herein one may know whether he is on the path to mastery or not.

To hold the mind and every part of the mind in this serene, strong state, and to hold it there at all times, is a very high art, and is made possible only through the training of the will to act upon the principle of the real will.

When the will wills to be what it is — the ruling power, and wills to feel the action of this power, the mind will enter the strong, serene state, because the action of the real will is perfectly serene, and its power is immensely strong.

Mastery of Self

TO MASTER oneself is to cause oneself to be what one wishes to be. To eternally become what one desires to become means a perpetual transformation of self because all becoming is change — eternal change for the better; and to perpetually transform the self, a higher order of life and thought must be constantly expressed in the self.

This, however, is made possible only through awakening of higher and larger states of consciousness, and as consciousness responds only to the actions of the will, the true use of the will becomes indispensable in the attainment of the mastery of self.

To train the will to act upon consciousness, will-power should be concentrated upon every individualization of consciousness in the personality as well as upon consciousness in general.

If we wish to produce a certain effect in any part of the personality, the will should act upon the consciousness that permeates that part, and the cause that can produce the desired effect should be impressed upon that state of consciousness.

Consciousness permeates every atom in your entire being, and every atom responds to the action of that part of consciousness that is centered within the atom; it is therefore possible to produce any desired physical or chemical effect in any part of the personality by producing in the consciousness within that part the desired cause.

There is a special centre of consciousness in every organ of the body, and in every faculty of the mind; therefore, to produce any desired effect upon any special organ or faculty, the will must act, not upon the organ or faculty itself, but upon the centre of consciousness that is within that organ or faculty.

The reason why the average person fails to control his body or mind is because he uses will-power upon the body and the mind instead of upon the consciousness that permeates both. Control the consciousness that permeates the body and you control the body as well; and consciousness is readily controlled when the will acts directly upon consciousness while strongly desiring to secure certain results.

To cause the will to act directly upon consciousness, concentrate attention upon the finest substance or life that you can picture as permeating that part of mind or body where you desire the effect to be produced.

To illustrate, when concentrating upon the brain do not think of the brain itself, nor use will-power upon the brain, but turn will and attention upon the finer life-forces that permeate the brain. Likewise when concentrating upon any organ in the body, do not direct the will upon the physical organ, but upon the finer forces that permeate that organ. In this way you will act directly upon the centre of consciousness within that organ, and whatever you impress that centre of consciousness to do, the organ itself will do.

Through the same process the centre of consciousness in any organ or faculty may be so strongly individualized that it will respond instantaneously to any action that may be made by the will. The stronger the centre of consciousness in any part of the personality the stronger the subconscious action of the will in that centre; and as it is the subconscious action of the will that controls, the value of developing strong centers of consciousness in every part of the personality becomes evident.

Mastery of Self

When attention is being concentrated upon the various centers of consciousness, the will must never try to control those centers, or domineer, in any way, over consciousness itself. The object of the will is to impress upon consciousness those actions or qualities that are desired in personal expression.

To promote this object, the force of will and the force of desire should be combined into one action, and this action should be directed where results are to be secured.

The true will and the true desire are the two halves of the same whole; they are therefore indispensable to each other, and the more thoroughly they are trained to work as one, the sooner will the mastery of self be attained.

Desire receives, and the will directs action upon the object that the mind wishes to receive. Before the mind can receive, consciousness must come in contact with the object desired, and to direct consciousness into that contact, the will is required, because the will is the only power that can direct.

When desire acts without the will, it fails to bring consciousness into contact with the object desired; nothing is therefore received; and this explains why most desires are never fulfilled. When the will acts without desire, the mental attitude that receives and appropriates is absent; there is no receptivity, therefore, nothing is received; and this explains why mere will-power is powerless to gain the object in view.

When the will acts upon a certain state of consciousness, there should be a very strong desire to awaken into positive action what may be latent in that state; and, conversely, whenever the mind feels a strong desire for something, the will should act directly upon the inner or subjective state of that centre of consciousness that contains that something.

Through these methods, what we desire to receive will be received, and what we will to accomplish will be accomplished.

The desire that is aimless, and the will that domineers but never directs — these two actions in mind are responsible for nearly all the failures in life; it is therefore evident that failure could be reduced to a minimum in every sphere of life when the force of desire and the force of will were combined into one perfect action.

Such an action would be irresistible, and would invariably gain what it willed and desired to gain. It would be the action of complete mastery wherever it willed and desired to act.

We may desire power for ages, but so long as consciousness is not placed in touch with the inner source of power, we shall desire in vain. We can receive nothing from any source, until we place mind in contact with that source, and to produce that contact, the will must direct consciousness to become conscious of that source.

It is the truth that we may gain possession of anything in the external world that we may require, if we unfold the necessary capacity and ability from the internal world; but again, it is only the true use of the will, combined with a strong desire, that can place mind in touch with the limitless power of this internal ability.

To use will-power without desire is to stupify the mind; and here we have one reason why so many minds lack brilliancy.

To use desire without will is to place the mind in a negative state, where it may be controlled by anything that may appear in its environment.

To combine the force of will and the force of desire into one action no particular method is required, except to will to desire whatever you desire to desire, and to desire to accomplish whatever you will to accomplish.

Whenever you desire to unfold and express a certain condition, state, or quality in your being, cause the will to act upon the inner consciousness of that condition, state, or quality; and when you employ the will in any way whatever, desire something definite at the time, with the very strongest desire that you can possibly arouse.

When causing the will to act upon consciousness, think of the soul of things; consciousness is always reached when attention is concentrated upon the soul of things, because consciousness is that finer something that permeates the soul of things. It has neither shape nor form, yet it is in all shapes and forms.

Mastery of Self

WHAT is termed the soul of things is the inner world of limitless possibility; therefore, by causing will and desire to act upon the inner world of consciousness, the greater things that are latent within are unfolded, developed, and expressed.

We thereby train ourselves to promote the purpose of self-mastery to a greater and a greater degree, because we attain the mastery of self only by eternally bringing forth a superior self.

It is therefore evident that every attempt towards self-mastery must have the superior self always in view; and this is accomplished perfectly when the forces of will and desire act invariably upon the inner consciousness of everything in the human system.

When the self is perfect, as far as its present requirements are concerned, it needs no control; it will be right and do right because it is right. When a certain organ in the body performs its function perfectly, it needs no attention; it needs no control in order that it may do its work; it is already subconsciously controlled by its own state of harmony with the real will.

It is the same with everything in the system; no mastery is needed over anything while it is doing its work perfectly, because it is already in the hands of mastery; but if it is not doing its work perfectly, it needs transformation, not control.

You cannot control the wrong to be right; but you can transmute and transform the wrong into the right; you can gradually transform the inferior into the superior, and it has been demonstrated that when the entire system is being steadily transformed, every part of the system will not only per- form its function properly, but will perpetually improve the work of that function.

The best way to keep the entire system in order, is to constantly improve the entire system; and this is the purpose of self, mastery.

To master self is not to try to control self, but to perpetually transform self; it means continuous advancement for every part of the being of man; it is the elimination of evil through a constant growth in the realization of the good; it is overcoming the imperfect by creating the perfect; it is the passing out of the lesser through the passing into the greater; it is the prevention of retrogression through the perpetual pro- motion of progression.

The law of continuous advancement, how-ever, is based upon the principle that every change or improvement that is to be produced in life must come from the unfoldment of the greater possibilities that are latent in life. We advance in the without by unfolding and expressing the greater from the within; and we master the self by causing the self to eternally become what is latent in the superior life within the self.

The mastery of self may therefore be promoted only through the practical application of this principle; that is, every action of mind, desire, or will must act upon the greater within. Before a desired effect can be secured in the without, the corresponding cause must be created in the within; and to create this cause, action must be concentrated upon the consciousness of the within.

To control the forces of the system, the mind, through the united action of will and desire, must act upon the finer forces that permeate the finer elements throughout the

Mastery of Self

system. Produce any desired impression upon the finer forces while mentally entering into the inner world of the finer forces, and the outer forces of the personality will act exactly as the impression desired. Discord, confusion, irritability, restlessness, or pain among the forces of the system can be removed instantaneously by impressing upon the finer forces the desire for peace, serenity, harmony, and poise.

When the mind enters the finer forces while in the attitude of harmony, perfect harmony will immediately be established throughout the personality.

This is how adverse conditions in the system may be mastered; not by trying to control those conditions, but by entering into the finer consciousness and creating there more perfect conditions. Whenever you wish to change physical action, direct attention upon the subjective side, that is, the finer consciousness that permeates that part of the physical form through which the new action is to appear, and desire that subjective side to act the way you wish the physical part to act; and as soon as the desired subjective action is produced the corresponding physical action will immediately follow.

In this way, the body can be controlled completely, and caused to act in any way that we may desire. To remove physical pain or disease, concentrate attention upon the finer consciousness of that part of the body where the pain is felt. Do not think of the body itself, nor the ailment, but cause the mind to enter into the finer elements and the finer forces that permeate that part of the body where the adverse condition appears.

While in the attitude of concentration, use the will in drawing all the forces of that part of the body into the finer vibrations, and desire, with deep feeling, to realize the health and the wholeness of this finer life into which the mind has entered.

The reaction will soon follow, and the adverse condition will be caused to disappear by the coming forth of a strong, wholesome life from within.

Every unpleasant sensation in the physical system can be removed by refining the vibrations in those parts where the sensations are felt; and the vibrations of any part of the system will be refined when attention is concentrated upon the finer forces that permeate those parts.

To master your mental attitudes, turn attention upon the silent within. There is a state in the inner field of consciousness where absolute peace prevails at all times; to become conscious of this state is to become calm and serene, and by directing attention upon this state the realization of peace will immediately follow.

When in the midst of confusion, do not permit your mental forces to run towards the surface; to do this is to become confused, and thus be controlled by the confusion that exists about you.

Draw all your mental forces towards the within, while in such surroundings, and think towards the peaceful within; you will thereby realize peace, and be in peace. You will master yourself in the midst of the storm; you will remain untouched, unmoved, and undisturbed.

To control your thoughts, do not try to control those thoughts that you are thinking now, but use the will in producing a new line of thinking. If the will is well trained this can be done at once, and as the mind becomes active in new fields of consciousness, those thoughts that we did not wish to entertain will disappear of themselves.

To think of something different becomes simplicity itself when the mind enters into the finer consciousness of new thought. It is only when the mind continues to act upon the surface that it is difficult to change the mind.

To control your feelings, enter into the finer feeling of the opposite states of feeling. Having decided upon the way you want to feel, turn attention upon the finer consciousness of the state of feeling desired. The desired state will soon be felt in every part of the system.

To control desires, transmute the forces that are trying to express themselves through those desires; then turn the transmuted energy into those parts of mind or body where expression may legitimately take place now.

To transmute the energies that are alive in any desire, concentrate attention upon that part of mind or body where the desire is centralized, and with the action of desire and will draw all the finer forces of that part towards the subjective side.

When the finer forces are felt, attention may be turned upon any part of the body or into any faculty where added power can be used with profit. Wherever attention is directed, there the finer forces will accumulate, that is, when the consciousness of those forces has been attained.

Through this same process all the finer elements and forces in the personality or the mentality may be called into action, and superior results secured in everything one may undertake to do.

Mastery of Self

All the forces of the system are creative, and the creative process may be promoted anywhere in the system by any of the forces of the system; therefore, if the creative function cannot now take place in the personality, the same force may be employed now in any part of the mentality. This being true, it is wasted effort to try to subdue one's physical passions; when physical desires are felt, and it is not possible to express them physically at the time, the force of those desires should be transmuted, and concentrated upon some mental creative process.

To apply the principle of self-mastery to the moral nature, the true method is, not to say no to the wrong, but to say yes to the right.

To control yourself in the midst of temptation, divert your attention from those things that you do not want, and cause the will to act upon the inner consciousness of those qualities and virtues that you do want.

To resist temptation is to fix attention upon the very thing that you do not wish to do; the mind will think more and more of the wrong until it becomes oblivious to the right, and will consequently do what it was tempted to do.

To concentrate the whole of attention upon the wrong is to cause all the tendencies of mind to move towards the wrong; the mind will think the wrong and be placed in bondage to the wrong; it will follow the wrong and act accordingly.

The secret of overcoming temptation is to refuse to give the wrong step a single moment of attention; do not resist it; do not even think about it, but give the whole of attention to the right step.

Mastery of Self

This will not be difficult if the mind, when concentrating upon the right step, will look within and view the superior side of the right step; because when its superiority is discerned, the interest in the right step will become so great that nothing could persuade the mind to think of anything else.

The various mental states of depression, gloom, despondency, worry, etc., are produced by the mind coming down to inferior planes of action. To control those states, that is, to remove them completely, turn all the forces of mind upon the highest state of consciousness that the imagination can picture. Then direct the will to act upon the finer consciousness of this state, and into the finer state the entire mind Will go.

No attempt should be made to control the temper; this will simply place the mind more completely in bondage to the forces of tern- per. It will also give life and power to the present personal will.

When a person becomes angry he throws his thoughts out towards the object of his ill-will, thereby bringing consciousness to the surface, away from the real will and into the personal will. His energies are wasted, poise is lost, and practically all the actions of mind are misdirected; to try to control anything while in such a state would, therefore, be useless.

To avoid becoming angry under every circumstance, do not permit the actions of the mind to move outwardly against anything when antagonized, but direct all the forces of mind inwardly at once. This will prevent the antagonistic attitude, and so long as there is no antagonistic attitude there will be no feeling of anger.

Mastery of Self

To prevent thoughts from going out when provocations appear, impress daily upon mind the most perfect conception of a wholesome nature that can be formed, and train all the tendencies of mind to focus upon this ideal.

This will not only cause the creative energies of mind to build a sweet and wholesome nature, but the tendency of all feelings and emotions to move towards this inner ideal will become so strong that nothing can cause the force of feeling to go out against anything.

When this state has been established, all temper has been mastered, because all those forces that were previously wasted in temper have been turned in their courses, and are now engaged in the development of kindness, sympathy, tenderness, and love.

To master anything is to turn it to better use; and all things are turned to better use that are trained to work in harmony with the law of continuous advancement.

To control circumstances, the principle is to establish in yourself what you wish your circumstances to be. The mind that has created the ideal mental world will gravitate, through absolute law, into an ideal physical world.

However, before man can create an ideal internal world he must attain that state of self-possession where he will not be influenced by the adverse in the external world.

He must control himself in the midst of circumstances before circumstances will respond to his control.

In the midst of adverse circumstances, it is your thought and feeling that must be controlled, and to control thought under such circumstances all thought must be given to the ideal circumstance that you have in view.

To meet and overcome adversity it must be approached, not as an enemy, but as a force that can be turned to a better use. Adversity is but misdirected energy; but if you remain calm and strong, it will follow you, and do what you may desire to have done.

When you become stronger in your own conscious being than the forces that are about you, those forces will obey your will. For this reason, he who has mastered himself has mastered the universe. The forces about you will not obey your will when you try to control them; they will follow you and obey you only when you have become stronger than they.

Circumstances do not have to be controlled; when the forces that are active in our circumstances are used intelligently, which means constructively, those circumstances will be in our hands without our trying to place them there.

It is necessary, however, to be calm and self-possessed in order to use those forces intelligently; therefore, the principal essential in the midst of circumstances is to control the mode of thinking. He who can do this can turn everything to good account that may enter his path.

There is only one mode of thinking that is conducive to self-mastery, and that is scientific thinking; therefore, to control thinking is to think scientifically.

To think scientifically is to cause all the forces of mind to work together for the object that one has in view; and when all the forces of mind work for this object, the forces of circumstance will work for the same object; that is, if the force of mind is stronger than the force of circumstance.

Every person that thinks scientifically, and that unites all his forces upon the one object in view, will be stronger than his circumstances, and will thereby control those circumstances absolutely. In the last analysis, therefore, the control of everything depends upon the control of self, and must necessarily follow the control of self; but he who would control himself must not try to control himself; he must not try to control anything; in brief, he must eliminate completely every desire that desires to exercise the power to rule. Instead, he must place himself absolutely in the consciousness of that power within that does rule — the power that is supreme.

He who gives himself to supreme power, will give expression to his own supreme power; and the expression of supreme power through every part of the self constitutes the mastery of self.

My Ideal of Marriage

My Ideal of Marriage

THERE is a power at work everywhere in the world today, the one supreme purpose of which seems to be to change everything. And this power is not working in vain. It has already succeeded remarkably. There is scarcely an institution anywhere that has not been affected by the persistent influence of this power; and the indications are that the work of this power, irresistible as it certainly is proving itself to be, will, before the end of this century, eliminate every trace of the passing order.

New demands are arising everywhere. The spirit of the new. age refuses absolutely to be satisfied with things as they are; and therefore is looking to the near future for a complete transformation of everything that pertains to the life and the welfare of the race.

What the cause may happen to be for this unceasing and universal desire for change, is a matter that is open to much speculation. But of one thing we are all convinced; and it is this, that this planet is now good and ready for something entirely different along all lines. The law of life is eternal progress. We have been moving forward with the invincible demands of that law. We have outgrown the old. We are facing the new. But what is all of that new going to be?

Another program is in press. Another play is to be staged. The curtain of human destiny may rise at any time and reveal a scene that may startle even the most radical among the progressive thinkers of today. But whatever the scene or the play may be, it will be the result of the demands of human progress. And therefore cannot be otherwise than good.

Everything is good that tends to further the advancement of man; and that which shall have the power to enrich and enlarge the life of the whole race, can certainly not be evil or

My Ideal of Marriage

wrong in any form or manner. The new play, therefore, which will, according to the signs of the times, be staged shortly upon this planet, cannot be evil, neither in its nature, nor in its final effect. But it may be "shocking" to those who have always believed that the customs of the past were sacred. The new is always shocking to those who have been drilled, all through life, to think that change is dangerous, and that mental growth is fatal. The greater good never fails to shock the minds and souls of those who are convinced, beyond the shadow of a doubt, that the lesser good is perfect.

However, the law of human advancement does not consider the pet feelings or overwrought sensibilities of those who are wedded to the tender memories of bygone days. The law is working for the greatest good of all; and when the time is ripe for a great change, that change must come, even though everything we have cherished and adored be swept from off the face of the earth. The law of progress does not stop at mere sentiment; but there is much consolation in the fact that when we are on the path of progress, the losing of the lesser love invariably means the coming of the greater love.

All in all, therefore, whatever may come, the future will be richer and larger and greater and better, provided we always continue on the upward and onward path. For this reason, we have nothing to fear from change. We need not feel disturbed about the coming of the new order. Any change will be a change for the better so long as we continue to face the visions of the ideal. And there never was a time when the ideal attracted as much attention as now.

This being true, the great change that is near at hand will be a decided change for the better. And every institution that will be affected by that change will be improved remarkably, and lifted many degrees in the scale. We may

My Ideal of Marriage

look forward therefore to the coming days with great joy. Those days hold invaluable treasures in store; and those days will be intensely interesting; for the fact is, that the most fascinating period the race has ever known is just beginning to dawn.

Among the many institutions that will be affected, directly and immediately, by the great changes that are rapidly coming over the world, the institution of marriage is by no means the least important. In fact, the changes that must inevitably come to that institution may well be considered the most important, touching as they will do, the very source of human existence upon this planet.

For many years the coming of these changes have been clearly evident; and the situation has been viewed with alarm by the conservative everywhere. But there need be no occasion for alarm anywhere. Nothing serious is going to happen. All that will happen will be the realization of new and higher ideals in everything pertaining to the marital state; and such a prospect should certainly be welcomed with more than usual joy.

The coming changes in this connection, however, will not simply affect the institution of marriage itself, but will also affect everything pertaining to sex. And what we are to do with all the customs, beliefs and institutions that are connected, directly or indirectly, with the elements of sex — this is indeed a great question — a question that must be answered in a thorough and satisfactory manner before we can proceed much farther with the progress of the race.

Many attempts have been made to give this great question the practical and scientific consideration required; but these attempts have not proven successful because the subject has been viewed almost entirely from the physical

My Ideal of Marriage

standpoint. The real element of sex, however, is not physical; it is psychological; and therefore we must give our attention to the psychological side of this subject before the true answer can be found.

In giving due attention to this important subject there are several facts of a most vital nature that we should constantly bear in mind; and the first of these relates to the function of marriage in the social order, and the place that the institution of marriage must necessarily occupy in the life and the progress of the race.

We all know that the family and the home constitute the very foundation of human civilization; and we also know that the human race must have civilization — higher and higher degrees of civilization — if the greater destiny of man is to be realized; but there can be neither family nor home, in the true sense of the term, without marriage; and marriage can exist only by virtue of the elements of sex. Thus we find that human civilization is directly related to the elements of sex. And the same is true of human progress; for the fact is, that we cannot further the advancement of the race as a whole without perfecting the family and the home; and to perfect the family and the home we must improve upon marriage, which implies the better use of everything pertaining to sex, or that may be related thereto in any form or manner.

The institution of marriage today does not measure up to the new ideals of life; and the modern home, with a few noble exceptions, does not possess those finer elements that alone can lift the race to a higher level of conduct and existence. A decided change therefore must come, both in the ideals of the home and in the ideals of the marital state; but we must understand the psychology of sex before we can proceed to bring about the change required.

My Ideal of Marriage

The current views of sex, marriage, love, courtship, conjugal attraction, and all other subjects of a kindred nature, are thoroughly materialistic, and therefore unsuited to the new time and the new order of things. The materialistic age is gone; we have taken, or are in the process of taking, a decided step forward — a step that will culminate in an age that will be idealistic in the best sense of that term. But that which had its origin in the materialistic cannot serve in a state that is becoming idealistic. Therefore, every materialistic tendency must and will be eliminated from the life of the race.

Another subject of vital importance is that of health and morality as related to the elements of sex. And this is something of serious concern, knowing as we do that such a large percentage of ills of the world, physical, mental and moral, have their origin in the misuse of sex. But how are we to know the true use of sex? And having learned the secret, how are we to gain the necessary power and mastery over mind and body to apply that secret?

This leads us to the consideration of a fact of exceptional importance — the fact that nature is constantly giving to all healthy men and women an enormous amount of creative energy — energy that produces a multitude of desires, both in mind and body — desires that become in many instances irresistible. And the question is, what are we to do with those desires, and with that creative energy?

What constitutes the true use of those elements and forces when we live in the marital state? And what constitutes their true use when we are not living in that state? We all want to know. Those forces and desires are there. Nature refuses to cease in her creation of such forces and desires. We must learn how to deal with them, for if we misuse those forces, or misdirect those desires, we bring all kinds of suffering and distress upon ourselves, and upon our children and children's children. But if we learn the true use of those forces and desires, we may not only eliminate a large percentage of the physical, mental and moral ills in the world, but we may also increase our own personal and mental power to a remarkable degree; and, in addition, become the progenitors of a greater race than this planet has ever known.

In the face of these facts, and scores of equally important facts, we cannot ignore the subject under any circumstance. We cannot permit abnormal timidity or fossilized conventionality to stand in the way of the knowledge we need. We want to know these things. And we will secure the information desired. However, the real facts can only be gained through a thorough study of the psychological side of this entire subject.

In trying to solve the many problems that we come in contact with in our study of this great question, one of the most prominent is that of unhappiness in marriage, or the lack of real happiness among so many who are living in the marital state.

When we look at this problem from a general point of view, we naturally come to the conclusion that, where love is lasting and strong the marriage state ought to be perfectly happy; but inasmuch as love does not prove lasting in so many cases, we naturally inquire the reason why. The majority of those who enter the marital state begin with an abundance of love, and therefore we are interested to know why their love does not continue as it began originally.

Many answers have been given to this question, and all of them are possibly true from certain points of view, but there is one answer that has received but little attention; and this answer we are convinced contains more of the truth than all the others combined.

When we observe the general customs of modern courtship, we discover something that gives much light on this subject; that is, where we examine it all from the psychological point of view; and this is necessary in any case, because the psychological side is not only the most vital side and the largest side, but is also the one factor that invariably determines both the course and the natural outcome of every action.

We agree that the usual method of winning a wife is more or less strenuous; and that mental force as well as many modes of persuasion are frequently employed in direct violation of the natural law of attraction.

When we examine the feminine mind, we find that fully seventy-five per cent of such minds are so constituted that they can be readily persuaded, not only to do certain things, but also to feel that those are the very things they want to do, even though they had no inclination along that line in the beginning. Therefore, if a man proceeds with strenuous and positive methods in the pursuit of the girl of his choice, using every means possible to persuade her that she does love him — we find that three out of four can be persuaded in that way, at least for a time; that is, where the man is fairly desirable. In such cases the love of the woman for the man is not natural, but is induced by suggestion, special attention and persuasive methods of all kinds.

In this connection, it is well to pause and consider a very important law in psychology; and it is this, that if a certain mind can be impressed with the idea that a certain thing is the very thing to do, then that mind may be so influenced by that impression as to actually come to feel a desire to do that very thing, even though it may be artificial in every form and manner, and not the thing for that person to do tinder any circumstance.

In pursuing the usual method of winning a wife, the man selects the woman because she may seem desirable; then he persuades himself, through repeated suggestions, to love her, and by constantly thinking to himself what a fine wife she would make, how proud of her he would be, and how much she would add to his happiness. In most instances he judges entirely from appearance, and does not consider the vital elements involved. However, he persuades himself to think that she is the one wanted, and goes in pursuit of her, determined to get her — filling her mind, day after day, with the idea that they belong to each other and that they must marry by all means.

Here we find an artificial love in the man, produced by auto-suggestion, inducing an artificial love in the woman through the use of all sorts of suggestions; and if they marry, the result will be a marriage based, not upon natural attraction, but upon artificial and temporary emotion. Those temporary feelings or emotions, however, will in time wear off, and then will come dissatisfaction, which frequently becomes painful repulsion.

In many instances, both parties hide their repulsive feelings for each other, and try to get along, or try to bolster up their artificial love for each other by more autosuggestion — trying to convince themselves that it is all right after all, and will work out all right. Thus they manage to live in reasonable peace; but the real joys of love are not there in any form or manner. In other instances, however, where temperaments are different, those states of dissatisfaction, resulting naturally from mere artificial love, tend to go from bad to worse, until complete separation is sought; and herein we find the real reason for a majority of the divorces that we deplore so much at the present time.

When we examine carefully the difference between love that is produced by natural attraction, and love induced by suggestion or strenuous modes of courtship, we soon realize that we have found one of the principal causes of unhappiness in marriage; but the question is, how such unions may be prevented. In any case it is a delicate subject; but to begin, we must change our attitude towards that wonderful something that we speak of as love between woman and man.

It is quite true that most women have, in the past, been so constituted that they preferred the idea of being pursued, not knowing that they might, through such a method, become merely a hypnotic victim; and a large percentage of such women have chosen men who are the most strenuous and the most persuasive in their love-making, regardless of the fact that the heart was elsewhere.

Woman still permits herself to be pursued in this manner; and the man thinks that the woman is something to be captured and taken possession of; accordingly, the law of natural attraction is ruled out completely in most instances, and mental force, persuasion, and even certain forms of mesmeric power are employed, consciously or unconsciously, in bringing about the results desired. We find, therefore, that a large percentage of those who marry are in love with each other, because they have been taught to love, and not because they are really made for each other. Later they wake up to a loveless marriage; and the consequences we are all familiar with.

We may consider the subject from any point of view, and we can come to only one conclusion; and it is this, that a

My Ideal of Marriage

happy marriage can only be realized where the two are made for each other; that is, where they are adapted physically, mentally and spiritually. And where the two are made for each other, they are naturally drawn together by the fascinating power of attraction, but by no other method whatever. This law therefore should be left free to express itself perfectly under every circumstance, regardless of social positions, accepted conventionality, or anything whatever that may tend to involve outside influences in connection with this sacred procedure.

We know that this law of natural attraction does not always operate at first sight, although it does in some instances. As a rule the actions of this law will only follow more perfect acquaintance, especially along mental and spiritual lines; but in many instances, especially where the two people involved are perfectly natural in their feelings, the presence of this law will be felt almost immediately after the two have met and exchanged sentiments and ideas upon the general problems of life.

There is one thing, however, in our present civilization that may interfere considerably with the full and natural expression of this law; and it is this, that human society, as a whole, is permeated with unnatural and artificial customs, feelings and conventionalities; in fact, there are very few people who really know how they feel in their own natural self; and there are very few who think their own thoughts, or feel privileged to carry out their own sacred rights in connection with love and marriage, because the public has such a strong tendency to judge, and friends will almost invariably step in and lend their so-called superior advice.

We realize, therefore, that in order that love-making in the future may become natural and that those who are made for each other may come together in a natural and wholesome manner, modern society will have to change largely, both with regard to its views upon this subject and with regard to its leading customs. In brief, we must, as far as we can, eliminate the artificial from our feelings, desires and aspirations, and try to get into more perfect harmony with the higher and finer feelings of mind and soul.

Those higher feelings, when permitted to express themselves, will inform us invariably as to what is best, and who truly belongs to us; and therefore, the more we inspire those feelings to act in everything we undertake to do in life, the fewer will our mistakes become.

It is not what may seem best from an external point of view that we should carry out or pursue, but what we know and feel to be best through the deeper consciousness of our own real individual need. And our understanding of real individual need, as well as the laws involved, will become more and more perfect the more fully we study the psychological side of this vital and most interesting subject. Turning our attention briefly to the subject of divorce, we find that the seeming increase in the number of separations is viewed with alarm by a great many, especially those who cling more or less to the old order. Others, however, look upon it as a good sign; that is, the breaking up of states that are not states of love, but bondage instead. And in many instances this is true; but on the whole the increase of divorce in itself is not a good sign. It is simply an indication of monumental ignorance upon the most important subject in the real living of life.

We know that a great number of couples marry every year by mistake; and to be just to others, we should permit these mis-mated couples to separate when they awake from their delusion; but we find that separations frequently occur between couples that are naturally adapted, and that should,

My Ideal of Marriage

under true circumstances, live more happily together all through life.

The reason why unhappiness comes into such unions is due to several causes. The first cause, and the principal cause, may be found in the fact that the natural laws that govern the physical side of marriage are violated almost continuously; and we know enough to realize that harmony and happiness cannot remain where the principal laws involved are violated to such a vast extent; in fact, where such laws were violated only at rare intervals, we might expect discord; but where they are violated almost continuously, it is impossible to expect anything but unhappiness and separation.

We know that the right use of any particular law may bring the greatest harmony and the greatest joy, while the violation, the misuse, or the excessive use of that law may bring the reverse — first unhappiness and then repulsion. This being true, we should never judge the merits or the demerits of anything unless we understand the true use of the laws involved. It is only the right use of anything upon which we can base judgment, because the wrong use is no use at all.

We find thousands of people denouncing the institution of marriage on account of the unhappiness that arises in that state; but we cannot justly denounce an institution on account of its misuse. It is the right use of that institution that alone can be considered; and we know that the right use of any natural institution, or law, must work for greater good, for greater happiness and for greater welfare to all persons concerned.

Concerning the physical side of marriage, we shall speak in detail later; but it can be stated as a positive fact that the

My Ideal of Marriage

larger percentage of unhappy marriages can be traced to the misuse of laws involved in the physical side of the marital state. No married couple therefore should delay in seeking thorough and scientific information on that most important subject.

Another cause of unhappiness in the marital state is found in the lack of character in one or both persons; and this has been the direct cause of a great many separations. However, we are not to infer that we have more weak characters in the present age than in the last; the reverse is the truth; but in the past there were many unhappy couples who remained together because, according to custom, it was a disgrace to separate. Then another thing that should be considered in the present is this, that suggestion plays a most important part in the increase of divorce. The fact is that every new divorce suggests the idea of separation to many who are not as happy as they would wish to be. And those who understand the psychology of the human mind know that after a suggestion has begun to work in minds that are not as strong in character and in will as they should be, will soon give way to those suggestions; and all their feelings and desires will succumb completely to the idea that has been suggested. We find this law operating all through life. Many people get the idea that they ought to do thus or so, because others have taken the same course; and they come to this conclusion without realizing the consequences, or without considering the fact that their own case may be entirely different from that of those from whom the suggestion was received.

It is highly important, therefore, that every individual learns to decide his own course from his own point of view, and take every means to strengthen his character and improve upon his mode of living, so that his life may become more and more of an inspiration to others, instead of being more or less of an aggravation.

We know very well that there are people whose lives are constant aggravations to everybody, especially to those with whom they associate intimately; and it is not to be expected that such people can long retain the respect or love of others; nor can they contribute to harmony and human welfare in any institution or state of society.

We understand therefore that since such a large percentage among average men and women are more or less aggravations to their associates instead of inspirations — as they should be and could be — discord instead of harmony will be produced in the home to an extent that is by no means complimentary to the usual type of human beings.

Pursuing our study along this line, we will soon come to the conclusion that if we made up our minds to develop loveliness of disposition, strength and quality of character, and trained ourselves to become inspirations to everybody, our presence would be conducive to harmony wherever we might live or choose to act; and accordingly, discord and unhappiness would be reduced to a minimum in nearly every home in the land.

Regardless of this fact, however, we must not forget that those alone should marry who are made for each other; and also that those alone should marry who understand the purpose, the significance and the vital essentials of an ideal marriage.

We should not enter into any state unless our purpose be to make that state ideal; for the fact is, that nothing is worthwhile unless it is made ideal; and therefore, the very first thought to be considered in this connection is how to

My Ideal of Marriage

make marriage ideal — what kind of a marriage can be made ideal, and what the man and woman should be and do in order that such a marriage can be continued all through life.

In our study of this important subject, there are several principles to which we shall give special attention, principles that are of vital importance to the life, the happiness and the welfare of all; and one of the first of these principles is this, that what we do not understand, we will misuse. It is of the highest importance, therefore, that we understand everything that we are to meet or contact in personal or social existence.

This principle is vitally related to the subject under consideration; but as we know, this is a subject that the majority have not tried to understand; and herein we shall find the principal reason why there are so many opinions and such uncertainty of feeling concerning the institution of marriage. We know that it is easy to theorize and draw conclusions from individual instances; but we do not understand a subject until we consider that subject from the viewpoint of the real factors involved. And this leads to another principle that we must consider carefully herewith; that is, that we must not draw conclusions from abnormal cases.

However, we have been in the habit of judging marriage almost entirely from the consideration of abnormal cases. When we discuss marriage we usually single out certain couples that have had most disagreeable experiences; and simply because those striking cases have come under our observation, with their discord and unhappiness, we are liable to judge the whole subject accordingly, and conclude that it is either a lottery or all a mistake. But if we seek to understand the subject of marriage we shall have to proceed in an entirely different manner.

My Ideal of Marriage

We can never know the truth about anything unless we study the natural law involved; and natural law everywhere finds true expression only through the normal. We know there are many abnormal people who are married; but such people have no right to marry because they are incapable of complying with the requirements of such an institution. Abnormal people will make mistakes wherever they may try to act; and therefore their experiences in marriage prove nothing with regard to the ideal of marriage itself.

It is the purely normal that alone are in a position to say what is right and what is best in any institution, or in any mode of life; but we know that the larger part of the unhappiness met with in marriage at the present time appears in families where one or both parties are abnormal in some form or other. They do not have, what we may call, the natural ability to relate themselves properly to the demands and privileges of marriage; and their conception of the responsibilities involved in such an institution are, as a rule, so perverted that they misdirect every move they make in connection with the matrimonial state. They have entered that state for certain personal or special reasons, without considering what it really means; and besides they may be, and frequently are, under the influence of some mental or nervous ailment.

There are a great many people, both men and women, who are so constituted that they cannot possibly relate themselves harmoniously to anyone with whom they come in daily contact. Their minds are abnormal; and therefore, they take the wrong view of everything, and rub everybody the wrong way. But such people, through their experience, can give us nothing that is true concerning the subject of marriage.

My Ideal of Marriage

Our rule should be, whenever we meet unhappiness in the marital state, to ask ourselves, "Are those people normal; are their minds wholesome; are they living a life that is true to life; is there something wrong with them in mind or body; do they have abnormal desires and unreasonable tendencies; or do they lack in normal desires and personal power?"

These things must be known before we can say anything about the case under consideration; and we shall find that a large percentage of the people who are unhappy in the matrimonial state are unhappy because they are not normal; or because there is something that is unnatural about them, either physically or mentally. However, such people have no right to marriage; and we can gain nothing by analyzing their experiences. When such people enter matrimony, it is all a mistake, and all we can learn by considering such cases is this, that they should not have married. Moreover, such unions should not continue. They are mistakes, and should be discontinued at once. If one of the two happens to be abnormal, the other should not be called upon by society to continue in such a state. No individual should be compelled to live a life that is wrong from every point of view; and the sooner that individual seeks freedom from such a mistake the better.

We know that conventionality has compelled a great many people to live together under conditions that are simply intolerable; but conventionality is, in too many instances, based upon prejudice and ignorance, and cannot be relied upon to a very great degree. But we are all emancipating ourselves more and more from crude conventional notions, and gradually becoming more educated on all these subjects.

We are now coming to the conclusion that there is no reason why a state or condition of life should continue, if that state be based upon ignorance and wrong, even though it might have continued for five, ten or twenty years. The fact that a mistake is an old mistake does not prove that it has a right to continue indefinitely; and therefore, it should be put out of the way at the earliest possible moment.

Before we decide, however, that an unhappy couple should separate, we should consider another principle that is vitally important herewith. We know there are many people who imagine that they are not properly mated in marriage simply because. they have met disagreements now and then; but here we should remember that it is an easy matter to get nervous about the various adversities that come up in life, and to blame it on our associates or companions, thus coming to the conclusion that life under such circumstances cannot be otherwise than wrong.

The living of life involves many problems; and simply because we may not be able to solve every problem the very day it appears, we should not imagine that the life we are living is all wrong, or that the people we are living with or working with are not suited to our needs. We should not permit trouble and adversity to distort our minds, cloud our judgment, or develop conclusions that are purely imaginary.

Our rule should be, that whenever we do not feel right physically or mentally; or when we come to places where we have lost interest in everything — we should stop right there, and take a brief rest. Whenever any mind comes to such a state, the remedy is rest. There is nothing serious the matter; but under such conditions we do not see anything properly and cannot judge anything justly. The only time that we can judge correctly of any situation is when there is sufficient energy and ambition in the system to keep the mind wide awake and fully alive to every purpose and function. When we are down in the "dumps" we are unable to view anything correctly; and although we ought to know enough never to permit ourselves to get down into the "dumps," still, when we come to such a place, we should understand that in that place we are not fit to judge anything or anybody; and therefore should stop thinking and take a rest, thus permitting nature to recuperate.

Here we should remember that whenever we are "down" mentally, or when our nerves are upset, or when the system is deeply disturbed, our view of everything will be largely mistaken; and what we think or imagine at such times will be mostly wrong. The conclusions we may come to, therefore, under such circumstances, should be thrown upon the scrap heap, as they are absolutely worthless.

Let us make this one of the permanent rules of life — never to judge anything unless the mind is brimful of energy, and every faculty fully alive. The time to judge and draw conclusions is when the mind is in the upper story — in the full light of reason, judgment and clearness of thought; and we shall find, if we judge the subject of marriage only when we are in the upper story, that we will develop conclusions far different from the pessimistic views of the world; and as we analyze those conclusions we will find them to be absolutely true.

When people live together or work together, it is important that they dwell as much as possible upon the better side of life as well as upon the better side of each other. We know full, well that if we continue to dwell on the wrong side of everything, and continue to think of the weakness of the people with whom we associate, we will soon come to a place where we not only see everything from the wrong point of view, but we will misjudge and mistreat everybody with whom we come in contact; therefore discord must follow; but discord of every description must be avoided if we seek happiness.

My Ideal of Marriage

When we take a broad and sensible view of this entire subject, we shall find that the larger part of the unhappiness that is found in marriage is due to the fact that one or both of the people involved in the union are abnormal in some form or other; or have such a small, or such a distorted view of life that they are incapable of adjusting themselves properly to anything or anybody in the world; and therefore, the study of marriage cannot be pursued with any satisfaction unless we eliminate abnormal cases absolutely, and proceed to consider this state as it may exist where the people are normal, and where the circumstances are conducive to the best application of every principle involved.

In the past we have given so much attention to the mistaken side; and not having found a satisfactory remedy for that mistaken side, we have decided that marriage is a problem for which no real solution can be found; but in the future, we must examine more carefully the normal side, and dispose of mistakes in the most orderly fashion possible.

Individuals that find themselves unhappy in marriage should be given the privilege to correct the matter, but under the guidance of the best information that society can furnish on the subject. However, we cannot lay down definite rules that will cover all cases. There are many reformers who have adopted such a method, but it is always a mistaken method under every circumstance. Each case is different from the others, and requires individual attention.

Society should, however, take an active part in deciding whether unhappy marriages are due to abnormal conditions, or whether they are due simply to nerves, bad habits, or a distorted view of life. If the cause is found among the latter conditions, let both parties involved repent and decide to become real human beings, henceforth. But if the cause is found to exist in abnormal states of mind or body, there is only one way out, and that is separation; although in this connection it is important to remember that if a better understanding of life, including the privileges and responsibilities of life, were attained by everybody living in the marital state, the number of separations would gradually be reduced to a minimum.

When we proceed to study marriage as it really is, and as it may become according to still higher ideals, we must begin our study according to natural law — natural law as expressed both physically and mentally. We must give special attention, however, to the mental side, because marriage is more of a psychological factor than a physical factor. It is the psychological side that will determine whether the marriage is to be happy or not, and also whether it is going to be a wonderful union, or a union that will simply prove ordinary. But here we must not forget the principle, that what we do not understand that we will misuse. Therefore, we must gain a better understanding of the psychological side of marriage, including the normal and the natural laws involved; otherwise, we will misuse that state of relationship both in the physical and the mental spheres of action.

In our study of an ideal marriage, the first proposition that we will make is this: "We must have both an ideal woman and an ideal man before we can have an ideal marriage." But this proposition has never received proper attention. We know a great many people, especially young girls, who dream about an ideal marriage, and the wonderful marriage which they expect to realize some day, but they never ask themselves what they are able to give to such a marriage. They do not think of what they are going to contribute to that institution after they have entered into it; and we must remember that we can never receive, from any source, any more than we give. If we want to realize the ideal,

My Ideal of Marriage

we must become ideal and be able to express the ideal in every form and manner. This idea therefore must be considered first of all.

The two people must be ideal; and by that we do not mean that they have to be perfect physically, mentally or spiritually, because none of us are as yet perfect in any manner, although most of us are surely moving in that direction. When we speak of ideal men and women in connection with marriage, we refer to those who enter that state with a certain definite object in view, and who have certain lofty aims that they are determined and able to express under every circumstance.

In the first place, the man and woman must be willing, ready and able to respect each other's individuality and each other's freedom. They must have good character and must be inspired with a living desire to express in life the ideal life, no matter what external conditions may be. They must be willing to overlook each other's shortcomings, and think as little as possible of the lesser side of human nature. They must proceed upon the principle that we are all human, and liable to mistakes now and then, but also that we are all growing, and that we must steadily improve. They must consider it a pleasure to give as little attention as possible to the weak points of personality, mind or character, and more than desirous to magnify the strong points, and give so much attention to the good qualities that they become actual inspirations to each other.

When we consider the requirements of an ideal mind, we shall find that one of the first of these is to have the tendency to give more attention to the good qualities than to the weakness we may find in others. In fact, such a mind will naturally give so much attention to the good qualities that practically no attention whatever will be given to those

My Ideal of Marriage

qualities that may seem weak or inferior at the time. The purpose of the ideal mind is to give the whole of attention to the development of the best there is in personality, mentality, character and soul. And therefore, an ideal mind is always looking for the best in everybody, always magnifying and encouraging the best, always adding to the life and the power of the best; and we know that in marriage it is absolutely necessary that the two members of the union look only for the best in each other — in fact, magnify the best to such an extent that they actually idealize each other to the highest possible degree.

We know that the tendency to idealize everybody is always productive of great good and great happiness; but we are sometimes told that if we idealize people, we may form incorrect opinions of their present nature, and accordingly they may never come up to our expectations, which fact would result in disappointment on our part. This view, however, is but temporary and limited; and in truth, does not consider the real facts involved. When we look more fully into this idea of idealizing everybody, we find that, instead of forming incorrect opinions of people, we do, on the contrary, form opinions that are nearer the truth than any kind of opinion that we could form otherwise.

When we look on the surface of life, we may not find a great deal to arouse our enthusiasm; in fact, we may not see much character or much ability in the individual thus considered, and there may be nothing about either mind or personality that is very attractive; but then we must remember that the individual is not simply a physical body.

The personality of that individual may, or may not, be attractive; but there is something else in that individual besides what appears on the surface. We know that that personality contains within itself wonders and marvels that have never been understood or comprehended by the physical side; and therefore, however limited the expression of the ideal may be on the surface, the real man or the real woman is so wonderful in mind and soul that no matter how we may idealize that man or woman, we cannot possibly do justice to the true life and the vast possibilities that really exist back of and above the physical personality.

The fact is, that we are all so wonderful in the potential that it is impossible to picture an idealization as wonderful as we really are. The idealist therefore is on the right path; and no matter how lofty our ideals may be of anyone, the real truth is far more wonderful and far more ideal than we can possibly picture.

Let us remember this, that the real truth is more wonderful and more marvelous in every individual than our highest ideal of that individual could possibly be; therefore, we are not violating the laws of truth in the least when we idealize other people, or when we magnify their good qualities, even though we should magnify those qualities to the very highest degree. Neither are we violating the laws of truth when we see a great many things in people that do not appear on the surface; for the fact is, that the surface of life reveals only a small fraction of the good, the beautiful, the ideal and the wonderful that does exist in life.

Accordingly, we may proceed to idealize everybody, knowing that the more we idealize all men and women, the farther we advance towards the real truth — the truth as it is in the real mind, the real character and the real soul of every individual.

The practice of idealizing people must also be considered from another point of view; that is, the effect that it will have upon our own minds. The fact is, that when the mind begins to idealize everything, then it is that that mind begins to become a beautiful mind, a rich mind, a large mind and a finer mind than it ever was before. We know, through experience and observation, that the most beautiful minds and the most wonderful minds in the world are invariably those minds that have made it a practice to idealize everything all through life. We also know that the materialistic mind, that is, the mind that simply judges according to appearances, and that is constantly looking on the bad side and the weak side, is never a very fine mind nor a very rich mind; and never develops to any marked degree. The statement may be made, herewith, that we know of brilliant minds that are very critical, that have the habit of tearing everything to pieces, and that deal more with facts as they are than with the ideal; but we must consider the whole truth in the matter; and the whole truth is this, that if we should watch those minds, we would find their brilliancy disappearing, gradually but surely; and their fine qualities diminishing until they had become very ordinary.

This very thing has happened in history thousands of times. Therefore, no matter how brilliant a mind may be today, if that mind continues to give undue attention to the weak, the wrong and the critical, that mind will finally weaken and lose both its power and its brilliancy. In every instance, such minds go down the scale every year both as to ability and brilliancy; and frequently, before they pass middle life, they become quite ordinary in all of their mental qualities.

Thus we realize that no one can afford to continue in the purely materialistic attitude. It is not good for the mind, and leads invariably to the decrease of all that is rich and good in that mind. We know that many things are wrong in the world, and that most things are not as desirable as they might be; but we can consider the defects of life and give

My Ideal of Marriage

them proper attention without constantly dwelling upon the dark side, the bad side, the wrong side and the perverted side.

The problem is to take life as we find it and proceed to improve upon everything; but we cannot improve life unless we first improve ourselves; and we know that there is nothing that will improve mind, character and soul so wonderfully as the practice of idealizing everything and everybody. The practice of idealizing all things will tend to refine the mind, to illumine the mind, and to make the mind more powerful, more brilliant, more capable and more effective in every form and manner. We steadily rise in the scale through such a practice, and become superior in all our qualities and capabilities.

In addition to this, we shall find that the practice of idealizing everything will tend to lessen our tendency to make mistakes; and also furthering the tendency to harmonize more perfectly with all kinds of people and conditions, which will reduce discord and unhappiness to a minimum. It is always the truth that the individual who idealizes everything in life, will find light and freedom much sooner than the one who goes out and battles with adversity, or who tries to remove the wrong with force. Therefore, in any state or relationship, the practice of idealizing everything and everybody will tend to improve upon conditions, steadily and surely, until the very ideals we seek will be realized; and we know that in marriage nothing could be more important than this beautiful practice of idealization.

We all are liable to express weakness in many respects, or to mistake in some of our thoughts and actions; but such conduct can only be temporary among people who are trying to rise in the scale; and if we make it a practice to idealize those people who are closely related to us, we will exercise a most beneficial influence upon them, helping them every day to outgrow their weakness and attain to a higher and finer understanding of all life, all thought and all conduct. The process of idealization always tends to beautify and refine. It always tends to harmonize and perfect; and therefore can have nothing but a most wholesome influence upon everybody that may practice idealization or that may come in contact with those who apply this sublime art.

In the family, idealization should be one of the prime factors, both between husband and wife and between parents and children. If the parents would idealize their children, and the children idealize their parents, everybody would improve, and everybody would enter into a greater joy and a richer life every day. In fact, the practice of idealizing our children is a practice that will prove more beneficial to their advancement than any one other thing that we could do.

In the past, however, it was the very reverse of idealization that was practiced in the family; or if idealization were practiced occasionally, it was alternated with the reverse so frequently that no good could follow. In the practice of idealization, however, it is not necessary to tell the child repeatedly how perfect or how wonderful it may be, although every child should be encouraged to know and realize that there are far more wonderful things in his deeper nature than have ever been apparent on the surface. These facts, however, should not be repeated too frequently, or in a purely mechanical manner, but should be considered too sacred to mention except at rare intervals, and under most favorable conditions. This, however, is another subject, and is related to child culture more than to the institution of marriage itself. But the practice of idealization should be taken up in every family, and should be practiced more and more until it becomes one of the fine arts of the world.

My Ideal of Marriage

Considering further the principle of idealization, which we admit is of vital importance in marriage, we might imagine a couple that would practice this principle all through life, idealizing each other in every mode and manner, and always being true to their very highest ideals of each other as well as of themselves individually. If they both would practice that sublime art, we realize that they would not only influence each other for good to a remarkable degree, but the practice would also react upon themselves, tending invariably to refine their minds, strengthen their characters and elevate all the elements of thought, life and soul.

The result would be that this couple would, from year to year, become finer and superior; and in consequence, they would, with the passing years, find more in each other to love and admire. There would be a steady increase in the power of attraction between them; and when celebrating their fiftieth anniversary, or even their seventy-fifth anniversary, they would love each other better than at any time in the past.

The more we study this principle of idealization, the more convinced we become that it is not only helpful to others, but is one of the great secrets through which we may help ourselves. When the husband idealizes his wife he is at the same time refining his own mind. He is bringing out into expression, in his own life, the finer elements and the superior qualities of his nature; and when the wife idealizes her husband she is bringing about the same desirable results in her mind and personality. Therefore, these two will develop continuously in life, character and soul, so that each one will find more and more in the other to admire and worship.

My Ideal of Marriage

In addition, this practice of idealization will largely prevent every form of misunderstanding, discord or inharmony between the members of the family. This is evident, because if the process of idealization is carried on steadily and continually, neither member is going to find much fault with the other, or get out of patience, no matter what the circumstance may be. True, moments may come when the better nature of each one may be tested to the very extreme, but such moments cannot remain sufficiently long to produce discord, if the process of idealization is strong and continuous in both minds. In the first place, therefore, an ideal man and an ideal woman would be a man and a woman that idealized each other in this continuous and wonderful manner.

In the second place, the ideal man and the ideal woman must respect each other's individuality and freedom; but when we speak of freedom we do not mean that the individual is to be free to do what he pleases. He should recognize the higher form of freedom; that is, to be free to do that which is best for both individuals concerned. In married life the idea that one person is the property of the other must, of course, be eliminated completely, because such an idea is the very contrary to the ideal conception of life, love and freedom. True, it may be difficult, especially for men, to eliminate this idea from their consciousness; but it is absolutely necessary, for we shall never have an ideal marriage so long as that belief continues. It is a belief that is wrong from beginning to end, and originated in those dark ages when the savage claimed his mate by force and carried her off as personal property.

The man of today, however, should have too much regard for himself and his chosen companion to imitate the savages of thousands of years ago; and the man of today will find that the sooner he eliminates from his mind the idea of

My Ideal of Marriage

personal property in marriage, the happier he will become, and the more happiness he will give to the woman.

In modern times we have come to the conclusion that every individual should be free to live his or her life according to the highest desires, aspirations and ideals of the individual; and an ideal individual, which is the individuality we all seek, is an individual who aims to be all that is best in life; and therefore such an individual can have no desire to misuse the privileges of freedom under any circumstance.

In this connection it is well to note that one reason why so many people go wrong is because they are restricted too much. They are hemmed in with all sorts of trivial rules and regulations; and in consequence their minds become cramped, thereby decreasing that finer consciousness of individuality which is absolutely necessary to self-respect, justice and the proper placing of one's self in the best order of human society. The fact is this, that if we confine people in a prison of ordinary rules and regulations, they will finally lose their capacity to live their own life they will become mere machines in the hands of conventionality, and cannot branch out, so to speak, as distinct individuals — individuals that will be a credit both to themselves and to the race.

We should therefore reduce social rules and regulations to a minimum, and should devote more attention to the higher development of each individual, to the end that he may become sufficiently strong and self-possessed to live an ideal life without the need of artificial restrictions of any form. We must, of course, have our laws and our social customs, but these should, at all times, be looked upon as secondary. Our one supreme purpose should be to develop strong, powerful, self-respecting masterful individualities; and such individualities flourish the best where the higher conception of freedom obtains.

My Ideal of Marriage

In the marital state the same principle should be observed; that is, the husband should not formulate a number of petty rules for his wife, nor should the wife take such a course with her husband. On the contrary, these two individuals should have such a high regard for each other that they would count it a pleasure to give, one to the other, perfect freedom to live the best life possible in the present state of human development. Each individual must feel, at all times, that the life companion has the privilege to live an individual life; and there must be no interference with the full expression of the highest and the best that may exist in real individuality.

To analyze this subject would take much time, and it would lead us into a thousand details; but this will not be necessary. In this age we understand fully the meaning of this higher state of freedom, and we know that if married couples would observe that higher conception of freedom, they would never be untrue to each other. The attraction, the regard, the respect and the love would be too strong under such circumstances to breed disloyalty of any kind. In addition, they would be far happier than would be possible under the old order; and here it is well to remember that when you give a genuine individual his freedom to be his best, he will consider it his highest privilege to serve you so that you may become your highest and best. Human nature invariably works that way; and it would work that way to the very highest degree in an ideal married state.

Another thing to be considered in the same connection is the effect that this idea of freedom would have upon the advancement of the individual. We know that whenever we give an individual freedom to develop thoroughly and constantly along natural and wholesome lines, he will soon become superior, and we will find more in him to love, respect and admire. The contrary is true, however, where the individual is hemmed in with rules and regulations, or is living more or less under bondage.

We have found in hundreds of instances that the woman, after having been kept under a glass case, so to speak, or confined to menial duties and given no permission to develop along any line, has continued to remain in the same cramped mental condition all through her married life. And in most instances the husband discovers, after twenty or thirty years of marriage, that his wife has not improved as he has improved. She has not kept up with the times; she is still a quarter of a century behind him in development, and compared with himself is more or less of a mental dwarf. The result is that he finds no satisfaction in her companionship, and therefore seeks diversion elsewhere.

We know the consequences of such a circumstance; and here let us remember that, in the majority of instances, where the husband, after a considerable period of married life, seeks companionship elsewhere, the cause is invariably to be found in the fact that the wife has not developed; she has confined herself to household duties, or to a mere superficial social life, and therefore is incapable of satisfying the needs of companionship in a husband who has forged to the front all those years.

We know that in this age it is absolutely necessary for a man to advance steadily if he is going to retain his position in the commercial or the professional world. He simply must advance and improve himself; he must keep up with the times in every mode and manner; and the more rapidly he develops, the more perfectly will he be able to fill his position in life. And the wife must advance with her husband, or there will come a time when they will no longer be companions to each other.

My Ideal of Marriage

In giving more definite attention to this subject, we might inquire where the blame may be found for this lack of advancement on the part of so many wives; and in many instances the husband may be to blame, although unconsciously, as a rule. In other instances, however, the wife is to blame, or rather womankind in general, because there is a tendency — too strong a tendency — in the feminine mind to settle down to mere household duties when the honeymoon is over. But this tendency must be eliminated completely; and although there is much truth in the fact that the average woman finds little time to study or improve herself, still we must not forget that "where there's a will there's always a way." When we realize the fact that the husband and the wife must advance and develop together along mental, intellectual and spiritual lines, they will certainly find the opportunity to further such advancement, no matter what their position in life may be.

In the meantime, it is highly important that this fact be proclaimed far and wide, as it is too evident that, if we permit a gulf to develop between husband and wife, the day will come when they will find no pleasure in each other's company; and such a day cannot be otherwise than sad for everybody concerned; therefore it must be prevented.

When we consider this subject from the viewpoint of the natural advantages arising from individual development, we realize that instead of the husband trying to discourage the development of the wife, or vice versa, it is the reverse that we shall find to be to the best interest of both parties of the contract. We clearly understand that if the wife develops more and more each year the husband will have a better companion and a better wife. She will become superior to what she was, and he will become more proud every year to say that she is his wife. The same is true where the husband develops continually; he will become more and more of a

My Ideal of Marriage

man, and his companion will take far more pleasure in the fact that he is her husband.

It is decidedly and directly to the interest of both parties concerned, therefore, to see that the full development of individuality in each one is encouraged to the fullest degree possible; and it is also to the best interest of both parties to increase that perfect freedom in life that tends to bring out the best, the richest, the highest and the finest that the wonder-world of human nature may contain.

Another matter of importance is the effect we feel in the mind when we have given freedom to those who are closely related. In truth, it makes all the difference in the world when we feel that our nearest relatives have been given their freedom. We feel that we have not only given them a higher position in life, but we have also expanded our own minds, and have taken a much higher view of everything that may pertain to the world in which we live.

But the tendency to restrict the thoughts and feelings and movements of others has a most unwholesome effect upon our own minds; for when we are constantly resisting mentally the actions of others we are wasting energy and literally tearing down portions of our own minds. It is highly important, therefore, for our own good, and for our own healthy mindedness, that we live in that feeling and consciousness where we give absolute freedom to everybody with whom we associate. It is the free state of mind that is the most conducive to the ideal state of mind; and a free state of mind is that state in which we live when we respect others so highly that we want them to be their best, believing that they have the intelligence and the power to do their best; and also knowing that they can be their best only when they are permitted to express themselves individually without

My Ideal of Marriage

being influenced in this direction or in that direction by an interfering or resisting force.

When we consider the flowers of the field, or the trees of the forest, we discover that they all grow and develop into that which nature intends them to be only when they are free to be themselves. If we should try to compel an oak to try to be an elm we should find that the death of the tree would result. The same would happen if we should try to compel a lily to become a rose. Such restrictions and such interference is contrary to nature everywhere, and invariably produces death or retrogression.

The great principle is this, that each individual can develop and advance to the fullest degree, and in the most thorough manner, only when permitted to grow naturally along the lines of his highest ideals, and not forced in this direction or that by those who might wish him to become something else than what his own individuality intends.

The effect of trying to influence others in their belief or in their conduct is detrimental under every circumstance. And to illustrate, suppose you have a number of friends, all entertaining different beliefs about life. Suppose you have been trying to influence those people to believe as you believe on all those subjects. You know the result that must necessarily follow. You are wasting your time and energy, and at the same time harming your own mind by trying to influence those people. But aside from that you are not as good a friend to them, nor are they as good friends to you as they would be if you all decided to agree to give perfect freedom to each other in thought and belief. We know full well that true friendship, and that finer companionship that we desire so much, cannot exist so long as we are trying to influence each other to be or become something different from what the highest aspirations of each individual may indicate; but when friends come to a place where they give each other absolute freedom to be their own best selves, and live according to their own highest light, they will not only respect each other more, but will enjoy each other's companionship far more than previously.

The idea, therefore, of giving freedom to others, in this higher and more beautiful manner, is something that should be cultivated and expressed everywhere, both in marriage and in all other states of human relationship.

Emphasizing briefly the essentials to an ideal marriage, we must first have an ideal couple; and an ideal couple would be a man and a woman properly mated, deeply in love, who have married to live for something worthwhile — a rich life, a beautiful life, an ever-advancing life; who respect each other's individuality and freedom, and who have given each other such freedom absolutely. An ideal couple would be a man and a woman that had married for the very highest and best that marriage can produce, and who have united for the purpose of working out the most ideal and the most lofty state of existence possible upon this planet.

Such a couple would also proceed in marriage with the one desire to give each other happiness; not merely pleasure, but real happiness, the highest happiness conceivable; and we know that whenever two well-mated people proceed in life to work for some lofty and wonderful goal, remaining faithful to that goal under all circumstances, they will finally reach, not merely the goal, but a much higher goal than they ever dreamed of in the beginning.

When we consider the factor of happiness, we must remember that no life is real or true to the principles of life unless it is a happy life. Happiness invariably proceeds from the highest order of living; and we may state it as an absolute fact that if we do not realize the very highest happiness conceivable we are not true to life. We have not found the real path of ever-ascending existence, and therefore should instantly look into our mode of living, so as to find the secret of the larger, the richer, and the better.

In the realization of happiness we must not forget the ancient statement that "we must first give happiness before we can receive happiness"; and it is self-evident that the more thoroughly concerned we are with the desire to give happiness to others, the more happiness we shall receive in return. In married life the principle that each individual should adopt is this: "I AM here to give you happiness, and will do everything I can that may prove conducive to your happiness; and in addition I will do nothing that may in any way decrease your happiness." We know that if this were made a positive rule, there would be a wonderful difference; and we all can live up to that rule if our desire to do so be genuine, whole-hearted and continuous.

Then we must remember that whenever we proceed along any particular line, we shall find it easier to act in that direction the longer we continue; therefore, if we begin with certain sublime principles, and remain faithful to them all for a time, we shall find that, after that time, it becomes almost second nature to live up to those principles; and we shall also find that the living up to lofty principles will not imply self-sacrifice of any form. It is the reverse that will happen. If we give up insignificant pleasures in order that we may give greater happiness to others, we find that we will be repaid by greater happiness in return; so that in all those circumstances we are simply giving up the lesser in order that we may secure the greater; and there is no self-sacrifice in such a process; on the contrary, it is immense gain.

My Ideal of Marriage

When we have an ideal marriage in view, we must provide the best possible for that life. It is not sufficient simply to give yourself in marriage. You must bring something into marriage; and the more you bring from the richness of your own character, your own mind and your own soul, the more you will receive from such a life. Therefore, when a man or woman is contemplating marriage, the first thought should be, "What can I give to that marriage; how much can I bring to that marriage state that is really worth while?" And if those questions are considered seriously, and every effort made to bring to the marital state as much as possible of those things in life that are lasting, that are true, that are genuine, that have real worth — the result can only be what we have desired — something very good and very beautiful in return.

However, in considering the question of what we can bring into marriage, the monetary factor should occupy a secondary place by all means. There is at the present time too strong a tendency to look upon the financial worth instead of the mental and the spiritual worth of the individual; and there is also too strong a tendency to look upon personal appearance instead of upon personal quality, character, refinement and beauty of soul; or to disregard the higher and the finer elements while in search of the purely materialistic.

The truth is, we must pause here in our consideration of what constitutes a desirable husband or a desirable wife. It is not wealth, social position or personal appearance; nor in fact anything that appears merely on the surface. It is the real man and the real woman that we seek. It is only a real woman that can make a desirable wife; and it is only a real man that can make a desirable husband. The search for the real, the genuine and the ideal, therefore, both in the man and in the woman, must occupy our first thought and attention. True, we are all entitled to the best that life can give on all planes, and we all should become as attractive personally as possible. In consequence, we are justified in demanding external means, and also attractiveness in personal appearance; but these things must not receive our principal or exclusive attention.

It is the real men and the real women that are of the first importance whenever we think of marriage; and herein we shall find a parallel to the great statement, "Seek ye first the kingdom of God and His righteousness, and all these things shall be added," which may be expressed in this fashion — give your first thought to real worth in personality, real quality in character, real power in mind and real richness in soul; in brief, seek first those finer things in the one that you desire as your life companion, and you will find that all that is desirable in external life must necessarily follow. We realize perfectly that a real man, even though he may have no possessions today, does have the power to make a place for himself in the world; and we also know that a real woman, although she may not be exceptionally attractive in personality today, still, being a real woman, she has awakened the more beautiful in mind and soul; and it is only a question of time when the beautiful in mind and soul will find expression in personality. Then the personality will have real charm, and become possessed of an attractiveness that is a thousand times more beautiful than that which dwells on the surface alone. But aside from all this, the one great essential in marriage is happiness; and happiness can live, grow and develop only when a real man marries a real woman — when the greater in the man mates with the finer in the woman.

Turning attention to the various elements and conditions that may tend to prevent the realization of ideal marriages, there are several in particular that should be mentioned; and although we need not speak in terms of criticism, still these facts must not be overlooked.

We shall refer in the first place to the tendency of a large percentage among marriageable women to think more of the wealth-producing power of the man in question than they do of his character. We know that this tendency is entirely too prevalent at the present time, and no woman with such views of life can become an ideal wife or take part in the creation of an ideal home. True, we blame no one for wanting the best there is in life. We all are entitled to every pleasure that is good, and to a reasonable supply of the luxuries of this state of existence; but all of those elements must be secondary.

We agree that no woman should be expected to marry a man that was incapable of providing for human comfort and welfare; but, on the other hand, if a woman persists in looking more at the side of material welfare than she does at the other and more important factors in marriage, she will turn her mind in the wrong direction. The whole institution of marriage will become perverted in her thought, and she will not be able to bring her best to the marital state. Every woman, therefore, who has an ideal marriage in view should begin at once to realize that the material side, with all its joys and pleasures, although thoroughly legitimate, must occupy a secondary position.

Among men the tendency is to look upon marriage as a purely physical institution, ignoring almost entirely the mental and spiritual side. We know, however, that real marriage is a mental and a spiritual state fundamentally. The physical side is secondary and must always be looked upon as such. It is the mating of souls that we have in view; and no real marriage does take place unless the true mating of souls has been accomplished. But this fact has been

My Ideal of Marriage

overlooked by women who think too much of superficial pleasures and material luxuries, and by men who look principally for physical attractiveness and personal enjoyments. The result is that the institution of marriage does, among a great many people, occupy a very common position; and those who enter marriage with such views in mind gain practically nothing through that institution, although we know that marriage does have the power to give, both to men and women, the highest joys imaginable in this sphere of existence. In this connection it will not be out of place to relate the experience of a well known character in history, and how he was made great and remarkable through the efforts of his wife. This particular man, previous to marriage, had no ambition whatever, although he had considerable talent. He was of that type of young men who do not care to work, and if left to himself would never have amounted to anything in the world. The woman that he chose for a wife, however, saw, through her fine intuition, that there was much in him, and, in fact, far more than appeared on the surface; and she married him in the faith that she might help him to become all that he had the power to become.

We admit that if a woman who marries a man under such circumstances, thinking she may make something out of him, undertakes a considerable risk; but this particular woman had faith and courage, and one of her first rules was to make her husband remain in his study at least thirteen hours every day. Her aims and desires were quite different from those of the average girl of this age. The girls of modern times — a large percentage of them — would rather devote the greater part of the day to superficial pleasures than give continuous thought and attention to the more practical side of life. However, times have changed, and in some ways they have not changed for the better.

My Ideal of Marriage

This particular woman made her husband work, and she encouraged him in every form and manner, inspiring him with the faith that he had the making of a great man; and she was determined to make him realize his greatness to the very highest possible degree. She was gentle, but firm in all her ways, and succeeded, not through forceful methods, but through the well-known methods of kindness, courage and love. In consequence, her husband obeyed, and remained long hours in his study, thereby developing himself into one of the greatest thinkers and one of the most powerful orators that modern centuries have known.

The husband of this good wife became great and famous, and his name will go down in history as one of the greatest forces for good in his age and time. His wife thought a great deal more of the possible achievements of her husband, and the wonderful good that he could do, than she did of material pleasures; and we realize full well that she secured a thousand times more out of life, through the great work that she accomplished — through and with her husband — than do those butterflies of modern days that are more of an obstacle to the achievements of their husbands than otherwise.

We do not agree with the idea that a woman should deny herself the pleasures of the present day. It is her privilege to come in contact with the best that is going on in the world; and she should by no means confine her attentions to the kitchen or the nursery. But regardless of this, we do feel that if we had a million young women today with the same lofty ideals, with the same faith and the same noble intentions as this little woman had that we have just mentioned, it would be a glorious day for the coming generation.

There is one thing in this connection that every woman should remember, and it is this: that if she marries a man who has some ability, or worth, or genius, she has it in her power to make that man a wonderful man. Every woman, if she will try, can double and treble the ability, the working capacity and the achievements of her husband. But if she aims to accomplish these greater things she must be inspired with the most lofty ideals, and must live constantly in the spirit of the great, the sublime, and the beautiful.

It is also true that even though a man may not seem to have much ability, or promise of future attainment, still a good woman can, in nine times out of ten, bring out a great deal that is latent in the mind of that man. Women do not, as a rule, realize their power in bringing out the finer elements and the superior qualities in human nature. They are positive adepts in this fine art, and all of them could become wonder workers in this art if they would give their attention more devotedly to its wonderful possibilities instead of frittering away so much of their time on the useless, the small and the superficial.

The more we consider this subject, the larger becomes the gulf between these two types of women; the one simply looking for physical comfort and superficial pleasure, while the other is looking for a great life, not only for herself and her husband, but also for her children. And although we must re-emphasize the fact that we all are entitled to recreation and enjoyments of every description, still the man or woman that lives exclusively for superficial pleasure is of no value whatever to the race. We all have potential qualities and powers that are truly remarkable; and surely no woman could realize greater enjoyment than to see herself bring out, in her husband, all the talents and marvels that are hidden in his mental and spiritual domain.

In like manner, no man could realize a greater joy than to see his wife develop steadily and continuously into an exceptional human flower — unfolding all that was sweet, tender, beautiful and ideal in her nature.

However, the modern woman gives very little attention to the bringing out of the marvels that are latent in her husband's mind; and the average man gives practically no thought to the bringing out of the beautiful and the ideal in the mind, soul and personality of his wife. We realize, therefore, that here is where one of the highest and greatest ideals in marriage may find expression. And where two well-mated souls unite in marriage, making this their principal purpose in life, we can imagine what the outcome of such a life will be. It can become nothing but wonderful, and will become an inspiration to all the world.

Considering further the elements of pleasure and enjoyment, we must remember that we cannot enjoy anything as we should unless we are in the right frame of mind; and in order that we may be in the right frame of mind, we must enter more and more into the finer, the higher and the ideal in life. Therefore, the average individual, who looks only for superficial pleasure, and does not seek to develop the richer and the greater in his nature, will find but fragments of the real thing in life and pleasure. Men and women, however, who give first thought to the development of the lofty, the noble and the sublime, will surely enjoy the many pleasures of life — physical, mental and spiritual — to a far greater degree.

The study of life, from any point of view, will indicate that growing minds always realize the most in life, and enjoy more of the best that can be found in life. Such minds have a finer appreciation of everything in the world that can produce enjoyment; and they have the capacity to appropriate, in larger measure, the richness and beauty that real pleasure may convey. We know that one hour of appreciative enjoyment, where the mind is in touch with the rich, the worthy, the lofty, the beautiful and the sublime, will bring more real pleasure than a year of empty experience with the superficial and the material.

There are certain things in life that come first; all other things occupy a secondary position; and whether we deal with marriage, or with life in any of its phases, we know that soul, character, growth, human advancement, the lofty, the noble and the sublime — these invariably must come first. When we blend all of these, and aim to bring out into realization the finest and the best there is in human nature, we shall provide every essential to a life worthwhile; and we know that an ideal marriage gives greater opportunity for the bringing out of the highest and richest and best in soul, mind, character and personality than any other condition of life; indeed, the power of marriage, herewith, is nothing less than wonderful.

There is no possible relationship where two individuals can help each other so much on the pathway of life, growth and higher realization as the relationship provided by an ideal marriage; but no marriage can be ideal unless it gives first attention to the soul side of life.

We know that any man who has ambition, who works hard, who is faithful to his vocation, who proceeds with determination and enthusiasm, ignoring all obstacles and difficulties — we know that such a man will accomplish much in life; but we also know that if such a man had a life companion who fully appreciated what he was trying to do, who really understood his purpose, who was in perfect harmony with his lofty aim, who could work with him toward the high goal he had in view, who could aid him and inspire him at every step of the way — we know that, under such circumstances, that man could accomplish two or three

My Ideal of Marriage

times as much. We all realize this fact. It is not mere fancy, or merely a pretty dream. It is a scientific truth that has been demonstrated again and again, although it can be demonstrated in a far more wonderful manner in the future, provided we give just consideration to the greater possibilities of an ideal marriage. Here, then, we have much to think about; and they who will think wisely along this line will do much for themselves, and for the race, in days to come.

The real basis of a true marriage must invariably be that of companionship. The two must be companions in the highest and best significance of the term. When they are true companions, then they have it in their power to make for themselves an ideal marriage; but if their companionship be not perfect, they are not made for each other, and the sooner they look elsewhere for their ideals the better.

Herewith remember, that no matter how much you may think of someone, the fact is that if that someone is not mutually attracted to you, you should change your mind at once, and turn attention in another direction. All attraction between man and woman must be mutual. The fact that you are in love with somebody does not prove that that somebody can be in love with you, or vice versa. And if we have proper control over our feelings, something we all should have, we will not permit our feelings to dwell upon the possibility of securing the love of those who do not, and cannot, think of us in the same way. We should, therefore, banish all such feelings, and go in search of the true ideal elsewhere, knowing that they who seek will surely find.

We understand that the element of companionship involves mutual attraction, mutual admiration and mutual worship; and there are many experiences that indicate the presence of true companionship. To illustrate: When you are in the presence of a person of the opposite sex, and feel perfectly at ease in mind and soul, and perfectly at home in the company of that person, realizing that your soul is at rest, and discerning the fact that there is an invisible something in the atmosphere that makes you say, "It is good to be here" — when you enjoy that higher and finer experience, you may know that the element of companionship is present to a considerable degree; and if the two souls involved feel the same ease and rest and joy in each other's presence, the indications are that the foundation for a true marriage may be established in that very place between those very people.

Another experience that indicates the presence of real companionship may be enjoyed when two people find it possible to be in each other's company for any length of time without finding it necessary to entertain each other with conversation, or in any other mode or manner. If they feel perfectly happy just to be in each other's presence, they are surely ideal companions; and if such companionship continues uninterruptedly, under various circumstances and conditions, the indications are that those two people are admirably adapted to each other, and therefore they could establish, an ideal marriage if they both understood the meaning of such an ideal.

We know that real companionship between the man and the woman invariably brings into expression that higher and finer feeling of mind and soul that means so much, and that tends to increase all the joys and qualities worthwhile in life. In brief, real companionship has a tendency to develop all that is beautiful, superior and sublime in human nature; and it always acts as a refining influence — an influence that is upbuilding and inspiring to a wonderful degree.

My Ideal of Marriage

In marriage, therefore, the principle of real companionship should be selected as the foundation; and we know that such companionship will involve a powerful attraction between the personalities of the two as well as between the minds and the souls of the two. The power of attraction in real companionship is triune, and acts irresistibly on the three great planes of consciousness — the physical, the mental and the spiritual.

Analyzing the chief essentials to an ideal marriage, there are many things that will have to be considered, and among these the physical side of marriage is by no means the least important. We shall not go into details, however, as that will not be necessary. It is only the vital principle that need receive attention, because those who understand the vital principle will be able, through their own judgment, to regulate the physical side of marriage according to their highest ideals.

We find that the majority of those who have written upon this subject have dealt almost entirely with the physical side, thinking that the solution of the question involved was to be found in a better understanding of that side; but this does not happen to be true, although there is a very important law involved in the physical side of marriage that must be observed, and observed absolutely under every circumstance.

The vital principle involved in the physical side of marriage and the law to which we refer is this: That the physical side must, at all times, and all through life, be in the keeping of the woman; and the reason why is found in the fact that nature has so created man and woman that it is absolutely necessary to observe this law in order that happiness and harmony may continue.

My Ideal of Marriage

We know that in most marriages this law is violated continuously; and it either leads to unhappiness and final separation, or leads to that condition in married life where very little attraction can exist between the man and the woman; and we know that marriage ceases to serve its divine purpose the moment this higher and finer attraction between the man and the woman begins to dwindle into indifference. It is something, therefore, to be avoided at any cost.

It is true that in many instances the character of the two people is so fine, and their admiration for each other so strong, that they succeed in overcoming the ill-effects that naturally follow the violation of this law; but in dealing with the ideal side we cannot afford to place any obstacle in our way; and at all times we must be true to nature — physically, mentally and spiritually. And we repeat, that nature has so created human life that the physical side of marriage must be in the keeping of the woman. She is the natural queen of that kingdom, and must have the privilege to decide what is to be done in that kingdom — where and when and how.

We admit that a materialistic man would object to such an idea; but a materialistic man is totally incapable of providing those essentials that are required in the building of an ideal marriage. With him the privileges of marriages are, as a rule, synonymous with physical pleasure, and therefore he does not discern the higher, the more beautiful and the more sublime relationship that can exist between a man and a woman when love is strong, and the law referred to is complied with under every circumstance.

Here we are glad to note that the purely materialistic man, as far as marriage ideals are concerned, is gradually disappearing from view. We now find that a large percentage of the men of this age are beginning to recognize the great law just mentioned, and count it a privilege to comply with that law. This is perfectly natural because the higher type of man does not seek women for physical pleasure alone, but for the sake of love; and we know that love will do anything for anybody regardless of cost or personal privilege.

When the man really loves, he will sacrifice all his own pleasures for the good of the woman; and when a woman loves, she will indeed do the same. However, where love is true and strong between the two, and where the law referred to is complied with, there need be no real sacrifice on either side. The contrary will be the truth, because in complying with this law the joys of marriage will be lifted to a finer plane and, therefore, those joys will be increased to a remarkable degree; in consequence, there is no loss but much gain, and the man gains fully as much as the woman.

We might note in passing that if our forefathers had obeyed this law, we all should have been far better off physically and mentally; because our heritage would have come, not through ignorance and mere impulse, but through the expression of the highest and the finest elements in human nature; and here we may add that the greatest joy and the highest happiness, as well as the greatest welfare to everybody concerned, can only come when we are true to nature. Therefore, the man who violates natural law will defeat his own purpose, becoming a stumbling block to his own aspirations and ambitions, to say nothing of the unhappiness and confusion that he may create in the lives of others.

Such men may think that they are helping themselves, but the truth is that they are steadily decreasing their power to help themselves. They imagine they are enjoying themselves because they are giving in to their desires; but they soon find that they have defeated all the objects of real joy for the mere sake of doing what they imagined at the time would be conducive to the greatest joy; but nothing can be conducive to the greatest joy where natural laws are being violated. Nature therefore must be first considered; otherwise the end we have in view will be defeated. It would be interesting to go into detail along this line, and if such were our privilege, we could prove conclusively that the law referred to is absolutely true to nature, and that its observance is absolutely necessary to the future welfare of the human family.

A very important essential, therefore, to be considered in connection with an ideal marriage is to give the woman the privilege to rule absolutely over the kingdom of the physical side. This is not only her privilege, but it is best for everybody concerned that she have the right to exercise this privilege; and we may count upon the good judgment and the love of the woman to so rule in this kingdom that no real joy will be lost at any time. In this connection we must remember that the normal woman has the capacity to enjoy all the pleasures and privileges of a real marriage to the same degree as the normal man; but in order that all this enjoyment — physical, mental and spiritual — may be complete, she must have the right to govern the physical side at all times.

When we proceed with our study of the psychological side, which is indeed both vast and interesting, there are several principles that will require thorough consideration. In the first place, we find that the love between the man and the woman should be given freely, and without the slightest reserve under any circumstances; but this principle is seldom observed, even among the best of marriages, and the reason is found in the fact that past training and heredity have given the mind of the woman a tendency to restrain or repress her feelings. She thinks it is her duty to place a check upon her affections for fear she might make it known

My Ideal of Marriage

to the man that she is deeply in love. Such a course, however, can lead to nothing but discord and disappointment to both parties concerned.

We have heard much about the tendency of the woman to deceive the man, and her effort to hide the fact that she is in love; and the observations of the race along this line have brought us all to the conclusion that deception in matters of affection has always been a part of the nature of the woman. This, however, is not absolutely true; but she has been trained so long in this practice that it has become a part of certain phases of her characteristics.

Many psychologists have stated that it was necessary for the woman to deceive the man, or at least to hide a larger portion of her feelings and desires, their arguments being that the woman becomes more attractive to the man if her charms are partly hidden or revealed only through the veil of deception or tact; and it may be true that men in prehistoric ages, or even in recent ages, were in that state where they would feel greater attraction for that which was partly hidden than for that which was fully revealed; but the human race at the present time is changing remarkably in this regard.

The truth is, that it is only to the crude mind, or to the materialistic mind, that those things that are partly hidden seem the most attractive. The reverse is true, however, where the mind has attained the understanding of the truth, and is no longer groping in the dark. The reason for this is found in the fact that the crude mind cannot appreciate the whole truth; therefore, it is better to hide a portion of the truth while in the presence of such a mind.

The highly developed mind cares less for that which is partly hidden, because to such a mind it is only the whole truth that has real value and worth. This being true, and it is fast becoming more and more true in the minds of all the enlightened races upon this planet, we realize that woman will find it necessary to change her tactics decidedly. In the past she made it her practice to hide her charms at least to some degree. She aimed to give a suggestion only as to how she felt and as to what her desires might be; and she has been drilled, for so many centuries, along that line that it has become a sort of second nature for the fair sex to practice deception in connection with her affections, and to do so unconsciously. But the time is at hand for a decided change in this direction. A large percentage of the masculine minds of this age are coming to a place where they understand life and nature in all its phases, and are developing the power to appreciate the higher and the beautiful in every form of expression. And such minds are reaching that high degree of appreciation where they are attracted only to the whole truth — and are not fascinated by the glaring arts of feminine deception.

This is self-evident because the mind that is in the light wants the truth, and the truth only. Such a mind is not attracted to deception in any form; but, on the contrary, will lose interest whenever in the presence of deception. When a woman meets such a man she will do well not to try to deceive him, because if she employs the methods of the past, she will no longer manifest an attraction for him. If she practice deception she will not be true to herself; and the more enlightened man wants a woman to be true to herself, and to give expression, not only to a part of her affections, but to all of her finer feelings, thus revealing the full beauty and charm of her mind and soul. Then, indeed, will she become tremendously attractive to the man who can appreciate the sublime and divine in the feminine soul; and such a man will be attracted far more to the soul of such a woman than to her personality, although personal attraction will be sufficiently strong at all times to make the two feel that they are absolutely one in body as well as in mind and spirit.

It may be argued that such men are not sufficiently numerous to make it safe for the modern woman to change her tactics, but the truth is that such men are far more numerous than we imagine; in fact, they are already in the majority among the more civilized races; and therefore the woman of the future will find it necessary to forget all the advice that she has secured, previously, on the art of pleasing men — advice that was written out by men or women who lived in the belief that we are attracted the most to that which is partly hidden, or to that which does not reveal itself but simply suggests itself.

Such advice is of no further value among the enlightened; and the woman of the future will find that the best masculine minds will want the pure truth in all its forms and manifestations. Such men will be far more attracted to the woman that reveals her real soul than they will be to the woman who hides her real soul and simply reveals a few superficial charms that are more physical than otherwise.

Herewith we ask ourselves a most important question: that is, if we can be true to ourselves when we are not true? Again, can we find the whole truth anywhere so long as we are trying to hide some of the most beautiful and sublime expressions of truth? And again, can we develop the highest feelings, the highest sentiments, the truest aspirations and the most beautiful expressions of life so long as we try to hide those finer feelings, or try to make others, as well as ourselves, believe that we are not what we really are?

All of this we realize is a contradiction of terms; and here we shall find one of the most important reasons why the human race with regard to love, affections and the finer feelings, has been so confused; for the truth is that any effort toward suppression of the higher and the finer in human nature invariably leads to confusion. It is not the suppression of our finer feelings that will protect us; nor do we gain protection from the reverse; that is, from the free and uncontrolled expression of our feelings. True protection in the best sense of the term can come only through the full expression of all of our highest feelings, and when such expressions are under the direct control and mastery of the superior in mind and soul.

In this place we discover why the race has found it impossible to understand the woman. In every age the statement has been made that woman is never understood; and the reason is that she has not revealed herself; she has tried to suppress the highest, the finest and the most beautiful in mind and soul; but suppression does not lead to revelation. We cannot understand that which is hidden, or that which is covered up under deception and suppressed states of mind. It is out of the question to understand women under such circumstances; and it is true that no woman can be herself, or secure her full rights and highest privileges upon this planet until she is understood.

We also realize that if the woman refuses to be true to her thought, her feelings and her affections, or to the one man upon whom she has promised to bestow her affections, she cannot give expression to her true worth. Such a woman will always be less than what she can be. And here we should emphasize the fact that, if the most attractive and best developed among women would give full expression to all their higher and finer feelings and affections, they would become far superior to what they now are, both in personal charm and spiritual power.

My Ideal of Marriage

In an ideal marriage it will be absolutely necessary for the woman to give all of her love. Such a marriage cannot be created under any circumstances if she only gives a fraction of her affections; but it has been said that if she does give fully of her whole life, then mere material man will take advantage of her position; and this may be true with mere material man; but we are not dealing with mere material man when we are speaking of an ideal marriage; besides, that type of man is disappearing; he is steadily losing ground and is decreasing in number everywhere.

The woman of today need not be disturbed about the man who is purely material; she can single him out instantly at any time. The other man, however, the new type, although alive with physical energy and virility, lives just as much for the mental and the spiritual, and will express his affections, not through the body exclusively, but equally through mind and soul. This type of man also appreciates the finer feelings and the sacred privileges of the true woman. Such a man, therefore, would not under any circumstances, take advantage of woman simply because she is trying to be true to herself. The truth is that he would appreciate her new position to the fullest degree, and therefore admire and love her far more than he possibly could if she revealed simply a portion of her affections and tried to suppress the remainder.

Then again we must remember that where love is real, whether on the side of the man or the woman, there will be no desire to seek pleasures or enjoyments that cannot be entered into, to the same perfect degree, by the other person concerned. When you love someone you only want to do what gives pleasure to that someone; and we know that the new type of man is developing real love. Considering this matter further, we shall find it interesting to note that one of the chief desires of the feminine soul is to become more and more attractive; and we have all observed what a transformation for the better invariably takes place, in the personality of the woman, when she really begins to love. She becomes far more beautiful than she ever was before; and her personality becomes charged with a wonderful something that we cannot define; but it does make her wonderfully attractive in every form and manner.

A certain woman may not be attractive in personality, but the moment she begins to love she becomes beautiful. We find, however, that in many instances she does not continue in this beautiful mode of expression, and we know the reason why. When she marries she sometimes finds it necessary to suppress her finer feelings, due to the fact that she married a mere man, or because the marriage was the result of physical attraction only; and she begins to suppress more or less those finer feelings and those sublime sentiments that were so wonderfully awakened in her soul when she first began to love. Accordingly, she decreases to that extent the charm of her personality, and also the attractiveness of her mind and soul. This proves conclusively that the very moment a woman begins to love with her whole heart and soul she becomes infinitely more beautiful than she was before; and on the contrary, the moment she begins to suppress her feelings, she begins to become ordinary, both in appearance and in mentality.

We understand fully that, in the past, many a woman found it necessary to suppress her finer feelings in the marriage state in order that she might not be taken advantage of by mere man; but such is not an ideal marriage, and we are not dealing with the misuse of love, or the violations of the principles of marriage; we are dealing with an ideal marriage. And when a woman marries she should remember that the moment she begins to suppress her affections and her finer feelings, she will become less and less attractive. In consequence, she will receive less and less admiration from her husband, so that the attraction between the two may in time become so insignificant that the man, if he be a mere man, will seek affection elsewhere.

Under such circumstances, instead of seeing his wife develop into a more and more beautiful woman, the man will discover that she is beginning to wither. He realizes that her finer feelings are being suppressed, and that he is not receiving all the love of her mind and soul. All that remains, therefore, is her physical body; and that in itself becomes unattractive, and begins to age quickly, the moment the elements of love are no longer given full and free expression.

In this very connection we might go into minute details and analyze the most important principles that are involved in the increase of affection between some couples and the decrease of affection between others; but we all can see that unhappiness in marriage, as well as separation, can and do find their origin in this very place; that is, where love is not given fully and freely; or where some of the finer feelings of the woman are suppressed for fear she be taken undue advantage of by the man.

Such a situation, we realize, is all wrong; and both the man and the woman should face the facts as they are, and come to an understanding immediately as to what would be right and natural. The answer to their problem would be this, that henceforth, the woman should give the man all the love of her heart and soul, and should, at every opportunity, show him, not only real love, but bestow upon him all those delicate affections and attentions that a woman in love can express in such a wonderful and such a beautiful manner. In response to this rare privilege, the man should comply with the law previously mentioned, that the physical side of marriage should be absolutely in the keeping of the woman. Then if the two complied with such an agreement, the man would realize a hundred times greater joy through married life than before; and the woman, in addition to the increase of her happiness, which would be extraordinary, would become more beautiful and more attractive every day. This change would react upon the husband's admiration, and he would love her better and better all through life.

We all can appreciate such a situation; and we agree that, if such a course were pursued in married life, an ideal marriage would follow in nearly every instance; happiness would multiply again and again every year; and the most beautiful, the most perfect, and the most worthy that does exist inherently in the mind and soul of the human entity, would find a finer and a larger expression. Thus we should have the constant development of the man and the woman along all those higher and finer lines in which the awakened of this age are so deeply interested.

Briefly stated, happiness would be increased; human advancement would be increased; the intellectual power of the man would be increased; the charm and attractiveness of the feminine personality would be increased; the good and the true and the beautiful on all planes — physical, mental and spiritual — would be steadily developed; and the expression of the ideal in life would come forth, through all the channels of thought and action, in an ever-increasing measure. And the fairest dream of life — the dream of love — would be realized in all its glory and joy.

Nothing Succeeds Like Success

Nothing Succeeds Like Success

THIS is a statement with which we are all familiar; and we all know it to be true; but do we know why it is true?

When we begin to think of this statement, really think, we find it to be pregnant with facts and possibilities far beyond anything the majority ever imagined; and when we understand these facts and possibilities we shall find the real secret to all success.

The understanding of these things, however, cannot be gained until we study carefully the psychology of success itself, as well as the psychology of the above mentioned statement. And we realize beforehand that we shall, through such a study, find facts that will positively prove invaluable.

When we think of success, we usually think of the accumulation of wealth, but this can never be more than a small fragment of success, because success in reality signifies any form of attainment or achievement that is truly worthwhile. And it is very important that we realize this larger meaning of success before we attempt to comprehend the psychology of success.

The fact is this, that anyone who is advancing in their work, is successful to that degree, whether their recompense be large or small; and no one can be spoken of as successful unless steady advancement is clearly evident. It is only the mind that is moving forward, or rising in the scale, that can succeed, because success invariably implies the adding of more and more to what we already possess, whether those possessions be tangible possessions, achievements and attainments or riches of mind and soul.

When we understand the full meaning of success, we shall find that the reason why nothing succeeds like success is due to the fact that the psychological process of success contains, within itself, the real power for success; and when that power has actually been placed in action, it tends invariably to produce greater and greater success.

This is something we shall understand perfectly before we are through with this important subject, and we shall find it interesting to the extreme.

When we examine any movement in life that is steadily advancing, or examine a successful enterprise, or some great achievement in the process of development — when we examine these things, we find two factors that are chiefly concerned. One of these is the human mind, or group of minds, directly responsible for what is being accomplished; and the other is the effect produced by this particular accomplishment, upon other minds, near or far, interested or unconcerned.

In other words, when you examine success, you will first meet the mind that is promoting that particular success; and it will be very interesting to note how success affects that mind, and how the process of success is affected in return. In fact, it is right in this very place that we shall discover why nothing succeeds like success. And when we make this discovery, then the real secret to success will be a secret to us no more.

We know that whenever an individual begins to succeed, certain things begin to transpire in his or her mind — certain things that have not transpired in that mind before; that is, not in the same degree; and this is particularly significant.

In the first place, that individual begins to appreciate themselves; and the moment real self-appreciation enters any mind, the power to become and achieve actually doubles in that mind. Thus we realize how success, in this regard, gives the mind the power to succeed more.

In like manner, there is increase of self-confidence, ambition, aspiration, and the desire to attain and achieve on a larger scale. All these things arise more and more in the mind that has begun to succeed; and they all are positive forces for still greater success.

Then we discover that the coming of success tends to produce greater harmony of action among all the forces and faculties of the mind; and this is extremely important, because the mind that can work in a state of active harmony has from three to ten times the capacity of the mind that is unstable, confused or chaotic.

This fact illustrates very clearly how success, when once begun, actually creates within itself the power to produce greater success; and that is one reason why nothing succeeds like success.

More important than any of the foregoing is this: that whenever the individual begins to succeed, then their mind begins to act more successfully. When you find that you are a success, you begin to infuse your mind with the idea of success — with the feeling, the consciousness and the spirit of success. And accordingly, your mind will proceed to work more successfully, thereby giving you the power to succeed more largely than before.

This very thing we all can appreciate perfectly; and we fully understand how the success of the individual must increase in the tangible world as the mind is trained to act more successfully in the mental world. Like causes produce like effects. A mind that is a success in itself — that operates successfully as a mind — will naturally produce success when called upon to act in the practical world; and this practical success will naturally increase with the increase of successful action in the mind itself. These are all self-evident facts — facts that illustrate most forcefully the importance of the subject under consideration.

Thousands of young men and women go out into the world expecting to succeed, not having given a single thought to the great principle, that the mind must be a success before the man can be a success. And therefore the majority do not realize their cherished ambitions nor their lofty dreams.

We must have efficiency in the mind before we can have it in the shop. The workmen of the mind must be trained in efficiency and skill, and inspired with the spirit of success, before the man himself can produce success. But paradoxical as it may seem, success itself, when once begun, invariably creates, in the mind, the power to produce still greater success.

A most important fact is this, that when you begin to succeed you begin to feel, more and more, that you can succeed; that is, you begin to think that you can; and we are beginning to understand the real reason why he can who thinks he can.

When you begin to think that you can, then you will find that all your faculties and talents begin to act, with greater ability and power, upon the one thing you are trying to accomplish, and results will increase remarkably in consequence.

We can readily note the difference between the man or woman who thinks that he or she can, and the one who doubts their own ability. The latter will not put forward a great deal of energy; in fact, they will express but a small fraction of their ability and power; but success does not come in that way. The former, however, will turn on more and more of the current; he or she will apply themselves more and more effectively; they will become thoroughly enthused, and will express their very best under every circumstance.

We may state the fact in this fashion: He who thinks he can, will arouse within him the power that can. And whenever we begin to succeed, we will begin to think and know that we can. This will lead to greater and greater success; and here we find another reason why nothing succeeds like success.

Every individual mind can reach the goal in view, and accomplish what is desired, if all the power of that mind is concentrated upon the one thing that is to be done. In other words, if all the talents and energies of any mind are directed upon the one object in view, that object simply cannot fail of realization, no matter how difficult it may seem to be, for the fact is, that there is enough power in any mind to realize any human desire, provided the all of that mind is correctly applied. And he who really thinks that he can will apply more and more of that all.

The psychology of the statement, "He can who thinks he can," is very simple, but in the application of the principle, the individual must be absolutely certain that he or she does think they can.

To illustrate, you may have a great achievement in mind, and you may have come to the conclusion that you positively can see it through successfully; but here is a fine point. You may think that you can; but if the undertaking is very difficult, one that will require much talent and time, you may, the more you consider the magnitude of the project,

Nothing Succeeds Like Success

find all sorts of little doubts coming up in your thoughts; and these may be followed by a score of "if's" and "but's"; so that really, after all, you are not exactly thinking that you can. You are simply on the outskirts of the "can," and not as yet in the very spirit of the real I Can.

Here we must remember that mere hope or a general belief is not sufficient; nor will it avail to pretend that you can, or try to "bluff" your mind into the idea that you really do think you can. The fact is, that when you actually think that you can, and think so in the very spirit of that conviction, there will be no doubts; absolutely none; and where there are no doubts, there are no impossibilities.

When we analyze this state of the mind thoroughly, we shall find that every force, every element and every atom of the mind becomes imbued with the spirit of "I can" whenever you really think that you can. The whole mind, and the real life and essence of the whole mind, becomes aroused with the same positive conviction; and this means that the whole mind and everything in the mind will begin to concentrate positively upon the object in view, and proceed to work with full force for the one thing you wish to accomplish.

Here, then, we find the very thing we all have been looking for; that is, the secret of causing the whole of the mind to work with full force for the object we have in view; for we all agree that when all of the mind — every force, faculty, element and power in the mind — when all these work together upon any project, then genuine success will positively follow.

This may seem to be a farfetched statement; but we know that every mind contains undreamed of possibilities and latent forces beyond all limitation. Then we have the vast subconscious field; so that every mind has sufficient upon which to draw for the realization of any goal or ambition conceivable. And there is nothing that creates a greater draw upon the marvelous powers of the mind, than the deep interior feeling that you can.

Another fact of vital importance in the same connection is this, that the human mind has the power to reproduce itself again and again on a larger scale; that is, your own mind has the power to make itself twice as large, twice as powerful and twice as brilliant as it is now; and then rebuild itself a second time on a larger scale, a third time, a fourth time, and any number of times for an indefinite period. Every individual faculty or talent also has the same power; and, than this fact, there is possibly nothing more stupendous in the entire psychology world.

When we appreciate this fact, we shall never hesitate when facing difficult or gigantic undertakings; and under no circumstance will we ever say, "It cannot be done"; for every individual mind has the power within itself to make itself large enough and great enough to achieve anything.

Illustrating this fact, you may have an exceptional ambition, an ambition that refuses to be "downed"; but your common sense informs you that your mind will have to be twice as large, twice as able, twice as powerful as it is now before that ambition could be realized. Should you give up? The average person would; but here we come face to face with this stupendous fact — your own mind can reproduce itself on a larger scale, and become twice as powerful and twice as able. Then should you give up your cherished ambition? Positively not. On the contrary, you would proceed to rebuild your mind again and again until it became large enough to make that ambition come true.

Nothing Succeeds Like Success

There are thousands of promising men and women who declare, "I would like to do this"; "I have that particular ambition; but I have not the talent; I AM not able enough to do what I want to do." But what of it? The mind can grow. You can become able enough. That which is small today can become great and powerful tomorrow. The force that can produce this increase in your own mind, or in any special faculty or talent, does exist now in your own mind. And the first step necessary to cause this great force to proceed with its wonderful work, is to awaken within yourself the deep interior feeling that you can.

Nothing Succeeds Like Success

WHEN you begin to succeed, and are actually producing results, you will find that you are awakening within yourself, more and more, the feeling that you can; and this feeling invariably arouses the desire to succeed still farther. In addition, this feeling convinces the mind that greater success is possible; and, in fact, proves to the mind that greater success can be achieved now.

Here is where we meet the real psychology of success; that is, the underlying forces that determine success; and we find, first, that the very force or consciousness of success itself tends to produce, both the power and the opportunity for greater success; and, second, that the more perfectly we succeed in producing results in the external world the more perfectly will our own mental elements and faculties work for success. In other words, when you begin to succeed — begin to feel that you are a success, you stimulate all the forces and talents within yourself to do better work — to work more successfully for greater and greater success.

The reverse is also true; that is, when you live in the idea that you cannot succeed, you place a check upon all your faculties and capabilities; and you may, in this manner alone, reduce your own ability and working capacity, for the time being, from ten to fifty percent, and sometimes more. Therefore, you wrong your mind, yourself and everybody concerned whenever you tolerate the belief that success is not for you.

In this connection, we should remember, that there is nothing that is more effective in prompting your mental elements to do better work, and more work, than the positive conviction that you can — the deep interior feeling that you can.

Nothing Succeeds Like Success

We realize, therefore, that when we constantly live in that attitude, knowing that we can, and work in the understanding of the fact that the mind, and all the faculties and forces of the mind, can reproduce themselves, again and again, on a larger scale — when we know these things, and in that knowledge proceed with our work and our development, there is nothing we cannot accomplish — no height in the scale of achievement we cannot reach.

The psychology of it all is this, that when you get into the real current of success, you will draw, from a hundred different sources, more and more force and power with which to increase the volume and capacity of that current, thereby proving the law — "nothing succeeds like success" — and illustrating, on every hand, the fact that it is only in the life, spirit and force of real success that we find the secret to greater success.

When we work and live constantly in the feeling and conviction that we can succeed, we naturally concentrate more perfectly and more positively upon the goal we have in mind. We also turn on, so to speak, more of the current; that is, apply a greater measure of the power we possess. And these things aid tremendously, both in the realization of present success and in the building for still greater success.

Our analyses of all these facts illustrate how the realization of success affects the individual themselves — how the individual's talents and powers are inspired to still greater efforts when they know that they actually have become a success; and also, how their talents and powers are given increased capacity through the living presence of the spirit of success in his or her mind and soul. And we all appreciate the vast importance of this gain for the individual within themselves; but there is another side to the process that is equally important — something with which we all are

Nothing Succeeds Like Success

quite familiar; that is, the effect that the success of the individual will sooner or later have upon the world in general and upon his or her immediate associates in particular.

On every hand we find evidence of the fact that the successful man or woman invariably becomes the center of attraction in their own world, and among all minds that appreciate the merit of his or her achievement; and the psychological value of such a situation we can clearly understand. In the first place, he or she will realize that they have become a power in the sphere of their influence; and this realization will tend directly to increase their own consciousness of power, thereby causing greater power to awaken and develop in their mind and soul. Thus, he or she becomes more powerful in their own world, and among their associations, by constantly giving evidence of power in their life and work. Another illustration of the great fact that nothing succeeds like success.

In the second place, they will, through their own success, create increased confidence in the minds of all with whom they may come in contact And this increased confidence will not only add to his or her prestige, but also give them all kinds of opportunities for the attainment of still greater success. We say that much gathers more, and that, "To him that hath shall be added." Here we find some of the reasons why; and we meet evidences every day of the fact, that it is the man or woman who is making a success of their life who is given the best opportunities to succeed on a still larger scale.

Furthermore, when the world begins to have more faith and confidence in you, you will naturally begin to increase your faith and confidence in yourself. And the more faith and confidence you have in yourself, the more you will accomplish under any circumstance. Therefore, when you have proven your faith, and your real merit, by producing tangible results — results of actual value to the world, results that the world can appreciate — when you have done these things, the world will, through its larger faith in you, help you, by increasing your own faith, to produce still greater results. And this process of increase may continue all along the line for an indefinite period, or until you reach the very climax of attainment and achievement upon this planet.

In this very place, however, we may, with profit, pause to consider a serious obstacle in the way — the tendency of the average individual to "lose their head" when real success begins, so that instead of taking advantage of those greater opportunities that invariably appear on the pathway of success, he or she "falls down" and soon will be moving in the wrong direction.

To avoid such a calamity it is only necessary to distinguish clearly the difference between the "exaggerated ego" and genuine self-confidence. Then, to develop the latter, and completely eliminate the former through absolute neglect. And here it is well to remember that an "exaggerated ego" lives on the surface, is always puffed up, never substantial, while real self-confidence is of the soul, filled through and through with quality, superiority and worth.

In the third place, the successful individual will, through a peculiar tendency in human nature, receive direct aid, encouragement and cooperation from a large percentage among those who are interested in his or her project or aim; for it is very strange, but true, that mankind seems to feel impelled to help the successful man or woman to succeed more.

People in general wish to associate themselves with success, and invariably prefer to do business where they find the greatest evidence of success. They have a natural aversion, however, for a man or an institution that is not making good. In other words, the human race instinctively works on the side of the successful — is vitally interested in making success greater success, but takes very little interest in helping make success out of failure. And, although this fact may not speak well for the large-hearted-ness of the race, still when considered carefully is found to be the correct attitude.

It is one of the great laws of life that no man should expect help from others until he first has proven that he can help himself. In other words, you must make good use of the talent you have received before you can enlist the cooperation of additional talent. You must prove your power in little things before you can be given jurisdiction over greater things. This is the law, and it is a law that is absolutely necessary to human advancement.

We remember the proverb, "God helps those that help themselves"; and the same is true of nature, and also of mankind. In fact, everything in life complies instinctively with this law — to enlist with those who are moving forward, to add power where they are successfully using power, to increase the good where they are actually making good, to add to them that have, to help produce greater success where they are positively demonstrating success — and help build where genuine building is now in progress.

Is this a heartless law? On the contrary, it is the very reverse, because it impels the race to work with the forces of construction and thus further the advancement of everything in life. Then we must remember, that any individual who will proceed to really help himself — to make the best use of the talent and power he may possess, will soon secure the benefit of this great law — will soon receive cooperation from

Nothing Succeeds Like Success

all sides — will soon come to a place where he will have all the aid and opportunity necessary to make his own success a still greater success.

First prove that you are worthy; first demonstrate the fact that you can stand alone in your smaller kingdom; then all the forces of life will come with you to give you place and position in a larger kingdom. The original step, therefore, depends upon the individual; and the individual who does prove true to his or her own talent need not feel disturbed over the future. All the building forces of life, as well as the interest, thought and expression of other individuals, will soon come over to his or her side. But under every circumstance he/she must continue to be their best. He or she must continue to be success within themselves; and success will come to them from every source in the outer world.

When we take simply a superficial view of life, we may meet many apparent exceptions to these rules; but all these exceptions are merely apparent, and arise, either from neglect along certain lines, or from the imperfect application of principles and methods along other lines. The main rule always holds good no matter how ignorantly or imperfectly we may apply the laws of life on the right or the left. And therefore the successful individual invariably receives, both from nature and from mankind, all kinds of means and opportunities to create for themselves still greater success.

This is as it should be; there are many psychological reasons why, a few of which have been mentioned; and every individual has the privilege to take advantage of this very situation. You can also become a vital center around which, and with which, the great forces of life and humanity may work; and by taking such a course, you will not only further,

Nothing Succeeds Like Success

most remarkably, your own advancement, but also the advancement of everything worthwhile upon this planet.

Nothing Succeeds Like Success

IN our study of the psychology of success, with a view of finding why nothing succeeds like success, we discover many facts and phenomena; and among these we find that whenever an individual begins to give full and effective expression to their own talent and power, they tend to place themselves in greater harmony with the constructive forces of nature, so that everything in nature will begin to work with them according to the power and determination of their aim.

We all have realized moments, and even days and weeks, when we could feel as if the finer forces of nature were working with us; and we have always noted that such moments followed periods of persistent endeavor on our part; so that we, ourselves, were originally the cause of this exceptional aid from the great kingdoms of nature.

The reason for this phenomenon is readily understood, because we have found in our experiments, as well as through observation, that whenever a certain force is placed in positive, constructive motion, it tends invariably to attract similar forces into the same current. We know that we are literally surrounded with natural forces of various degrees of fineness and expression, so that we can readily understand how a large number of those forces will naturally be drawn into our own life current whenever we make a determined effort to achieve and attain along a certain line.

Thus we discover how nature helps those who helps themselves; and we shall find that it is through the same law, in a higher degree of expression, that God helps those who helps themselves.

We realize that whenever an individual soul is beginning to give expression to the highest and best that may exist in body, mind or spirit, that soul will naturally be placed in more perfect harmony with Higher Power, or Infinite Power; and we understand that the more perfectly we harmonize with Infinite Power, the more of that power we will receive and appropriate, as far as we are able to use and apply at the time.

This is a law that holds true all the way upon the ever-ascending scale. We find it in the purely physical, where a powerful force attracts similar forces — where a determined individual tends to attract the cooperation of other individuals having the same aims and sympathies — where a determined mind tends to arouse and call to action similar forces from throughout the mental world — where a highly developed and positive individual tends to draw into the current of his or her life the finer life currents that may exist in nature all about them, and where the human soul, in proceeding to give expression to its highest and best, harmonizes, through that expression, with these superior forces that are continually giving expression to the highest and best.

We may be familiar with the expression, "In Tune With The Infinite"; but we should know that no individual can enter into tune with the Infinite unless that individual be literally filled with harmonious and constructive forces, all tending toward higher and greater things. We find, therefore, that the very secret of entering into harmony with Supreme Power, or realizing perfect tune with the Infinite, is found in the full application of all our talents, powers, tendencies and forces, acting harmoniously, constructively and continuously for the realization of some lofty goal.

Briefly stated, it is harmonious action, constructively applied, that can place us in harmony with similar forces, both in physical nature and in the higher realms of nature; and we know that whenever a group of forces enter into harmony with each other, they begin to work together for the one supreme goal that originally inspired the state of harmony that has been attained.

It is well to note in this connection that a state of harmony is impossible where there is not motion. Harmony invariably implies actions that are in concord. So that if you wish to enter into harmony with the forces of nature, or with the higher forces of life, or with the power of the Supreme, you must act, and you must act with all the power within you, and according to the highest and finest aspirations that you can possibly arouse in your soul.

When we consider the above, we find some very striking reasons why nothing succeeds like success, because the successful individual — the individual who is forging to the fore, making the best use of his or her energies and powers, is thereby securing reinforcements, so to speak, from the world of force and energy all about them, both in the visible and in the invisible realms of nature.

Again we find positive illustrations of the fact that much gathers more, and that wherever accumulation has begun, there the tendency to accumulate will become stronger and greater so long as the ruling force in the midst of that accumulation continues to live and work for the object in view. Recapitulating briefly, we find that whenever an individual begins to succeed, producing positive evidence of success, they will inspire faith and confidence in their associates, and also in the public in general; and accordingly, he or she will not only be in a position to attract aid and cooperation for all kinds of success, but will also meet with new opportunities at every turn of the way. This effect then, upon the outside world, is of a definite, positive nature; and that effect tends to enlist assistance, in every form and manner, from the outside world.

Nothing Succeeds Like Success

Human nature is so constructed that it invariably follows the most successful; and circumstances are so constructed that the best opportunities invariably appear upon the pathway of those who have already made good.

When we go deeper into the subject we find how the successful mind effects the forces of their own mind, arousing them all to more successful effort, and in the same way attracts valuable forces from nature, thereby steadily increasing their own power and their own capacity, so that they may achieve on a much larger scale in the future. In other words, the successful mind inspires success all along the line, attracts assistance and cooperation all along the line, and gathers and accumulates additional power all along the line. It is clearly evident, therefore, why nothing succeeds like success.

These things we appreciate perfectly. Now the question is, how shall an individual proceed who has not, thus far, made a success of their life. The world is doing nothing for them, and in fact may be against them in some respects; and nature is almost wholly indifferent, not having been called upon to act in his or her behalf; and furthermore, having made practically no use of their talents, and not having helped themselves, they are not in a position, to receive help from higher power, or from the Supreme, because it is absolutely true that God helps only that individual who helps themselves — that is, that individual who already has used the talents in their possession, and who already has made the best possible use of every power and possibility that they originally received from Supreme Creative Power.

To state it briefly, when you have made perfect use of your original talents and possibilities, then the Infinite is ready to give you more, and help you on further, so that you may advance in life; but there is no need of your praying for more until you have made perfect use of what was received originally.

This explains why most prayers are not answered. The average individual prays for help from the Supreme while the tremendous forces within them are still dormant. He or she is looking for outside aid while the marvelous possibilities within them remain untouched and undeveloped. No aid will come, however, from the outside, or from above, until he or she has made full use of the riches that already exist in the vastness of their own mental kingdom.

But the question is, what is the individual to do who has not thus far succeeded. The first step would be to proceed to make their own mind a success; that is, he or she should proceed to train their own talents and powers to work successfully. They should begin by thinking that they can, and they should dwell upon that idea until it takes positive hold of every force and element in their mind. They should decide definitely upon some great goal that they expect to reach, and should proceed to concentrate upon that goal with all the desire, force and determination they can possibly arouse. Briefly stated, they should awaken to positive and constructive action the best that is within them, and continue to use that best according to their higher understanding, regardless of circumstances and regardless of whatever difficulty or obstacle they may encounter.

Any individual, by taking such an action, will find that their faculties and talents will enter into more and more perfect harmony with each other, and thereby develop both their power and capacity, working themselves out in such a way as to actually demonstrate practical results in the external world.

Nothing Succeeds Like Success

Above all, he or she would develop in their mental world the positive conviction that they can succeed; and although this feeling might at first be more or less honeycombed with doubt, still, all such doubts would be overcome as the greater and deeper forces within them were coming to the fore, demonstrating the fact that they have within themselves tremendous talents and powers — talents and powers sufficiently large and great to accomplish anything. Such an individual would, within a reasonable time, succeed in making their own mind successful; and whenever an individual mind begins to work successfully within his or her own world, that is, within the mental world, it is only a question of a short time and further application along practical lines, when actual success will be realized externally.

Such a course would mean that all the elements of the mind would become united, and would fit themselves for greater things than had ever been thought of before; and even though some time may elapse before actual results are attained, still if the elements and forces of the mind continue to work with greater and greater force and animation for the object in view, they are actually producing the very secret, or we might say, the vital germ of success. Accordingly, they have already become successful, and they will proceed from that time on to demonstrate, more and more effectively, that nothing succeeds like success.

In this connection we should remember that we sometimes judge people unjustly because they have not achieved wonderfully in an external sense, when possibly those people have been working themselves up in the mental world to a place where they are becoming ready to take unusual action, and actually do something that is far greater than we have ever accomplished, or even dreamed of.

Nothing Succeeds Like Success

All great things must be developed first in the within; so, therefore, we must not judge according to appearances. There is many a mind today who has thus far accomplished practically nothing, externally speaking, but who has been in preparation, internally speaking, for a wonderful work, and will be heard from in the very near future.

When we understand the psychology of success we become fully convinced of the fact that when the mind has been trained within itself for successful action, that mind can positively succeed in the practical world, regardless of what the past or the present may indicate. The same is true of the mind that may have failed externally any number of times; for the fact is, that even though such a mind did not meet success along other lines, still, if success does exist in an active sense in the mind itself, that mind will, sooner or later, find a channel of expression in the external world, where wonderful success will positively follow.

We should remember this, that if the talent and the power for success does exist in the within, it will in time find its way out into the practical world, and will find the proper channel for expression. It is most important, therefore, that we continue to develop a greater and a greater measure of successful action within the mind itself, making the mind more powerful, training all the faculties and forces of the mind to work more successfully along all lines of action throughout the mental kingdom, because in this way we produce the actual cause of success; and the effect, external success, must inevitably follow.

We frequently meet people who succeed immediately after undertaking something new, and we marvel how they could grasp the situation in such a short time; but the reason is that their minds have been in preparation, possibly for years, never succeeding in anything else, but were now ready for this very thing, and demonstrated success immediately.

When we appreciate the importance of creating the spirit of success within ourselves, and also the importance of creating faith and confidence within ourselves, even before we have accomplished anything externally, we understand why we must have faith in ourselves before we can expect the faith and the confidence of the world.

In this very place, however, thousands make a serious mistake. They expect the world to approve of them before they have approved of themselves. They expect outside encouragement before they have learned to encourage their own mind. They expect help and opportunity from the external before they have proven, in their own mental world, that they can take hold of any opportunity that may appear. And here we might ask, "What is the first opportunity that naturally comes to any mind?" The first opportunity that can come to any mind is the opportunity to place all the forces, elements and talents of that mind in positive constructive action, and to train the whole mind to think that you can.

This opportunity any mind may take advantage of, and prove itself worthy; and any mind who does prove equal to this first opportunity will have a number of external opportunities; in fact, more of the best opportunities than anyone could possibly use. But if we expect this very thing to happen to us, we must consider well the law, that it is only they who prove their power in simple things that are given the privilege to apply their power in complex and greater things.

In our study of success, we have looked largely upon success as an external process, something to be achieved on the outside through the use of purely external elements, forces and methods. We have been in the habit of saying that, "This is the way to do business; this is the way to accomplish things in this place, or in that place;" and we have become so accustomed to such ideas that we overlook, almost entirely, the real power of success and the real source of an ever-increasing success.

True, there are certain external methods that must be employed in any line of endeavor, but those methods are, at best, only instruments in the hands of the mind of man; and the more we develop and train the mind, the greater becomes its capacity to use those particular methods. The external side, therefore, is always secondary, although absolutely necessary; but in the past we have given ninety percent of our attention to external methods; and the ten percent that we have given to the inner source of success has been given largely in a helter-skelter fashion.

However, when we begin to understand why nothing succeeds like success, we will begin to appreciate the fact that ninety percent of our attention should be given to the psychological side; and the psychological side involves the thorough understanding and the scientific application of certain definite factors in the mind, a number of these factors to which we have given brief consideration in the preceding pages.

We know that any skilled workman can build a good piano, but such a piano will never give forth its best until it is played upon by a genius. It is the same with so-called practical and indispensable business methods. Any practical mind can work out a business system, but no business system can produce the greatest possible results until such a system is employed by a mind that is, in every sense of the term, a genius in the world of success.

Steps in Human Progress

Steps in Human Progress

Table of Contents

Steps to the Higher Self -   450
Steps to Higher Truths -   470
Steps to the Spiritual   -   491

Steps in Human Progress

Steps to the Higher Self

IN the presence of modern thought and aspiration what may we consider the greatest, the worthiest, the most important and the most inspiring thing that man can do. This is one of the leading questions of today, and we are face to face with a new answer, an answer that has never been given before. In the fields of invention, art, discovery, music, literature, industrial achievement and special mental attainment, man has accomplished much, and he will, in all these fields, accomplish vastly more. But there is another field, the most important that was ever known, which we are about to enter; and it is in this new field that man will do his greatest work — work, indeed, that will cause the wonder works of history to pale into utter insignificance.

The age of real wonders has just begun. The next one hundred years will witness achievements so extraordinary that the terms "marvelous" and "miraculous" will not begin to describe them. Everything that the master minds of today are dreaming about will be realized, and infinitely more. Even much of what can now be discerned in the light of the soul's vision will come to pass, and hundreds of worlds, as yet closed to the minds of the many, will open their limitless possibilities to the race. Accordingly, the welfare, the happiness and the progress of man will be promoted as never before. All these things, however, will simply mark the continuation of fines of progress already in action; they will naturally follow the further development of fields that are well known, and therefore will not necessarily be the result of a new step in advancement. But man is on the verge of a new step. Among all the known wonders there is a new wonder, far greater than all the others, just appearing at the dawn of the new day, and it heralds the next step in the progress of the world.

Steps in Human Progress

Thus far human attainments and achievements have concerned themselves principally with things, and with those mental faculties that act directly upon things; and the reason why is found in the fact that we have understood only those forces in man that can be applied to things. But the coming of modern metaphysics and the new psychology has opened our minds to the consciousness and the understanding of other forces — higher and more powerful forces — forces that can be applied to elements that are above things, in brief, the creative elements within man himself. In the past, the various steps in progress have been taken in those worlds that lie outside of the being of man; but the next step will be taken in those worlds that lie within the being of man. The next step in human progress will be to gain complete mastery over the creative forces and the creative elements within the human personality so that we can transform our interior nature and our personal appearance into what may be termed an Edition de Luxe of man.

Men and women are something like books — all kinds of editions, all styles of binding and every imaginable subject introduced in the contents; but there is one difference. Among books we find editions that have quality, richness and worth, both as to contents and general appearance. The subject matter in some of these books constitutes the very essence of inspirational power, while the physical appearance is all that high art can cause it to be. Among people, however, it is almost impossible to find rich interior quality and rare personal appearance combined in the same person. The finest characters and the greatest minds do not always dwell in beautiful personalities, while persons who are exceptionally attractive to physical sight do not always possess unlimited riches of mind and soul. True, there are exceptions to all general rules; but the fact remains that Editions de Luxe of the being of man have not as yet appeared. However, if we can have Editions de Luxe of books we can have Editions de Luxe of men and women. Man has the inherent power to do far more with himself than he ever did with things; and the next step in his progress is to learn how. When we look at the human family we find any number of paper editions, cheap cloth editions and the like; although occasionally we find a few that approach something far better, and it is the psychological study of the creative elements that are active in the personal natures of these few that has given us the secret to the next step in human progress. What one person can do, all can learn to do; what a few have accomplished more or less unconsciously, all can learn to accomplish consciously and intelligently. And where unconscious action has, under favorable conditions, produced results to a certain degree, intelligent action can, under any condition, produce results to the very highest degree. This is the law, and no law in life can ever fail when properly applied.

The reason why people who are extremely attractive physically are not always competent mentally or highly developed spiritually, is readily explained. When the creative process in the human system tends to build up and perfect the outer personality, nearly all the energy generated in the system will be used for that purpose, and in consequence there will be but a fraction remaining with which to build up mind and soul. In like manner, when the creative process tends to produce mental brilliancy, most of the energy of the system will be drawn into the mind, and the development of the physical personality will necessarily be retarded. In some people we find this energy dividing itself into several forces, one of which tends to build up the personality, while the other tends to develop the various phases of mind, character and soul. And this is the ideal arrangement; therefore people who are built on these lines, are always attractive in body, brilliant in mind, strong in character and beautiful in soul;

that is, if they are well supplied with energy and do not waste their forces in any form or manner.

When the creative energies of the system naturally divide themselves among the various factors in human life, the greatest possible results are not always produced in anyone place of action; the reason being that in the average person most of the energy generated in his system is wasted; and if what remains is to be divided among several factors, the amount given to each will be small. There is enough energy, however, generated in the system to develop to the highest degree desired, everything that exists in the entire being of man; therefore, when a person properly saves his energy and applies it according to the laws of human development, he can secure just as great results in all the factors of his being as is usually secured in but one. In fact, he can do far better because he will act consciously, and will personally control the laws through which results are to be gained.

When a person has learned to save all the forces in his system, and has learned to personally control the creative elements of his being, he can develop a more attractive personality than was ever seen before; he can develop a more powerful and a more brilliant mind than was ever known before; and he can develop the very highest states of character and soul that the finest consciousness has ever discerned in the ideal. He can do all these things at the same time; he has sufficient energy when he saves it all; and what is so strongly in his favor is the great fact that when we develop the whole man we secure greater results through anyone part than we possibly could if we developed that one part alone. In this connection it is well to remember that no chain is stronger than its weakest link; but when every link is strong — exceptionally strong — the strength of the whole chain will be great indeed.

Steps in Human Progress

There are many inspiring scenes in nature — scenes that lift the soul to the very heights of empyrean realms; but the most inspiring scene of all is the sight of a human personality that reveals, in visible form, all that is pure, all that is rich, all that is high, all that is worthy, all that is beautiful and all that is ideal in existence sublime. When we are in the presence of a human personality where "the elements are so mixed" that we feel as if we have met the very climax of workmanship divine, our thoughts of man cease to dwell upon earth. Man, to us, is no longer a mere human creature; he is something more, and we begin to gain glimpses of what can be done with that "something more." And as those glimpses reveal the possibilities that he before us, we realize that we are beginning the study of the most interesting, the most profitable and the most fascinating theme that has ever presented itself to the mind of man.

When we meet people who express, even to a slight degree, the richness and the beauty that is inherent in human nature, we realize that we are in the very presence of the kings and queens of earth; and new faith is awakened within us. We no longer think of the human race as "depraved," or as "almost hopeless," or as "mere weaklings" of little more consequence than the leaf that comes with the wind, and with the same wind is blown away. We can see in man the Real Man; and as this Real Man appears before us in all his majesty and power, we begin to understand why "thou art mindful of him." We also begin to see, as never before, how much time and energy we have wasted in building up and tearing down useless things, while the greatest world of all worlds — the world within — has remained undeveloped and unexplored.

The greatest ambition of the coming day will be, not to write the best book, not to invent the most wonderful machine, not to paint the most inspiring picture, not to conduct the largest enterprise, not to amass the greatest amount of gold, but to develop and express the finest, the strongest, the most perfect, the most beautiful and the most inspiring personality in the world. To have the power to manipulate the creative elements in the world of things is truly a mark of greatness; but to exercise that same power upon the creative elements in human life is a mark of far greater greatness. And to enter this new field and develop the marvelous possibilities that are contained therein, is the next step in human progress.

We must remember, however, that to enter this new field is not to neglect other lines of progress and achievement. You may write an extraordinary book, or any number of them, and at the same time build and rebuild yourself, until you become an Edition de Luxe, both in human quality and in personal appearance. You may paint the most inspiring picture that the world has ever seen, and at the same time apply the divine art within your own being until you become the most inspiring living picture that the world has ever seen. You may conduct a great business enterprise and be a power in the world of practical things, and at the same time so direct the creative elements in your own being that you become as rich in personal quality as the possessions over which you exercise control; as noble in bearing as the kingship that rules in your mind; as strong in personal expression as the power that governs your vast domain; and as attractive in personal appearance as the richly adorned mansion you call your home. Whatever you do, you can become a genius in your sphere, and reach the highest places in practical achievement; but you can, at the same time, do even greater things with yourself. You can so rebuild and perfect your own personality that you become an Edition de Luxe in living, human form.

The personal worth of the man should at least be as great as the actual worth of his possessions; otherwise, he is not in keeping with his world. And his personal worth should be fully expressed through every atom in his being. He should "look" it in every sense of the term. The woman should at least be as beautiful as her gowns; otherwise, she is not true to the matchless charms of her nature. But this is but the beginning for her. The adorner's art is as nothing compared with the beautifying power that is latent in the feminine soul. People in general should at least be as attractive in themselves as are the houses they build or the surroundings in which they live. True, some are more attractive, but such attractiveness is born, not made. Henceforth, we must not depend on what we receive through heredity, but must proceed to make ourselves, and continue to remake ourselves until we become precisely what we wish to be. Nor is this a "mere dream" or a "useless desire." Man positively can remake himself according to his highest ideal of himself, and to do this will be the next step in his progress.

The purpose we have in mind is to consciously control and direct the creative elements in the system so as to rebuild the human personality according to our highest conception of what we personally should wish to be. These creative elements can be trained to act not only upon that finer field of life that lies back of and within the personality, but also upon the tangible personality itself, even the cell-structures of the physical body. The use of these creative elements in furthering the purpose we have in view will, at first, result in a strong, attractive personality in man, and a beautiful, charming, fascinating personality in woman. But this is but the beginning; when man learns to control the building power that is inherent in his mind, and when woman learns to control the beautifying power that is in her soul, there is no ideal in connection with the perfecting of the human entity that cannot be realized. Then every individual may certainly become an Edition de Luxe, and according to his own ideal of what such an edition should be.

This new and wonderful goal, however, is to be reached, not by acting upon the personality from without, but by unfolding the strong, the beautiful and the ideal from within. The finer elements of mind, thought, feeling, consciousness and soul are to be given predominance in every action and phase of life. And when these elements are given the first place in all that pertains to actual living, they tend to work themselves out into actual expression through the personality. Thus the personality gradually changes from a state of weakness and inferiority to a state of richness, quality and high worth. You no longer present a "common" personal appearance; the ordinary has entirely disappeared from your life, and you become one of the "rare products" of creative art divine. In other words, you remove the cheap binding from your personal appearance; you remove the cheap paper, page after page, from your nature; you insert high art illumined pages instead, and you have your entire personal self bound in de Luxe.

Man has the power to remake himself and cause both his interior nature and his external appearance to become as far superior to the "average person" as the highly cultivated rose is superior to the weed. And the day is at hand to begin. We are now in possession of the necessary principles, the necessary methods and the necessary facts; we are ready for this next step in human progress; we are ready to remake ourselves in the image and likeness of our highest ideals, and thus become, in the true sense of the term, the crowning glory of Nature's sublime creative art.

The same power, the same efficiency, the same insight and the same genius that we have demonstrated in the world of things, we can now demonstrate in that world that is above things — the world of ideal human life; and we can cause everything that is ideal in that finer life to become ideal in actual, personal life. This finer life, and the world from which it springs, is within man; therefore, it cannot be acted upon through physical means; nor can it be reached through the channels of objective actions. To act upon that world subjective actions, applied through the elements of mind, thought, feeling, consciousness and soul, become necessary. That world, however, is almost wholly undeveloped; it is virgin soil, but its productive capacity is limitless. Rich rewards, therefore, are in store for those who will learn to cultivate the new fields of that vast domain. And anyone can learn to begin at once. Moreover, to be just to ourselves and the people with whom we come in contact, we must learn to begin at once.

The fact is that no person has the right to present a cheap, common, ordinary personal appearance to the world when he knows how to build in himself a superior personality. If we carry upon us a commonplace personal appearance, we invariably produce a cheap impression upon the mind of every person we meet; and cheap impressions lead to cheap thinking and inferior living. It may seem somewhat farfetched, but it is the truth that every person who presents a cheap personal appearance tends to draw the race down into inferior thought and life. The idea, however, is not that every person, to produce good impressions upon others, must be elegantly dressed; dress does not constitute personal appearance; besides, it is those things that are alive — the living appearance — that produces the deepest impressions upon our minds. Dress as well as you possibly can; it is very important to do so, and remember, it is not the price of your clothes, but the way you wear them, that constitutes wholesome appearance. But dress is secondary; real personal appearance is in yourself, in your countenance, in your bearing, in your conduct, in your attitude, in your movements and in the general expression of your personal life. This being true, we all can have a fairly good and wholesome personal appearance, and when we learn to use the finer creative elements within us, this appearance may become extraordinary.

When you develop a superior personality, you become an inspiration to every person you meet; which fact we shall admit when we realize that a superior personality does not simply constitute a well-shaped physical form, but a refined, wholesome physical form, that is actually alive with the richest qualities and the highest states of sublime worth that can possibly be found in body, mind and soul. Shape is secondary; any shape becomes strong and attractive when alive with supreme power and high worth; and any shape becomes charmingly beautiful when animated with the very life, the very essence and the very soul of the beautiful. But the shape of any personal form can be so modified as to correspond exactly with the ideal personality we have undertaken to build. The human form is not only very plastic, but is constantly being reconstructed by the renewing forces in nature; therefore superior creative art from within will find no difficulty in remolding the personal form according to the finest pattern that we may have selected.

A beautiful woman, if she be truly beautiful in body, mind and soul, is doing more for the race than the richest and most liberal philanthropist. She is awakening those finer things in human life that alone can make living truly worthwhile. And every man who is in possession of a strong, attractive, wholesome, spirited personality, is leading hundreds, possibly thousands, to greater things. There is nothing that is more conducive to greater things than a human personality so constituted, that it tends to inspire in everybody a living desire to do greater things. And all men and women can exercise this inspirational power through their personal appearance as well as through their thoughts and deeds. These are facts, therefore it is not only what we think or say or do, but also "how we look," that determines our value to the race. But personal appearance has been ignored, or simply dealt with in the most superficial manner. An attractive personality has been looked upon as a luxury; now we know it to be a necessity. And the reason why is found in the fact that the power of appearance is one of the great powers in the world, not only in the life of the individual himself, but also in the life of every person that he may meet.

The world is governed by mental impressions, and everything we meet, in any manner whatever, produces a mental impression; but those impressions we gain from the people we meet are the strongest of all, and therefore exercise the greatest power upon our mode of life, thought and action. Happy, then, is the man whose personality gives only impressions of the strong, the worthy, the high, the superior, the beautiful and the ideal to every person that may come his way.

The foregoing facts prove conclusively that the next step in human progress is a necessity if we are to promote general progress as perfectly and as extensively as we would have the power to do if we could take advantage of all our present possibilities. But we cannot take advantage of all those possibilities so long as we, ourselves, continue to be, in many respects, an "inferior product." So long as the human personality produces inferior impressions upon the mind of the masses, the progress of mankind in general will be retarded. But, on the other hand, the more inspiring personalities we have in the world, the greater will become that power in the world that leads upward and onward. And here is our opportunity.

In taking this next step in human progress, however, we are not simply becoming benefactors. It is the individual who takes this next step who will realize the greatest gain. To prove this we might mention hundreds of incontrovertible facts, and shall at the outset present two of these, though these two are by no means the most important. First, we know that a man who has a strong, wholesome, attractive personality can accomplish fully twice as much, and more, with the same talent as the man who is personally weak, spiritless or unattractive. Second, we know that a woman who is beautiful in person, sweet in disposition and lovely in soul, can get almost anything she may want in this world. And there is a reason why — a reason that is not based upon selfish love, physical desire or personal vanity, but a reason that can only be found higher up in the finer life of ideal soul existence.

Should we have no other grounds upon which to base the value of this next step than the two great facts just presented, the subject before us would deserve all the time and attention that could be possibly given; but we are yet to look into the vast realms that this new step will open up to the mind, to the intellect, to the soul, to the fields of consciousness, to the physical senses and to all the faculties, functions, forces and elements in the entire being of man. In fact, the human world will be so enlarged, so enriched, so beautified and so perfected that the joy of living will be multiplied even hundreds of times.

We have found unlimited interest and fascination in exercising creative power in the world of things; we can imagine what our interest and fascination will be when we learn to exercise this creative power in the limitless domains

Steps in Human Progress

of real human life; and also the supreme delight that we shall naturally enjoy when we begin to note results. Surely, we can think of no step in human progress that could add so richly to the happiness and the welfare of life as this next step before us; we shall therefore proceed with more interest and with more pleasure than we ever knew before.

To proceed, begin in the beginning; and the first essential is to picture in your mind your ideal of yourself. Then continue to see this ideal picture, no matter what external circumstances or conditions may be. You will daily grow more and more into the likeness of that picture until you become in the real what you have seen in the ideal. And the reason why is found in the fact that the energies of the system invariably select your predominating thought, or leading mental picture, as the pattern for their work. What you habitually think of yourself is your predominating thought of yourself; and it is this thought that your creative energies use as their model in building and rebuilding you. Therefore, when you improve your thought of yourself by picturing in your mind your highest ideal of yourself, your creative energies will have an improved model, and will, in consequence, begin to rebuild you according to the likeness of this new and better model. This is the basic principle in all human advancement, and there is absolutely no limit to its possibility and power. And as it is very easily applied by anyone, there is no reason why we all should not make a beginning now that will culminate in far greater results than we ever dreamed

To picture in your mind that ideal of yourself that you wish to realize in personal form, it is necessary to incorporate in that picture every ideal quality that you can think of. The imagination governs completely all the creative forces of the system; therefore the imaging faculty must be trained to picture only those qualities and conditions that you wish to express in the new and improved personality.

To give all these ideal pictures predominance in consciousness, live in the consciousness of every ideal quality that you have begun to picture. This will so deepen the ideal in your life that all the elements of the ideal will become living elements throughout your being. You thus cause ideal qualities to become actual parts of your personality, and as you continue, you personally will be composed entirely of such qualities. When this is accomplished, you will have eliminated the cheap and the inferior from your personality, and the very cells in your body will have become as rich in texture as the petals of the highly cultivated rose.

When you have clearly formed in mind a complete picture of the new personality that you have begun to build, that is, when you can distinctly see yourself as you would actually appear after you had become an Edition de Luxe in human form, live with a deep, constant desire to build and express such a personality. What you constantly desire to do, you will inspire your creative energies to do, but this desire must be so deep and so strong that it becomes, not only a permanent power, but a ruling power in your life. The entire system must continue in perfect health and in perfect harmony. When the health is not perfect, the natural building processes of the system are interfered with, and it is not possible to build the strong, the beautiful and the ideal without perfect harmony.

To eliminate all adverse mental states is one of the first essentials; the reason being that everything that is taking place in the human system is more or less affected by the states of mind. Anger wastes energy and invariably tends to produce a mean expression. But you will need all the energy you possess if you wish to remake yourself; and if you wish to produce in your personality a superior expression, all your expressions, even the slightest, must be of the very best. Worry dries up the cells and produces old age conditions as well as those "dried up" conditions that are so detrimental to health, youth, vigor and personal charm. Every dried-up cell is a dead cell, and every dead cell adds so much more to personal weakness and personal inferiority. Fear retards natural and full expression; it also produces negative conditions and weakens the entire personality. No one can develop a strong, powerful, attractive personality until he has overcome fear, because every action of fear is an action of retreat; it moves to the rear; it gives up and drifts further and further back toward nothingness. The way to strength, power and higher development of every description, however, leads forward and forward continually. It is therefore most evident that no person can take the next step in human progress until anger, fear and worry have been removed from his life absolutely. But this is not impossible. Anger, fear and worry can be eliminated completely by anyone without any difficulty whatever.

Among other mental states that must be removed, we find grief, disappointment, discouragement, excitability, moroseness, the negative attitude, the critical attitude, the antagonistic attitude and states and attitudes of a similar nature. Cultivate the opposite states in every case, and the adverse ones will disappear. Live in perpetual sunshine; in fact, be sunshine; be the very spirit of joy, as there is nothing that is more conducive to the purpose you have in view than real, wholehearted joy. Live in perpetual happiness, and inwardly feel the fullness of unbounded joy. And you can, when you learn to look at life from the proper point of view.

Another great essential is to love with every fiber of your being. The power of love is a great building power, provided it is love — the love that loves because it is love, and not because it wants something in return. Love that demands recompense or reward is not love; it is a misuse of the forces of mind, and therefore an obstacle in the way of greater things. Love with the love that wants to love; love all things with such a love, and with every fiber in your being; you thus, not only arouse the finest creative elements in your system, but you direct those elements to build in yourself the strong, the beautiful and the ideal.

The rebuilding of your personality must be carried out from within; the interior life must be reconstructed according to the ideal before the ideal can be made real in the external personality; and since the interior life is almost entirely controlled by the power of feeling, it is necessary that you train yourself to deeply feel every quality, condition or force that you wish to express. In the last analysis "you look the way you feel," and the way you feel depends upon what you imagine concerning yourself and what you habitually and subconsciously think about yourself. So long as you habitually and subconsciously feel ordinary, you will look ordinary; but as soon as you have trained your deeper feelings to feel the richness, the worth and the superiority of your true being, you will begin to express superiority and high worth in your personal appearance.

Continue to feel mean, ugly, miserable or disgusted, and you will finally look these things. Continue to feel disagreeable every hour for a year, or even less, and you will not only look disagreeable, but you will become personally repulsive. These are well-known facts; but the law works both ways. Continue to feel within yourself all those qualities that naturally attract admiration, and you will become so attractive, first in your nature and then also in your personality, that you will attract the admiration of every person you meet. Continue to feel any desirable quality, and that quality will become a living power in your nature. Later it will express itself in your personality, and you will look what you feel. This feeling, however, must be continuous; it must become habitual and subconscious, and must be thoroughly alive every hour.

Continue to feel life, power, purity, refinement, sweetness and loveliness, and these qualities will be expressed more and more in your personality. By feeling these things you cause them to become living forces in your interior life; and whatever is made alive and built up in the life within, will at once begin to work itself out and build itself into the external personality. You thus, through the elements of deep feeling, cause the ideal to actually become real; or, in other words, you cause the possibilities within to become living factors in the without.

To cultivate this high art of feeling in the within that you wish to express and build up in the without, live in the consciousness of the ideal and constantly feel the fullness of the ideal. When you feel the interior fullness of a quality you develop that quality, and the development will be similar in every respect to the ideal that animates what you feel. At first, special attention must be given to the continuous feeling of every quality that you wish to develop in your nature and in your personality; but gradually, as every feeling becomes subconscious, it will be second nature for you to feel the way you want to feel; and when you feel the way you want to feel you will look the way you want to look.

To apply the principle of feeling to the best advantage, the man should live in the consciousness of strength, power, capacity, quality and worth; and the woman should live in the consciousness of purity, refinement, beauty, loveliness and soul. Continue to feel inwardly the beautiful, and the beautiful will unfold itself in every atom in your being.

Steps in Human Progress

Continue to feel the thrill of loveliness, fascination and personal charm in every fiber of your being, and you will not only become charmingly beautiful in personal appearance, but you will also gain that irresistible fascination that all the world admires so much in the truly developed feminine soul. Train yourself to feel refined, and you will express refinement in life, thought, speech, action and outward appearance. Train yourself to feel the sweetness of your ideal feminine nature, and you will become, in body, mind and soul, all that the term "human sweetness" can possibly imply.

Continue to inwardly feel strong and you develop a strong, attractive, masterful personality. Continue to feel in the within the fullness of strength and power, but do not permit this strong feeling to become overwrought or aroused beyond your absolute control. Be calm and poised while masterful and strong. Feel inwardly calm and inwardly strong, and you have the secret.

To continue to possess a personality that may rightly be termed an Edition de Luxe in human form, it is necessary to perfect such a personality more and more so long as we remain in personal existence. When we cease to promote progression we return to the ways of retrogression. An ideal personality can come only from an ideal life that is inwardly, actually and continually lived. When we cease to inwardly live the ideal and outwardly apply the ideal, our personal charms will begin to fade away. But those charms, when once gained, can be retained as long as we live, provided we continue to live charmingly, and continue to develop more and more every ideal quality that may exist in our nature.

You will never lose your strength or your power so long as you live to gain more and more strength and power. You will never lose your beauty, your loveliness or your sweetness so long as you live to become sweeter, more lovely and more beautiful than you ever were before.

The principles, methods and ideas presented in the preceding pages constitute the bridge, so to speak, over which we may pass into that new and vast domain where we may begin the next step in human progress; and having entered this domain, we are ready to take possession of the finer creative elements in the wonderful being of man, and direct those elements in such a manner as to produce any desired results in any special part of this new field. To begin, subjective concentration becomes the practical instrument through which these finer creative forces may be successfully applied; and we shall appreciate the great value of this instrument when we learn what can be accomplished through its scientific use.

Concentrate subjectively — in deep feeling — upon any part of the body, and you change the form of that part of the body to correspond with the ideal you clearly hold in mind during the concentration. This is a scientific fact, and one of the most important that this age has produced. You can prove it yourself. If there is a certain part of your face that you desire to have filled out, concentrate subjectively upon that part for a few minutes every hour, and in a few weeks you will note the desired change. You can do the same with any part of your body, because, through subjective concentration, you gain control of the finer creative elements of your system — those elements that are within and back of the cell structures, and that can produce any amount of new or improved cell structure as desired. Through subjective concentration you cannot only modify the shape and the form of the body and build for yourself a more beautiful body, but you can also improve the quality of every fiber in your system; that is, you can increase or decrease the number of cells in any part and also change the fineness of those cells, just as the horticulturist develops a common looking group of leaves into a most beautiful and highly cultivated flower.

Concentrate subjectively upon any quality in your nature, and you increase the power as well as the worth of that quality. And here we have a method through which any person can entirely change, for the better, his nature, his disposition, his character and his entire mentality. Concentrate subjectively upon any force in your system, and you not only increase the active power of that force, but you gain perfect control over the force itself, as well as its sphere of action. Concentrate subjectively upon any mental faculty or talent, and you awaken the real, interior power of that talent — that power that produces genius.

Concentrate subjectively upon any phase of consciousness, and you expand that consciousness continuously until you become conscious of worlds, realms and domains that you never dreamed of before. In brief, through subjective concentration, we may gain control of all the elements and forces that exist in the vastness of human life, and direct those elements in the remaking of ourselves according to our highest ideal. But this concentration is not the mere holding of attention here or there as we may elect. Subjective concentration is a special art — a very high art, and a most extensive art; it is the entering into the real essence of all substance and all force; it is the conveyance of a mental state or an ideal condition to any special part anywhere in the human system; it is the living of the superior in that part where you wish the superior to be expressed.

Steps in Human Progress

Steps to Higher Truths

WHEN we proceed to consider what we know about the highest truth conceivable in our present state of development, we shall meet a very great paradox, and we shall also meet the reverse of this truth; that is, what we may term the only real sin possible to the human ego — the coming down from the perfect consciousness of this highest truth, which would constitute the great fall. And when we inquire to what this highest truth has reference, our answer must be that it is the truth concerning the most sublime principle of which we are conscious; and this can be nothing less than our own real or supreme self.

We understand that we may know many things concerning the external, but we may naturally know more about our own innermost nature than anything else that may have existence in the universe. Therefore, this highest truth necessarily declares something definite concerning our innermost or supreme self; and when this highest truth reveals itself we discover that the real or eternal self, that is, the soul or spirit of man, is now in possession of what we may term the All in All, and accordingly, has no needs or requirements whatever.

When we consider life in the external we find that existence has seemingly many needs and requirements; but we find that the spirit of man, the real eternal you, does not need anything whatever, being supplied abundantly with the All in All. Accordingly, the soul of man can, in justice and truth, ask for nothing, pray for nothing, desire nothing, hope for nothing, because the soul does have everything — "All that the Father hath is mine."

However we may consider the life of the individual, the needs of the personal man, or the requirements of the human phases of existence, we come invariably to the conclusion that everything that the personal or human side of life can possibly desire or require does, even now, exist in the human soul. The great kingdom has been given to man. The eternal I AM is in itself sufficient unto itself — having all life, all wisdom, all power, all joy, and is complete, perfect, and finished in the largest and highest significance of those terms.

When we consider this great truth, admittedly the highest truth that we can discern at the present time, we will, if our analysis be complete, meet the reverse; that is, the ignoring of this truth, which would involve the desire of the ego to seek for things in the external. And here is where we find the original sin, or the fall of man — going out or down into the external for anything whatever, when the soul or the spirit is already in possession of everything heart could wish for, or that the most perfect states of life might require.

Realizing the great truth that the human spirit, or the I AM, has everything needful for eternity, then we understand that if the Human Ego goes out into the external in search of pleasure, or wisdom, or power, or possessions, or help, or anything whatever, the Ego falls; and this is the only fall, the original fall, or the original sin of which we have heard so much during centuries past.

In the last analysis, there is only one sin possible to the Human Ego, and only one real mistake that the human entity can possibly make; and that sin is to leave the marvels and the riches of the spirit, wherein everything may be found — to leave the joys of the kingdom and the glories of the heaven within, and go out in search of lesser things.

Thus we must come inevitably to the conclusion that whenever we seek pleasure, or wisdom, or power directly and exclusively in or through external sources, we are committing again the original sin — we are repeating once more the great fall. And here is where we meet the great paradox; that is, what we should do with external things; if we should seek anything in the external; or try to enjoy any phase of existence that may appear on the outside of spiritual consciousness.

The great problem is this, if the soul in its glorified state always is in full possession of the Great Good, why should we seek anything whatever in the external. Why should we care for anything existing upon the outside. Indeed, could this be right under any circumstance. And how would it be possible to seek external joys, external wisdom and power, or anything that might seem of value in the external — how would it be possible to seek those things if the mere going out in search of them would constitute a sin or a fall? This is the great paradox, a seeming contradiction of the highest truth.

Turning our attention to an expression that reveals much light in this connection, we may quote a familiar statement, which declares, "Whenever you come to a place in supreme spiritual consciousness where you actually know that you are in need of nothing whatever, then you will find that everything in external life will begin to come into your world from every source conceivable."

There are a great many enlightened and powerful souls that have applied the principle of this law; and it proves itself invariably; but it is only the enlightened that can understand the reason why.

Considering another phase of the same idea, we realize that so long as we are going out, here and there, in search of what we need or desire, we are not true to ourselves; that is, we are not true to our highest and best self — that highest and best self that does possess everything we need. Briefly stated, we step down from our lofty position whenever we seek anything in the external; and accordingly, we become confused and lose our power. Therefore, whatever we may try to secure under such a circumstance, we shall fail, or at best we shall secure only fragments; and what comes into life through a mere attempt to search in the external for the needs of life will neither give real joy nor higher power.

This explains why the multitudes are never satisfied, because if they do not have what they want they are dissatisfied, and when they do receive what they thought they wanted, they are, in like manner, dissatisfied, because what they do receive under such a circumstance is but a fragment of the All in All. The soul, however, must be filled with the highest and best, and must be conscious of the All in All, if real joy is to obtain; and as the soul does possess inherently the All in All, being sufficient unto itself, we can readily imagine how we violate all the laws of life when we go out into the external in search of anything whatever.

Another great truth, or a vital phase of the same highest truth, is this, that so long as we retain our lofty position, realizing that we have everything, being all sufficient, having need of nothing from any source, and being so complete in ourselves, in our real supreme self, that we do not even need the universe, but could abide in serenity and perfection even though the universe should disappear — when we continue in that sublime realization, we establish ourselves in the very midst of the greatest power that the soul can possibly exercise. Indeed, at such a time consciousness lives and moves and has its being in the very center of the Great Life, in the very light of the Great Wisdom and at the very heart of Limitless Power. Accordingly, the I AM, at such a time, is related perfectly to the Infinite, to the cosmos and to the entire world of things; that is, the I AM has its hold, so to speak, upon the entire situation, and can, not only master everything within its own world, but functions from that divine center of consciousness in supreme existence toward which the All-Good is moving eternally.

To state it differently, when you ascend to that supreme state of consciousness where you know that you have all things, including all power, you come into possession of the power to bring to yourself anything whatsoever, if you should so wish or desire.

When we appreciate this highest truth to the fullest degree, we shall indeed inquire again and again what we are to do with external things. But the problem is readily solved because the question is, not whether we are to ignore the external or to try to adapt ourselves to the external according to the light of this highest truth — these are not the questions involved; but the question is, whether we are to consider the external as of first importance, or look upon the manifested universe as something that is not absolutely necessary to our real existence, but that is a coming forth into external appearance of the All in All, the full possession of which we now have, and always will have for all eternity.

To use another expression, external things are not necessary to our happiness or wisdom or power any more than the rays from the sun are necessary to the existence of the sun; but because of the existence of the sun, the rays will continue to come forth perpetually; and in the same manner, because of the existence of the All in All in the soul and in the spiritual world, the manifestation of things will continue perpetually; and we can enjoy them as an expression, just as a genius enjoys his work, although knowing that his work is simply the result of what he is in himself, and of what he is doing with what he does possess within himself.

Steps in Human Progress

When we consider the element of happiness, which has been described as the highest good, we learn that we never find happiness if we go in search of happiness itself. True, we may find a few momentary pleasures through such a search; but those pleasures invariably produce undesirable reactions. The truth is, that we find happiness, not by seeking happiness directly, but by doing something that will result in happiness; and in all our doing, that is, if we wish to exercise our highest and greatest power in whatever we do, we must ascend to the consciousness of the Great Power existing in the soul. Therefore, by reasoning correctly, we understand that if we would live and work in the consciousness of the highest power of the soul, we would naturally produce those activities in consciousness that would result in the greatest happiness. In other words, the greatest happiness comes from the greatest work; and the greatest work is possible only in the consciousness of the greatest power — the power that we exercise and apply when we live and think in the realization of the great truth that the soul now is in possession of the All in All.

We may consider all forms of conditions and things, and we invariably find that they prove unsatisfactory so long as we go in search of them directly; that is, by seeking things in the external that we imagine may minister to our needs, we never find more than fragments; and the personal mind is half starved most of the time. However, when we remain in our lofty position, realizing that the soul is all-sufficient, having no need whatever — "All that the Father hath is mine" — then we discover that all kinds of desirable conditions, things, environments and situations begin to aggregate in our world — not because we need them absolutely, but because we invariably produce the aggregation of desirable conditions and things in the without whenever we begin to dwell in the consciousness of their spiritual correspondents within. In other words, while we are deeply conscious of the All in All within, we will attract the all-good from all sources in the without. Thus we explain the great mystery; that is, why the soul in its lofty position, where it feels that it has need of nothing, begins to draw towards itself everything.

To state the same truth in a different manner, we may emphasize the statement that when we enter that place in spiritual consciousness where we find everything, and where we find everything in its true and perfect position — when we live in that place we find that external conditions and things will begin to readjust themselves on every hand, working themselves out right, transforming themselves in every form and manner so as to harmonize, in their external state, with the perfect harmony and right position of what we have become conscious of, in that sublime state in the soul, where all is always well.

Here we discover how we create for ourselves a new heaven and a new earth, and how all things become new in the external when we have realized that which is forever new in the sublime within; that is, when we find the real heaven within, or become conscious of the newest and the highest states of being that we can realize in our present state of development, we observe that all external conditions will change to correspond; and thus we have a new earth — an external life as ideal and as perfect in the external as the new heaven is in the realms of interior consciousness. Furthermore, when we arise to this lofty state and assume our true position, which is to be conscious eternally of the supreme self, the Human Ego will again place itself in the midst of the Great Power — the Power that can do anything in the within or in the without — cause all things to rearrange themselves harmoniously, beautifully and perfectly to correspond with the perfect vision of the soul.

Steps in Human Progress

When we look upon the world in the without, we observe that vast multitudes are constantly looking in the external for what they think they need, never finding what satisfies, or coming in contact with what they describe as "the real thing." And the reason is, that the Human Ego in each one has stepped down, committed the original sin, searching in the without for that which we already possess in the within, and has repeated again and again the great fall. Thus every individual has, for the time being, lost the great power, come down from the lofty position of spiritual consciousness, and is to that degree out of place, out of tune and out of harmony, more or less, with everything and everybody. Thus multitudes go through the world dissatisfied and heart hungry — miserable creatures physically and mentally, never finding exactly what they desire, and always dreaming of some future time when all needs shall be supplied and all wrongs shall be righted.

This is the condition of vast multitudes; but how readily they could change their condition — how soon they could absolutely transform their personal life and their entire world of manifestation, changing everything, causing everything to become as they wish it to be; for indeed, the very moment they would arise and reestablish themselves in their true position, in the full consciousness of this highest truth, they would know that we have the All in All now — that the All in All does exist in the spiritual life of every individual this moment and forever; and that we all may live in the spiritual, should continually live in the spiritual, upon the heights of supreme consciousness, in the realization of the limitlessness inheritance of the Supreme Self.

When we understand these things we realize the uselessness of working so hard to change conditions and environments in the external, as many do, literally working the body to death in order to produce certain external conditions that we imagine to be desirable — wearing life away in producing conditions which in the end prove themselves to be entirely inadequate to the real needs of the real man. We understand clearly how useless it is to pursue such a course when the eternal I AM, the spirit of man, already is in possession of the All in All, being sufficient unto itself, having its true being in that lofty state where the soul has received the kingdom — where we fully realize the largest and highest significance of the great statement, "All that the Father hath is mine."

When we proceed to apply in practical life the principle of this highest truth, we may in the beginning inquire whether or not we can accept that principle in full, when we see on every hand in the visible world the lack of things needful, as well as any number of unrealized ideals; and the answer is, that so long as we continue to live down among things, expecting to secure what we desire through the search of things, we shall not be able to appreciate the real meaning of this highest truth. But the moment we arise to that lofty position of the spirit wherein we know "what God has prepared for them that love Him," we find ourselves in the very midst of the great fight of this truth, and in consequence we can say, in all conviction and sincerity, "I have everything."

Whenever we have made efforts in the past to cause consciousness to transcend the temporal and enter into the light of the spiritual, we have met with experiences of a very striking nature; that is, so long as we lived down in the temporal, or in that state of material consciousness that has been described as "this world," we were constantly confronted with what we might term the awfulness of adversity, trouble and wrong; and upon many instances seemed so engulfed in confusion that we did not know where to turn; and all of those distressing conditions seemed, not only very real, but seemed to combine sufficient power to overcome us completely. However, when we began to look up towards the lofty places, and began to lift the mind, causing consciousness to rise more and more until we found ourselves upon the heights of the spiritual — when we found ourselves in that position, we realized that adversity had become so insignificant as to mean practically nothing. Trouble and sorrow had vanished into the distance and was scarcely discernible any more, while confusion and darkness had completely disappeared beneath the glory and the light in which Ave now were living, moving and having our being.

We all have had experiences of this kind, illustrating how real adversity and confusion seems to be while we are down among things; and how insignificant trouble, evil and wrong become when we permit the soul to take wings and ascend to the loftier heights. In other words, while we are down among things, we do not seem to have anything that is satisfactory, and mostly everything seems to be against us; but when we transcend "this world" and enter the light of the spirit, then everything changes. We find ourselves in possession of everything that we wanted — we are conscious of the fullness of the all-good; and instead of conditions being against us, everything is for us, coming more and more into our world, bringing from every source the spirit and truth of the heart's desire.

Considering this experience we may justly inquire as to its real significance, whether or not it is a demonstration of the law, or merely a seeming change for the better due to a change of attitude; and it may seem to be the latter at times; that is, we may enter into a state of mind wherein everything seems better, although in the world of hard cold facts there may be no change whatever; and this may be true at times and for a period; but we all shall discover most positively that even the hard cold facts of the practical world will respond and change absolutely provided we continue to live upon the spiritual heights, and continue to affirm this highest truth that we have everything now — that we have the all in all, being sufficient unto ourselves, created as we are in the image of the Supreme, and having in our possession the riches of the Infinite.

We shall find, through actual demonstration, that so long as we maintain our lofty position in the spiritual consciousness of this highest truth, never under any circumstance coming down, or giving way to any seeming contradiction of this truth — so long as we continue in that lofty position, we will gradually and surely cause everything, both in the without and in the within, to change more and more until our entire world, visible and invisible, tangible and intangible, has become exactly similar to our own sublime realization of truth.

Approaching again the great paradox — when you realize in spiritual consciousness that you have everything, and therefore need not go in search of anything, it is then that everything that you have ever desired, or wished for, or asked for, will come to you in boundless supply from every source — when we consider this paradox from other viewpoints, we may well ask ourselves, "Why should it be necessary for everything to come to us that we might have desired in the past when we have become conscious of that sublime state of being where we feel that we are not in need of anything?" This, however, is something that we can understand only as we become spiritually conscious, and discern clearly the true relationship between that which remains forever in the absolute, and that which is forever coming forth into manifestation.

In reality the soul or the spirit is not in need of things; and therefore if we wish to live in perfect harmony with the life of the soul, we must not think it necessary to go in search of things in order to secure pleasure, wisdom or power. But aside from this great truth, the soul, when living its full life, will give expression to its own joy, to its own wisdom, to its own power; and all such expressions will find manifestation through those external things that correspond to the life and the ideals of the soul.

Again, the soul is sufficient unto itself in every form and manner; and yet it is not the purpose of the soul simply to five merely in the consciousness of that state of all-sufficiency. It is also the purpose of the soul to bring forth, in ever-increasing measure, the elements and qualities of that state of all-sufficiency; and this bringing forth will cause life in the personality to be related to the world of things, and related harmoniously in proportion to the perfection of our consciousness of this all-sufficiency of the soul.

To state it differently, if we are only partially conscious of the all-sufficiency of the soul, we will be harmoniously related to the world of things only in isolated places, while more or less at variance with the larger part of the visible world; but as we grow in the consciousness of this all-sufficiency of the soul, we will manifest more and more of the life and wisdom and power of the soul, and thereby cause a larger measure of the world of things to be related harmoniously to our own personal existence. To use a kindred expression, the more of the harmony of the soul we become conscious of, the more harmony we will establish in our own world of things; and also the more of the fullness of the life of the soul we become conscious of, the more of the good and the true and the perfect will we realize in the outer world of things, proving the law that external things, as they exist or act in our personal world, will correspond exactly with our state of consciousness in the within.

It may require much deep thought to discern the significance of this analysis; but if we look upon external things as merely channels for expression, and never think of things as absolute necessities to the real life of the soul, we will understand more perfectly the meaning of this highest truth. To use a simple illustration: We cannot find real pleasure among things provided we seek such pleasure among things exclusively, being at the time unconscious of the real joy of the soul; but when we become conscious of the real joy of the soul, and proceed to express that joy through external things, it is then that things serve their true purpose, adding thereby to the joy of the soul; because here it is most important to understand that the inner consciousness of the higher joy of the soul increases in proportion to the measure of that joy we express.

We can find an illustration of this truth in the world of music; that is, however great the joy and the privilege of the musical genius may be in the mere fact that he is conscious of his power to give music, his joy and privilege will increase remarkably the moment he proceeds to express that music through a perfect instrument. In like manner, the joy of the soul, in its own sublime consciousness of the all joy, may be marvelous beyond words; nevertheless, when the soul begins to express that joy in the world of things, immediately the feeling of joy in the within will increase accordingly.

Thus we understand that, although the world of things is not necessary to the full life of the soul as lived in the spirit, nevertheless, the life of the soul becomes infinitely more wonderful and enjoyable as it is given expression in the outer world; and that is why we have the manifested universe with its innumerable spheres, visible and invisible.

The same truth, if applied in another direction, would lead us to the conclusion that all the souls in the cosmos, frequently described as "the great white throng," are as necessary to God as God is necessary to that innumerable host; and to express this idea briefly, we would simply say that, although the Infinite is sufficient in the fullest and highest significance of that term, nevertheless, the expression of Divine Life, individualized in countless millions of human entities, is a privilege far beyond the power of any mind to conceive; because the joy of Infinite Life increases in proportion to the measure of expression of that life in the consciousness of human souls who have the power to partake and manifest that joy. If we are spiritually conscious we can discern this very clearly; and it is a truth that is wonderfully rich with spiritual wisdom — a truth which when discerned will change remarkably our understanding of the Supreme. Furthermore, when we know that we exist as spiritual entities, not in some vague, indefinable realm only, but because we are necessary to the greatest joy and privilege of the Supreme — that we are necessary in this manner throughout eternity — when we realize this great truth, we shall indeed pause to think as we never thought before.

Returning to that phase of the subject that we shall have to consider in living up to this highest truth, we must constantly bear in mind the principle that we must become conscious of the allness of life and power in the within before we can demonstrate the power to cause all things desired to come to us in the without; and when we realize further that things have no value in themselves, but become valuable only as channels for expression, we understand how absolutely necessary it is to continue in that lofty position where we are fully conscious of the possession of everything that can possibly exist in the life of the soul. But as the soul lives perpetually in a desire to express its all-sufficiency — it is when we become deeply conscious of that desire that we can really appreciate the true purpose of things; and it is then that we make a most important discovery concerning the true relationship between the spirit of things and things themselves. And through this discovery we find that we do not secure power from things; but we can, when we live in the spirit, give power to things — give power to everything, and thereby manifest our own power in the external in perfect accord with our consciousness of that power in the within. And again, we must remember that however great our joy our wisdom or power may be in the perfect consciousness of the soul, that joy wisdom and power will consciously increase through expression.

In this connection we might with much interest consider another phase of the same principle; that is, that the privilege of being alive, although very great, is not nearly as great as the privilege of living life; and the reason is, that when we are simply alive we are conscious of life only in its passive or inactive state; but when we begin to live life, then we cause life to go forth in a thousand different directions; and accordingly, life becomes a thousand times more interesting. This fact, if considered in connection with all other modes of expression, will give emphasis to the statement made, that the soul although all sufficient in itself, finds far greater joy in its all-sufficiency when that all-sufficiency begins to manifest throughout the visible and tangible world of things.

To consider this idea in a very practical manner, we will turn our attention to the fact that nearly every mind of ambition is constantly in search of external advantages or more worthy opportunities. Accordingly, we find all such minds going out in search of greater opportunities, or in search of external channels for more worthy or more wonderful accomplishments; and in a measure these things are found; but only in a measure, and for the time being — no permanent satisfaction ever arising from such a mode of procedure. However, if these minds would first search for the greater power within, that is, the all-sufficiency of power, realizing that every advantage, opportunity or privilege exists potentially in the life of the soul even now — if the mind would first enter into that extraordinary realization, the power desired would at once arise in consciousness; that is, that power within through which every individual can create his own opportunities, his own privileges and his own channels of richer expression. Thus, instead of going out into the external in search of something that will have to be created from the within before it can possibly exist in the external — instead of taking that roundabout way, usually finding nothing, we may, by entering directly into the consciousness of the all-sufficiency of the soul, secure the very power through which we can create for ourselves any external opportunity, privilege or advantage that we may wish to apply in connection with any object or ambition we have in mind.

When we understand these things we realize that there is no contradiction in the statement that, having everything already we should not go in search of anything. But there is a seeming contradiction so long as we view this highest truth from the consciousness of the personal only. The fact is, we should not go in search of things for the mere sake of possessing things, or in the mistaken belief that we can find in things what we need or desire. We should take another course entirely, and first seek the consciousness of that higher power within that can, when manifested in the without, do anything desired with things — a power that can create any condition among things, or attract any combination of things or quality of elements or forces whatever according to the object we have in view.

To use a familiar statement, we can do anything desired with effects when we gain the power to master completely the original cause of all such effects. But that power we cannot gain so long as we live down in the world of things, believing that we are subject to things or dependent upon things, or that we can secure happiness, wisdom, power or a richer life through a certain peculiar combination of things. Such a belief is the very reverse of the highest truth, which declares, that we are not directly dependent upon anything in the external, because we have, not only the all in all in spiritual consciousness, but through the possession of the all in all we have that power that can, when applied externally, do everything conceivable with the external world.

Another important statement to hold constantly before mind is this, that we secure a certain desirable combination of things in the without only as Ave gain the consciousness of the ideal of that combination in the higher life of the real and the true. But we cannot become conscious of that ideal excepting in this sublime state where we know that we have everything.

When we consider the needs of the personal life, as found among those who live exclusively in the world of things, we discern on every hand persons that feel as if they could not exist another day unless they secured certain conditions, certain privileges or certain tangible things that seem absolutely necessary. And they live constantly in that attitude, receiving temporary satisfaction upon occasions, but never securing what they think they positively must have in order to live. And the reason is, that they are looking in the world of effect for that which cannot appear in the world of effect until it has been created by the natural cause in the within.

We may grope in darkness for ages, thinking we cannot exist another moment until we receive the light, and yet so long as we continue to grope in darkness, never thinking of how we might produce the light, we will continue in the blackness of the darkness without change. But the very moment we go to the source of light, and give attention to that source, we produce the light, and the awful darkness disappears completely.

However, the great source of everything that we may desire or need can be found only in that sublime state of consciousness wherein we know that the soul is in possession of the all-sufficiency — in need of nothing, having within itself the limitless life, wisdom, power and riches of the Infinite. It is then that we can give real action to the sublime source of the Great Light; and when we do give such action, the Great Light will go forth throughout the entire world of consciousness. And what we become conscious of, that we shall invariably bring forth in the visible world.

When we understand this highest truth, we discover for the first time the meaning of that wonderful statement, "Be true to yourself," because it is only as you take this lofty position where you realize that you are the true self, that you become conscious of the all-sufficiency of the soul; in other words, we can be true to the self only when we know what the self really is, and what the self really can do. But on the contrary, we cannot be true to the self so long as we go in search among things for those needs of life that the self alone can provide. This is what it means "to grieve the spirit away"; to deny Higher Power, believing that we can find what we want in "this world." However, when we arrive to that higher consciousness where we realize that the all in all is in the spirit only, in the spiritual life of the supreme self, then we no longer deny the Holy Spirit, nor the Christ, nor the Infinite. We rely upon the whole truth, the highest truth; and we receive that greater power that invariably appears in consciousness when we discern this highest truth.

To state it differently, when we find our true position in life — and we find our true position only as we establish ourselves in our loftiest position — when we begin to live in that lofty position, which is the true position, we understand that it is then and then only that we can live life as life should be lived, and relate ourselves to things in such a way as to use all things according to the law of manifestation and the law of growth and advancement in personal life; that is, it is only after we have taken our true place in life and consciousness that we can do anything right. And when we begin to do everything right, then we can readily understand what a marvelous change must come over our entire world.

The more we think of this highest truth the more clearly we appreciate its real significance; but while we are on the way to the full understanding of this highest truth it is well to consider the immediate value of accepting this truth, even though its greatest power has not as yet become manifested. To illustrate: When we accept the idea that the human soul, being in possession of everything necessary to life, and when we realize that the spirit of man can, therefore, need nothing, or lose nothing — when this startling truth is realized, we shall never be depressed, dissatisfied or disappointed with external conditions, no matter how disappointing those conditions may for the time being seem to be.

When we take that lofty position, realizing that we have it all, and therefore, we can in reality experience neither loss, grief nor disappointment — when we take that higher ground, what an immense change we will produce, not only in our own attitude towards life, but in our own state of mind, in our own feelings, desires and mental actions; in fact, our mode of thought and action will change absolutely; and instead of grieving when conditions seem to be adverse, we will continue in the consciousness of the great truth that we have everything and that all is well.

Steps in Human Progress

In the beginning, the practical value of such an attitude will simply be to give us sublime peace of mind no matter what may transpire; but the taking of that higher ground will work wonders in the course of time, because if we continue to live in the conviction that we have it all, and that all is well, we will continue to create the perfect and the ideal in our own consciousness, creating the perfect and the ideal more wonderfully, and upon a grander scale every day; and according to the great law, whatever we create in consciousness we will invariably experience, attract, produce and possess in the external in due time. In consequence, we do not simply give the mind peace by living in the conviction that the soul is all-sufficient now, in need of nothing, beyond all loss, grief or disappointment. We accomplish infinitely more than merely this peace of mind, because, while living in that lofty position, we continue to live the highest truth — to express and manifest the life, the wisdom, the light and the power of the highest truth. And in due time, such expression will appear in the visible and in the tangible, which will mean the transformation of the external according to the image and likeness of the highest truth — the consciousness of which we have lived so faithfully and so well.

Thus we realize that whatever the person may think or feel, or however conditions may appear in the external, we have everything to gain by taking this higher ground now; and we all can. Then as we proceed, we will demonstrate more and more that the law is absolutely true; we shall not have to live very long in that lofty place, in the consciousness of the power of the spirit, until that power will begin to make changes for the better in mind and body and in external conditions. Furthermore, we will demonstrate continuously the power of that great statement, "When one is lifted up, hundreds and thousands will be lifted up." When we take this great step, we will become instrumental in leading, first, a few to do the same, then a larger number, until later we

Steps in Human Progress

may inspire a vast throng to take the same higher ground, the final results of which will be marvelous beyond words to describe.

We know that the greatest movements in the world have originated in this manner — some great soul taking higher ground, and a few coming up to the same lofty place later; and gradually a larger number began to apply the same idea until the movement itself became an inspiration to the race. We can do this very thing now upon a larger scale than anything ever attempted in the past, because we are not dealing simply with the light of some valued idea — we are dealing with nothing less than the light of the highest truth; and therefore, the possibilities of a spiritual movement having for its purpose the living up to this highest truth — the possibilities of such a movement are so numerous and so wonderful that we shall, in order to appreciate the outcome, cause our imagination to extend its power into the highest and largest realms conceivable; and even then, we shall be able to imagine only a part of what we may accomplish in taking such a course — proceeding now regardless of time, circumstance or condition to live up to this highest truth — to know that we have everything that heart can desire — living in the very life of the Supreme.

Steps to the Spiritual

THE first essential in giving scientific attention to the study of the spiritual world is to realize that, what we speak of as the spiritual world, is not necessarily synonymous with the invisible world. And here we find one of the chief obstacles to spiritual advancement; that is, that we have, in too many instances, made the terms "spiritual" and "invisible" synonymous, and accordingly have come to the conclusion that an experience in the invisible is also a spiritual experience, or that a gain made in our understanding of the invisible would also imply a gain in our understanding of the spiritual.

The fact is, however, that these two terms are not synonymous — the invisible does not necessarily contain any more of the spiritual than does the visible; but wherever we do proceed in the belief that the invisible is synonymous with the spiritual, we are very liable to turn our attention away from the spiritual, instead of entering into higher realizations of the spiritual.

We must begin this study by understanding, in the first place, that the invisible world, so-called, is only an extension of the visible world; and therefore, what we speak of as the invisible universe is simply elements and forces found in the physical universe manifesting in higher grades of vibration.

As an illustration, we may take the force of light, which manifests in the visible through certain grades of vibration, but manifests also in a number of higher grades of vibration, spoken of as the higher octaves of light; but the only difference between visible light and the higher octave's of light is this, that the vibrations in the latter are more rapid than in the former. Therefore, we cannot speak of the invisible rays of light as spiritual, any more than we can speak of the visible rays of light as spiritual. The only difference between the visible and the invisible is a matter of speed in the vibrations.

We are surrounded with elements on every hand that are purely physical, and yet not visible to physical sense — the atmosphere, as an illustration; but we have learned, through experiments, that there are also finer grades of atmosphere so delicate and so high in the scale of vibration that they cannot be discerned through any of our physical senses. However, those finer grades of atmosphere are not necessarily spiritual simply because they are beyond the discernment of physical sense.

We might analyze the entire tangible universe in the same manner, and we would find, in each instance, that forces and elements manifesting in the physical universe may and do manifest through higher and finer grades of expression, as high in the scale as we may wish to go; but in no instance are these so-called higher expressions of force or substance any more spiritual than those expressions of force and substance that we can feel, weigh and measure upon the physical plane.

The reason for this is found in the fact that spirituality is something entirely different from the mere manifestation of life, force, substance or power upon any plane, no matter how high, delicate or wonderful that plane may be.

We may illustrate the same principle by comparing two human beings, one very crude in expression and appearance, while the other very refined and highly developed, so far as mind and personality are concerned; but this would not prove that the refined personality would necessarily be more spiritual than the crude personality, although if the individual of refinement should undertake the development of spirituality, he would advance far more rapidly towards the spiritual heights than the individual who was still lacking in refinement of personality, thought and mind.

You may examine two distinct forms of intellect in the same manner, one developed to a very high degree, as far as intellect is concerned, while the other decidedly undeveloped in the intellectual world; but again the intellect with high development would not necessarily appreciate the spiritual, nor even the moral any better than the intellect that was lacking in purely intellectual development. But the same would be true as in the former illustration, with regard to possibility of spiritual development; that is, the finer the intellect the more rapidly can the mind develop along all lines, even spiritual lines, provided such development is undertaken.

We know, however, that a great many highly intellectual people are absolutely lacking in spiritual appreciation and cosmic consciousness; although their minds are wonderful in the intellectual world, still they are practically blind when it comes to things spiritual.

Then on the other hand, Ave find a great many people who are not developed intellectually, but who may have a certain degree of appreciation of the spiritual. This does not prove, however, that intellect is an obstacle to spiritual development. On the contrary, it is a most important essential, provided we undertake spiritual development in earnest. But, knowing all these things, we realize that intellect itself, no matter how refined or how wonderful it may be, does not, in itself, constitute spirituality.

The truth is, that an individual may be wonderfully developed in personality, in mind, in talent, in genius and in all the higher and finer elements and qualities of life, and yet be totally unconscious of the spiritual side of life.

In like manner, an individual may be highly developed in the so-called psychic world and be practically master of all the phases of the sixth sense, thereby having the power to look into the invisible world as if it were an open book, and yet be totally unconscious of the spiritual world and without the least spiritual development.

All these facts prove that what we speak of as the higher, or the finer or the invisible, does not produce or constitute spirituality. The truth is, we may rise to the very highest states of attainment in the so-called invisible universe, without taking a single step in advance into the spiritual world. And the reason why we understand when we realize that spirituality is something entirely different from anything that appears anywhere in the manifested universe, no matter how high in manifestation the appearance may come forth.

Regardless of our development along any line, we must add something entirely different if we wish spirituality, or if we desire to enter into the spiritual world.

In many instances, that something else appears in minds that are neither refined nor developed; but minds that are lacking in refinement and development cannot go very far into the spiritual; so that we shall find it an advantage to further our own development along all lines when we have higher spiritual attainments in view.

We may know something about the spiritual without having gone very far in the development of mind, personality, life or character; but the farther we go in the development of personality, life, mind and character, the higher we may go in spiritual development, provided we find the key to the spiritual world.

But we must, under every circumstance, have that key; because if we do not have the key to the spiritual world, we shall not find spirituality, no matter how wonderfully we may be developed along all other lines, including the understanding of the invisible universe.

On every hand we find people who have undertaken the study of the invisible, thinking that they may, through that source, gain absolute knowledge of life, and in that manner find the real solution for all the problems of life. But here we must remember again that the so-called invisible universe does not contain the secret, because the invisible, as well as the visible, is merely an effect. The cause of all manifestation is found only in the great within of the spiritual world. You will not get any nearer to the real principle of life or wisdom by furthering your study of the so-called invisible forces and elements of life, nor will you become more deeply conscious of the presence of the Infinite through development along these invisible lines.

The reason is, that in any case, you will be dealing simply with manifestation; and you will not enter into that marvelous something that exists back of manifestation until you enter into the real consciousness of the spiritual world.

The power of the spirit can be found only in the spiritual world, and may not be found in matter or force, no matter how high in the scale of the invisible world matter or substance or force may manifest.

To find the spirit of things, we must enter into the spirit of things; and we enter into the spirit of things only when we become conscious of the spiritual world — that world of reality and principle and life that has its being within the entire cosmos, but that does not appear in differentiated form anywhere in the world of manifestation.

We also realize that we can understand cause only by entering into the consciousness of cause; but here we should remember that cause does not exist in the invisible any more than in the visible. On the contrary, cause exists back of the invisible as well as back of the visible, these two being, under every circumstance, merely effects of the Real Cause of everything, which may be found only in the spiritual world.

It is clearly evident, therefore, that we cannot understand the spiritual world merely through a study of the invisible. We must turn our attention in another direction; and when we do, we shall find that there is just as much spirit in the within of visible substance as there is in the within of invisible substance; and also, we shall find the power of the spirit expressing itself just as fully in visible force as it does in invisible force, although a greater measure of this power may sometimes be found expressing itself in the higher grades of invisible life, the difference there would be, not in kind, but in quantity.

When we consider the subject from this true understanding of life, we will naturally inquire what we really do know about the spiritual world. It is quite true that we know a great deal about the invisible world. Modern science is making it possible for an individual to gain direct information concerning what we have spoken of as things invisible. We may, through certain instruments, discern higher octaves of light, such as the XRays and the NRays — forces of light that cannot be discerned through the physical eye unaided. We are also able to measure higher vibrations of sound that cannot be heard by the physical ear unaided. In like manner, we are able to detect substances and elements higher up in the scale of manifestation — elements that appear intangible to physical sense, and yet prove themselves, through experiments, to be just as tangible as the solid rock with which we all are familiar.

We are exploring the unknown in every realm of the invisible universe, and we are finding facts and information of inestimable value; but this information gives us absolutely nothing about the spiritual world, the reason for which our preceding analysis has demonstrated conclusively.

A scientist may be able to use the XRay and the NRay, and any number of higher and finer rays of light, understanding them perfectly, comprehending the laws through which they manifest, but this power does not make him spiritual.

An occult scientist may be able to discern some of the finest forces in the invisible world, and may be able to detect, through the sixth sense, all kinds of manifestations and modes of life upon higher planes; but this does not make him spiritual, or give him the least added insight into the spiritual world.

In many instances, this so-called higher knowledge of invisible things will, for a time, become an obstacle to real spiritual understanding, because the individual may imagine for a time that he has found, through his knowledge of the invisible, the real secret of spiritual things.

The same may be true of the physical scientist. He may become so enthused over his ability to penetrate the unknown with his wonderful instruments that he may imagine for a time that the unknown is nothing more than an extension of the known, and that it is all force and matter after all, appearing in different grades of vibration. He defines the invisible, or the unknown, as simply more rapid vibrations of force and matter; but, to his mind, it is all force and matter; and in consequence, he remains, in his conception of things, as materialistic as he was before. We realize that knowledge along all lines will, in the long run, prove advantageous, both in our ability to master the visible and the invisible, and in our ability to discern the spiritual. But, as stated previously, we must find the key to the spiritual world before we can enter that world; that key, however, cannot be found simply through a knowledge of visible or invisible elements or forces. We must search in an entirely different direction.

The first essential will be to realize clearly and absolutely that the spiritual world and the invisible world are not the same. The second essential will be to realize that we cannot find the spiritual world by going up in the scale of vibration of manifested expression; but that we can find the spiritual world only by entering into the spirit of the unmanifested within that exists back of all manifestations; or in other words, that has its being in the Changeless Soul of the universe. When we enter the spirit of all life, we find a state wherein all being is as it is for all time; and in that state we find the All in All — a state to which nothing can be added and nothing taken away.

On the other hand, whenever you meet a state of existence wherein you find that something might be added, or taken away, you are not dealing with the real spiritual world, but with the manifested world, the world of change and growth and development, existing as it does, not only upon the visible plane, but upon millions and millions of invisible planes, ascending higher and higher in the scale of ever advancing manifestation.

Steps in Human Progress

When we enter the spiritual world we find real being itself; but real being is something that cannot be defined in words. It is something that we must become conscious of individually; and we do become conscious of real being when we experience that consciousness of being that reveals to us unmistakably the great truth that to this being nothing can be added or taken away.

When we analyze the great universe of manifestation, visible and invisible, we find that it is eternally becoming; it is incomplete everywhere, and subject to development along all lines for eternity. But this is not true of the spiritual world. The spiritual world is finished even now; it is complete in the absolute sense, containing within itself the All in All; and when we actually enter into the spiritual world, and become conscious of the All in All, we shall know for ourselves that within the spiritual world nothing can be added or taken away. Thus we may declare with the illumined Mind of other days, "It is finished, and it is all very good."

When we approach the study of the spiritual we must invariably bear in mind the truth that everything existing in, or pertaining to, the spiritual is in itself complete; and also that our mental attitude, when undertaking such study, must proceed in the conscious recognition of this great truth — recognizing definitely and continually the principle of absolute perfection and completeness in everything that involves the elements of the spiritual. In approaching the study of the soul we must employ the same method, because the soul is absolutely spiritual, and therefore contains within itself everything that is necessary to the life and eternal existence of the soul. We know that mind and body are incomplete, which is true of everything finding expression in the external; that is, wherever we find expression, there we shall find completeness, because expression is at best only a partial coming forth of the limitless that exists in the spiritual within.

This being true, we realize that development and advancement would involve the continual increase of expression in every form and manner — an increase that is necessarily perpetual, because there can be no end to the increase of that which is, in reality, limitless.

When we proceed with the analysis of anything in life, we meet the same principles and conditions; that is, we find incompleteness in the external no matter how high in the scale the external may manifest; and we meet absolute completeness in the within of everything, whether it be a quality, a principle, an entity or a universe. The spiritual within of everything is complete and changeless, and that is the reason why it is spiritual.

To consider the more practical side of the subject, we may examine the principle of health and wholeness; and we shall discover the existence of a principle of health having its being within the life of all kinds of health, and that this principle contains every element of health that is conceivable or possible. In other words, the principle of perfect health contains so much health that it would be impossible to contain any more; and therefore the real principle of health is purely spiritual, containing within itself an unlimited measure of real or absolute health.

This being true, we realize the necessity of going to the inner or spiritual source for health, wholeness, life, vitality, power, if we would secure the largest possible measure and the finest and most perfect conceivable quality.

We may examine any quality in the same manner, or any state of the mind, or of consciousness; and we shall find that even though the external expression may be incomplete, the inner source is absolutely complete, so that the without can continue to draw upon the within for an endless period of time, constantly receiving more without at any time exhausting the source of supply.

This being true, we realize that no matter how much we may possess of the richness or perfection of life, either in personality, in mind or in soul, we can always receive more from the spiritual within, and continue to receive more without any end — rising thereby in the scale along all lines perpetually. However, we must, before we can apply this wonderful law, understand perfectly the great truth that the spiritual is perfect, complete and inexhaustible, and that the spiritual is the real, immeasurable source of everything that appears in the outer world.

When we consider individuals in the light of this idea and speak of them as spiritual, Ave cannot possibly mean that they are spiritual through and through, or in the absolute sense, but that they are growing in the consciousness of the spiritual, and thereby drawing more and more upon the perfection of the soul for external expression in mind and personality.

The outer life is always incomplete, always growing, always developing, always advancing, while the inner life is constantly giving forth more and more from its inexhaustible perfection for the purpose of increasing the perfection, the richness and the worth of external life; and any individual who is constantly bringing forth from the spiritual within more and more of the richness, the quality and the life of the spirit, is constantly becoming more spiritual in consciousness and in realization; and therefore we can speak of such an individual as being upon the great spiritual path.

An individual, however, who has not become conscious of the spiritual within, and is accordingly depending exclusively upon the limitations of the outer life, has not as yet entered upon the spiritual path, and therefore reveals in personality, in mind and in thought only those elements that pertain to personal life, or the earth, earthy. But we all are destined in due time, to become conscious of the spirit, and thereby begin the expression of the spiritual through every phase of external life; but as this is an endless process, no individual soul will, at any time, come to a place where the full expression of the spirit will become tangible in external life; and this is well, because if we should reach such a state, then life would come to a standstill, and there would be nothing further to live for in the future.

When we realize the full significance of life and its development, we find that we live in two worlds, or that we all should live in two worlds if we would be true to the great purpose that existence has in view. These two worlds constitute the great within and the great without, or the spiritual within which is inexhaustible perfection, and the external without which is eternally receiving a greater and a greater degree of expression from the spiritual, and thereby ever becoming more wonderful, more beautiful and more ideal.

The majority, however, live almost entirely in the without, and only upon rare occasions come into conscious contact with the spiritual within. That is the principal reason why the majority is materialistic and live in bondage to illness, adversity and pain, meeting the wrong on every hand and gaining only fragments of that which is conducive to goodness and joy

To live in such a state of mind, however, is to depend almost exclusively upon the limitations of the without, and therefore such an existence will not mean very much under any circumstance. But when we proceed to live as much in the spiritual within as we do in the tangible without, we shall find that every moment will become larger, more wonderful and more desirable, because we are constantly drawing upon the richness of the spiritual for perpetual increase in the external; and we know that there can be no greater joy than the consciousness of continuous ascension into the larger, the richer and the higher in life, thought and sublime realization.

To make practical application of this mode of living, we should enter as frequently as possible, and as deeply as possible, into the consciousness of the purely spiritual — into the realization of that world wherein all things are absolutely perfect and inexhaustible, so that we may receive an ever-increasing measure, not only of life, but of all the elements and qualities of life, thereby increasing constantly the value, the worth, the meaning and the power of personal existence; that is, we should be conscious of the spirit continually, and should continually aim to build up, refine, develop and perfect everything in mind and personality. But in order that we may proceed in the application of this principle, we must live in two worlds at a time; we must live in the tangible without and also in the spiritual within.

When we appreciate the real significance of the spiritual world, and know that it is a world permeating all other worlds in the vastness of the cosmos, and that this spiritual world is so constituted that it contains within itself everything that eternity may require for life, advancement and ascension, we will naturally inquire how we may know more about the spiritual, and also examine our minds with a view of ascertaining how much we know about the spiritual at the present time.

Steps in Human Progress

When these questions have been answered, we will ask ourselves how we learned what we know about the spiritual, or how we became conscious of those spiritual elements that we know we are conscious of in our present stage of realization. When we know these things we shall be better able to proceed further, and therefore such questions are most important.

When we attempt to define the spiritual we begin by declaring that the spiritual world is absolute; and we know that that which is absolute is in a state wherein nothing can be added; but we do not find it possible to conceive of such a state so long as our consciousness is purely personal. The appreciation of the spiritual, therefore, is something that cannot be gained until we first develop at least a measure of spiritual discernment; but we all do possess a certain measure of spiritual discernment, and therefore we have a foundation upon which to build the great structure of limitless spiritual consciousness.

We speak of the Divine as absolute because we realize that we can add nothing to the wisdom, the power, the life, the light and the glory of the Supreme. We say that God is All in All, but we can say the same of the spiritual world.

When we examine the external world, however, we find the very reverse. We may ascend continually in the scale of development until we become marvels, far beyond the power of imagination to picture, and yet we can still go higher. We can still attain greater power, greater wisdom, greater attainments. The same is true of everything that exists in the great without. No matter how wonderful it may be, we can still make it more wonderful, and we can continue to make it more and more wonderful during the innumerable aeons of eternity.

Steps in Human Progress

Thus we appreciate the fact that that which manifests in the great without, no matter how marvelous or how high in the scale it may be, whether it exists in the visible or in the very highest phases of the invisible, it is nevertheless external — you can always add something more, you can always make it more perfect or more wonderful.

But this is not true of the spiritual world. The spiritual world is, even now, at the apex of absolute perfection, so that there is no law in the cosmos through which anything could be added to the completeness of that world.

However, the spiritual world, even though it appears to be the very reverse of the external world, is not a thing apart. It is not a universe that exists beyond or away from the physical or external universe. The spiritual world is, in truth, the very soul of the external world, and therefore is present everywhere. But it cannot be found by going up, so to speak, in the scale of development, nor can it be found by entering the invisible, because the invisible spheres are also in the external.

We can find the spiritual world only by entering into the spirit of the within; and spirit is neither visible nor invisible — spirit is neither high nor low in the scale — spirit neither changes nor disappears, but always is what it is — the All in All.

This being true, we find the life and the principle of spirit everywhere, in every quality, in every manifestation, in every expression; and for an illustration, we may consider the spirit of music. We know that music, as generally appreciated, is an external expression, involving harmonies of tone; but that expression has a source in what we speak of as the soul of music. And we know that whenever we enter into the soul of music, or enter into that state of appreciation where we feel that we discern the spirit of music, it is then that we appreciate and enjoy music far beyond previous experience.

We know that those who appreciate real music are familiar with the fact that the finest artists invariably approach the spirit of music, and also that the more deeply an artist enters into the spirit of music, the more wonderful his music becomes. We say that the music of such and such an artist has soul — in brief, it is something more than the mere harmony of tone — something infinitely more — something that can never be defined or described. And the reason for this we understand when we know that the soul of music contains within itself all the music of existence; that is, so much music that it would not be possible to add to its volume, quantity or quality in any form or manner.

In this very place we will make a great discovery, if our minds are open to the higher and the greater. We will discover the secret of becoming a great or a wonderful musician; and this secret consists of the power of entering into the soul of music instead of simply performing in the external. We know that an artist invariably gives expression in the without to what is felt in the within; and therefore, if the artist can enter so deeply into the spiritual within of the soul of music that the real divine source of music is felt and discerned, we understand that such an artist would naturally give expression to music that would be far superior to anything we had ever heard before. We know that there are any number of musicians who are technically perfect in their expression, but there are only a few who reveal the real spirit of the Great Symphony.

However, if all these musicians who are technically perfect would realize that music has soul, or that there is a spiritual world within the tangible world of music, and then try and become conscious of that spiritual world so as to feel and realize the marvels, the wonders and the indescribable beauty of music as it is in its sublime perfection — if our technically perfect musicians would take such a course, we can well imagine what the music of the future would be.

We may examine any art or any quality in life, and we will discover the same principle. To illustrate again, we may take human character, and we shall find that certain characters are strictly proper in their conduct and in their relationship with human life, but there is something about their conduct that appears to be purely mechanical, and therefore they produce no special impression upon those with whom they come in contact. But occasionally we meet characters who have soul, and we are aware of the fact that they are not only living in harmony with the great laws of life, being true to the truth in all their actions and expressions, but in addition they are giving soul not only to everything they do, but they are also giving soul to their very presence, so that when we find ourselves in the presence of such characters we are wonderfully impressed with the beauty, and we might say divinity, of the life that is being expressed through them.

We meet the same conditions in the human mind, and also in the various faculties of the mind. Some minds are brilliant, but are purely mechanical in their brilliancy, while other minds add what we might call a "finer touch" to every thought or expression; and the reason is that such minds are in touch with the soul of life — such minds are becoming conscious of the spiritual world existing everywhere, within the mind, within all things.

In any individual mind we may find certain faculties that are spiritualized, so to speak, while the other faculties remain purely material; and the reason is that the majority of those faculties have not been sufficiently developed to discern or express the soul of mentality, while one or a few of these faculties may have received such development. That is why certain individuals sometimes are so extraordinary and so superior along one or a few fines of expression, while very ordinary or even inferior in every other respect.

Thus we appreciate the importance of training the entire system to give expression to the life and the power of the spiritual world that permeates all things; but again we cannot find spirit by trying to go up into the invisible, as so many have tried to do; but only by directing consciousness upon that wonderful state within where everything is changeless, absolute, complete, containing eternally the All in All.

Illustrating further, we find this same wonderful principle revealed in our idea of the beautiful. We may think that we appreciate the beauty of things, and yet our appreciation may be insignificant compared with what it might be if we were conscious of the soul of the beautiful everywhere.

The more we analyze the subject, the more perfectly we realize that within everything that is beautiful, or back of every expression of the beautiful, we shall find the real soul of the beautiful, and this soul is infinitely beautiful; that is, the soul of the beautiful involves so much of the beautiful, and to such a wonderful degree, that it can only be described as infinitely beautiful — beyond all thought or expression in its splendor and glory.

We find the same to be true of the ideal; that is, we shall find that every ideal has soul, and that the ideal of the soul is infinitely higher than the ideal itself. Therefore, if we would learn to approach the soul of every ideal, we should find that our ideals would become higher and higher eternally; and we know that the higher our ideals ascend, the higher we shall rise, not only in life, but also in expression and true spiritual attainment.

In our personal development, and especially in the development of the powers or talents of the mind, we shall find in this connection a most practical idea. Briefly stated, if you have a certain talent, and know that that talent is but a partial expression of an interior or spiritual talent which is so wonderful that it contains within itself the absolutely limitless, you are on the verge of a wonderful experience in development. You realize, in the first place, that the more deeply conscious you become of the limitless and infinitely perfect talent within you, the more you express from the within through the external manifestation of your talent. You thereby not only give your external talent soul and spirit and a greater measure of life and power, but you continually bring forth into the external an ever-increasing measure of talent, so that in the course of time the external expression of your talent will necessarily become prodigious. But again, we shall have to remember that we cannot find the spirit of anything unless we direct our minds towards the spiritual within and recognize the great truth that in the spiritual within we shall find the All in All.

We may apply the same principle in personal development along any line, or with reference to any quality or any power, or any possibility we may possess. Within them all we shall find the spirit, or the soul, or the spiritual world; and the more deeply conscious we become of the perfection and the limitlessness of the spirit within everything, the more we shall express through everything; and this is especially true of life itself, the greatest and most wonderful gift that the individual has received from the Supreme.

Steps in Human Progress

The majority, however, live their life in the external, almost unconscious of the spiritual source, and therefore they never realize the life more abundant. But the moment we begin to become conscious of the inexhaustible life in the great within, or discover the very spirit of life itself — the very moment we meet this experience, we find that the gates are ajar, and we proceed to enter a state of existence that is infinitely larger, more wonderful and more desirable than anything we have ever experienced before.

In other words, when we enter the spirit of life, we find that we become conscious not only of life in its highest and most wonderful state of being, but we also become conscious of limitless, inexhaustible life — the glory and splendor of which the illumined soul, in its master state, alone may behold and understand.

For the purpose of illustration, we may again consider the quality of health; and we find that the principle of health in itself is in truth the spirit of health, or has its origin and existence in that something that we may define as real and unchangeable and invincible health — a state or spirit that contains health to such a perfect degree that it would not be possible for anything to contain health to a more perfect degree; and furthermore, that the health of the spirit is so powerful that it could not be changed or removed by any power in the external world with which it might come in contact.

If we could realize absolutely such an idea of health, we understand what a difference we would experience in our possession of health. The majority feel that they have reasonably good health, but have no idea as to what the ideal of absolute health might signify, nor do they for a moment think that there is a deeper and a finer state of health which constitutes in itself the perfection of health. Accordingly, the majority are in a condition where their health is not fully established, and frequently their possession of health is limited or uncertain.

With this condition we may well compare that consciousness of perfect being into which we enter when we realize that we possess, within ourselves, a principle or spirit of health that is absolutely perfect and complete; and having made this comparison, we will inquire as to how we may pass from the condition of the former to the consciousness of the latter. The answer is this, that when in search of health, and we all are in search of more health, we must begin with the realization of the great truth that the source of absolute health is found in the spiritual world, that wonderful state of being that exists everywhere and that permeates all things. Furthermore, we must realize that health itself is spiritual; that is, real health, which is experienced by the few as compared with the limited expressions of health, which is experienced by the many.

When we understand that real health is spiritual, and that such a state of health contains so much health and such perfect health that it could not be increased or improved upon in any form or manner, and then proceed to enter into the consciousness of the spirit of real health, we understand fully that the expression of health throughout our entire system will steadily increase until in time the personality will become so powerful with the real spirit of health that it would be immune under every circumstance.

For further illustration, we may consider the attitude of peace, or the consciousness of the serene; and although many have the power to become peaceful and quiet to some degree, nevertheless there are only a few who ever become conscious of the peace that passeth understanding. The reason why is this, that real peace is spiritual, existing only in the consciousness of the spiritual world, a world into which the mind may enter only as spirituality is developed.

When we understand that the peace that passeth understanding is so perfect and so deeply calm that it possibly could not contain higher or finer or more perfect elements of peace, we have an ideal of the consciousness of peace that is so wonderful that we shall have to think for days and weeks and months upon its possibilities before we can really comprehend its full significance.

In like manner, we may consider the state of harmony; and we shall find that what the majority call harmony is not real harmony itself, but just a limited expression of concordant activities. If we would experience real harmony, we must enter the spirit, because such harmony is spiritual, and exists only in the spiritual world. Accordingly, real harmony is so complete and perfect in itself that it could not become more harmonious.

Here again we have an ideal that deserves deep and sublime thought; and we shall find that the more we think of real harmony as existing in its perfect state in the spiritual world, the more harmonious we shall become in thought, life, feeling and action until we shall have gained remarkably in this direction.

When we consider these various qualities or states of being, we find invariably that in reality they are spiritual; and as we trace them out to their source and origin, we invariably enter the spiritual world, that world in which every quality or state of being is so perfect and so complete and so ideally placed, in its own existence, that it could not be improved upon in any form or manner.

We may trace any quality in the same way; and if we try to find that quality in its perfect state, we invariably enter the spiritual world; and here we begin to understand what we mean by the term "spiritual." It is not a state of invisibility, or something that is beyond the external merely; but it is that world in which all things are perfect and complete, wherein nothing can be added or taken away — a world that exists in all things, and surrounds us everywhere, permeating everything, from the simplest of the visible to the highest and the most marvelous of the invisible.

When we look into the soul, or into the inner life, we find this spiritual world established there as it is established in every entity; and we find all the qualities of life existing in the soul in a spiritual state, that is, absolutely perfect and complete; and when we ask ourselves what we really know about the spiritual world, we shall find the answer in those experiences that we have enjoyed while the mind took wings, so to speak, and we transcended the incomplete and entered into the realization of things as they are in the perfect — in the sublime — in the real spirit of all that is.

To state it differently, whenever we have experienced a joy that we might describe as the fullness of joy, or a state of harmony that we might describe as the fullness of harmony, or a state of health that we might describe as the fullness of health, or any state that we might describe as the fullness thereof, we have been conscious of the spiritual world.

Therefore, it is not what we may speculate concerning the invisible that gives us the key to the spiritual world, but what we become conscious of in that realm of being wherein all things are eternally perfect, absolute and divine. And the word "divine" may be employed only when referring to qualities or states of being that contain so much of their own reality that they could not contain any more; that is, they are, in truth, the fullness of their own nature.

Therefore, perfect health, or the fullness of health, is divine health. Likewise, perfect joy, or the fullness of joy, is divine joy; and perfect music, or what we may describe as the full expression of harmony through music, would be divine music. Briefly stated, perfect expressions of anything in nature, are divine expressions, provided we use the term "perfect" as implying the fullness of expression, realizing that the fullness of anything is all there is of that particular thing — a statement that becomes too large for objective comprehension when we realize that the all of anything is limitless.

When we develop spiritual consciousness, we may take many journeys into this inner world, either into our own interior nature, or into the spirit of everything existing in nature; and we shall find that the spirit of a flower is as much a part of the limitless spiritual world as is the spirit of our own soul. In brief, the spirit of everything does exist in the spiritual world, and is a part of the spiritual world, just as a drop of water in the sea is a part of the sea itself, no matter where that particular drop may be found.

Wherever we may turn our attention, therefore, if we go into the spirit of the thing itself, into life itself, into harmony itself, into peace itself, into music itself, into art itself, into any quality as it is in itself, we shall meet the spiritual world, the world in which all things exist in their fullness — without limitations or imperfections or incompleteness in any mode or manner.

Realizing this important truth, we may learn infinitely more about the spiritual world if we will continue to seek for the real source of every quality, or expression, or manifestation of which we may be conscious.

To illustrate: When we try to be peaceful, we should turn our attention towards the spiritual within, and try to realize the great eternal calm. In like manner, whenever we try to be harmonious, we should turn attention to the spirit of harmony, and try to experience more and more of that state of harmony that is so wonderful that it could not possibly be more harmonious. Then when we think of health, we should, instead of thinking about the body, turn attention to the spirit of health, which exists in the soul, or in the spiritual world, permeating all things.

We know that the majority, when in search for health, think too much about the body, believing that health has its origin and expression in the body only; but this is not the truth. We know that it is well to care for the body in the best manner possible, to follow all the laws of life on the physical plane and be in perfect harmony with nature as manifested either mentally or physically; but when we think of real health, or go in search of real health, we should realize that health itself does not have its origin in the body. Real health has its origin in the spirit of health, and the spirit of health abides in the spiritual world.

Accordingly, the more deeply we enter into the consciousness of the spirit of health, the more perfect and more powerful will become the expression of health through the mind and body, because when we find the limitless source of any expression, the expression itself will increase more and more as we become more deeply conscious of that source.

Here we should remember the great law — whatever we become conscious of in the within, that very thing we will manifest in the without.

When we are in search of power we must realize that the source of power is not found in the physical world, nor even in the mind. The source of power is found in the spirit of power which exists in the spiritual world; and if we will search in that direction we will not only find greater and greater power, but we will, at the same time, develop our spiritual consciousness, so that we may become better equipped for the finding of the spiritual source of anything that we may desire in life. This is clearly evident, because as we become more and more conscious of real power in the spiritual world, we will not only grow in power, but also grow in the consciousness of the spiritual world itself, which is indeed our purpose, whatever our external object at the time may happen to be.

Our one continuous aim, therefore, in this study should be to find more and more of that wonderful something that exists back of, or within, or at the source of all things; that is, the spiritual world itself — not a world that we may define as something finer than the physical — not an invisible world merely, but a state of being existing within everything, back of everything, beyond everything, and containing the fullness of everything.

When we consider the term "in all its fullness," we may well ask ourselves if we really appreciate its vast significance. We may repeat this expression "in all its fullness" again and again, in our own mentality, trying to comprehend everything that it might imply; and the more we think of it, the more vast and more wonderful it becomes. And when we realize that any quality or state of being becomes spiritual only when it appears in all its fullness, we begin to understand, not only the real meaning of the term "spiritual," but what an immensity that term represents; and not only immensity, but degrees of perfection beyond degrees of perfection, going deeper and higher perpetually into infinity.

When we pause to consider life in all its fullness, joy in all its fullness, health in all its fullness, harmony in all its fullness, power in all its fullness, wisdom in all its fullness — when we pause to consider all these things, we realize that we are in the presence of wonderful ideals; and the more deeply we enter into the consciousness of those ideals, the more closely we approach the spiritual world, until finally we enter into the full significance of the spiritual world.

The pathway to the spiritual, therefore, is not as difficult as we have thought in the past, although it implies everything that is ideal and wonderful and marvelous. The moment we begin to take our spiritual journey upon this path we realize that we are in the presence of elements and possibilities that are too vast, too immense and too sublime for the outer mind to comprehend; but we know that so long as we continue to search for the fullness of things, or to enter into the consciousness of the spirit of things, we are upon the straight and narrow path; that is, the path that leads directly, without wavering or turning, into the full consciousness of the spiritual.

In consequence, we should no longer think of the invisible, or any phase of the invisible, when we are in search of the spiritual; but should, instead, think of the perfect, the complete, the absolute, and that state in which everything exists in all its fullness — a state where life is so perfect that additional life could not be added; where peace is so perfect and so deeply calm that it is beyond all understanding; where light is so brilliant that it could not become more brilliant; where harmony is so perfect that it could not become more harmonious; where all the elements of life, consciousness and being are so wonderful and so divinely ideal that they could not become more wonderful or more ideal — this is what it means to be spiritual; and as we grow into this deeper and finer and higher understanding of all things, it is then that we develop real spirituality.

www.ingramcontent.com/pod-product-compliance
Lightning Source LLC
Chambersburg PA
CBHW031358290426
44110CB00011B/206